Daoism, Meditation,
AND THE
Wonders of Serenity

SUNY series in Chinese Philosophy and Culture
Roger T. Ames, editor

# Daoism, Meditation,
## AND THE
# Wonders of Serenity

*From the Latter Han Dynasty (25–220)
to the Tang Dynasty (618–907)*

STEPHEN ESKILDSEN

STATE UNIVERSITY OF NEW YORK PRESS

Cover illustration: *Laozi Riding an Ox*, hanging scroll, light color on paper, 101.5 x 55.3 cm. National Palace Museum, Taiwan. Laozi is carrying a copy of the *Dao De Jing*. Source: Wikimedia Commons.

Published by State University of New York Press, Albany

© 2015 State University of New York

All rights reserved

Printed in the United States of America

No part of this book may be used or reproduced in any manner whatsoever without written permission. No part of this book may be stored in a retrieval system or transmitted in any form or by any means including electronic, electrostatic, magnetic tape, mechanical, photocopying, recording, or otherwise without the prior permission in writing of the publisher.

For information, contact State University of New York Press, Albany, NY
www.sunypress.edu

Production, Dana Foote
Marketing, Michael Campochiaro

Library of Congress Cataloging-in-Publication Data

Eskildsen, Stephen
  Daoism, meditation, and the wonders of serenity : from the latter Han dynasty (25–220) to the Tang dynasty (618–907) / Stephen Eskildsen.
      pages cm.—(SUNY series in Chinese philosophy and culture)
  Includes bibliographical references and index.
  ISBN 978-1-4384-5823-6 (hc : alk. paper)—ISBN 978-1-4384-5822-9 (pb : alk. paper) ISBN 978-1-4384-5824-3 (e-book)  1. Meditation—Taoism.  2. Taoism—China—History—To 1500.  I. Title.
  BL1923.E845 2015
  299.5'1443509—dc23
                                                     2014045580

10 9 8 7 6 5 4 3 2 1

# Contents

| | |
|---|---|
| Acknowledgments | vii |
| 1. Introduction | 1 |
|    Opening Comments | 1 |
|    The Ancient Precedents | 4 |
|    Overview | 19 |
| 2. The Earliest-Known Daoist Religious Movements | 29 |
|    The Taiping Group Texts 太平經 | |
|      (*The Great Peace, GP Synopsis, GP Instructions*) | 31 |
|    The *Laozi Xiang'er zhu* 老子想爾注 (*Laozi-Xiang'er*) | 62 |
| 3. Dramatic Physical and Sensory Effects | 75 |
|    Surges of Primal *Qi*: The *Xiandao jing* 顯道經 | |
|      (*The Manifest Dao*) | 77 |
|    The *Rushi si chizi fa* 入室思赤子法 (*Contemplating the Baby*) | 104 |
|    The *Taishang hunyuan zhenlu* 太上混元真錄 (*The True Record*) | 118 |

4. INTEGRATING BUDDHISM: EARLIER PHASE  143
  The *Xisheng jing* 西昇經 (*The Western Ascension*)  143
  The *Xuwu ziran benqijing* 虛無自然本起經
    (*The Original Arising*)  161

5. INTEGRATING BUDDHISM: EMPTINESS AND THE
   TWOFOLD MYSTERY  181
  The *Benji jing* 本際經 (*The Original Juncture*)  181
  The *Wuchu jing* 五廚經 (*The Five Kitchens*)  194
  The *Qingjing jing* 清靜經 (*The Clarity and Calmness*)  201

6. SERENITY AND THE REAFFIRMATION OF
   PHYSICAL TRANSFORMATION  211
  The *Zuowang lun* 坐忘論 (*Sitting and Forgetting*)  211
  The *Dingguan jing* 定觀經 (*Stability and Observation*)  230

7. SERENITY, PRIMAL *QI*, AND EMBRYONIC BREATHING  241
  The *Cunshen lianqi ming* 存神鍊氣銘 (*The Inscription*)  241
  The *Taixi jing zhu* 胎息經註 (*Embryonic Breathing*)  254

8. CONCLUSION  277

NOTES  305

BIBLIOGRAPHY  353

INDEX  373

# Acknowledgments

I have never taken up the practice of meditation because I seriously lack patience and bodily flexibility. Attempting certain meditation postures such as the full lotus position would probably kill me. The restricted dietary regimens that frequently accompany meditation practice are also problematic, as I tend to require more nutrition than the average person. However, the experiences of people who meditate—especially if they are Daoists—somehow fascinate me.

This book developed over the course of the past ten years as my constant curiosity toward Daoism, meditation, and mystical experience drew my attention toward specific texts that vividly attest to the variety and magnitude of sensory and physical phenomena that may be brought about just by making the mind clear and calm. Actually, such texts range in date from the Latter Han right down to the modern period, and I had originally envisioned a volume of much broader chronological scope than this one. However, I eventually came to realize that the Han-through-Tang material easily yielded enough interesting data to fill a monograph, and that a proper, careful analysis of the Neidan (internal alchemy) materials of the Song period onward was an endeavor that needed to be deferred to the future.

Most of the material in this book has not been previously published. Exceptions to this are found in parts of chapter 3 and chapter 4. Some of the discussion on *The Manifest Dao* has appeared in my article "Some

Troubles and Perils of Taoist Meditation" (*Monumenta Serica*, no. 56 [2008]: 259–291). Some of the discussion on *Contemplating the Baby* and *The True Record* has appeared in my recent article "Red Snakes and Angry Queen Mothers: Hallucinations and Epiphanies in Medieval Daoist Meditation" (in *Hindu, Buddhist and Daoist Meditation: Cultural Histories*, ed. Halvor Eifring [Oslo: Hermes Publishing, 2014], 149–184). Some of the discussion on *The Original Arising* appeared in my article "Mystical Ascent and Out-of-Body Experience in Medieval Daoism" (*Journal of Chinese Religions* 35 [2007]: 36–62).

The people I need to thank on this occasion are many. My gratitude goes out to all of my teachers of past years, especially Daniel Overmyer and Joseph McDermott. I am grateful to the University of Tennessee at Chattanooga for providing me with a happy work environment for many years, and for providing me with a Faculty Research Grant to do fieldwork in China during the summer of 2010. I thank all of my friends and colleagues in Chattanooga for their kindness over the years. I thank Nancy Ellegate and her fine staff at the State University of New York Press, along with the two anonymous readers who took the time to read the manuscript carefully and provide helpful, insightful feedback.

Perhaps the main reason for why I was finally able to complete this book this year was that I had the outrageous good fortune of receiving a one-year Visiting Research Fellowship from the Käte Hamburger Kolleg, "Dynamics in the History of Religions between Asia and Europe" situated at the Ruhr-University Bochum (Germany). My stay in Bochum has been extremely intellectually stimulating, and has allowed me the time and resources to complete my project. I would like to particularly thank Volkhard Krech, Licia DiGiacinto, and Lucia an der Brügge for their generosity.

But my most constant companion and supporter over the past decade has been my wife, Eiko Namiki. I thank her for her love and encouragement, and look forward to her future scholarly monographs. I also thank Hana-chan and Kobuton (the ascended) for all of the furry, cuddly comfort that they have provided. Finally, I send my love and gratitude to my parents Edward and Marion Eskildsen, my brothers Tom and Walter, and my Aunt Lucile—all of whom have been a blessing to me for my entire life.

# ONE

# Introduction

## OPENING COMMENTS

Daoism has always emphasized mental serenity and maintained that good effects will come about from it. To be serene means that the mind is clear (*qing* 清), or free of any thoughts that confuse it; it also means that the mind is calm (*jing* 靜), without any emotions that agitate it. Daoism maintains that you should foster serenity at all times and in all activities. Activity itself is best limited to only what is most natural (*ziran* 自然) and necessary—"nonaction" (*wuwei* 無爲) is thus frequently enjoined.

For Daoists, meditation has been a primary means of fostering serenity and bringing it to greater depths. The greatest depths of serenity are entranced states of consciousness wherein mystical insights or experiences are said to come about,[1] or where vital forces of both mind and body—typically conceived as spirit (*shen* 神), *qi* 氣/炁 and essence (*jing* 精)[2]—are said to be activated and mobilized in most salubrious and wondrous ways. However, for such wondrous occurrences to come about in full abundance, it is frequently maintained—as we shall see—that your method of meditation ought to be simple and passive, apparently so as not to hinder the wonders that can only arise naturally. Less is more in all things, including meditation.

An immense variety of meditation methods and regimens have been devised within Daoism. Many of these have actually been very complicated, and have involved the active manipulation of the psyche and physiology by means of techniques such as visualizations (especially of deities inside and outside the body), invocations, mental guiding of *qi*, controlling and holding of breath, swallowing of breath, swallowing of saliva, knocking of teeth, self-massages, bends, stretches, drawing or swallowing of talismans, and such. Techniques of this sort—which we refer to as *proactive* (as opposed to the sort that most concerns us, which we refer to as *passive*)—are presented in particular detail and abundance in a category of Daoist scriptures called the Shangqing 上清 or Maoshan 茅山 scriptures, which originated out of divine revelations that are said to have occurred in the latter half of the fourth century in Jurong 句容, not far from present day Nanjing. These scriptures were widely acknowledged as the highest of divine revelations in medieval Daoist circles, to the extent that in the structure of the Daoist canon as conceived in the early fifth century, the canon's first section—the Dongzhen 洞真 section—was reserved for them. Modern scholarship has rightfully devoted a great deal of attention to the Shangqing scriptures, and Isabelle Robinet has provided us with particularly detailed and illuminating studies on their meditation methods.[3]

However, such elaborate, proactive meditation techniques are not described or endorsed in ancient Warring States (Zhanguo 戰國; 403–221 BCE) period Daoist texts such as the *Laozi* 老子 (The Old Master, aka *Daode jing* 道德經 [Classic of the Way and the Virtue]), the *Zhuangzi* 莊子 (Master Zhuang) or the *Neiye* 內業 (Inner Training). These texts endorse the habitual fostering of serenity throughout all circumstances and activities; if and when they do specifically speak of meditation, the method seems to involve little more than just calming and emptying out the mind.

As we shall see in this book, despite the profusion of proactive meditation techniques in Daoism during the first millennium of the Common Era, there also continued to exist and develop more passive approaches to meditation that calmly observed the processes that unfold spontaneously within the mind and body. Theorists and practitioners of such methods claimed that through deep serenity one could variously attain profound insights, experience numerous sorts of visions, feel surges of salubrious *qi* in the body, overcome thirst and hunger, be cured of all ailments and decrepitude, ascend the heavens, and gain eternal life. While they did not necessarily reject or disdain the proactive methods, they often viewed them as conferring lesser blessings, or as being rudimentary methods that should or can be practiced in preparation for undertaking the more sublime passive methods.

This book is a historical overview of Daoist religious texts of the late Latter Han 後漢 (25–220) through Tang 唐 periods (618–907) that describe meditation methods of the passive kind, along with the various effects that serenity—particularly that of the deep sort—was believed to bring about. These texts, in emphasizing serenity and promoting passive approaches to meditation can be said to follow the legacy of Warring States period Daoism to a significant degree, though they also draw inspiration from other sources, and attribute to serenity effects of far greater variety and magnitude. Also, this material is crucial to our understanding of the subsequent development of some of the major types of Neidan 內丹 (Internal Alchemy) meditation that emerged from the Song 宋 period (960–1279) onward,[4] which also put a prime emphasis on deep serenity and passive observation. This subsequent development is intended as the subject of a sequel to our current study.

Daoist theories on deep serenity and its effects developed under the influence of far more than just ancient Daoist philosophy. During the Han dynasty (206 BCE–220 CE) and throughout the medieval period (covering roughly the years 220 through 960), the increasing emphasis put on the quest for physical immortality, and the incorporation of various macrobiotic theories and methods developed by various immortality-seeking lineages, led to the development of a much greater variety and complexity of meditation techniques, as well as more extensive, concrete, detailed, and audacious claims regarding the sensory and physical effects that can come about. From the fifth century onward certain key Buddhist doctrines and notions such as rebirth, the Dharma Body [*fashen*] 法身, compassion, skillful means, and Emptiness [*kong*] 空 came to be firmly incorporated into the Daoist worldview. There also emerged a renewed interest in the philosophy of the *Laozi* as reinterpreted through a mode of discourse (the so-called Twofold Mystery [Chongxuan 重玄]) modeled upon that of the Mādhyamika school of Mahāyāna Buddhism. The incorporation of Buddhist ideas provided Daoists with new reasons for laying prime emphasis on mental serenity, as well as new insights and strategies for the cultivation of serenity. It also caused some Daoists to reexamine the nature and relationship of mind, spirit, and body in a way that apparently engendered a tendency to emphasize the cultivation of the spirit over that of the body. This latter tendency would come under explicit criticism from fellow Daoists, who lamented what appeared to them as an abandonment of the cherished goals of physical longevity and immortality.

The primary scope of this book is Daoist religion of the late Latter Han through Tang periods. To try to ascertain the original teachings and intentions (and identity) of the author(s) of the *Laozi* or other Warring States period Daoist works is a task that has been ably and strenuously undertaken by many others; it is not my objective to try to provide groundbreaking insights to this discussion. However, before proceeding with proper subject matter, it is necessary to overview what some of the Warring States period texts had to say regarding serenity, meditation, and the effects thereof. The ideas on these matters occurring in these texts were carried on and further developed in Common Era Daoist religion. Both the *Laozi* (especially) and the *Zhuangzi* are quoted by Daoist religious authors for inspiration and support of their teachings. The *Neiye*, on the other hand, has been virtually ignored by them. However, the groundbreaking research of Harold Roth has brought it to the attention of modern scholars as a rare and crucial text for understanding the mysticism and praxis of Warring States period Daoism.[5] The *Neiye* contains some noteworthy observations on the cultivation of serenity and its resultant effects on the condition of the body and its vital forces—observations that anticipate theories that get developed in Common Era Daoist texts.

THE ANCIENT PRECEDENTS

The *Laozi*

In the first chapter of the received version of the *Laozi* (ca. third century BCE) is a passage that relates to the absence of desires (an essential condition for serenity) and that can quite readily be understood as describing a sort of mystical apprehension that can result from having no desires. The *Laozi* famously starts out by describing the eternal Dao (*dao* 道) as something that can be neither spoken of nor named, and states that this nameless Dao was at the beginning of Heaven and Earth (it also states, in what seems like a more ambiguous statement, that the "named" [*youming* 有名] is the "mother" of all things). After thus speaking of the elusive, ineffable quality of the eternal Dao, it states:

常無欲 以觀其妙 常有欲 以觀其徼

If you are always without desires, you thereby observe its marvels. If you always have desires, you thereby observe its outer fringe. (1/1b)[6]

To see the Dao's marvels may or may not mean to actually observe the elusive, ineffable Dao itself; however, it would at least seem to mean witnessing something extraordinary that pertains to or is proper to the Dao. To always be without desire is really also something quite extraordinary, for in practice we seem to always be harboring some sort of desire. When we are in our ordinary desire-laden state, we cannot see the Dao's marvels, but only its "outer fringe" (*jiao* 徼; here I follow the rendering of James Legge).[7] Meant here by "outer fringe" are perhaps empirically observable natural phenomena, all of which come about through the power and workings of the mysterious Dao, but none of which manifest the Dao itself. By somehow becoming free of desires, it would appear that you are supposed to acquire a capacity to apprehend what eludes the grasp of ordinary consciousness.

At the outset of our discussion it was proposed that serenity is a mental condition where clarity and calmness prevail, and the Chinese words *qing* 清 and *jing* 靜 were presented as designations for these two attributes. The two words do quite often get joined into the compound *qingjing* 清靜, which is used in Daoist literature to describe the cherished state of mental serenity. (One also often finds the homophonic compound *qingjing* 清淨 ["clear and pure"] used interchangeably with it.) One of the most popular and influential scriptures of the Tang period that presents itself as the utterances of Lord Lao is the *Qingjing jing*, or the *Scripture of Clarity and Calmness* (to be discussed in chapter 5). In the ancient *Laozi* itself, the compound *qingjing* is indeed found, but just once. It is found in the 45th chapter, and occurs within a phrase that reads, "By means of clarity and calmness, you can bring about rectitude under Heaven" 清靜以爲天下正 (3/8b). The meaning of the passage would appear to be that mental serenity—on the part of the king, or perhaps the people more generally—can bring about optimal social harmony. Perhaps the idea is that if the ruler habitually keeps his mind clear and calm, he will be able to see every situation objectively for what it is, and respond in the most fair, appropriate, and effective manner. Or, perhaps, the idea is that if mental serenity prevailed among people in general, the world would be free of conflict and strife.

Separately, the words *qing* (clear) and *jing* (calm) occur four and ten times respectively in the *Laozi*; one of the passages containing the word *jing* is found in the sixteenth chapter, and is of particular interest to us, as it lends itself—intentionally or not—to an interpretation that relates to passive meditation. The passage reads:

致虛極 守靜篤 萬物並作 吾以觀其復 夫物芸芸 各復歸其根 歸根曰靜 是謂復命

Bring forth the utmost emptiness, and guard your calmness steadfastly. The myriad things arise all together, and I hereby observe their return. The things that grow forth in profusion, each return back to their roots. To return to the roots is stillness. This is called returning to life/destiny (?). (1/13a–b)

"Emptiness" (*xu* 虛) here can be understood as referring to a condition where the mind has been emptied of all its thoughts and desires. When the mind has been thoroughly emptied out and made calm, it simply observes things as they are, without imposing its own biases and wishes, and without interfering. But what is being observed here? Is it your own mind and body as you experience it in meditation, or is it the world out there as habitually encountered in everyday experience? How you chose to render the meaning of the character *ming* 命 ("life" or "destiny"?) seems to be contingent upon which of these lines of interpretation you take.

If one is to adopt the view that the above passage pertains to meditation, it could be interpreted as saying that when you bring the mind and body to the condition of utmost emptiness and calm in meditation, this will lead spontaneously to a fresh movement of vital force from your "roots" or the depths of your being. This surge of fresh vitality serves as the key agent for constantly restoring your "life" (*ming* 命). Thus, it is necessary to enter the depths of calm so as to bring about this resurgence, and to calmly witness it so as to harness it for the maximization of your vitality. This, anyway, is the sort of meditation-based interpretation that would come to be given to this passage of the *Laozi*.

It is also plausible that the passage does not by original intent pertain specifically to meditation, and that the things that it tells you to calmly observe are those you see around you in the world. The idea is perhaps that when you observe things around you clearly and calmly for what they are, you realize that it is basic to the nature of all things to flourish and decline. Knowing that such is the inevitable nature of all things—yourself included—enables you to understand and accept your destiny (*ming*).

What subsequently follows in the *Laozi*'s 16th chapter seems to support the latter, non-meditation-specific interpretation, because it states that the "returning to *ming*" is what is "constant" (*chang* 常), and that to understand this constant nature of things is to be "enlightened" (*ming* 明). Not understanding the constant principle will make you deluded and prone to malignant behavior, while understanding it will make you "tolerant" (*rong* 容) and "public-minded" (*gong* 公) in a manner befitting a king, or Heaven, or even the Dao itself. As for what happens when this magnanimous virtue attains to the level of the Dao, the text goes on to state that you will be "long-lasting" (*jiu* 久). However, the text then follows with a phrase (*moshen budai* 没身不殆) that is open to conflicting interpretations. One possible rendering of the phrase could be, "you will be without danger till the day that you die"; another could be "you will die, but will still not be in danger." Rendered in the latter manner, the phrase could be taken as referring to some sort of eternal life that occurs after actual or apparent death (such as is indeed the case in the *Xiang'er* commentary to the *Laozi* [see chapter 2]). Rendered in the former manner, the phrase appears to nicely summarize the 16th chapter as a whole, and the gist of the chapter would seem to be as follows: If you keep your mind serene you can see the nature of things for what it is and peacefully accept your own destiny. This wisdom will make you into an unselfish, magnanimous person who will not engage in malignant or reckless behavior. Such a person stays out of dangerous situations and lives a long life that concludes only with a peaceful, natural death.

In sum, a coherent message best seems to emerge from the sixteenth chapter of the *Laozi* when it is understood as referring to the habitual serenity that witnesses the world for what it is, and to the resulting wisdom and practical benefits that accrue thereby. Although such might be the reading most truthful to the *Laozi*'s author's (or authors') intentions, the other interpretations—those pertaining to meditation, vital force, and immortality—are actually more important to our study, for these were interpretations that were seriously put forth and that impacted the methods and aspirations of subsequent Daoists who cultivated deep serenity through passive meditation methods.

## The *Zhuangzi*

In the Inner Chapters ("Neipian" 內篇; chapters 1–7) of the *Zhuangzi*—the portion of the text generally thought most likely to issue from the hands of Master Zhuang (Zhuang Zhou 莊周 [ca. 369–286 BCE]) himself—we find some noteworthy anecdotes pertaining to clearing out and calming the mind. Interestingly, and perhaps oddly, two of these feature Confucius (Kong Qiu 孔丘; 551–479 BCE) and his favorite disciple Yan Hui 顏回 as the protagonists. In both of these anecdotes we encounter what is apparently a fictional Daoist Confucius who expounds teachings contrary to what one would expect the actual Confucius to have expounded.

In the *Zhuangzi*, chapter 4 ("In the World among Humans" [Renjian shi 人間世]) we are told about the time Yan Hui went to Confucius to ask his permission to go to the state of Wei 衛 and remonstrate against its tyrannical ruler. Confucius does not approve, because he doubts that Yan Hui could ever succeed at reforming the Lord of Wei, and even more fears that he could lose his life by angering the tyrant. Yan Hui then proposes to Confucius a few different strategies by which he might approach the Lord of Wei, persuade him, and go home unharmed. However, Confucius explains that these strategies have no hope of success. Yan Hui then concedes that he has no more ideas as to how to proceed, and begs Confucius for his advice. Confucius advises him that he must undertake "fasting" (*zhai* 齋)—not ordinary fasting, but rather, the Fasting of the Mind (*xinzhai* 心齋). As for what this is, Confucius explains:

> 若一志 無聽之以耳而聽之以心 無聽之以心而聽之以氣 聽止於耳 心止於符 氣也者 虛而待物者也 唯道集虛 虛者心齋也
>
> You must unify your will (concentrate yourself). Do not listen to it with your ears, but rather listen to it with your mind. Do not listen to it with your mind, but rather listen to it with your *qi*. Listening goes no further than [what] the ear [can hear]. The mind goes no further than [things that] tally [with what it already knows]. *Qi*, however, is something that is empty and which waits for things. Only the Dao gathers where it is empty. To be empty is the fasting of the mind. (1/18b)[8]

It would appear that Confucius wants Yan Hui to keep his mind concentrated and to listen carefully and properly. It is not quite clear here whether Confucius is speaking specifically about Yan Hui's prospective interview with the Lord of Wei, or whether he is speaking more generally about how to engage the world with the mind and senses. Whatever the case, Confucius maintains that it is better to "listen" with the mind than with the ears. This probably means that he ought to use his mind to discern the true intent that lies behind the surface of words that the ears hear. However, even a clever mind can only understand things in terms of its own past experiences, preconceptions, and agendas. Thus Confucius maintains that it is even better to employ the *qi* 氣 in "listening." Here *qi* is perhaps best understood as referring to the air that you inhale and exhale, and that sustains your bodily existence. Air in itself has no solid or liquid form that can be seen or grasped, and will accommodate any other object into the space that it occupies—hence it is described as "empty." To undertake the Fasting of the Mind apparently means to make the mind empty like air—free of any thoughts or desires of its own; it then somehow comes to possess a capacity to apprehend things more accurately and respond more effectively than when it relies on rational thinking or ordinary sense perception. This capacity is there because somehow the mysterious, wondrous Dao "gathers" inside a mind that is empty. The

Dao then seems to somehow function in a manner that generates an intuitive wisdom.

The text then continues with Yan Hui remarking that previously, before knowing about how to carry out the Fasting of the Mind, he had "regarded himself as Hui" 自回, but that now that he is able to practice the Fasting of the Mind, "there has not yet begun to exist any Hui" 未始有回. In other words, he has emptied his mind of even the notion of his own selfhood, and has transcended egocentric concerns that are the source of so much anxiety and conflict (though one wonders how this is possible when he has only now just heard of the Fasting of the Mind; perhaps something has been skipped in the narrative here). Confucius now feels reassured, and tells Yan Hui that he can try visiting the Lord of Wei if he likes. However, he also gives him a few more words of advice, the gist of which seems to be that in his interaction with the Lord he should take care not to become involved or concerned with matters pertaining to reputation, and should not persist in expounding his message if the Lord shows himself not to be receptive to it. Amid such words of advice, Confucius also states, "As for he who stares into that closed space, that empty room will produce whiteness (i.e., brightness), and auspiciousness will abide there; if it does not abide, this is to sit and hurry" 瞻彼闋者 虛室生白 吉祥止止 夫且不止 是爲坐馳 (1/18b–19a). The closed, empty room spoken of here would seem to be the mind of the person who practices the Fasting of the Mind, and the radiance that emerges would seem to be the intuitive wisdom that issues forth. Good results ensue when this sort of wisdom guides you, rather than your own ego-laden thinking processes. To "sit and hurry" seems to mean that the mind is hurried and busy with thoughts even while the body sits still, which means that the mind is not empty and thus the "auspiciousness" cannot abide therein.

In the *Zhuangzi*, chapter 6 ("The Great and Most Honored Master" [Dazongshi 大宗師]) it is described how one day Yan Hui came before Confucius and declared that he was making progress. Confucius asks him why he thinks this is the case, and Yan Hui explains that it is because he has "forgotten benevolence and righteousness" 忘仁義. Confucius acknowledges that this is indeed progress, but also tells Yan Hui that more progress is necessary. Yan Hui comes back another day to report further progress—he has "forgotten the rites and music" 忘禮樂. Confucius once again approves, but encourages further progress. Yan Hui comes back yet again on another day to report progress. This time, he states that he "sits and forgets" (*zuowang* 坐忘). Confucius is puzzled, and asks him what he means by this. Yan Hui explains:

墮肢體 黜聰明 離形去知 同於大通 此謂坐忘

> I destroy my limbs and body and I eliminate my intelligence. I separate from my body and I do away with knowledge. I become identical with the Great Pervader. This is called "sitting and forgetting." (2/9a)

What Yan Hui seems to mean by this is that he is able to sit down and empty his mind of all thoughts and desires, to the point where he is oblivious to even his own mind and body (clearly, his body has not been literally destroyed). It is by such self-oblivion that he is able to become somehow directly conscious of the Dao (the Great Pervader [*datong* 大通]; again following the rendering of James Legge)[9] and of the fact that he partakes of and participates in it.

Having been told this, Confucius can only admit that his disciple has surpassed him. This is because such a person who transcends all concern with the mortal, personal self and instead identifies with the eternal Dao that works through all natural phenomena, no longer prefers one thing ("has no likes" [*wuhao*] 無好) over another, and no longer has any set opinions ("has no constants" [*wuchang*] 無常). It can further be surmised that such a person can adapt smoothly to all situations and interactions, and cannot be brought to despair by any circumstances—not even death. It is to be noted that this particular *Zhuangzi* anecdote and its key concept of "sitting and forgetting" were deemed particularly important by certain medieval Daoists, resulting in the appearance of an important treatise entitled *Zuowang lun* 坐忘論 (Treatise on Sitting and Forgetting), which is attributed to one of the most eminent Daoists of the Tang dynasty, Sima Chengzhen 司馬承禎 (647–735). This text has been translated and extensively discussed by Livia Kohn,[10] and is discussed in chapter 6 of this book.

The beginning of the *Zhuangzi*, chapter 2 ("Making things Equal" [Qiwu 齊物]) depicts another apparent practitioner of self-oblivion in the person of Nanguo Ziqi 南郭子綦. One day he was leaning on his desk, looking up toward the sky, breathing softly and in a swoon. Yancheng Ziyou 顏成子游 sees this and asks him what he has just been doing, and whether it is possible for the body to become like a "withered tree" 槁木, and the mind like "dead ashes" 死灰. Nanguo Ziqi replies that he had in fact just "lost" (*sang* 喪) himself. He then turns around and asks Yancheng Ziyou whether he had ever heard the "pipes of earth" 地籟 or—even better— the "pipes of Heaven" 天籟, rather than just merely the "pipes of humans" 人籟. Yancheng Ziyou, curious, asks what the method for listening to those pipes might be. Nanguo Ziqi proceeds to describe how sounds of various pitch and volume sound forth from the earth when the wind blows through formations that it encounters on the landscape, such as a forest of trees with their various branches, leaves, apertures, and crevices. From this Yancheng Ziyou understands what Nanguo Ziqi means by the "pipes of earth," but is still compelled to ask what exactly the "pipes of Heaven" are. To this, Nanguo Ziqi says, "It blows upon the myriad differences, and makes them what they are. All things take their own, but who rouses them?" 夫吹萬不同 而使其自已也咸其自取 怒者其誰邪 (1/6a). The pipes of Heaven apparently is a metaphor for the workings of the mysterious Dao that gives rise to all things and makes them what they are, but which is itself utterly imperceptible and incomprehensible. It seems that Nanguo Ziqi had acquired this insight into the pipes by virtue of his ability to make his body like a "withered tree" and his mind like "dead ashes" and thereby "lose" himself; perhaps when in full trance he could even somehow hear the pipes of Heaven?

In *Zhuangzi*, chapter 23 (Gengsang Chu 庚桑楚)—one of the so-called Miscellaneous Chapters (Zapian 雜篇)—we find another mention of the body that is like a withered tree and the mind that is like dead ashes. This occurs within a conversation that is depicted occurring between the wise Old Master, Laozi, and Nanrong Chu 南榮趎, who was a student of Gengsang Chu—himself a former student of Laozi. Gengsang Chu had sent the elderly Nanrong Chu to visit and learn from Laozi, for under his own tutelage he did not seem to be making good progress toward becoming the "Ultimate Man" (*zhiren* 至人). The instructions that Laozi proceeds to give Nanrong Chu are full of themes, terms, and phrases resembling or matching those found in the *Laozi* and the *Neiye*. Among these are the injunction (apparently culled from the *Laozi*, chapters 10 and 55) that one ought to become like a baby or a very small child, whose vitality is so full that he or she can clench the fists firmly and cry all day without getting hoarse. Further expanding on the virtues of the small child, Laozi tells Nanrong Chu:

兒子動不知所為 行不知所之 身若槁木之枝而心若死灰 若是者
禍亦不至 福亦不來 禍福無有 惡有人災也 宇泰定者 發乎天光

> The little child moves without knowing what he is doing. He goes without knowing where he goes. His body is like the branches of a withered tree and his mind is like dead ashes. He who is like this does not come to misfortune, nor do blessings come to him. How could he be subject to human misfortunes?
> He whose house is peaceful and stable emits a heavenly light. . . .
> (4/32a–b)

Here, then, the withered tree/dead ashes condition described is not one of a man sitting in trance, but of a small child going about in a clueless and carefree manner, utterly lacking in self-awareness. The idea seems to be that if you just go about your activities without any self-conscious thoughts, desires, or aims, none of the circumstances you encounter will seem like misfortunes to you—nor like blessings, for that matter. Nothing can thus bring you to anguish or despair. The "house" here would seem to refer to your mental house or mind. The "heavenly light" that emerges when the mind is kept peaceful and stable would again seem to be some sort of intuitive wisdom. Perhaps this is in part so, but from what follows after this in the text it would appear that this "heavenly radiance" is something of an aura that you unwittingly exude, and which brings a particular sort of reaction from people and Heaven, respectively. As for what the reaction is from people, the text's wording is difficult to comprehend, and could be variously interpreted as saying that people will "abandon" you, or that they will "take up lodging" with you (the key here lies in how to translate the character *she* 舍). However, in regard to Heaven's reaction, it clearly says that it will aid (*zhu* 助) you. Thus, it would appear that you are immune from disaster not only in the sense that you maintain equanimity under all circumstances, but also because there is some mysterious principle at work by which harm evades you and good happens to you, all by no effort of your own. It should be noted that such an uncanny principle is also described in the *Laozi*'s 55th chapter (3/15a–16a), which praises the abundant virtue of the baby (*chizi* 赤子) that enables him or her to never be stung by poisonous insects, or attacked by ferocious beasts and birds of prey.

In chapter 11 (Letting Be [Zaiyou 在宥]), one of the *Zhuangzi*'s so-called Outer Chapters (Waipian 外篇), we find an anecdote in which the Yellow Emperor (Huangdi 黃帝) twice visits Guangchengzi 廣成子 (Master of Vast Accomplishment) on Mt. Kongtong 空同山. Upon his first visit, the Yellow Emperor asks Guangchengzi to instruct him on the "essence of the ultimate Dao" 至道之精, so that he can apply it to the bringing about of prosperity and order throughout the Empire. Guangchengzi sternly rebukes him and refuses to respond to the query. The Yellow Emperor then abdicates the throne and dwells in retreat in a grass hut for three months, before visiting Guangchengzi for the second time. This time he asks him about how to "govern the body" 治身. Guangchengzi responds warmly and enthusiastically with the following words:

至道之精 窈窈冥冥 至道之極 昏昏默默 無視無聽 抱神以靜 形將自正 必靜必清 無勞女形 無搖女精 乃可以長生

The essence of the ultimate Dao is profound and dark. The limit of the ultimate Dao is dark and silent. Do not look, do not listen. Embrace your spirit with calmness; your body will thereby naturally be rectified. You must be calm, you must be clear. Do not belabor your body and do not agitate your essence. Thereby you can live long. (2/25a)

Guangchengzi further goes on to admonish against hearing, seeing, and knowing too much, and reassures the Yellow Emperor that if he just focuses on governing his body in this way, the world and the myriad creatures will flourish on their own. He then reveals that he himself has thus cultivated himself for 1,200 years, and has not declined at all in physical vigor (!).

Whereas the previous anecdotes that we examined from the *Zhuangzi* (all but one were from the "Inner Chapters") speak primarily of the noetic and psychological benefits that come about from clearing out the mind, this anecdote from the "Outer Chapters" trumpets the immense physical benefits of serenity. Guangchengzi proclaims that keeping the mind clear and calm makes the condition of the body what it ought to be, and enables you to harness your "essence." What is unclear is whether essence means seminal essence specifically (as is often the case in Common Era Daoist religious texts) or vital essence as the basis of individual and cosmic vitality (as employed in the *Neiye*, as we shall see); if the former interpretation is taken, the passage entails a specific admonishment against sexual desire and excess. Another nagging question is whether the author here really wants readers to believe that it is possible for a human being to live 1,200 years, or whether this is mere literary hyperbole or a metaphor of some sort (these are very common in the *Zhuangzi*). Whatever the case, the physiological emphasis of this anecdote that distinguishes it from the anecdotes of "Fasting of the Mind" and the "Sitting and Forgetting" can perhaps be taken as betraying the fact that it, like most of the material in the "Outer" and "Miscellaneous" chapters, was probably not written by Master Zhuang himself, but rather by a disciple, follower or admirer of the third century BCE. This, however, in no way diminishes the interest of the anecdote for this book. The teachings conveyed in the anecdote anticipate what Common Era Daoist religious texts would have to say about the physiological necessity and benefits of serenity.

The *Neiye*

The discourse in the *Neiye* more fully explains how the cultivation of serenity facilitates longevity by bringing about a plenitude of vitality in one's person, along with sagely wisdom. The *Neiye* was never a lost text, and yet was virtually ignored by the Daoist religious tradition. The reason for this was apparently because the received version of the text is found in the 49th *juan* of the *Guanzi* 管子,[11] a highly eclectic anthology of treatises, many of which relate to statecraft and present a Legalist tendency of thought. By being in effect "buried" within such an anthology, the *Neiye* was habitually overlooked by Daoist readers and authors who might have otherwise recognized its coherence and resonance with their own convictions and aspirations. Yet, unbeknown to them, some of their basic ideas seem to have derived and evolved out of those in the *Neiye*.

The first section of the *Neiye* (I follow the section divisions proposed by Harold Roth in his critical edition)[12] talks about the "essence of all things" 凡物之精 that brings all things to life, from the five varieties of grain that grow down in the earth, right up to the stars that shine in the sky. It also states that the essence brings about phenomena that we refer to as "ghosts and spirits" 鬼神 when it flows about in space, and that it makes a person into a Sage 聖人 if it is stored inside that person's bosom. The *Neiye*'s second section is about "this *qi*" 此氣—meaning apparently the essence extolled in the first section—which it explains as being something that cannot be harnessed by means of force or speech, but rather must be "put at ease by virtue" 安以德 (or "inner power") and "welcomed by awareness" 迎以意 (see Roth 1999, 47).

It is to be noted that in the *Neiye* "essence" (*jing* 精) denotes *qi* 氣 of a more pure, refined quality. The eighth section states, "That which is [known as] 'essence,' is the essence of *qi*" 精也者 氣之精也. In other words, it is the purer, subtler essence of *qi* that you obtain by removing its coarser constitution, much in the way one removes the husks and polishes rice to obtain shiny white kernels. (The character *jing* 精 for essence is composed of the character *mi* 米 denoting rice or kernels of grains more generally, and the character *qing* 青, that here denotes clarity or purity.) This essence is what gives vitality, consciousness, and intelligence to living beings. This usage of the term *essence* and its perceived relationship to *qi* is actually different from what becomes common in Daoist religious literature, where essence is usually associated with nourishment, procreation, and bodily (especially sexual) fluids, and generally stands below both *qi* and spirit in the ascending scale of refinement. However, the *Neiye* and the Common Era Daoist religious texts that are examined later fully agree that essence and *qi*—whatever their mutual relationship may be—must be cherished, and that mental serenity is most essential for this purpose. Thus, the first six lines of *Neiye* section 8 (those directly preceding the sentence quoted earlier) read:

能正能靜 然後能定 定心在中 耳目聰明 四肢堅固 可以爲精舍

If you can be rectified and calm, you can subsequently become stabilized. If you stabilize your mind within, your hearing and sight will be clear and acute, and your four limbs will be firm and solid. You can become a dwelling for the essence. (Roth 1999, 61)

Thus, the essence dwells in you if you are good at making the mind calm, stable, and inwardly concentrated. Crucial yet problematic here for understanding the passage is the exact sense of the characters that I rendered respectively as "rectified" (*zheng* 正) and "stabilized" (*ding* 定). This has a direct bearing on whether we understand the passage as related specifically to meditation exercise. Roth renders the character *zheng* as "aligned," meaning that the body is maintained in a well-aligned, balanced posture of the sort usually recommended in seated meditation practice. Plausible though this is, it also seems possible that the character could mean something to the effect of maintaining a proper state of mind or of following proper conduct in daily life. The character *ding* would during the Common Era come to be used in Chinese translations of Buddhist scriptures to refer to states of *samādhi* or meditative trance. It is thus certainly tempting here to interpret *ding* as bearing a similar sense. However, it is probably more reasonable within a pre-Common Era context to understand *ding* as simply meaning that one is calm and under control.[13]

In any case, we are told that the positive effects of this rectified, calm stability will include enhanced sensory acuity and a strong, healthy body. Section 15 of the *Neiye* further explains that when you thus store the essence inside of you, you form within you a "wellspring" (*quanyuan* 泉原) and "pool" (*yuan* 淵) of *qi* that is "flood-like" (*haoran* 浩然; an expression famously used by the Confucian luminary Mencius [Meng Ke 孟軻 372–289 BCE])[14] and inexhaustible (see Roth 1999, 75). Section 16 describes how being "rectified and calm" (*zhengjing* 正靜) improves the texture and appearance of your skin, the suppleness of your muscles and the strength of your bones, along with the acuity of your hearing and vision (see Roth 1999, 77).

In section 13, this all-important essence gets described as a spirit:

有神自在 一往一來 莫之能思 失之必亂 得之必治 敬除其舍 精將自來

> There is a spirit that does what it will. Now going and now coming, nobody can fathom it. If you lose it, you will certainly be in disorder. If you obtain it you will certainly be in control. Reverently clean out its dwelling, and the essence will thereby come of its own accord. (See Roth 1999, 71)

The "dwelling" that you need to clean out is your mind, which needs to be freed of all thoughts and desires. What you yourself need to do is just empty out the mind. The actual coming of the essence/spirit is something that it does on its own, and that you passively await with a clear, calm mind.

Elsewhere in the *Neiye* this life-giving force that can be made to stay through steadfast serenity is referred to simply as the *Dao*:

夫道無所 善心安愛 心靜氣理 道乃可止

The Dao has no place. It rests within and cherishes a good mind.[15] If the mind is calm and the *qi* is regulated, the Dao can be made to stay there. (*Neiye*, section 5; Roth 1999, 55)

道也者 口之所不能言也 目之所不能視也 耳之所不能聽也 所以修心而正形也 人之所失以死 所得以生也

The Dao is what cannot be spoken of with the mouth. It is what cannot be seen with the eyes. It is what cannot be heard with the ears. Therefore you cultivate the mind and rectify the body. People who lose it die. People who obtain it live. (*Neiye*, section 6; Roth 1999, 57)

靈氣在心 一來一逝 其細無內 其大無外 所以失之 以躁爲害 心能執靜 道將自定

Numinous *qi* is in the mind. It comes and it goes. In its minuteness there is nothing it cannot enter. In its vastness there is nothing that it does not extend beyond. The reason you lose it is due to the harm brought forth by agitation. If the mind can hold to calmness, the Dao will thereby naturally be stabilized [in there]. (*Neiye*, section 26; Roth 1999, 97)

The Dao, then, is a most numinous *qi* that can reside within you and sustain your life, but does not have to; it can and will go anywhere to work its wonders. The only way to ensure that it will dwell in you is by keeping the mind clear and calm. This same notion (more or less) is forcefully expounded in the *Laozi Xiang'er zhu* 老子想爾注, one of the important extant texts of early (ca. 200 CE) Daoist religion, and is echoed repeatedly in subsequent texts.

The earlier discussion of the *Laozi*, the *Zhuangzi*, and the *Neiye* certainly has not covered all that these texts have to say that might be relevant to serenity and its effects. Furthermore, these are not the only ancient materials that represent or preserve views of the Daoist persuasion (among some of the other sources that might be culled are the *Xinshu* 心術 Parts I and II [*Guanzi, juan* 36, 37], the *Liezi* 列子, the *Huainanzi* 淮南子, and the *Lüshi chunqiu* 呂氏春秋). However, we have shown how these ancient texts endorse mental serenity variously as a means of gaining apprehension of the Dao's subtleties; generating intuitive wisdom that guides spontaneous, effective action; overcoming stress, fear, and anxiety; staying out of harm's way; and filling and maintaining oneself with vitality. While the serene state is certainly something that should be fostered in all activities and circumstances, there is also considerable evidence suggestive of meditation exercise wherein deep serenity is fostered.

## OVERVIEW

In chapters 2 through 7 we highlight fourteen different Daoist texts that range in date between roughly the second and ninth centuries CE. They have been selected for examination because they offer interesting and important discussions on serenity and/or passive meditation, or offer particularly detailed or vivid descriptions of sensory and physical phenomena that are supposed to come about from deep serenity. Note, however, that these texts, despite sharing certain themes, characteristics, or propensities, do not collectively represent a self-conscious tradition. "Passive" and "proactive" are my own analytical categories, and some of our texts endorsing methods describable as "passive" are not necessarily disdainful or critical of methods describable as "proactive." Their authors may have practiced both sorts of methods and perhaps did not perceive a distinction of the sort (namely, passive versus proactive) that I do.

Grouping and ordering the texts for a discussion that properly traces the historical evolution of Daoist methods and theories of passive meditation is a somewhat difficult and perilous enterprise, because most of the texts to be discussed are not easy to date with much precision, and some of them—most notably the Taiping Group texts—underwent some fairly complex processes of redaction. Although the intent here is to try to present the material in approximately the proper chronological order, this ordering is imprecise and is based largely on the internal doctrinal and thematic contents of the texts, and the degree to which they match with certain tendencies that we associate with particular known movements and events in Daoist history.

Chapter 2 starts with texts that have long been of interest to many scholars due to their possible connection to the earliest Daoist religious movements known to history—the Way of Great Peace (Taiping Dao 太平道) and the Way of the Five Pecks of Rice (Wudoumi Dao 五斗米道; aka, the Way of the Heavenly Masters [Tianshi Dao 天師道]) that arose in the second century. The Taiping Group texts (meaning primarily *The Great Peace* [*Taiping jing*太平經],[16] *GP Synopsis* [*Taiping jing chao* 太平經鈔] and *GP Instructions* [*Taiping jing shengjun bizhi* 太平經聖君祕旨]) contain material that has survived from a lengthy second-century text known as the *Taiping qinglingshu* 太平清領書—or more simply the *Taiping jing*—and which according to the standard histories was cherished by the Way of Great Peace that undertook the notorious Yellow Turban Revolt of 184. The *Laozi-Xiang'er* [*Laozi Xiang'er zhu* 老子想爾注] is a partially surviving commentary to the *Laozi* that has been ascribed variously to Zhang Daoling 張道陵, the founder and first Heavenly Master of the Way of the Five Pecks of Rice, or to his grandson, the third Heavenly Master Zhang Lu 張魯.

Because the Taiping Group texts and the *Laozi-Xiang'er* bear such possible connections to the two large and influential organizations at the dawn of Daoist religious history, one might surmise that what these texts say on any matter would set precedents and have a profound bearing on how the religion would subsequently develop. This indeed seems to be the case in regard to matters related to serenity and meditation. The Taiping Group texts offer descriptions of meditation methods of various sorts, both passive and proactive in tendency, and rank the different sorts of methods in a manner that places in the highest position the methods that do *not* involve the visualization of complex, concrete forms. The Taiping Group texts emphasize an underlying inner clarity and calm as fundamental to meditation in general, and also claim that all thirst and hunger can be overcome. They also contain interesting statements on the serene, innocent mental states of fetuses and of humans at the dawn of creation who are/were able to survive and flourish without food, and who do not breathe, or breathe only very softly. These discussions seem to represent precedents to later theories pertaining to dietetics and to so-called embryonic breathing (*taixi* 胎息) methods. The *Laozi-Xiang'er*, in stark contrast to the Taiping Group texts, seems—at least at first glance—to disapprove of meditation practice in general, in favor of faithful adherence to moral precepts. However, it carries out a discussion of profound, fundamental importance on how a pure mind ensures that the *qi* of the Dao will abide in you and keep you alive.

Chapter 3 discusses texts that have received much less interest from modern scholars, but which may be quite early (mid-fourth century or earlier?) or contain early material, and which give very vivid and concrete descriptions of dramatic sensory and physical phenomena that result from deep serenity. The criteria for surmising an early origin pertains mainly to the absence of internal evidence of influence coming from well-known Daoist scriptural corpuses such as the Shangqing and Lingbao 靈寶 that emerged from the latter half of the fourth century onward, or especially from Buddhism, which despite entering China as early as the first century seems to have begun to leave a profound impact on Daoist beliefs and practices only during the late fourth and (especially) fifth centuries.

*The Manifest Dao* (*Xiandao jing* 顯道經) has been selected for examination in chapter 3 because it features a discussion—presented as the utterances of Laozi—of a simple, largely passive method of confined, reclining meditation called the "Plain Way." This discussion is strikingly concrete and vivid in its descriptions of extraordinary physical symptoms, sensations, and visions that occur as a result of the activation of what gets referred to as the primal *qi* (*yuanqi* 元氣) or the Dao-*qi* 道氣 that issues from the "Elixir Field" (*dantian* 丹田) inside the belly, as well as the activity of spirits both benign and malevolent. *Contemplating the Baby* (*Rushi si chizi fa* 入室思赤子法) has been chosen for examination primarily because of its vivid descriptions—also presented as the utterances of Laozi—of a more or less spontaneously arising vision sequence in which the practitioner encounters among other things a fiery red snake and the famous goddess of ancient immortality lore, the Queen Mother of the West (Xiwangmu 西王母). While the meditation method of *Contemplating the Baby* is rather unique—particularly in its emphasis on specific hours and days for practice—its vision sequence, or something closely resembling it, is something that can be found in at least five other texts, which in date of authorship range between the seventh and twentieth centuries.

Among these other texts containing such a vision sequence we have selected *The True Record* (*Taishang hunyuan zhenlu* 太上混元真錄) for examination in chapter 3. Actually, this text probably dates to the seventh century, when Buddhism had already deeply influenced Daoism. However, the text in content consists largely of materials that are culled from earlier sources and that betray no Buddhist influence in the doctrines and practices they describe. These are packaged and presented by the compiler as teachings that the Most High Lord Lao (the divine Laozi) conferred upon his disciple, the Keeper of the Pass Yin Xi 關令尹喜, who he had encountered while on his way toward western lands with the intent to convert the "barbarians." Among these teachings we find described a lengthier, more elaborate version of the same sort of vision sequence described in *Contemplating the Baby*. There are also descriptions of various meditation techniques, both passive and proactive, but it is difficult to determine which or any of them is the specific method that is supposed to generate the vision sequence in question.

Chapter 4 begins with a discussion of *The Western Ascension* (*Xisheng jing* 西昇經), which is another text that presents itself as teachings that Laozi/Lord Lao conferred upon Yin Xi during their momentous encounter (and which is quoted extensively in *The True Record*). This text is estimated as dating to the fifth century, and its teachings certainly betray significant Buddhist influence, particularly in how it fully incorporates the doctrine of rebirth (*saṃsāra*—"flowing" or "wandering from existence to existence"—in Sanskrit) into its worldview. Inferring from this doctrine the presence of an immortal spirit that transmigrates from body to body (in a manner incongruent with the fundamental Buddhist teaching of no-self [*anātman*], though Chinese Buddhists themselves sometimes made this same inference), *The Western Ascension* sets out to assess the relative worth of the spirit and the body, as well as the manner of their interrelationship. In regard to meditation it proposes—at least according to the interpretation of its earliest commentator—that inner bodily deities can and ought to be visualized, but only in preparation for ultimately moving on to the higher level of meditation where no thoughts or forms are purposely entertained.

We then move on to examine *The Original Arising* (*Taishang Laojun xuwu ziran benqi jing* 太上老君虛無自然本起經).[17] This text sets forth as its principal assertion the necessity, possibility, and supreme soteriological benefit of bringing the human mind to a condition described as the "Naturalness of Empty Nothingness" (*xuwu ziran* 虛無自然), and thereby fully embodying the Dao and its sublime attributes. As a means of realizing this condition it forcefully endorses a simple, passive form of meditation, and provides a vivid description of a type of out-of-body experience that is supposed to spontaneously come about through it. This text is also interesting and unique for the manner in which it redefines the supreme Daoist soteriological ideal as something highly reminiscent of the condition of the eternal Buddha of Mahāyāna Buddhism, who abides perpetually in the realm of *saṃsāra* to guide sentient beings, and in doing so makes it seem as though he undergoes deaths and births.

Chapter 5 examines three texts that integrate Buddhist insights on nonself (*wuwo* 無我; *anātman* in Sanskrit) and Emptiness (*kong* 空; *śūnyatā* in Sanskrit) and apply them as means of facilitating serenity by enabling one to mentally detach from all things and concepts (including even "Emptiness" and "detachment"). *The Original Juncture* (*Taixuan zhenyi benji miaojing* 太玄真一本際妙經), which dates to around the year 600, was a text that was widely read in its time, and which engages in a manner of discourse known as the "Twofold Mystery" (Chongxuan 重玄), which applies the principles of Mahāyāna Emptiness ontology to the interpretation of the *Laozi*. This text lucidly sets forth highly Buddhistic doctrines that constitute significant innovations in Daoist cosmology, soteriology, and praxis. These teachings on cosmology and soteriology follow along similar lines with what is articulated in *The Original Arising*, but are formulated around a theory regarding the nature and role of its supreme deity, the Primordial Heavenly Worthy (Yuanshi Tianzun 元始天尊). The teachings on praxis revolve around the themes of devotion, along with the cultivation of correct insight based on mental clarity.

What is notably absent in this text is any sort of discussion on the health and longevity of the physical body, and the means by which one can cultivate it.

Such a heavily mental emphasis can also be noted in the cases of *The Five Kitchens* (*Wuchu jing* 五廚經) and *The Clarity and Calmness* (*Taishang Laojun shuo chang qingjing jing* 太上老君說常清靜經)—though both of these texts were interpreted and applied in ways more related to the body. *The Five Kitchens*, a scripture authored some time prior to 735, is itself very short, consisting merely of five sets of verse, each consisting of four five-character lines. These verses simply enjoin the maintenance of inner calmness and harmony, which simultaneously involves the elimination of all desires and attachments. However, these verses came to be widely regarded—by both Daoists and Buddhists (!)—as possessing the efficacy of subduing hunger. *The Clarity and Calmness* was also in circulation by the eighth century and is also very brief. It enjoins the cultivation of inner clarity and calmness, and maintains that such cultivation can and ought to succeed because the human spirit or mind is fond of clarity and stillness to begin with. It further maintains that by making the mind clear and calm you can come to apprehend the Empty nature of all things and concepts. Among the various first millennium texts examined in our study, *The Clarity and Calmness* is by far the one that maintained the most popularity and influence into modern times, perhaps particularly because its study and recitation was promoted by the founders of the influential Quanzhen 全真 School that emerged in the late twelfth century.[18] Within this tradition, *The Clarity and Calmness* was given a creative interpretation relating to the salubrious inner movement and solidification of essence and *qi* that will result from the cultivation of inner clarity and calm.

Chapter 6 examines two texts of the Tang period that are also conversant in the discourse on Emptiness and thoroughgoing detachment, but at the same time issue protests against a perceived lopsided emphasis on spiritual cultivation. *Sitting and Forgetting* (*Zuowang lun* 坐忘論) is a substantial treatise ascribed to Sima Chengzhen 司馬承禎 (647–735), one of the most acclaimed and influential Daoist masters of the Tang period. It carries out a fairly wide-ranging exposition that covers not only the proper manner in which to meditate, but also discusses matters pertaining to the proper faith, simplicity in lifestyle, and moral comportment that are necessary as a foundation for fostering mental serenity. It argues that if deep inner serenity is thus cultivated, the Dao will enter, abide, empower, and transform the person in both mind and body. Unfortunately, the text laments, too many people disregard the body and cultivate themselves only to the point where the mind alone is transformed by the power of the Dao. *Stability and Observation* (*Dongxuan lingbao dingguan jing* 洞玄靈寶定觀經) is a shorter text that is of particular interest due to its thoughtful discussion on the cultivation of mental serenity and wisdom that addresses some of the problems and detrimental effects (such as delusion and insanity) that can arise when one's way of practice is anxious and unbalanced. The last portion of the text consists of an enumeration of the Seven Phases (*qihou* 七候) of physical transformation that you can undergo when you "obtain the Dao," and concludes with statements criticizing those misguided practitioners who think that the mere attaining of wisdom is what constitutes "accomplishing the Dao."

Despite their apparent pleas to fellow Daoists for a renewed emphasis on physical cultivation and immortality, *Sitting and Forgetting* and *Stability and Observation* have little to say about physiological processes. The two texts that are the principal subjects of chapter 7, *The Inscription* (*Cunshen lianqi ming* 存神鍊氣銘) and *Embryonic Breathing* (*Taixi jing zhu* 胎息經註) are roughly contemporary to *Sitting and Forgetting* and *Stability and Observation*, and also endorse simple, passive approaches to meditation that are expected to transform the body. However, in their respective discussions, the harnessing of vital *qi*, the Elixir Field, and the spontaneous overcoming of hunger figure prominently, and the method is presented as a means of "embryonic breathing" by which the pristine vitality of the fetus is recovered.

*The Inscription* is attributed to the great physician Sun Simiao 孫思邈 (581–682). It thus shares with *Sitting and Forgetting* the trait of being attributed to a monumental figure in Tang Daoism, though the authenticity of the attribution has been called to question in both cases. *The Inscription* also resembles *Sitting and Forgetting* in the way its author takes recourse to Buddhistic terminology and discourse pertaining to the cultivation of wisdom, and concludes with criticisms of practitioners who do not take their cultivation to the level where the body gets transformed and immortalized. *The Inscription* also contains an enumeration of the

Seven Phases of physical transformation that matches considerably that in *Stability and Observation*. However, it also speaks of the harnessing and refining of *qi* and the importance of concentrating on the Elixir Field in this process, and of overcoming the hunger that will result thereby, in a manner reminiscent of what is taught in *The Manifest Dao*, as well as in Neidan literature of later periods. In one place toward the end, *The Inscription* refers to its method as "the meditative stability observation of the embryonic breathing" (*taixi dingguan* 胎息定觀).

By the Tang period there existed an extremely wide variety of longevity-immortality methods that were claimed to constitute embryonic breathing, and many of these were highly proactive procedures that entailed the gulping of air or saliva, or the holding or controlling of breathing. However, *Embryonic Breathing*, which consists of a brief main text with a somewhat more detailed commentary (datable to the latter half of the eighth century or the early ninth century), endorses what appears to be a simple, highly passive approach to embryonic breathing closely resembling what is recommended in *The Inscription*. The main text of *Embryonic Breathing* tends to give the impression that keeping a calm mind is the prime—perhaps even sole—thing that is required. The commentary states that when you subdue the *qi* beneath the navel and guard the spirit within the body, spirit and *qi* merge to form the Mysterious Womb. Doing so, it claims—most significantly—constitutes "Internal Alchemy, the Way of Immortality" 內丹不死之道. It also claims that if spirit and *qi* are thus harnessed, you will no longer hunger nor thirst.

The commentary to *Embryonic Breathing* also mentions that you need to "internally circulate" (*neiyun* 內運) the primal *qi*, and suggests that there is something fundamentally wrong with how ordinary people breathe; unfortunately, it offers no further discussion of what the "circulation" of primal *qi* is, or what the correct technique of breathing might be. For clarification on these matters we consult four other embyonic breathing-related treatises, *The Embryonic Origins* (*Changsheng taiyuan shenyong jing* 長生胎元神用經), *The Embryonic Subtleties* (*Taixi jingwei lun* 胎息精微論), the *Holy Embryo* (*Zhuzhen shengtai shenyong jue* 諸真聖胎神用訣), and *Bodhidharma's Lesson* (*Damo dashi zhushi liuxing neizhen miaoyong jue* 達磨大師住世留形內真妙用訣). From these texts we learn about methods that the commentator of *Embryonic Breathing* may have had in mind, which entail—while breathing normally through the nose and mouth—first mentally directing the primal *qi* toward the Elixir Field to conceive the inner "fetus," and then making the inner spirit and *qi* circulate, nourish, and transform the body. Doing so, we are told, will eventually naturally bring it about that air does not go through your nose, and you are able to completely control and suppress your sexual desires and functions.

The sort of Embryonic Breathing theory and method conveyed in *The Inscription, Embryonic Breathing, The Divine Functions, The Holy Embryo, Bodhidharma's Lesson,* and *The Embryonic Subtleties* represents an important precursor to major Neidan 內丹 methods of the "passive-reactive" sort that developed from the Song period onward, and which will be the focus of a sequel to this book. In these methods also the calm focusing on the Elixir Field that harnesses and merges spirit and *qi* is fundamental, and the elimination of hunger, the suspension of breathing, and the eradication of sexual desire and function are claimed to naturally come about in the case of accomplished practitioners. However, one can also say that these serenity-based Neidan methods are better described as passive-reactive than just passive, because at certain junctures within the regimen when new stirrings of psychic or physiological activity are observed emerging from the depths of stillness, you are supposed to resort to certain acts of mental volition, such as the guiding of the *qi* up the spine, or the projection of the spirit out of the top of the skull.

In this book I have tried to read the Latter Han-through-Tang sources in a straightforward manner that is coherent to the chronological context, avoiding any distortion that might come about by imposing anachronistic notions upon it. Because part of the interest in these materials does lie in how they may have anticipated or influenced the subsequent development of Neidan, there is certainly the danger that one might erroneously interpret them according to Neidan theories that only developed later. I have tried to exercise due caution toward this problem. However, I also believe there are cases where later (or even much later) Neidan theories may provide clues to interpreting some of the more ambiguous passages in our Han-through-Tang materials. Thus, I do in some places suggest such interpretations, albeit only tentatively.

If one greatly broadens one's scope, one certainly finds that the cultivation of serenity is a concern shared by far more than just Daoists. When one surveys the teachings of the contemplative mystics of the various major religious traditions of the world, one will readily find views extolling the state of utter mental clarity and calm—entirely free of any thoughts or images—as the optimal state for mystical illumination. It is hoped, thus, that this book can also be of use and interest to those who are concerned with mysticism as a universal human phenomenon. The data in this book should provide a further body of testimony as to how in seemingly all times and places, for whatever reason (psychological, biological, or supernatural?), mental serenity at its greatest depths can bring about experiences that strike their subjects as being sacred, illuminating, invigorating, or transformative.

However, it is also anticipated that the data in this study pertaining to the sensory and physical phenomena that results or is anticipated from passive meditation will speak to what is unique and quintessential to the Daoist religion. The Daoist religion, much more than any other well-known religion, has tenaciously held to the hope that the physical body can be made to overcome death. Daoism, more than any other tradition, it would seem, has always perceived of an inextricable link between the mind, the body, and their respective cultivation and wellbeing. Through the sensory and physical phenomena that unfold in passive meditation, Daoists hope to experience eternal life by gaining direct, tangible, evidence that the eternal Dao (*dao* 道; the Way) is alive within them, and that they are progressively conquering the limitations and frailties imposed by their egos and mortal bodies. The presence or absence of such phenomena has been considered a prime standard by which to gauge not only the progress and aptitude of the practitioner, but also the legitimacy of a meditation regimen. For this reason Daoist meditation literature sometimes refers to such phenomena as "signs of proof" (*zhengyan* 證驗). If the passive cultivation of deep serenity has survived the test of time better than (or at least as well as) any other approach to meditation devised by Daoists, it is perhaps because it has demonstrated to its practitioners a quite satisfactory propensity for rendering forth signs of proof.

TWO

# The Earliest-Known Daoist Religious Movements

The earliest organized Daoist religious movements that we know of appeared in the second century CE, during the Latter Han 後漢 dynasty (25–220). The accounts given in the standard histories indicate that participants in these movements were practicing certain methods of isolated contemplation. This contemplation tended to be something along the lines of penitential self-reflection. Pei Songzhi's 裴松之 (372–451) commentary to Chen Shou's 陳壽 (233–297) *Sanguo zhi* 三國志 (8th *juan* 卷) quotes Yu Huan's 魚豢 (third century) *Dianlüe* 典略 (now lost) to describe how during the late second century three different uprisings by "sinister bandits" (*yaozei* 妖賊) occurred. First, during the Xiping 熹平 reign era (172–178), there was an uprising in Sanfu 三輔 (Chang'an 長安 [Xi'an 西安] and vicinity) led by a certain Luo Yao 駱曜. During the Guanghe 光和 reign (178–184) Zhang Jue 張角 led an uprising in the "eastern direction" (portions of Shandong, Hebei, and Jiangsu), while in Hanzhong 漢中 (northern Sichuan and southwestern Shaanxi) there was the uprising of Zhang Xiu 張脩 (or Zhang Heng 張衡?).[1] Luo Yao taught people the method of "*mianni*" 緬匿, which could plausibly be translated as "pondering and hiding." Zhang Jue, whose group bore the name Way of Great Peace (Taiping Dao 太平道), engaged in methods of healing diseases, in which patients were required to reflect on their transgressions while prostrating themselves and "knocking their heads" (*koutou* 叩頭) on the ground, after which they were made to drink water in which the ashes of a burned sacred paper talisman had been dissolved. The methods of Zhang Xiu, whose group was known as the Way of the Five Pecks of Rice (Wudoumi Dao 五斗米道), were "roughly the same as those of [Zhang] Jue" (*lüe yu Jue tong* 略與角同). However, he did institute a number of additional features, one of which was to set up "quiet rooms" (*jingshi* 靜室) in which the patients were made to contemplate their transgressions. Another feature of Zhang Xiu's practices that gets described and that also merits mentioning here is that he appointed "libationers" (*jijiu* 祭酒), whose duty was to guide people in the study of the "5000 Characters of Laozi" 老子五千文 (i.e., the *Laozi*) (see *Sanguo zhi*, 1:264).[2]

The isolated contemplation thus described in the case of the Way of the Five Pecks of Rice (aka, Tianshi Dao 天師道 or the Way of the Heavenly Masters) was an act of contrition meant to facilitate the procedure of healing. It does not appear to have been a meditation technique intended for clearing out the mind or cultivating mystical experience. In light of the fact that they studied the *Laozi*, it is tempting to speculate that they may have also used the quiet rooms to practice some sort of meditation practice based on or inspired by it. However, we are far from being able to conclude from this information that they interpreted the *Laozi* and applied its teachings in such a way.

The most obscure figure is Luo Yao. Aside from what is mentioned in the *Dianlüe*, nothing is known about him or his movement. Whether his group was something aptly describable as "Daoist" is unknowable. The fact that his movement is enumerated along with those of Zhang Jue and Zhang Xiu under the designation "sinister bandits" could perhaps imply that his movement's beliefs and practices were similar to theirs in some way that made all of them appear strange or perverse to the eye of the historiographer. If so, it seems plausible to speculate that "pondering and hiding" was some sort of isolated contemplative method, be it of a penitent or serene sort.

Based solely on the description of the *Dianlüe*, Zhang Jue's Way of Great Peace would at first glance appear to have been a faith-healing movement that drew no particular inspiration from Daoist philosophy or the cult of a deified Laozi (a phenomenon that had emerged at various levels of society by the second century),[3] and which did not engage in any sort of meditation practice. However, this movement is regarded alongside the Way of the Five Pecks of Rice as one of the two earliest known Daoist religious groups, for reasons that are brought up shortly. Zhang Jue's Way of Great Peace did not enjoy a lengthy existence due to the failure of its massive armed revolt of 184 (the Yellow Turban [Huangjin 黃巾] revolt) and the subsequent suppression. The Way of the Five Pecks of Rice—aka, the Way of the Heavenly Masters—on the other hand, did survive to play a leading role in the subsequent evolution of the Daoist religion.

In this chapter we examine the Taiping Group texts and the *Laozi-Xiang'er*—texts that may provide us with a more detailed and concrete understanding of the serenity-related teachings and meditation practices of the Way of Great Peace and the Way of the Five Pecks of Rice, as well as perhaps other unknown Daoist movements of the second century or thereafter. We first discuss the Taiping Group texts, which tend to get associated with the Way of Great Peace, but were certainly not their exclusive property. We then move on to discuss the *Laozi-Xiang'er*, which appears to have been an important text of the early Five Pecks of Rice movement.

## THE TAIPING GROUP TEXTS 太平經
### (*THE GREAT PEACE, GP SYNOPSIS, GP INSTRUCTIONS*)

So on what grounds could one rightly describe Zhang Jue's Way of Great Peace as "Daoist"? First of all, one standard historical source does suggest that Zhang Jue either subscribed to some sort of Daoist philosophy, or perhaps worshipped Laozi. Fan Ye's 范曄 (398–445) *Houhan shu* 後漢書 (71st *juan*) states that Zhang Jue "venerated and served the Way of *huanglao*" 奉事黃老道. (*Houhan shu*, 8:2299)[4] The exact meaning and significance of this is hard to discern. During the Han period the term *huanglao* 黃老 often referred to the dual personages of the ancient Sage-Emperor *Huang*di 黃帝 (the Yellow Emperor) and the philosopher Laozi, and to a school of thought that sought to apply their putative teachings largely toward statecraft and the cultivation of longevity. However, by the second century Laozi had come to be deified and widely worshipped both by members of the ruling elite, as well as among popular sectarian movements; in such cases Huang Laojun 黃老君 (Yellow Lord Lao) was one of the names that he was individually referred to by.[5]

More significantly for us, Zhang Jue's Way of Great Peace has also been associated with an important Daoist scripture called the *Taiping jing* 太平經 (Scripture of Great Peace). The *Houhan shu*, in *juan* 30b, describes how a "divine book in 170 *juan*" 神書百七十卷 entitled *Taiping qingling shu* 太平清領書 (Book of the Pure Commands of the Great Peace), which had originally been acquired by a certain Gan Ji 干吉 by the banks of the springs of Quyang 曲陽 (in western Hebei), was on two occasions presented to the imperial throne by men who had hoped—alas, in vain—that their sovereign might employ its tenets and thereby rule in a sagely manner. First, a certain follower of Gan Ji named Gong Chong 宮崇 of Langye 琅邪 (southeast Shandong) presented the book to the Emperor Shundi 順帝 (r. 126–144). Later, Emperor Huandi 桓帝 (r. 147–167) was presented the book by Xiang Kai 襄楷. The text then goes on to state, "later, Zhang Jue very much had (?) that book" 後張角頗有其書焉 (*Houhan shu*, 4:1084). Although the exact meaning and nuance of this phrase is unclear (hence my awkward translation), it apparently means to say that Zhang Jue adopted the *Taiping qingling shu* as an important source of inspiration and reinforcement for his teachings and practices. Li Xian's 李賢 (654–684) commentary to the *Houhan shu* states that this *Taiping qingling shu* "is none other than the current *Taiping jing* of the Daoist school" 即今道家太平經也 (*Houhan shu*, 4:1080). (It also bears noting here that as early as the end of the first century BCE another text bearing the word *taiping* in its title had been submitted to the throne and ultimately rejected; however, the content of this text and its relationship to the *Taiping qingling shu/Taiping jing* is unknown.)[6]

The *Taiping jing* was indeed one of the most famous and cherished scriptures in medieval Daoism. While Zhang Jue's Way of Great Peace disappeared after the failure of his violent Yellow Turban Revolt in 184 and was by and large denounced or disowned by Daoists of later periods, the *Taiping jing* was not similarly discredited. This is probably because it was not the exclusive property of Zhang Jue's movement. The scripture and the legend of its revelation to Gan Ji are promoted in extant Heavenly Masters School texts of the third through fifth centuries.[7] When the

Daoist canon was configured (around 600 CE) into its standard seven-section (three "caverns" [*dong* 洞] and four "auxiliaries" [*fu* 輔]) format, one of these sections—the Taiping Section 太平部—was devoted to the *Taiping jing*. The extant Ming dynasty Daoist canon (referred to as the *Daoist Canon*)—which consists of the *Zhengtong daozang* 正统道藏 compiled in 1445, and its supplement of 1607, the *Xu daozang* 續道藏—contains a Taiping Section that features a text entitled *Taiping jing* 太平經 (from here on the extant text is referred to as *The Great Peace*).[8] Unfortunately, *The Great Peace* has not come down to us in its complete form; of its original 170 *juan* ("scrolls"), only 57 survive.[9] However, 57 *juan* is still quite a substantial quantity of material; furthermore, this material is supplemented in the *Daoist Canon* by the texts referred to as *GP Synopsis* (*Taiping jing chao* 太平經鈔; Synopsis of the *Taiping jing*)[10] and *GP Instructions* (*Taiping jing shengjun bizhi* 太平經聖君祕旨; The Sagely Lord's Secret Instructions of the *Taiping jing*).[11]

*GP Synopsis* is a synopsis in 10 sections of an entire, once-extant, 170 *juan* "*Taiping jing*."[12] *GP Instructions* is a short collection of instructions primarily on meditation that are presented as utterances pronounced by a certain Sagely Lord (Shengjun 聖君) and entrusted to the deity Lord Green Youth (Qingtongjun 青童君). As has been pointed out by the modern scholar Wang Ming 王明, many of its passages—amounting to about one-fourth of the full text—correspond in content and wording to portions of *The Great Peace* (71/2a–3a; 96/5b–6a) and *GP Synopsis* (10/10a–b; 2/5a–b), and it seems likely that many or most of its other passages were extracted from portions of the *Taiping jing* that are now lost.[13] Thus, in *The Great Peace*, *GP Synopsis*, and *GP Instructions* we have a large quantity of material that could originate from the *Taiping qingling shu* of the second century. This material can be further supplemented by passages quoted from the *Taiping jing* in other sources such as the early Tang period Daoist encyclopedias *Daodian lun* 道典論 (Treatise on the Daoist Standard Works; DZ1130/TT764)[14] and *Sandong zhunang* 三洞珠囊 (Pearl Bag of the Three Caverns; DZ1139/TT780–782).[15] In our discussion that follows, all of this textual material is referred to collectively as the "Taiping Group texts." (Wang Ming has assembled and organized all of this material into a single volume in a valiant attempt to reconstruct the original full text of the *Taiping jing*; this volume is entitled *Taiping jing hejiao* 太平經合校.)

It must first be noted, however, that the textual history of the *Taiping jing* and our Taiping Group texts turns out to be even more complicated than what has been described so far. Scholars such as Fukui Kōjun 福井康順 and Yoshioka Yoshitoyo 吉岡義豊 have argued compellingly that the 170-juan *Taiping jing* from which our *The Great Peace* has survived in its current total of 57 *juan* was itself not the original second century *Taiping jing* (namely, the *Taiping qingling shu*), but rather a reconstituted version produced around the year 572 by a certain Zhou Zhixiang 周智響.[16] Prior to that time the original 170 *juan Taiping jing* had become lost, while there remained fragments of a 144 *juan* version of the *Taiping jing* entitled *Taiping dongji jing* 太平洞極經 that was transmitted within the Heavenly Masters School. It appears likely that Meng Zhixiang produced a new 170 *juan Taiping jing* by expanding and embellishing what was left of the *Taiping dongji jing*.[17] *GP Synopsis* and *GP Instructions* are considered most likely to be Tang period compositions, and it is difficult to determine which version of the *Taiping jing* they are based upon.[18] The first section ("Jia" 甲) of *GP Synopsis* relates lore related to the Shangqing school that is blatantly anachronistic to a second-century setting; the editor of *GP Instructions* appears to have also embraced this sort of Shangqing lore, judging from how he ascribes his text's teachings to the Sagely Lord and Lord Green Youth. However, note that such clear evidence of Shangqing influence is otherwise not readily found in the Taiping Group texts.

Barbara Hendrischke, who has published an English translation of a significant portion of *The Great Peace* (*juan* 35–37, 39–49),[19] argues—cogently it seems—that the bulk of the material in *The Great Peace* only makes sense if understood as issuing from the context of the popular Daoist religious movements of the Han dynasty. Most of it bears the format of conversations between an anonymous figure known as the Heavenly Master (Tianshi 天師) and his disciples who are referred to as Genuine Persons (*zhenren* 真人). The Heavenly Master presents himself as being on a mission from "Heaven" (*tian* 天) to proclaim a message that can reform government and society in a manner by which the impending apocalypse can be averted, a peaceful, just and happy society can be realized, and the best of people can attain immortality. The main key lies in reforming the conduct of government and of the people in general, because natural disasters come from cosmic forces that respond aversely to the transgressions of human beings that have accumulated over the generations. Such a concern with human morality and its resonances on the cosmic order can be said to be characteristic of the Han period way of thinking; furthermore, as Hendrischke points out, the cosmology of *The Great Peace* attributes a dominant place to the color red and the agent of Fire—both of which bore an association with the Han dynasty. The style of writing throughout most of the text is verbose and inelegant—unlike anything seen elsewhere in the *Daoist Canon*—and seems almost certainly addressed to a nonelite audience. Hendrischke speculates that the redundant, verbose exposition results very likely because these are transcripts of actual conversations that occurred as preachers of a missionary movement repeatedly tried to convey key points of their message. As for exactly which missionary movement this was, this is never named. But the movement seems to be one not unlike the Way of Great Peace or the Way of the Five Pecks of Rice.[20]

In sum, although the Taiping Group texts are thus fraught with textual critical issues, they nonetheless offer us a wealth of information on early Daoist religious beliefs and practice that simply cannot be ignored. When reading them we can never be entirely sure that we are dealing with second-century Daoism; however, most passages we encounter in them do seem reflective of an early phase of Daoist religion that preceded major Six Dynasties period developments such as the major textual revelations (such as the Sanhuang, Shangqing, and Lingbao) or the intensive incorporation of Buddhist doctrines.

Meditation is a major theme (among many others) in the Taiping Group texts. In one passage in *GP Synopsis* is the following description of meditation that is to be carried out in isolation:

其為之法 當作齋室 堅其門戶 無人妄得入 日往自試 不精不安復出 勿強為之 如此復往 漸精熟即安 安不復欲出 口不欲語 ... 視 ... 食飲 ... 不欲聞人聲 關鍊積善 瞑目還觀形容 容象若居鏡中 若闚清水之影也 已為小成 無鞭策而嚴 無兵杖而威 萬事自治 豈不神哉 謂入神之路也 守三不如守二 守二不如守一 深思此言 得道深奧矣

The method for practicing this [meditation] is to set up a retreat room. Firmly shut the door so that nobody can carelessly enter in. Daily go [into the room] and put yourself to the test. If you cannot concentrate or if you feel uneasy, come out. Do not force yourself to do it. In this way continue to go [into the room daily]. Gradually your concentration will be thorough, and you will feel relaxed. You will no longer want to come out. Your mouth will not want to speak. See . . . eat, drink (a lacuna in this sentence?). You will not want to hear the voices of other people. Train in confinement and thereby accumulate merit. Close your eyes and look back upon the forms and appearances. The images will be like what resides in a mirror. It is like looking at reflections on clear water. This already constitutes the minor accomplishment. Without using a whip it is rigorous. Without using weapons you are mighty. All matters are naturally under control. Is this not divine? This is what is called "the road that enters divinity." To guard the Three is not as good as guarding the Two. To guard the Two is not as good as guarding the One. Reflect deeply upon this statement. You will thus attain the profundities of the Dao. (*GP Synopsis* 10/6a–b)

The meditation described here needs to be done in confined seclusion, and requires no small degree of concentration and effort. The loneliness and sensory deprivation will tend to make the average person feel uneasy and restless rather soon. You should not force yourself to withstand more isolation than you can bear, but rather gradually acclimate yourself to the practice. Eventually you will get to the point where you feel both concentrated and relaxed, and are no longer eager to come out of isolation and partake of human company. One portion of the passage seems to be mutilated, but seems to be saying something about seeing (*shi* 視), and about eating and drinking (*shi yin* 食飲). Speculating based on the context, one might surmise that the passage was meant to say something to the effect that once you are more concentrated and relaxed in the practice, you will lose your longing for sights outside the meditation room, and for food and drink (the Taiping Group texts, as we shall see, do in various places state that you should try to restrict your diet, feed on formless *qi*, and ideally consume no food at all). The actual meditation technique is not described in sufficient detail here either. However, you apparently are supposed to, while shutting your eyes, observe "forms and appearances" of some sort, which will at some point begin to appear before you vividly and clearly. The passage concludes by stating that it is better to guard the One than it is to guard the Two or the Three; "Guarding the One" (*shouyi*

守一) is a term frequently used throughout the Taiping Group texts—and in various other texts (both Daoist and Buddhist)—to refer to meditation. But what does it mean to "guard the Two" or "guard the Three"? Perhaps these, too, are meditation techniques that are of some significant benefit, but are just not as beneficial as "Guarding the One." By guarding "two" or "three" it would seem as though you are engaging your mind with something more complex and less essential than the "one." The statements here perhaps allude to a hierarchy of meditation methods—described more clearly elsewhere in the Taiping Group texts—that gives a higher ranking to methods involving less concrete mental imagery.

The One (*yi* 一) is a term that appears in the following famous passages of the *Laozi*:

載營魄抱一 能無離乎 (10th chapter)

Can you carry your soul and embrace the One without separation? (*Daode zhenjing* 1/3a)

是以聖人抱一爲天下式 (22nd chapter)

Hereby the Sage embraces the One and becomes a model for all under Heaven. (*Daode zhenjing* 1/6a)

昔之得一者 天得一以清 地得一以寧 神得一以靈 谷得一以盈 萬物得一以生 侯王得一以爲天下正 (39th chapter)

As for what obtained the One in times past: Heaven obtained the One and became clear. Earth obtained the One and became calm. Deities obtained the One and became divinely efficacious. Valleys obtained the One and became full. The myriad creatures obtained the One and came to life. Marquises and kings obtained the One and rectified all under Heaven. (*Daode zhenjing* 2/1b)

道生一 一生二 二生三 三生萬物 (42nd chapter)

The Dao produced the One, the One produced the Two, the Two produced the Three, and the Three produced the myriad creatures. (*Daode zhenjing* 2/2b)

Although the *Laozi* does not specifically say to "guard" the One, it does recommend "embracing" it. It is by "obtaining" the One that all things can exist and function as they ought to. In the sequence of cosmic generation, the One is the first thing produced by the ineffable Dao, and all else is produced by the One. The One is perhaps something like the primal, universal vital force of the Dao that endows all creatures with their essential nature and individual life. To hold firmly to this force is to be what you are supposed to be and to stay alive.

In one passage, the *Neiye* specifically speaks of guarding the One. That passage reads:

大心而敢(放?) 寬氣而廣 其形安而不移 能守一而棄萬苛

If you make your mind magnanimous and fearless (or, "and let it go"?),[21] and make your *qi* relaxed and vast, the body will be calm and will not move. You will be able to guard the One and cast off the myriad tribulations. (*Neiye*, section 24; Roth 1999, 93)

The One here most likely can be regarded as synonymous to that entity referred to elsewhere in the *Neiye* variously as "essence," "spirit," "Dao," or "numinous *qi*" that will keep you alive and well as long as it is maintained within. A mind that is "magnanimous and fearless" would seem to mean a mind that is free of the fear and anxiety that come with having too many selfish concerns. To "make the *qi* relaxed" may well mean to breathe slowly, deeply, or softly, and for the body to "not move" perhaps means that you can sit calmly in meditation.

*GP Instructions* contains numerous passages pertaining to Guarding the One. One of them reads:

守一之法為善 效驗可睹 今日為善清靜 神明漸光 始如螢火 久似電光

When you are good at the method of Guarding the One, you can observe its effects. If today you are good at being clear and calm, the divine radiance will gradually shine brighter. At first it will be like that of a firefly, but after a long while it will be like lightning. (*GP Instructions* 6a–b)

Apparently, being good at Guarding the One has much to do with being good at being serene. It also has to do with observing the sensory phenomena that emerge from within you. Mastery of the method brings forth observable effects, and the effect specifically described here is that you begin to see an inner light, which is but a faint flicker at first but which after a long while increases dramatically in its brightness. The vision of an inner light thus seems to be the initial, primary, tangible sign that the One is indeed alive and well within you. Another passage in the same text states:

守一明之法 未精之時 瞑目冥冥 目中無有光 守一復久 自生光明 昭然見四方 隨明而遠行 盡見身形容 群神將集 故能形化為神

The method of Guarding the One Light: when you are not yet refined at it, it will be pitch-dark when you close your eyes; there will be no radiance in your eyes. After Guarding the One for a longer time, you will naturally produce radiance. You will clearly see to the four directions. Following the light you will go long distances, and see all of the bodily forms and appearances. The throngs of deities will thereby gather. Thus you will be able to make your body transform into spirit. (*GP Instructions* 1b)

Here the meditation method is referred to as Guarding the One Light (*shou yi ming* 守一明). While closing your eyes, you hope to see an inner light emerge spontaneously. However, at first, when you are not accomplished at meditation, you will see only pure darkness. However, the text goes on to reassure you that through persistence you will see a radiance while closing your eyes, and that the obtaining of this inner radiance will confer supernormal visual powers on you and enable you to somehow perceive or perhaps communicate with deities. Furthermore, by persevering in this practice you can actually transform your physical body into spirit (*shen* 神).

In sum, the key to successful meditation is serenity, which can eventually cause an inner light to spontaneously emerge, which in turn attracts the company of deities, and which conduces to the refinement of the body. This general sort of scheme is also conveyed in the following passages found in *GP Synopsis*:

故樂者 天地之善氣精為之 以致神明 故靜以生光明 光明所以候神也 能通神明 有以道為鄰 且得長生久存

Thus, joy is something brought about by the good *qi* and essence of Heaven and Earth, which in turn brings forth the divine radiances. Thus, by means of calmness you produce radiance. Because of the radiance you can await the deities. You can communicate with the deities, and thus have a means of being in proximity with the Dao. Also, you can attain long life. (*GP Synopsis* 2/3a–b)

夫神靈出入 無有穴窠 清靜而無聲 安枕而臥 神光自生

The deities and spirits in their exiting and entering do not have burrows or nests. If you are pure and calm without a sound, and lie down peacefully on your pillow, divine radiance will naturally emerge. (*GP Synopsis* 2/15a–b)

The first passage states that "joy" (*le* 樂), which is bred from the good forces of the cosmos, is what attracts deities. Calmness of mind produces inner light, by which it becomes possible for you to expect the arrival of deities. The second passage describes deities and spirits as beings that exit and enter, and which have no fixed abode. Divine and spiritual beings can enter and inhabit the body, but are also frequently inclined to wander out. Through serenity and quietude you generate divine radiance, and this seems to be because the divine beings are happy and content to reside within you. Interestingly, it also says here that you are to lie down with your head on a pillow; thus it would appear that meditation was carried out at least sometimes in a reclining position, as opposed to a seated one.

In regard to the desirable duration of the meditative confinement, *GP Instructions* states:

守一之法 百日為小靜 二百日為中靜 三百日為大靜 內使常樂 三尸已落

The Method of Guarding the One: 100 days is a minor calm, 200 days is an intermediate calm, and 300 days is a major calm. Inside it makes you constantly joyful, and the Three Corpses are disposed of. (*GP Instructions* 5b)

Thus, one hundred days was perceived as a momentous milestone to aspire to, and three hundred days was considered truly impressive. It is worth noting again here the emphasis on serenity and joy as the prevailing condition and mood. The Three Corpses (*sanshi* 三尸), which are frequently mentioned in Daoist literature from the Six Dynasties onward (but are only mentioned this once in the Taiping Group texts; perhaps this is evidence of Six Dynasties embellishment), are three demons dwelling in the human body which desire the person to die, and thus have a constant propensity to tempt people towards immoral, self-destructive behavior, after which they periodically travel up to the heavens to report the person's sins (while he or she is sleeping) to the divine powers that punish evildoers by shortening their life spans.[22] In essence, to dispose of the Three Corpses means to purge the body of what makes it mortal.

Thus, the Taiping Group texts, in their instructions regarding meditation, indeed place a great emphasis on serenity, which is deemed instrumental in bringing about the tangible effects indicative of progress. These tangible effects primarily consist of visions of inner light that emerges spontaneously and that leads to visions of divine beings that are thought to be attracted by that inner light.

While the Taiping Group texts indicate that much spontaneous sensory phenomena can be passively observed through deep serenity, they also strongly endorse the proactive method of visualization in passages such as the following:

真人但安坐深幽室閑處 念心思神 神悉自來到

Genuine Person, you should just sit peacefully and relax in a deep, dark room. Mindfully think of the gods. The gods will naturally arrive on their own. (*The Great Peace* 96/25b)

故人能清靜 抱精神 思慮不失 即凶邪不得入矣 其真神在內 使人常喜欣欣然 不欲貪財寶 辯訟爭 競功名 久久自能見神 神長二尺五寸 隨五行五藏服飾

Thus, if people can be clear and calm and thereby embrace their essence and spirit, their contemplations will not err, and wickedness cannot enter in. The genuine deities will stay inside them, causing them to be always joyful. You should not covet wealth and treasures, engage in quarrels, nor compete for merit and fame. After a long while you will naturally be able to see the deities. The deities will be two feet and five inches[23] [tall] and will be clothed in garments that accord with the five agents (wood, fire, earth, metal and water) and five viscera (liver, heart, spleen, lungs and kidneys). (*GP Synopsis* 10/5a)

使空室內傍無人 畫象隨其藏色 與四時氣相應 懸之窗光之中而思之 上有藏象 下有十鄉 臥即念以近懸象 思之不止 五藏神能報二十四時氣 五行神且來救助之 萬疾皆愈 男思男 女思女 皆以一尺為法 隨四時轉移 春 青童子十 夏 赤童子十 秋 白童子十 冬 黑童子十 四季 黃童子十二

Make it so that in the empty room there is nobody around you. The pictures should be in accordance with the color of the organ [where they reside], and correspond to the *qi* of the four seasons. Hang up [the images] amid the light from the window(s), and contemplate them. Above is the image of the organ, and beneath are the ten homesteads (?). When lying down, contemplate and go near the suspended image. If you contemplate this way without ceasing, the deities of your five viscera will be able to respond to the breaths of the twenty-four times, and the deities of the five agents will also come to your assistance. The myriad diseases will be cured. If you are a man you should think of male [deities]. If you are a woman you should think of female [deities]. Each [deity thought of] is one foot [in height]; this is the method. [The object of contemplation] shifts in accordance to the four seasons. In the spring, [think of] ten Green Children. In the summer, [think of] ten Red Children. In the fall, [think of] ten White Children. In the winter, [think of] ten Black Children. In the four *ji* months (the third and last month of each of the four seasons; i.e., the third, sixth, ninth and twelfth lunar months), [think of] twelve Yellow Children. (*GP Synopsis* 2/3b–4a)

Thus we are told that by intensively thinking of specific deities in very specific forms, you will hopefully reach a stage where those deities will appear before you in the precise form that you had imagined. "Thinking of" (*si* 思) or contemplating upon these deities most likely involves conjuring a mental image of them. The ability to create a vivid, accurate, and appropriate mental image seems to be crucial, and this is why you need to set up pictures of the deities in your meditation chamber to study, so as to facilitate the correct visualization. Thus, although a mood of inner calm is deemed essential, the actual mental technique here seems to involve far more than passive inner observation.

There are a few passages in the Taiping Group texts that endorse visualization techniques that paradoxically exclude visual content. For instance, one passage in *GP Instructions* states:

守一之法 當念本無形 湊液相合 一乃從生 去老反稚 可得長生 子若守一 無使多知 守一不退 無一不知 所求皆得 端坐致之 子欲大樂 與一相知 去榮辭顯一乃相宜 子欲養老 守一為早 平床坐臥 與一相保 不食而飽 不德衰老

[To practice the] method of Guarding the One, you should contemplate the original formlessness. Bringing the fluids together and merging them together (?), the One thereby is produced. Going away from old age and returning to childhood, you can obtain long life. If you Guard the One, do not make yourself know much. If you Guard the One without relent, there will not be a single thing that you do not know. Everything that you seek for, you will obtain. You will bring it forth just by sitting upright. If you wish for great joy, get to know the One. Avoid glory and eschew fame, and the One will be compatible with you. If you want to nurture yourself in old age, Guarding the One is the thing to do early (in the morning?). Sit or lie on a flat bed, and preserve yourself with the One. Without eating you will be full. You will not acquire decrepitude and old age (or perhaps, "If you are not virtuous, you will become decrepit and aged" [?][24]). (*GP Instructions* 4b–5a)

The method described here does not require visualization of specific deities, forms, or shapes. Yet, it is not quite what one could call passive observation either, for you are given a subject to reflect on—albeit one that is formless. By keeping your mind free of forms—or perhaps by immersing yourself in the self-negating insight that you, like everything else, originated out of an original formlessness—it appears that you initiate some sort of spontaneous physiological process (if this is what is meant by the phrase tentatively translated as "bringing the fluids together and merging them together" [*couye xianghe* 湊液相合]) by which the eternal, life-giving force wells up within you. The passage then proceeds, much in the spirit of the *Laozi*, to claim that emptying the mind of all knowledge is the way to obtain a truly all-embracing knowledge. It further goes on to state that everything you really need will be obtained effortlessly as long as you Guard the One and maintain your rapport with it (through non-ambition and self-effacement). Notably, one of these benefits is the ability to be satiated and nourished without eating—a topic that we return to.

Another such minimalist sort of proactive meditation is described in the following passage in *The Great Peace* (with cognate passages also to be found in *GP Synopsis* and *GP Instructions*):

第一元氣無為者 念其身也 無一為也 但思其身洞白 若委氣而無形 常以是為法 已成則無不為無不知也 故人無道之時 但人耳 得道則變易成神仙 而神上天 隨天變化 即是其無不為也

其二為虛無自然者 守形洞虛自然 無有奇也 身中照白 上下若玉 無有瑕也 為之積久久 亦度世之術也 此次元氣無為象也

First, the [method of] the Non-action of the Primal *Qi*: Contemplate your body. Do not do a single thing. Just think of your body as hollow and blank, as though it were formless and entrusted to *qi*. Always make this your method. Once it is accomplished, nothing will be not done and nothing will be unknown. Thus, when people do not have the Dao, they are but people. When they obtain the Dao, they transform and become Divine Transcendents. Thus, your spirit will ascend the heavens and transform according to the heavens. This is whereby nothing is not done by you.

The second [method] is the Naturalness of Empty Nothingness. Guard the body that is hollow, empty and natural, and has nothing strange. Throughout the body is bright and white, from top to bottom like jade that is without blemish. If you practice this for a very long time, this is also a technique for transcending the world. This is next best to the form of [the method of] Non-action of the Primal *Qi*. (*The Great Peace* 71/2a–b)

The two methods outlined here are part of an enumeration of nine practices—or "Nine Degrees" (*jiudu* 九度)—by which you can practice the Dao (see *The Great Peace* 71/1b–3a).[25] The practices are enumerated in descending order of efficacy and holiness. The two methods outlined here are listed at 1 and 2, meaning that they are to be regarded as superior to the other methods. The supreme method—the method of the Non-action of the Primal *Qi*—involves "not doing a single thing." This being said, it turns out that the method does entail visualization—albeit visualization of something utterly blank and formless. What you are visualizing is the formless form that you hope your body will someday assume when you achieve transformation into the holiest type of immortal person that exists. The term "entrusted to *qi*" (*weiqi* 委氣) here in all likelihood refers to the class of person referred to in the Taiping Group texts as the Formless Divine Person Entrusted to *Qi* (*wuxing weiqi zhi shenren* 無形委氣之神人), whose function in the divine bureaucracy of the cosmos is to "regulate the Primal *Qi*" (*li yuanqi* 理元氣); this is because he or she "resembles the Primal *Qi* (*si yuanqi* 似元氣).[26] Through this method the transformation visualized is said to be indeed possible. Method 2—the Naturalness of Void Non-being—is similar, or in fact hard to distinguish from method 1. It also is a simple visualization in which you visualize the inside of your body not as the abode of deities, but as luminous, unblemished void. The anticipated reward is immortality and perhaps heavenly ascension (depending on how one is supposed to interpret the commonly used but ambiguous term "transcend the world" [*dushi* 度世]).

The other methods among the Nine Degrees consist mostly of what appear to be techniques for visualizing, communicating with, or commanding deities. Methods 4 and 5 involve visualizing and controlling the deities of the five viscera somewhat in the manner we saw earlier; here these methods are regarded as good primarily for prognostication and for subduing demons, rather than for longevity or immortality. Methods 6 through 9 appear to involve communications with various deities in the world outside one's body, and are not much recommended by the text at all; attached to their descriptions are warnings maintaining that such worldly deities are often deceptive, and that even worse, they have the propensity to possess people and drive them to insanity.

Most ambiguous—and perhaps without parallel in Daoist literature—is the description of method 3, "Counting and Measuring" (*shudu* 數度), which is considered a method for the "minor transcending of the world" (*xiao dushi* 小度世). It is described as:

積精還自視也 數頭髮下至足五指 分別形容 身外內莫不畢數 知其意 當常以是爲念 不失銖分

In a sustained, diligent manner, look back upon yourself. Count the hairs on your head and [keep counting your physical components] down to the five toes on your feet. Discern and distinguish the forms. On the surface and on the inside of your body count everything. Understand the meaning of this. Always keep this upon your mind. Do not miss the smallest details. (*The Great Peace* 71/2b)

What is described here is actually somewhat reminiscent of an ancient Buddhist meditation technique known as "mindfulness of the body" (*kāyagatā-sati* in Pali) wherein one is to reflect on one's body and its components in detail, from its hair, nails, teeth, skin, inner organs, and so on, down to its excrement, bile, phlegm, saliva, mucus, urine, and so on.[27] The objective of Buddhist mindfulness of body meditation is to foster disgust and detachment from the body. Such does not seem to be the objective of what is described here in *The Great Peace*. The meticulous "counting" of hairs, fingers, and so on is seemingly supposed to foster some state of mind that is conducive to "transcending the world," but that state of mind does not seem to be disgust or detachment. In some early Chinese translations of Buddhist texts the term *counting* (*shu* 數) is used to refer to particular meditation technique. However, that counting technique is a method of fostering inner calm and concentration by counting one's respirations (*shuxi* 數息); it is not the same sort of counting described here in *The Great Peace*.[28]

In *GP Synopsis* (5/13b–14a) we also find mentioned a set of nine practices called the "Nine Rooms" (*jiushi* 九室). The Nine Rooms appear to have been a series of meditation techniques that a high-aspiring adept was expected to carry out in ordered progression in isolation in a meditation room. Unfortunately, the text does not actually provide us with distinct descriptions of nine different meditation methods. The passage in question does start out by saying:

入室思存五官 轉移隨陰陽 孟仲季為兄弟 應氣而動 順四時五行 天道變化以為常矣

Enter the room to contemplate the Five Officials. Rotate and shift according to the *yin* and *yang*. *Meng*, *zhong* and *ji* (the first, second and third months of the three months constituting each of the four seasons) are brothers. Move in response to the *qi*, according with the four seasons and Five Agents. The way of heaven is to transform, and thereby be constant. (*GP Synopsis* 5/13b)

From this it appears that perhaps some or all of the Nine Rooms methods alluded to shortly further on in the text have something to do with visualization of divine, cosmic, or physiological forces or entities, the exact manner of which shifts and varies according to the natural processes of cosmic *qi*, the seasons, and the Five Agents of Wood, Fire, Soil, Metal, and Water. The biggest problem here is what is meant by the "Five Officials." Most likely it refers either to the deities that embody and command the Five Agents in the cosmos, or to the deities dwelling in the body's five viscera (liver, heart, spleen, lungs, and kidneys).

In any case, the passage continues by expounding on how you must maintain and accumulate *qi*, and states that through steadfast practice you can become long-lasting and can "transform in accordance with the *qi*" 隨氣而化. Further on it states, "In your own studies, after you have exchanged [one for another] the Nine Rooms you become a Divine Person" 身學 已更九室成神人. It then explains that the sort of people able to accomplish this are those whose thoughts and aspirations differ from common folk, and are always focused on heavenly things. Regarding such people we are told:

乃後可下九室 積精篤竭自化 易其形容 即是上天聖人也

[They] can subsequently undergo the Nine Rooms. Through accumulated diligence and thorough dedication they naturally transform. They change their appearances. They are the Sagely Persons of the upper heavens. (*GP Synopsis* 5/14a)

Unfortunately, specific descriptions of the nine different meditation methods of the Nine Rooms cannot be found among the Taiping Group texts. However, as described in chapter 3, such descriptions appear to have perhaps survived in a text that we refer to as *The True Record*. At the very least, that text is evidence that the notion of a regimen of nine consecutive isolated meditation techniques did survive among the *mileu* that promoted the hagiographical lore pertaining to Lord Lao (Laojun 老君; the deified Laozi) and his instruction of his main disciple Yin Xi 尹喜.

*The Great Peace* does not reserve its meditation techniques for the spiritual elite. Rather, it conveys the hope that all people, by Guarding the One as best as they can, can fulfill their allotted potential, and collectively contribute to the realization of a better society and world. In the 96th *juan* of *The Great Peace* we find the following passage:

是故夫守一之道 得古今守一者 復以類聚之 上賢明力為之 可得度世 中賢力為之 可為帝王良輔善吏 小人力為之 不知喜怒 天下無怨咎也

Therefore, in regard to the Dao of Guarding the One: You can take those of past and present who Guard the One, and organize them by category. If superior worthies wisely and diligently practice it, they can transcend the world. If intermediate worthies diligently practice it, they can become the worthy confidants and officials of an Emperor. If small people diligently practice it, they will know of no more delight and anger (they will have no drastic mood swings), and there will be no more enmity and transgression under Heaven. (*The Great Peace* 96/5b–6a)

In other words, it is only the most virtuous people who can attain immortality by Guarding the One; however, everybody still should practice it. Even if your virtue falls short of making you capable of attaining immortality, meditation can still endow you with the inner clarity and wisdom to contribute to the administration of the empire. Even people who entirely lack moral virtue (this is what is meant by "small people") can through meditation control their moods and become more amicable and obedient. Thus it is for the common good to widely propagate the meditation of Guarding the One. It is not an esoteric practice that should be concealed or withheld from anybody. This outlook is consistent with the broader social and cosmological vision of the Taiping Group texts, which maintain that human evil and transgressions create disharmony in the cosmic forces that naturally bring forth epidemics and natural disasters. The accumulated transgressions of past generations continue to bring repercussions on later generations. The solution to the problem must be the society-wide reform of human behavior, and this can be best accomplished by propagating the *Taiping jing* and its teachings (including Guarding the One). Fostering general mental serenity throughout society will lessen people's impulses to commit transgressions, and will lessen the frequency of illness and natural disaster for present and future generations; meditation is conducive to fostering this serenity.

Thus, in the 108th *juan* of *The Great Peace* is the following passage, which is quite interesting for how it provides a picture of people of seemingly mediocre virtue and fortitude being put into confinement for a designated number of days, with some degree of monitoring by others:

其為道者 取訣於入室 外內批之 滿日數 開戶入視之 於其內自批者 勿入視也 其內不自批者 即樂人入視之也 開戶入視 欲出者便出之

> As for practicing the Dao, the principle of it is to be found in entering the room. Critique them from outside and inside. When the designated number of days has elapsed, open the door and look at them. As for those who are critiquing themselves from within, you must not go in and look [at them]. [However,] those who are not critiquing themselves from within enjoy having [another] person coming in to look at them. [In such a case] you should open the door to go in and look [at them]. Those who want to come out you should thereby bring out. (*The Great Peace* 108/1a)

Unfortunately, the passage here lacks a specific description of what the "Way" is that is being practiced inside the closed room. Is it a meditation technique such as Guarding the One, or the Non-action of the Primal *Qi*, or is it something more along the lines of the confined penitential self-reflection that preceded the healing rituals administered within the Way of the Five Pecks of Rice? The usage of the term critique (*pi* 批) tends to suggest that it is a penitential practice. On the other hand, on the same page of the text we do find a short passage also pertaining to "entering the room" (*rushi* 入室), which strongly suggests that the practitioner is supposed to be carrying out a meditation technique:

其問入室成與未者 取訣於洞明白也 形無彰蔽 以為天信

> As for those who inquire as to whether the entering of the room has been accomplished or not yet accomplished, the principle is to be found in hollow, bright whiteness. If the form has no concealment of its brightness, this is the indication from Heaven. (*The Great Peace* 108/1b)

Although the meaning of the above passage is far from straightforward, it appears to be saying that the success of the "entering of the room" is to be gauged according to whether a particular sort of inner luminosity is witnessed as having resulted. This, then, could be the sort of standard by which the confined practitioners were being critiqued by self and others. Whatever the case, it would appear that many of these practitioners were not particularly suited for the practice, and were quite happy to be let out of confinement.

As was briefly noted earlier, in the Taiping Group texts there are various passages in which the reduction or (even better) elimination of food intake is put forth as an important objective to be attained, at least by the spiritual elite that aspire to immortality. This attainment amounts to a restoration of a pristine condition that humanity enjoyed at the time of creation. In the 36th *juan* of *The Great Peace*, in a section entitled "Guarding the Three Substantial Things" (Shou sanshi fa 守三實法; Section 44), we find the Heavenly Master telling the Genuine Man:

然天下人 本生受命之時 與天地分身 抱元氣於自然 不飲不食 噓吸陰陽氣而活 不知飢渴 久久離神道遠 小小失其指意 後生者 不得復知真道空虛 日流就偽 更生飢渴 不飢 (*sic.*, 飲) 不食便死

However, when the people under heaven were originally born and received their lives, their bodies divided off of heaven and earth. They embraced the primal *qi* naturally, never drinking and never eating. They lived breathing the *qi* of *yin* and *yang*, and did not know of thirst and hunger. After a long time their spirits separated far away from the Dao, and little by little they lost its principles. Those who were born later could no longer know the vacant emptiness of the true Dao. Daily they drifted toward the artificial, and gave rise to thirst and hunger. [So it came about that] they die if they do not drink[29] and eat. (*The Great Peace* 36/1b–2a)

Further on, in the 36th *juan*, in the section entitled "The Fortune and Misfortune of the Three Urgent Things" (Sanji jixiong 三急吉凶; Section 45) the Heavenly Master similarly states:

跂行始受陰陽統之時 同髣髴噓吸 含自然之氣 未知食飲也 久久亦離其本遠大道消竭 天氣不能常隨護視之 因而飢渴

When walking creatures first received the governance of *yin* and *yang*, they all in the same manner exhaled and inhaled faintly, and thus contained within them the *qi* of naturalness. They knew not of eating and drinking. After a long while they separated a long way from their origin, and the Great Dao disappeared and was exhausted. The *qi* of heaven was no longer able to constantly follow, protect and look after them. Thus they get thirsty and hungry. (*The Great Peace* 36/4b)

The message thus conveyed by the above two passages is that we originally did not need to eat and drink, because we were nourished by primal *qi* (*yuanqi* 元氣), or the *qi* of naturalness (*ziran zhi qi* 自然之氣) that we were able to somehow embrace or contain within us. All we did to stay alive was breathe, and this we did very softly. All of this was possible because we were spiritually in touch with the Dao; we went about our ways naturally and without artifice, and were thus protected and nurtured by the *qi* of heaven. Both passages are followed by statements proclaiming that after we had fallen into our mortal condition that required solid and liquid nourishment, heaven and earth, out of pity for us, began to produce things that we could eat and drink; our mortal condition also made it necessary for heaven to cause us to procreate through the union of the sexes.[30]

Another sort of pristine condition that seems to serve as a model and inspiration for not eating is that of the fetus. In *GP Synopsis* we find the following statements.

胞中童 不食十月神相通 自然之道無有上 不視而氣宅十二重 故反嬰兒則無凶 老還反少與道通

Children inside the embryo eat nothing for ten months, and yet their spirits come to interpenetrate. [In the following of the] Dao of naturalness, there is nobody superior to them. Without looking, they have a dwelling of *qi* in twelve stories (?). Thus, if you return to the condition of the infant, you will come to no harm. The elderly can return to youth and communicate with the Dao. (*GP Synopsis* 4/1a)

請問胞中之子 不食而取氣

在腹中 自然之氣 已生 呼吸陰陽之氣 守道力學 反自然之氣 反自然之氣 心若嬰兒 即生矣 隨呼吸陰陽之氣 即死矣

[The Genuine Man said,] "May I ask about how children inside the embryo do not eat, yet obtain *qi*?"

[The Heavenly Master replied,] "When they are in the belly, [fetuses are sustained by] the *qi* of naturalness. Once they are born, they breathe the *qi* of *yin* and *yang*. When you guard the Dao and study it diligently, you revert to the *qi* of naturalness. When you revert to the *qi* of naturalness, your mind is like that of an infant, and thereby you live. If you follow the way of breathing the *qi* of *yin* and *yang*, you will die." (*GP Synopsis* 8/19b–20a)

Fetuses obviously do not eat or drink in the manner we do, yet they not only survive but also grow rapidly in both their physical and mental capacities. Their condition of pristine vitality is one worth emulating, and that condition is one where they are nourished by the *qi* of naturalness. The *qi* of naturalness is in the second passage here contrasted to the *qi* of *yin* and *yang* that people breathe once they have been born, and this ordinary manner of breathing is condemned as something that brings about death. In the previous passages idealizing the condition of humanity at the dawn of our genesis, the primitives were described as breathing the *qi* of *yin* and *yang*, but were also described as breathing in a "faint" (*fangfu* 髣髴) manner. The implication here is that there might be some method of very soft breathing that one ought to practice in order to minimize the harm wrought by ordinary breathing, while maximizing the volume and efficacy of the *qi* of naturalness or primal *qi* within you. We have here, it seems, some fundamental ideas behind the various techniques of "embryonic breathing" (*taixi* 胎息) that developed in medieval times, and which is discussed in chapter 7. Equally or more importantly, what infants and primitives are assumed to share in common (rightly or wrongly; one wonders whether our earliest ancestors were really not quite fraught with anxiety over their bare survival) is the serenity that is borne by innocence, that enables them to successfully embrace the primal *qi* and stay in intimate communion with the Dao and the protective *qi* of heaven, all without any conscious effort or purpose.

The abilities to stop eating and to suspend breathing would come to be regarded in various Daoist texts as important effects that deep serenity was supposed to spontaneously bring about. In the Taiping Group texts there are a few passages that seem to suggest that the elimination of hunger can occur spontaneously as an effect of meditation, without any recourse to any deliberate technique of fasting or hunger-suppression. One such passage is the one quoted earlier from *GP Instructions* (4b–5a) where it describes how to Guard the One by contemplating the "original formlessness" 本無形, and further on states that by Guarding the One you will be full without eating. Another such passage can be found in *The Great Peace*, *juan* 98, in a section entitled "Lesson on Enwrapping Heaven and Earth, and Guarding the *Qi* without Interruption" (Baotian guodi shouqi bujue jue 包天裹地守氣不絕訣; Section 160). There we find the Heavenly Master offering the following advice on how to go about becoming everlasting as heaven and earth:

子欲不終窮 宜與氣為玄牝 象天為之 安得死也 亦不可卒得 乃成幽室也 入室思道 自不食與氣結也 因為天地神明畢也 不復與於俗治也 乃上從天太一也 朝於中極 受符而行 周流洞達六方八遠無窮時也

> If you do not want to come to an end, you should with *qi* make your Mysterious Female. Emulate heaven in doing this. How could you thereby obtain death? However, [this method] cannot be immediately obtained. Thus, you should make for yourself a dark room. Enter the room and contemplate the Dao. Naturally you will not eat and you will be bound together with *qi*. Because the divine radiance of heaven and earth is completed, you will no longer associate with secular governance. Thus you will up above follow the Great One of heaven. You will have an audience with the Central Extreme, receive a talisman and go about. Circulating about and pervading the six directions and eight distances, you will never come to your end. (*The Great Peace* 98/12b)

It is hard to say here what is meant by "with *qi* make your Mysterious Female" 與氣為玄牝. However, it should be noted that "Mysterious Female" (*xuanpin* 玄牝) is a term that famously occurs in the *Laozi*'s sixth chapter, and which is there used to describe a certain "spirit of the valley" 谷神, which "does not die" 不死. This terminology would come to be interpreted and employed in various ways in Daoist religious literature in relation to meditation and longevity practices. In any case, the Heavenly Master here seems to admit that this method, whatever it is, is probably too difficult for most people to undertake anyway. The method that he prescribes after this is what presently concerns us. He states that you are to prepare yourself a dark room in which to "contemplate the Dao" (whatever this specifically means), and that by doing so you *naturally* do not eat. In this condition you are somehow "bound up with *qi*," which we might surmise to be something like the condition of people at the dawn of creation or of fetuses, who embrace the primal *qi*.

Although there is thus some indication in the Taiping Group texts that the elimination of hunger can come about as a natural effect of meditation practice, one also finds various passages promoting a more deliberate, proactive method for eschewing food and drink. That method is the "eating of *qi*" (*shiqi* 食氣). In the 42nd *juan* of *The Great Peace*, in a section entitled "The Nine Heavens Method for Eliminating the Calamities of Previous Kings" (Jiutian xiao xianwang zai fa 九天消先王災法; Section 56), the Heavenly Master sets forth the theory that there are nine types of persons who need to each carry out their proper task and aid in the governance of the king, in order for a harmonious society of Great Peace (Taiping 太平) to come about. The most sublime of these are the aforementioned Formless Divine Persons Entrusted to *Qi* (*wuxing weiqi zhi shenren* 無形委氣之神人). Their task, as mentioned, is to "regulate the primal *qi*" (*li yuanqi* 理元氣), since they are themselves formless.[31] The Heavenly Master goes on to outline a method for controlling the *qi*, by which you are apparently, in the best scenario, supposed to transform into such a Formless Divine Person Entrusted to *Qi*:

調氣必先食氣 故上士將入道 先不食有形而食氣 是且與元氣合 故當養置茅室中 使其齋戒不睹邪惡 日練其形 毋奪其欲 能出無間去 上助仙真元氣天治也 是為神士天之吏也

To control the *qi* you must first eat *qi*. Therefore, superior gentlemen, when entering the Dao, first stop eating things that have form, and instead eat *qi*. This also is to merge with the primal *qi*. Thus, you should nourish and situate yourself in a thatched chamber, observing ritual purifications and precepts. Do not look upon wicked things. Daily refine your form, without slacking in your will. You will be able to depart and go amidst the space of nothingness, and above assist the Transcendent Genuine Ones in their celestial governing of the primal *qi*. This is a Divine Gentleman, an Official of Heaven. (*The Great Peace* 42/3a)

What is thus set forth is undoubtedly a rigorous practice in which you need to make yourself stop eating food and instead eat *qi* that is formless. It requires great effort, determination, and focus. Thus it entails seclusion and the observation of ritual purifications and precepts. It is a process by which the very constitution of your body is to be entirely transformed into a formless state in which it can mount the skies and perform the sublime *qi*-regulating tasks of the celestial bureaucracy.

Essentially, you eat formless *qi* in order to become formless; but what exactly is this formless *qi* that you are supposed to eat? It is most likely air. The technique probably consisted of swallowing air into your esophagus and down into your stomach. That such is likely the case is most suggested in a conversation recorded in the 86th *juan* of *The Great Peace*, in a section entitled "Lesson on Bringing the Good and Gathering the Documents from the Three Roads" (Laishan ji sandao wenshu jue 來善集三道文書訣; Section 127). There we are told of how the Heavenly Master was visited by the Genuine Persons of the Six Directions 六方真人, who had been doing a great deal of contemplating and discussing of things among themselves. On a prior occasion the Heavenly Master had declared that for the realization of a fair and open government and society all people should be encouraged to report in written documents all of the good and bad things that they saw around them, and that these documents should be collected for examination by the sovereign. The six Genuine Persons were deeply concerned about the prospects of this venture being successful, and had looked to certain omens to allay or confirm their fears. One variety of omens they had witnessed and contemplated was that of the astronomical sort. When they describe these astronomical omens to the Heavenly Master, the Heavenly Master confirms their fears that the omens reflect the dire situation where enlightened governance based on open, candid communication is severely inhibited. Interestingly, the six Genuine Persons also report on a certain omen they each witnessed when they undertook the eating of *qi*:

又六人俱食氣 俱咽不下通 氣逆而更上 當此之時 耳目為之眩瞑 無睹 俱怪而相從議之 不知其為何等大駭驚怖 唯天師為愚生說 之

Also, the six of us all ate *qi*, but all of us when swallowing it could not make it penetrate below, and the *qi* reversed itself and came back up. At this moment, our ears and eyes were darkened and could not observe. We all thought this strange and discussed it among each other. We could not understand the reason for it and were horrified. We request the Heavenly Master to explain it to us. (*The Great Peace* 86/5b)

What is described here sounds like an attempt to swallow air into the esophagus, which resulted only in the air coming back up, perhaps in a burp or belch. Apparently, the six Genuine Persons are experienced enough in the method to where they no longer expect this to happen; rather, the air is supposed to stay down in them, pervade their bodies and nourish them. But what seemingly perturbs them the most is that this failure in *qi*-eating also muddles the ability of their ears and eyes to "observe." It would appear as though their *qi*-eating was carried out in tandem with meditation, and that in the midst of this meditation they had hoped for some sort of mystical insight that might reveal what prospects for success lay in store for the Heavenly Master's initiative for open communication and enlightened governance. In any case, in what follows in the text, the Heavenly Master proceeds to confirm that their failure to keep down their *qi* was indeed an inauspicious omen; the failure of the *qi* to penetrate the inner conduits of the body was a result of a correlative, sympathetic response to the situation in society, where a culture of intimidation and fear inhibits the free communication of ideas and information (see *The Great Peace* 86/5b–6a).

There seems to be here the idea that the eating of *qi*, combined with quiet contemplation, can lead to profound, guiding insights. Indeed, in a few places in the Taiping Group texts we can find evidence of a notion of the existence of wise men of ancient times who employed this method to enable them to carry out effective government. In *The Great Peace*, *juan* 36, in the section entitled "The Fortune and Misfortune of the Three Urgent Things" (Sanji jixiong 三急吉凶; Section 45), the Heavenly Master states:

故古者聖賢飲食氣而治者 深居幽室思道 念得失之象 不敢離天
法誅分之間也 居清靜處 已得其意 其治立平 與天地相似哉

> Therefore, the Sages and Worthies of ancient times, who governed while drinking and eating *qi*, dwelled deep inside the dark room to contemplate the Dao. They contemplated the emblems of gain and loss, and did not dare to deviate from the heavenly laws on the exacting of punishment. They dwelled in a place of clarity and calmness. Once they had gained what they had intended, their government was immediately peaceful. They were just like heaven and earth! (*The Great Peace* 36/6a)

Thus here we see the eating of *qi* being described as something done in tandem with solitary contemplation in a dark room, during which "emblems" (*xiang* 象) constituting omens are somehow perceived. The abiding state of mind fostered through all of this is clarity and calmness—namely, serenity—and the result is a just and peaceful society under the Sage or Worthy who practices this.

Also, in a fragment attributed to "the 145th *juan* of the *Taiping jing*," now preserved as a quote in the early Tang Daoist encyclopedia, the *Daodian lun*, we find the following statement:

古者上真睹天神食氣 象之為行 乃學食氣 真神來助其為治 乃遊
居真人腹中也 古者真仙之身 名為真人室宅耳

> In ancient times the superior Genuine Ones observed the gods of heaven eating *qi*. They conducted themselves in emulation of them, and thus learned to eat *qi*. The genuine gods thus came to assist them in their governance, and wandered in to dwell inside the bellies of those Genuine Persons. In ancient times the bodies of Genuine Transcendents were known as "the houses of the Genuine Persons." (*Daodian lun* 4/9a)

Here we are told that the very idea of eating *qi* was inspired by observing the actions of celestial deities—certainly a mode of observing that requires significant prior attainment of psychic powers. We are further told that the subsequent eating of *qi* not only inspired gods to come and assist the ancient Genuine Persons in governance, but also caused the gods to dwell within them. It is as though the practice of eating only air somehow empties and clears out the body so as to provide room for the gods.

Speaking more realistically and practically, substituting air for solid and liquid nourishment is a horribly difficult and arduous task that cannot be undertaken by any ordinary person or novice. Understandably then, the Taiping Group texts do mention other dietetic methods that can be undertaken instead of or in preparation for the eating of *qi*. One of these is to start out by first eating small amounts of food, and gradually proceeding to the level of eating *qi*. This notion is neatly summed up by the Heavenly Master in the following statement, found in the 70th *juan* of *The Great Peace* (Section 106, "Lesson on the Gains and Losses of Students" 學者得失訣):

入室始少食 久久食氣 便解去不見者 是也

To eat little when first entering the meditation room, to begin to eat *qi* after a long while, and thereupon become liberated and invisible—this is good. (*The Great Peace* 70/2b)

Another method that stands somewhere in between the reduced food intake and the eating of *qi* in its degree of efficacy is the ingestion of drugs (*yao* 藥). In a fragment attributed to "the *Taiping jing*'s 145th *juan*" that is now preserved as a quote in the early Tang period encyclopedia the *Sandong zhunang* we find the following passage:

上中下得道度世者 何食之乎 答曰 上第一者食風氣 第二者食藥味 第三者少食 裁通其腸胃

[The Genuine Person asked,] "As for the people of superior, intermediate and lower levels of obtaining the Dao and transcending the world, what do they eat?"

[The Heavenly Master answered,] "Those at the first, highest level eat wind-*qi*. Those at the second level ingest drugs. Those at the third level eat small amounts of food, and thereby reduce and clear out their intestines and stomach." (*Sandong zhunang* 4/3a)

Presumably, the parties conversing here are the Heavenly Master and the Genuine Man. What can be first noted here is how the Heavenly Master refers to the highest practice as the eating of "wind-*qi*" (*fengqi* 風氣),

which seems to confirm our speculation that the *qi* to be eaten is air. The reduction of food intake apparently serves to both reduce the capacity of the digestive system (or at least this is how I have interpreted the character *cai* 裁) and to clear it out (if this is what is meant by *tong* 通). As for why the ingestion of drugs is considered better than eating small amounts of food, it is probably because the drugs you take would possess some sort of hunger-suppressing quality, meaning that the quantity of the drug you would ingest would be far less than the quantity of food that you would otherwise need to eat. For many practitioners it would have been reassuring to note here that a desirable level of salvation or immortality was attainable even if you did not quite actually stop eating all together. Even those who merely reduce their food intake still qualify as having "obtained the Dao" (*dedao* 得道) and "transcended the world" (*dushi* 度世).

In the *Sandong zhunang* the above passage is directly followed by another quote from "the *Taiping jing*'s 145th *juan*," which states:

天之遠而無方 不食風氣 安能疾行 周流天之道哉 又當與神吏通 功共為朋 故食風氣也 其次當與地精并力 和五土 高下山川 緣山 入水 與地更相通 共食功 不可食穀 故飲水而行也 次節食為道 未 成固象 凡人裁小別耳 故少食以通腸 亦其成道之人

> Heaven is remote and limitless. If you do not eat wind-*qi*, how can you move rapidly and circulate throughout the roads of heaven? Also, you need to correspond in merit and become companions with the Divine Officials. This is why you should eat wind-*qi*. To rank directly below this you need to combine your strength with the earth's essences and harmonize the five soils. High and low are the mountains and rivers. You climb the mountains and enter the rivers. In order to further communicate with the earth, you must share in its manner of eating. Thus you must not eat grains, but must just go about drinking water. At the next level you practice the Dao by limiting your food intake. You do not yet complete a solid form (?). Ordinary people are different in their degree of reduction. Therefore they should clear out their intestines by eating only small amounts of food. They also are people who accomplish the Dao. (*Sandong zhunang* 4/3a–b)

The interpretation of this passage can vary depending on whether one regards it as a direct follow-up to the passage quoted in the *Sandong zhunang* right before it. The Heavenly Master (presumably he is the speaker) here describes intermediate practitioners as those who drink only water and eat no grains, for they are beings in league and sympathy with the earth, which itself takes nourishment only from the rain water that comes down on it, and which does not eat grains (rather, it yields grains forth). The question here is whether the Heavenly Master actually means to say that you take small, prescribed potions of drugs with the water, because in the prior-quoted passage from the *Taiping jing*'s same 145th *juan* he had just said that practitioners at the intermediate level ingest drugs. In regard to the lower level practitioners, the Heavenly Master again speaks of the clearing out of the digestive system, and offers again the reassurance that even just reducing your food intake is an achievement worthy of the description, "accomplished the Dao" (*chengdao* 成道).

*GP Synopsis* (8/1a–b) relates a conversation that begins with the Genuine Man asking how one can become able to be full without eating, and thereby attain a lengthy lifespan. The Heavenly Master responds first by declaring that the method for doing so is the "way of bringing prosperity to the nation and preserving its people" (*fuguo anmin zhi dao* 富國安民之道); seemingly conveyed in this declaration is the idea that if such dietetics were practiced widely throughout society, the nation would flourish as result of both the improved general health of its populace, as well as the slower depletion of its resources. The Heavenly Master then states:

比欲不食 先以導命之方居前 因以留氣 服氣藥之後 三日小飢 七日微飢 十日之外 為小成無惑矣 已死去就生也

If you want to stop eating, first prepare yourself through the practice of the method for guiding life, and thereby make the *qi* stay. After you have ingested *qi* drugs (or "*qi* and drugs" [?]), you will have only minor hunger after three days, and only subtle hunger after seven days. After ten days you will attain the minor accomplishment that is to be without confusion. After you die, you will proceed to life. (*GP Synopsis* 8/1a)

Here, apparently, the Heavenly Master recommends prior to fasting a certain "method of guiding life" (*daoming zhi fang* 導命之方), which involves ingesting a certain *qi*-drug (*qiyao* 氣藥) that apparently supplements your *qi* and gradually reduces your susceptibility to hunger. After several days the drug will begin to take a noticeable effect, as the hunger you feel becomes "small" (*xiao* 小), and then "subtle" (*wei* 微). After ten days you are "without confusion" (*wuhuo* 無惑), which in this context would seem to mean that you are no longer confused by hunger. Reaching this condition apparently is supposed to guarantee some form of life beyond the grave, if such is what is meant by "after you die, you will proceed to life" 已死去就生也.

In any case, the Heavenly Master then proceeds to say:

服氣藥之後 諸食有形之物堅難消者 以一食為度 食無形之物 節少為善 百日之外可不食 名不窮之道

After ingesting the *qi*-drug, all foods that have form and are hard and are difficult to digest should as a principle be eaten [only] once [per day]. You should eat things that are formless. It is good to limit your intake. After 100 days you will be able to not eat. This is called "the Way of being unlimited." (*GP Synopsis* 8/1a)

Thus, over the course of the regimen after the initial ingesting of the *qi*-drug you are permitted to eat some solid food if you must, but no more than once a day. After 100 days it is to be hoped that all eating can be done away with, and the ability to do this is supposed to confer eternal life.

Clearly the Taiping Group texts convey the view that the reduction of food intake is a vital indicator of one's degree of progress in the quest for immortality, and that this process is closely related to the practice of meditation. However, the different passages vary in the extent to which they view reduced food intake as something facilitated by meditative calm, or rather view fasting—typically facilitated by *qi*-eating, drug-ingestion or gradual food-intake reduction—as a means of enhancing the psychic powers that are wielded in meditation. While Taiping Group text passages do emphasize the prime value of serenity in meditation, and at times show a preference for visualizations involving minimal sensory content, they also amply endorse the visualization of bodily deities and the eating of *qi*—two of the principal proactive methods that would flourish in medieval Daoism.

## THE *LAOZI XIANG'ER ZHU* 老子想爾注 (*LAOZI-XIANG'ER*)

*Laozi-Xiang'er* (*Laozi Xiang'er zhu* 老子想爾注; *Laozi*, with *Xiang'er* commentary) is another text crucial to our understanding of the beliefs and practices of organized Daoist religion in its earliest known phases. This text, strangely and unfortunately, is not found in the *Daoist Canon*. What survives of it is a damaged, incomplete manuscript that was recovered from the Mogao 莫高 Caves of Dunhuang 敦煌 (in far-western Gansu 甘肅 Province). This manuscript (kept in the British Library and catalogued as Stein Manuscript no. 6825) preserves less than half of the original book; it contains the main text and commentary of what corresponds to chapters 3 through 37 of the received text of the *Laozi*. At the end of the fragment is the title, "*Laozi daojing, shang, Xiang'er*" 老子道經 上 想爾 (*Laozi*, Scroll One: Book of the Dao, [with] Xiang'er [Commentary]). The first modern study and critical edition of the text was published by Rao Zongyi 饒宗頤 in 1956.[32]

Based on late Six Dynasties and Tang sources, we can know that *Laozi-Xiang'er* belonged to the Taixuan 太玄 (Great Mystery) section of the Daoist canon, and was among the texts that were ritually transmitted together with the *Laozi* to Daoist initiates.[33] There was also a set of moral precepts that was based on the dictates of *Laozi-Xiang'er*.[34] Sources of the late sixth- or early seventh-century name the third Heavenly Master Zhang Lu as author or possible author of *Laozi-Xiang'er*,[35] while sources of the eighth century or later name the first Heavenly Master Zhang Daoling 張道陵 (fl. ca. 142) as the author.[36]

Kristofer Schipper, due to what he perceives as discrepancies between the teachings of *Laozi-Xiang'er* and those of the Way of the Heavenly Masters, contends that the text issues from some other Daoist religious movement of the Han, and that the text could even date back to the first century.[37] Other scholars have contrarily argued for a later, Six Dynasties date of authorship.[38] However, scholars such as Chen Shixiang 陳世驤,[39] Ōfuchi Ninji 大淵忍爾,[40] and Stephen Bokenkamp[41] believe that *Laozi Xiang'er* indeed issued from the early Five Pecks of Rice/Heavenly Masters movement, and that its author quite likely was Zhang Lu. The most compelling evidence in their favor seems to be found in a Heavenly Masters movement text of 255 CE called *Daodao jialing jie* 大道

家令戒 (Commands and Admonitions for the Families of the Great Dao).⁴² This text contains the word *xiang'er*,⁴³ contains ideas and phrasing highly reminiscent of *Laozi Xiang'er*, and cites one of the *Xiang'er* precepts.

Regarding what the term *xiang'er* 想爾 means, there are contending views. One view, upheld by Schipper and supported by one late sixth- or early seventh-century source is that "Xiang'er" is the name of some now-obscure Daoist immortal or saint.⁴⁴ Ōfuchi and Bokenkamp contend rather that it probably is not (or was not originally regarded as) a person's name, but should be understood as meaning "thinking of you," in the sense that the Dao remains attentive toward and sustains those faithful people who are mindful of the Dao.⁴⁵

A full English translation of *Laozi-Xiang'er* with a masterful introduction and notes has been published by Stephen Bokenkamp.⁴⁶ His translations have been consulted for my own translations of selected passages in our discussion that follows. I have also consulted the modern Chinese translations of Gu Baotian 顧寶田, Zhang Zhongli 張忠利 and Fu Wuguang 傅武光.⁴⁷

What survives today of *Laozi-Xiang'er* does not, at first glance, seem to have much to say about meditation; indeed, in places it comes across as a decidedly nonmystical document. It is nonetheless highly relevant to our discussion because of what it has to say about serenity and the harnessing of the *qi* that *is* the Dao.

The first *Laozi* passage preserved in the Dunhuang *Laozi-Xiang'er* manuscript comes from what corresponds to the third chapter of the received *Laozi*. It reads, "Do not look at what is desirable, so as to not cause disturbance in your mind" 不見可欲 使心不亂. The commentary to it reads:

... 不欲視之 比如不見 勿令心動 若動自誡 ... 道去復還 心亂遂之 道去之矣

(2 or 3 characters missing) . . . , not desiring to look at it, is like not seeing it. Do not allow your mind to waver. If it wavers, admonish yourself. (2 characters missing). . . . The Dao goes and returns again. Disorder in your mind repels it, and the Dao leaves it. (*Laozi-Xiang'er*, 2; see also Bokenkamp 1997, 78)⁴⁸

In other words, if your mind is tranquil and free of desires, the Dao will come to you and stay with you.

The main text continues on to say "As for the governance of the Sage, he makes their minds numinous (empty?),[49] and fills their bellies." 聖人之治 靈（虛？）其心 實其腹 The commentary explains:

心者規也 中有吉兆善惡 氣常欲實 腹者道囊 心爲凶惡 道去囊空 虛去心中凶惡 道來歸之 腹則實矣 空者耶如入 便煞人 虛去心中凶惡 道來歸之 腹則實矣

The mind is the compass. Within it are auspicious omens, good and evil. The *qi* always needs to be plentiful. The belly is the sack of the Dao. When the mind is malicious and evil, the Dao leaves, and the sack becomes empty. If you empty the mind of all of its malice and evil, the Dao will come and return to it. The belly is thereby full. If wickedness enters into an empty [belly], it will kill a person. Empty the mind of its malice and evil, and the Dao will return to it. The belly will thereby be full. (*Laozi-Xiang'er*, 2; see also Bokenkamp 1997, 78)

Here the Dao is described as *qi* that fills your belly if your mind is good and pure. If your belly is depleted of this *qi* of the Dao, you are left vulnerable to attacks from "evil" (demons? noxious energies?) that can be fatal.

Of particular interest is what *Laozi-Xiang'er* has to say in regard into the phrase of the *Laozi* main text (corresponding to the beginning of chapter 10 of the received text) that reads, "If in carrying your soul you embrace the One, you will be able to be without separation." 載營魄抱一能無離:

一者道也 今在人身何許 守之云何 一不在人身也 諸附身者悉世間常偽技 非真道也 一在天地外 入在天地閒 但往來人身中耳 都皮裡悉是 非獨一處 一散形爲氣 聚形為太上老君 常治崐崙 或言虛无 或言自然 或言無名 皆同一耳 今布道誡教人守誡不違 即為守一 不行其誡 即爲失一也 世間常偽技 指五臟以名一 瞑目思想 欲從求福 非也 去生遂遠矣

. . . The One is the Dao. Where is it in the human body? What does it mean when one says to "guard" it? The One is not in the human body.

Those [methods] which assign it to the body are all nothing but the false techniques that are common within the world. They are not the True Way. The One is beyond Heaven and Earth, but enters into the midst of Heaven and Earth. It merely comes to and goes away from the human body. The entire space within your skin is it (the place where the Dao can enter). It is not any single place [within the body]. When the One scatters its form, it becomes *qi*. When it gathers together its form, it becomes the Most High Lord Lao, who always rules atop Mt. Kunlun. It is sometimes called "void non-being." It is sometimes called "natural." It is sometimes called, "the nameless." These [appellations] all point to the same thing. We now propagate the precepts of the Dao in order to teach people to hold to these precepts without disobeying. This is what it means to Guard the One. To not obey the precepts is to lose the One. In the false techniques common within the world, they point to the five viscera and call them the One(s). They close their eyes and think of it, wanting to thereby seek blessings. This is wrong. To go away from life to seek blessings is wrong. Remotely distant from life it is. (*Laozi-Xiang'er*, 37–38; see also Bokenkamp 1997, 89)

Thus the notion is reiterated once again that the Dao—also known as the One—is a life sustaining *qi* that will enter and stay within the body of a morally upright person. At the same time, this passage introduces themes and arguments that set it apart from some of the views of the Taiping Group texts, and that could even be regarded as polemics consciously directed toward *Taiping jing* proponents. Specifically, this passage attacks the practice of visualizing the deities of the five viscera, and even seems to deny the value of meditation more generally. To "Guard the One" means to obey moral precepts, and is not a meditation technique at all. It is by obeying the precepts that you retain the One. The One fills the entire body of the good person, but it also pervades and transcends the universe. It also exists eternally as a personal deity known as the Most High Lord Lao (Taishang Laojun 太上老君)—that is, the eternal, cosmic Laozi—perched upon the cosmic mountain of Kunlun (widely considered elsewhere to be the abode of the Queen Mother of the West [Xiwangmu 西王母]).

In commenting on a phrase in what corresponds to *Laozi*, chapter 14 ("It is the form without a form, an image of no-thing" 是无狀之狀 无物之像), *Laozi-Xiang'er* states as follows:

道至尊 微而隱 無狀貌形象也 但可從其誠 不可見知也 今世間偽
技指形名道 令有服色 名字 狀貌 長短* 非也 悉邪偽耳

The Dao is most lofty. It is subtle and hidden. It has neither countenance nor form. You can only obey its commandments, and you cannot see or know it. The false methods of the world today point to forms and call them the Dao. They cause it to have garments, colors, names, appearances and specific lengths. This is wrong. It is all falsehood. (*Laozi-Xiang'er*, 58; see also Bokenkamp 1997, 96–97)

This passage seems to deny the possibility of any mystical experience of the Dao. It asserts that our task is simply to obey the commandments revealed by the Dao, and that this is what it means to "guard the One."

Underlying people's actions is their general mental state encompassing their thoughts, emotions, desires, and impulses. The task of obeying moral precepts is greatly facilitated by keeping the mind calm and free of the sorts of thoughts and desires that motivate sinful behavior. As we have already seen, *Laozi-Xiang'er* states that evil thoughts in and of themselves—even before they can generate bad behavior—cause the *qi* of the Dao to leave the body and stay away from it. While *Laozi-Xiang'er* seems to clearly disapprove of meditation of the sort entailing concrete visualizations, it does recommend keeping the mind clear (*qing* 清) and calm (*jing* 靜). Doing so obviously requires no small degree of mental discipline and awareness at all times and in all situations. But in speaking of being "clear and calm," is *Laozi-Xiang'er* also at least in part referring to some sort of regular meditation exercise of a passive sort?

Perhaps instructive here are the comments to the phrase in *Laozi-Xiang'er* (corresponding to *Laozi* chapter 15) that reads, "[Their minds are] muddled like muddy water. Yet the muddy water, through stillness gradually becomes clear" 肫如濁 濁以靜之徐清. The commentary explains that "people who seek life" 求生之人 (worthy Daoists) are so devoted to the Dao and so indifferent to worldly benefit and honor that they may seem obtuse or insane. However, it is by being this way that they can recover their unadorned genuine natures. Then, "after this, through clarity and calmness they can observe the various subtleties" 然後清靜能 視眾微. In other words, if, on top of being oblivious to profit and reputation, you can make your mind clear and calm, you will attain insight into "subtle" things (See *Laozi-Xiang'er*, 65; also Bokenkamp 1997, 99). Here we are led to wonder whether "clarity and calmness" is not only a habitual state of mind, but perhaps also some sort of meditation exercise anticipated to bring forth mystical experience or insight.

The commentary goes on to draw a parallel between the natural world and the human being. It points out that when Heaven and Earth are calm, clouds form in the sky and dew settles on the ground in a manner that enables all things to be properly moistened and nourished. However, when there is tumultuous thunder and wind, creatures are harmed and "the *qi* of the Dao conceals itself and does not constantly permeate" 道氣隱藏 常不周處. In light of this fact, you should do as follows:

常清靜爲務 晨暮露上下 人身氣亦布至 師設晨暮清靜爲大要

> Make it your duty to always be clear and calm. At sunrise and sunset (or perhaps "from sunrise till sunset" [namely, all day long]) the dews ascend and descend. In the human body the *qi* also pervades. The Master(s) established the sunrise and sunset clarity and calmness as the great essential. (*Laozi-Xiang'er*, 65; see also Bokenkamp 1997, 99)

In other words, it is by keeping the mind clear and still that you can enable the *qi* of the Dao within you to properly pervade and nourish your body, much in the same manner that the world is naturally moistened and nourished by the dews when heaven and earth are at peace. Although the above passage starts out saying that you should always be clear and calm, it could also be understood as specifically designating sunrise and sunset as occasions during the day—established by the Master(s)—for practicing clarity and calmness in a manner that nourishes the body with *qi*. (This is how Bokenkamp interprets this passage.[50] However, it also appears possible to interpret the characters *chenmu* 晨暮 as "from sunrise till sunset" and to thus interpret the passage as prescribing serenity in all actions throughout the day). Perhaps, then, there was some sort of prescribed meditation exercise (presumably of a passive sort), that was supposed to be carried out on a twice-daily basis.

In its commentary to the opening phrase ("Arrive at the utmost emptiness, steadfastly guard the stillness" 致虛極 守靜篤) to what corresponds to *Laozi* chapter 16, *Laozi-Xiang'er* continues its criticism of those who visualize deities of specific sizes, garments, and colors in specific parts of the body, concluding that all such practices "are not as good as guarding your stillness and making yourself steadfast" 不如守靜自篤. The main text and commentary then read as follows:

萬物並作 吾以觀其復 夫物云云 各歸其根

The myriad creatures together arise. I thereby see them return. All the various sorts of things each return to their root. (Main text)

万物含道精 並作出生起時也 吾道也 觀其精復時 皆歸其根 故令人寶慎根也

The myriad creatures contain the essence of the Dao. "Together arise" refers to the moment they rise up to life. "I" refers to the Dao. [The Dao] observes that when their essence returns, it always returns to their roots. Thus [the Dao] commands people to treasure and take care of their roots. (Commentary)

歸根曰靜

To return to the root is called "calmness." (Main text)

道氣歸根 愈當清靜矣

When the *qi* of the Dao returns to the root, you must even more stay clear and calm. (Commentary)

靜曰復命 復命曰常

Being still is called "returning to life." Returning to life is called "constant." (Main text)

知寶根清靜 復命之常法矣

Knowing how to treasure your root in clarity and calmness is the constant method of returning to life. (Commentary) (*Laozi-Xiang'er*, 71; see also Bokenkamp 1997, 101)

Thus we are told that the Dao, described as both essence and *qi*, is contained in all living things, and is what gives them their life. This vital force (essence/*qi*) is by nature something that waxes and wanes cyclically. Phases of growth and increased activity (e.g., spring and summer, morning and afternoon, waking and rising) are followed by phases of decline and quiescence (e.g., autumn and winter, evening and night, fatigue and slumber), which are however necessary for the subsequent phase of growth and activity to occur. When the vital force is in the waning phase, it concentrates itself in the "root." (Thus with plants it is the case that when the leaves and flowers are withered away, the vitality of the organism is retained in the roots under the soil until the time comes again to sprout and bloom.) The Dao, which in *Laozi-Xiang'er* is also the supreme deity who has revealed the *Laozi* and various other teachings to the community of believers, for this reason commands that humans must, during the waning of the vital force, take particular care of their roots; also, the moment during which the quiescence has reached its limit and the vital force is completely concentrated in the root, is the moment when it is most crucial to keep your mind clear and calm. But, in terms of speaking about the human body, what is the root? The answer to this is apparently to be found earlier on in *Laozi-Xiang'er* (in the portion corresponding to *Laozi* chapter 6) in the following passage:

玄牝門 天地根

The gate of the Mysterious Female is the root of Heaven and Earth. (Main text)

牝地也 女像之 陰孔為門 死生之官也 最要 故名根 男荼亦名根

The "female" is earth. A woman resembles it. The vagina is the gate. It is the organ of death and life. It is most important. Thus it is called the "root." The man's penis is also called the "root." (Commentary) (*Laozi-Xiang'er*, 19–20; see also Bokenkamp 1997, 55)

Thus, the root to which you must pay utmost attention, especially during the utter depths of quiescence, is your genitals. Bokenkamp points to this as evidence that the author of *Laozi-Xiang'er* likely knew of and approved of the sexual rite known as the "Merging of *Qi*" (*heqi* 合氣) that is known to have been widely practiced within the Way of the Heavenly Masters during its early phases (though one could question whether the rite was being practiced as early as pre-215).⁵¹ Bokenkamp states, "The commentary does not state what was supposed to occur when the pneumas (his translation of *qi* 氣) of the Dao return to the sexual organs, but it is likely that this was regarded as the necessary precondition for the rite of 'merging the pneumas (namely, Merging of *Qi*)'" (Bokenkamp 1997, 46).

In what survives of *Laozi-Xiang'er* the Merging of *Qi* is never mentioned by name. Whenever the text does mention sexual practices in any clear terms, it is vehemently critical of them. Also, the *Laozi-Xiang'er* promotes sexual moderation or abstinence as means of preserving essence and *qi*. Nonetheless, Bokenkamp holds to his view, and could be correct. As he points out, the Merging of *Qi* was in its nature and purpose apparently something quite different from the sexual methods that *Laozi-Xiang'er* denounces—those that people at the time were attributing to legendary figures such as the Yellow Emperor, the Mysterious Maiden (Xuannü 玄女), Master Gong 龔子, or Master Rongcheng 容成子. These are described as being of the sort where you "copulate with girls without ejaculating" 與女子交合而不施泄, and "recycle the essence to supplement the brain" 還精補腦 (see *Laozi-Xiang'er*, 35). The text describes the practitioners of these things as people who "want to borrow" 欲貸 (see *Laozi-Xiang'er*, 139). These, in other words, were sexual methods of the sort meant to supplement one's vitality by drawing in that of one's partner. While the full method, meaning and purpose of the Merging of *Qi* rite still elude our full understanding, it does appear to have been something rather different. In the Merging of *Qi* neither partner was supposed to increase their vitality at the expense of the other. Rather, both partners were supposed to be enhanced in their vitality as well as their ability to command spirits, and were together ensured long life and survival of the anticipated apocalypse as "seed people" (*zhongmin* 種民).⁵² If the entire *Laozi-Xiang'er* had survived, we perhaps might have found in it some much less ambiguous references to and endorsements of the Merging of *Qi*.

It is thus possible that the returning of the vital forces to the "root" referred to in the above-quoted passage (from *Laozi-Xiang'er*, 19–20) was indeed the bodily condition that directly preceded the arousal and intercourse of the genitals of the paired practitioners. Because the quiescence and concentration of vital force in the genitals would be followed directly by arousal, it certainly would be important to retain one's composure and self-control, so as not to wastefully expend one's essence through ejaculation.

In sum, Bokenkamp's view is plausible, in spite of the unfortunate lack of further support within the rest of what survives of the text. However, in light of what can be seen within Neidan literature in (admittedly) much later periods—particularly that of the Quanzhen Longmen 全真龍門 tradition of Wu Shouyang 伍守陽 (1573–1644) and Liu Huayang 柳華陽 (fl. 1794)—it seems that there may be another possible explanation as to why, at the utmost extreme of quiescence, one needed to pay careful attention to one's genitals. What we could be dealing with here is spontaneous genital arousal or seminal emission that can occur during depths of serenity in solo meditation, or during sleep.[53] In any case, it would appear that the religious *milieu* that produced *Laozi-Xiang'er* saw the ebb and flow of the universal vital force or *qi* of the Dao as being intimately connected to the physiology related to reproduction and sexual arousal—thus meaning that sexual restraint is crucial.

*Laozi-Xiang'er*, in its portion corresponding to the *Laozi*'s chapter 6 reads:

谷神不死 是謂玄牝

If you want your spirit to not die, this [way that you should emulate] is called the Mysterious Female. (Main text)

谷者欲也 精結為神 欲令神不死 當結精自守 牝者地也 體性安 女像之 故不掔 男欲結精 心當像地似女 勿為事先

By *gu* 谷 (valley) is meant *yu* 欲 (want, desire). Essence binds together to become spirit(s). If you want your spirit(s) to be immortal, you must bind together your essence and guard it. The "female" is the earth. Its embodied nature is peaceful. Women resemble this, therefore they are not hard. If a man wants to bind his essence, his heart needs to resemble the earth and resemble a woman. He must not put himself first in things. (Commentary) (*Laozi-Xiang'er*, 19; see also Bokenkamp 1997, 83)

Here it is declared that the retention and "binding together" (*jie* 結) of essence is of the utmost importance for the immortality of the spirit (or, perhaps the multiple spirits or deities frequently said to inhabit the body in Daoism), since essence thus bound together somehow becomes spirit(s).[54] The way to facilitate this process is to be like the earth or like a woman, meaning at the very least that you should be calm, passive, and yielding in your attitude and behavior. Difficult to determine here is how we ought to understand the sense in which women are said to be "not hard." Bokenkamp interprets it as meaning that women's sexual organs do not get hard. If one follows this line of interpretation, one might also surmise that to emulate a woman means to not make your penis erect through sexual activity, although from the wording of the text here the emulation seems to pertain more to one's state of mind.

However, in the ensuing passages *Laozi-Xiang'er* proceeds to what is most definitely a discussion pertaining to sexual activity, and makes it quite clear that the essence that becomes spirit if bound together and retained in the body, is also something that escapes the body in the act of sexual procreation. The text glosses the next phrase, "the gate of the Mysterious Female is the root of Heaven and Earth," 玄牝門 天地根 by explaining that the root is the vagina or the penis, depending on the gender of the person concerned. It then goes into an extended discussion on sexual activity in its comments to the subsequent portion of the main text.

Concerning the phrase, "slight and subtle, and thus endure" 綿綿若存, it explains that at the age of "knowing the Mandate" 知命—meaning age 50—one ought to terminate all sexual activity (or at least that which leads to procreation, depending on how one interprets the text),[55] and that younger people should exercise great restraint (be "slight and subtle" in the manner and extent to which they do engage in sexual activity). The text goes on to explain that the Dao created our sexual functions and propensities only to enable us to "combine our essence and give birth to life" 合精產生 so as to continue our species; the Dao did not intend for us to belabor ourselves with too much sexual activity. Yet, people nonetheless belabor themselves with it and do great harm; the harm apparently lies in the fact that by squandering their bound-together essences in procreation, people are failing to create the immortal spirit(s). The text then states, "People of superior virtue are firm and strong in their will power and self-discipline. They are able to not crave procreative copulation, and put an end to it when young. Thus, their good spirits are completed early" 上德之人 志操堅彊 能不戀結產生 少時便絕 又善神早成. The text then further points out that "heaven and earth have no ancestral shrines, dragons have no children, Transcendents [have no][56] wives, and Jade Maidens have no husbands" 天地无祠 龍无子 仙人[无]妻 玉女无夫. In other words, the fact that these great beings are so long-lasting is in great part attributable to the fact that they are not engaged in sexual activity or procreation—or, perhaps vice-versa, they do not procreate because they themselves are immortal and have no need to produce offspring to perpetuate their own kind (see *Laozi-Xiang'er*, 20; and Bokenkamp 1997, 84).

In sum, *Laozi-Xiang'er* maintains that the reduction or elimination of sexual activity (or at least that of the procreative kind) constitutes an integral part of being a person of "virtue" and of "good spirit" who can attain longevity or immortality. Having this virtue entails possessing the will power and self-discipline by which you can overcome desire. Presumably, as far as indicated, over the course of your subsequent lengthy or eternal life, you will still possess the natural procreative bodily functions, which you will keep under restraint. At much later periods, in Quanzhen Longmen Neidan theory of the sort most clearly articulated by Wu Shouyang and Liu Huayang, your cultivation of deep serenity in meditation not only decreases and eliminates your sexual desires, but it also shuts down the essential sexual functions of erection and ejaculation.[57] Such does not seem to be the claim here.

Finally, concerning *Laozi-Xiang'er*, it bears mentioning that it also considers the ability to do without ordinary food to be a definitive characteristic of an immortal being. The portion of the text corresponding to the end of *Laozi*, chapter 20 states:

我欲異於人 而貴食母

I desire to be different from people, so I value feeding off the mother. (Main text)

仙人與俗人異 不貴榮祿財寶 但貴食母者 身也 於內為胃 主五臟氣 俗人食穀 穀絕便死 仙人有穀食之 無則食氣 氣歸胃 即腸重囊也 腹之為實 前章已說之矣

> Transcendents are different from worldly folk. They do not value fame, rank, money or treasures. The reason why they only value feeding off the mother is for the sake of their bodies. Internally, it is for the sake of the stomach, which is the master of the *qi* of the five grains. Worldly folk eat grains, and when the grains run out, they die. Transcendents eat grains if they have them, but if they do not, they eat *qi*. The *qi* returns to the stomach, which is the layered sack [among the] intestines. Regarding the belly becoming full, it has already been discussed in a previous chapter. (Commentary) (*Laozi-Xiang'er*, 97; see also Bokenkamp 1997, 112)

Daoists who partake of great longevity and immortality are thus the sort of people who care only about what is most basic, which is nourishing the body. The best way to nourish the body is to feed off the "mother," which here seems to denote the Dao, which as we have seen, is described earlier in the text (*Laozi-Xiang'er*, 2) as something that when dispersed is *qi*, and that comes to fill the bellies (or "sacks of the Dao") of people whose minds are free of evil thoughts. Here, then, it is apparently being claimed that people whose bellies are kept full in such a way do not need to eat grains or any other such ordinary foods for their nourishment and survival. (This is also how Bokenkamp interprets the passage.)[58] Note here that there is apparently nothing wrong with grains per se as nourishment, as long as you have them. The problem with grains, or any other commodity, is that they can at times become unavailable. Such is not the case with the Dao or its *qi*, which is eternal and ubiquitous. Now, as we saw in the case of the Taiping Group texts, the term "eat *qi*" (*shiqi* 食氣) seems to have denoted a method of swallowing air into the esophagus. Such also could be what is at least in part meant here. However, it would seem that the theoretical scheme of *Laozi-Xiang'er* pertaining to the *qi* of the Dao naturally filling the bellies of pure-hearted people might obviate the need for any deliberate method of suppressing hunger.

THREE

# Dramatic Physical and Sensory Effects

The previous chapter examined texts that have attracted the interest of modern scholars largely due to their likely connection to the earliest known Daoist religious organizations—the Way of Great Peace, and the Way of the Five Pecks of Rice/Heavenly Masters. *The Manifest Dao, Contemplating the Baby,* and *The True Record*, on the other hand, have received little attention and present us with theories and methods of obscure provenance. They are of interest because they offer extremely vivid and concrete descriptions of sensory and physical phenomena that occur in the deep serenity of meditation. These theories and practices thus described betray no discernible Buddhist influence and seem likely to originate prior to the fifth century. All of these texts present themselves as the teachings of Laozi or of his deified form Lord Lao (Laojun 老君).

A prominent feature of certain important early medieval Daoist texts such as the *Taishang Laojun zhongjing* 太上老君中經 (Central Scripture of the Most High Lord Lao; second century?),[1] or the *Taishang huangting waijing yujing* 太上黃庭外景玉經 (Most High Jade Scripture of the Outer Scenery of the Yellow Court; pre-255)[2] is the descriptions of the body's inner anatomy and the deities that inhabit it. These form the bases for methods of inner visualization by which you are supposed to retain the gods within you, actualize them in visions or mobilize them in a manner that ensures prolonged vitality and brings about transformation into an immortal, transcendent being. Methods of roughly this sort are promoted in the Taiping Group texts (and criticized in *Laozi-Xiang'er*); however, conspicuously lacking in the Taiping Group texts are references to special bodily locations known by terms such as Elixir Field (*dantian* 丹田), Crimson Palace (*jianggong* 絳宮), Yellow Court (*huangting* 黃庭), Hall of Light (*mingtang* 明堂), or Muddy Pellet (*niwan* 泥丸), or to key inner deities such as the Baby (Chizi 赤子), the Genuine Person (Zhenren 真人), or the Jade Woman of Dark Radiance (Xuanguang Yunü 玄光玉女). Terms and concepts such as these are featured in the *Taishang Laojun zhongjing* and the *Taishang huangting waijing yujing*, and would come to feature prominently in the proactive meditation theories and regimens of the Shangqing scriptures of the latter part of the fourth century.

The textual material examined in this chapter follows much of this theory on bodily anatomy and an inner pantheon. The Lower Elixir Field and the Baby figure prominently in this chapter. However, our texts describe meditation techniques that are simpler and more passive. These primarily involve calming the mind and focusing inward to witness certain physical and sensory effects that emerge spontaneously. There is not much volitional endeavor involved beyond just directing your attention to a particularly bodily location (such as the Lower Elixir Field). The sensations and visions that emerge can be of an alarming and disturbing quality because they arrive on their own accord on their own time, and do not take on a form that you have purposely visualized or invoked.

Having said this though, our textual materials do not criticize proactive, visualization-based methods in the way that *Laozi-Xiang'er* does. It is altogether likely that the same people who undertook the methods examined in this chapter also practiced the proactive, visualization-based meditation methods as well as various other longevity-immortality methods available to them, such as dietetics, drug ingestion, laboratory alchemy, rituals, and talismans. Although it is thus doubtful that we have in these materials any sort of attempt to promote passive meditation or sheer serenity as a supreme or exclusive practice, we do find deep serenity and its effects described in them with extraordinary vividness, and in ways at times anticipating or influencing what certain later authors would describe.

## SURGES OF PRIMAL *QI*:
## THE *XIANDAO JING* 顯道經 (*THE MANIFEST DAO*)

*The Manifest Dao*[3] (*Xiandao jing* 顯道經; The Scripture of the Manifest Dao)[4] is a text consisting of three sections that perhaps at one time did not constitute a single work, and may have circulated separately. The first section (1a–3a), which bears no heading, takes the format of eight short discourses by Laozi, each starting with the phrase, "Laozi said, . . ." (*Laozi yue* 老子曰). The second section (3a–12a), which primarily concerns us, is entitled "Sudao jie" 素道解 (Explanation on the Plain Way) and mostly takes the form of conversations in which Laozi responds to the questions of an anonymous interlocutor or interlocutors. The third section (12a–14a), entitled "Juegu shiqi fa" 絕穀食氣法 (Method of Eliminating Grains and Eating *Qi*), is a manual on fasting, and does not present itself as the utterances or instructions of Laozi, nor of any other named individual.

*The Manifest Dao* bears no preface or colophon, nor any references to dates, events or people that would betray its date of authorship. Its contents show no evidence of Buddhist influence. Kristofer Schipper dates the text to the third century, or at least prior to the Eastern Jin 東晉 dynasty (317–420). He does so based on affinities that he sees between this text, the aforementioned *Taishang laojun zhongjing*, and another early text, the *Taiqing zhenren luoming jue* 太清真人絡命訣 (The Genuine Man of the Great Purity's Lesson on Prolonging Life).[5] Specifically, he points out that a set of names given to the gods of the five viscera on page 10b of *The Manifest Dao* (discussed later) match with the names given to them in the other two texts. Sun Qi 孫齊 has recently given further support for a third century dating for *The Manifest Dao* by arguing that it largely consists of remnants of a long-lost scripture entitled *Daoji jing* 道機經. This scripture was known to Ge Hong 葛洪 (283–343), who considered it to be the work of Wang Tu 王圖, a military commander of the Three Kingdoms Wei 魏 dynasty (220–265).[6]

Laozi's discourses in the first section of *The Manifest Dao* overview a number of matters pertaining to the body, corporeal spirits, meditation, health, longevity, and immortality. The first discourse pertains to facial complexions and the physical conditions that they reflect. The second discourse pertains to the process of aging, and claims that people who "have the Dao" 有道 can transcend the normal heaven-allotted lifespan of 120 years. The key to this is to not "worry of distant matters and thereby damage your essence and spirit" 遠慮損精神, but instead to "calm your mind and maintain your peace in a state of empty nothingness that is placidly detached" 安心守靖虛無淡泊; in this way you will "naturally become a Genuine Person" 自爲真人 (See 1a–b). The third discourse has Laozi talking about how the Dao nurtures the human body by means of the activity of "the male and female" (*xiongci* 雄雌) that "follow each other but are not different" 相隨不別. These, "spirits" (*shen* 神) are the cloud-soul(s) (*hun* 魂) and the white-souls (*po* 魄).[7] When merged together, the cloud-souls and white-souls become the Baby (Chizi 赤子), which can nurture and maintain the vitality of the human body by circulating throughout it. How all of this is to come about is not explained, but it perhaps requires some sort of visualization method on the part of the practitioner.

In the remaining discourses of the first section we find Laozi admonishing against carelessly expending essence and *qi* through excessive activity or outward engagement of the senses. We also see him describing abstractly an inner contemplative method whereby you "enter the room of the Dao" 入道室 and guard the "origin of the mystery" 玄元, and find that "within the mystery is a mystery, and this is my life/destiny" 玄中有玄 是我命. Progressing further, you find out that inside this life/destiny is "my form" 我形, within this form is "my essence" 我精, within this essence is "my *qi*" 我氣, within this *qi* is "my spirit" 我神, and within this spirit is "my naturalness" 我自然 (2a).

In the next to the last short discourse he describes physical traits indicative that one has obtained the Dao. These include a luxuriant head of hair, abundant perspiration on the hands and feet, the ability to go day and night without lying down, the absence of thirst and hunger, the ability to "engage in embryonic breathing in the manner of turtles and dragons" 龜龍胎息, and the ability to feel warm in the winter and cool in the summer (2b).[8] In the final discourse of the first section are directions pertaining to "transmitting the Dao" 授道. It is stated that the Dao should be transmitted to people of "soft and benevolent" 柔

仁 temperament, and that even if you do not have "talent and skill" 才巧, you can "through accumulated learning enter the divine" 積習入神 (2b–3a).

The first section of *The Manifest Dao* thus talks in a general way of the great benefits of inner serenity and a generally mellow comportment, and refers to or describes briefly a few approaches to meditation. These are too brief and summary for a proper analysis, but it would appear that both proactive and passive methods are being endorsed.

The second section of *The Manifest Dao*, the "Sudao jie," relates a more thorough and detailed discussion of a particular method of confined, reclining meditation. This discussion is strikingly concrete and vivid in its descriptions of extraordinary physical symptoms, sensations, and visions that occur both as a result of the activation of what gets referred to as the primal *qi* (*yuanqi* 元氣) or the Dao-*qi* 道氣, as well as the activity of spirits both benign and malevolent. For the regimen to attain optimal results, you are supposed to abstain from sexual activity and restrict and limit your eating. This is probably why the "Sudao jie" section is followed by a description of the rigorous fasting regimen entitled "Juegu shiqi fa" 絕穀食氣法, although it is possible that the choice to combine the "Sudao jie" with this fasting manual was made by a later editor who considered such a combination appropriate and helpful. In any case, though, it would appear that the internal *qi* activated through the Plain Way of the "Sudao jie" was ideally supposed to be adequate on its own for nourishing and transforming the body, and did not need to be supplemented with any sort of deliberate *qi*-eating method, at least once the practitioner had reached a certain level of experience and prowess.

The format of the "Sudao jie" wherein Laozi responds to an anonymous interlocutor—or perhaps, interlocutors—is quite unique (but also somewhat similar to the format of *The Great Peace*). Typically, texts that claim to record the teachings of Laozi have him addressing the reader directly, or conversing with his eminent disciple Yin Xi 尹喜 within the setting of a hagiographical narrative.[9] The "Sudao jie," however, reads like a transcript of actual verbal exchanges. The language employed is colloquial, informal, and unpolished. It does not give the impression of being some individual author's idealized portrayal of a conversation that would have taken place many centuries prior to his or her own time. This fact in itself brings to mind a number of questions pertaining to the historical, social, and religious context out of which this text issues.

If it is a transcript of actual conversations—as opposed to responses to anticipated questions coming from imagined interlocutors—who is this "Laozi"? Are we dealing here with a teacher or sectarian leader who was a self-professed incarnation of the eternal Laozi? Or could this Laozi be some other "old master" (*laozi*) who did not claim to be that famous person traditionally credited with the authorship of the *Laozi*? Or, might we consider the possibility that Laozi was being channeled through the mouth or brush of a spirit medium? Who was the interlocutor? Is the interlocutor the same person throughout, or is Laozi speaking to an audience of multiple persons? In other words, are we dealing here with a small lineage where teachings were conferred in a limited and personal fashion, or are we dealing with some sort of sect where groups of people learned, worshipped, and practiced together? In any case, if we are dealing with such a sect, one can surmise (for reasons that become clearer) that it would have included both men and women, and was not of a monastic persuasion. (This is significant for the dating of the text, for a monastic setting would probably require a chronological setting of the fifth century or later.)

The regimen of the Plain Way requires that you practice alone in a clean, dry, fragrant (by means of burning incense), and austerely furnished meditation chamber, located amid the desolate quietude of the mountains. Yet, you are not entirely alone. You are assumed to have an attendant serving your various needs so that you may focus on the meditation regimen without distractions. The attendant's duties mentioned in the text include shooing away any birds, dogs, or chickens that may be making excessive noise in the vicinity of the meditation chamber (3b). Because you are required to be naked when meditating, and are not supposed to abruptly get up after the conclusion of a meditation session, it is the duty of the attendant to fetch your garments for you (5b–6a). One can also surmise that the attendant would be responsible for various other duties related to housekeeping, as well as the acquisition and preparation of food. Perhaps the adept is assumed to be wealthy or socially prominent enough to have servants in the household. A loyal junior family member could well be imagined as an attendant as well. Perhaps the attendant is a disciple, patron, or client, who in return for attending the adept—and perhaps providing accommodations and other resources—hopes to eventually personally benefit by being taught the contemplative regimen or by somehow receiving assistance through the wisdom and powers the adept attains.

Before commencing the regimen of secluded meditation, there are certain preliminary protocols, described by Laozi:

老子曰 初入道室法 先以破除之日 解五過七污 東流水上 沐浴齋戒 令身鮮潔五臟平安 志意和適 除損萬事 無爲淡泊 則可治道 明受師法

Laozi said, "The method for first entering the room of the Dao [is as follows]. First, on the day of elimination (last day of the lunar year?), expiate your five transgressions and seven defilements. At the banks of an eastward flowing stream, bathe your head and body and observe the abstentions and precepts. Make the body fresh and clean. Pacify the five viscera (liver, heart, spleen, lungs and kidneys), and make the mind at ease. Eliminate the myriad affairs, and be in a state of non-action and contented detachment. Hereby you can manage the Dao, and receive the master's methods with clarity." (*The Manifest Dao* 3a)

Thus, before even being taught the contemplative regimen, you must undergo a range of ritual procedures to guarantee a proper degree of purity, both physical and mental. As mentioned earlier, doctrines pertaining to sin and guilt, and the need to repent so as to avoid divine punishment, held a central place in late Han and early medieval Daoist religion, and contemplation in a secluded room was among the procedures of expiation resorted to. Although such expiation of guilt liable to divine punishment is almost certainly what is being spoken of here, it should be noted that the contemplative regimen that is to be described in the ensuing discourse of the "Sudao jie" is not itself expiatory or purgative in nature. Procedures of expiation must *precede* it, so that it can be undertaken in a state of mind that is content, placid, and at least relatively free of guilt.

The meditation itself is to be carried out in a supine reclining position. As Laozi explains, this is because it is the most relaxing posture, which allows the *qi* to circulate with the greatest ease. The pillow used has to be 4 *cun* (roughly 4 inches) in height; using a pillow that is too high is said to constrict the kidneys, while using a pillow that is too low is said to harm the lungs. Both the pillow and the resting mat need to be soft, so as to better facilitate deep, long breathing (3b–4a). As mentioned earlier, you should remove your clothing, or at most wear a small robe (*xiaoyi* 小衣). If the body begins to shiver in the chilly air, you can use a blanket. The reason for the nakedness is not stated, but one can best surmise that this requirement also pertained to the facilitation of proper respiration and *qi* circulation; perhaps it had something to do with exposing the pores on the body's surface so that *qi* can somehow enter or exit through them as needed (5b–6a).

Regarding the matter of how to breathe, we find the following verbal exchange:

或問 初道 氣息未習 欲長反短 欲散反疾 欲留反還 云何

老子曰 初道 務清務靜 無強無長

Someone asked, "When first undertaking the Way, one's breathing is not trained. You want it to be long, and yet it is short. You want it to be relaxed, yet it is rapid. You want it to stay, and yet it goes back. What do you say to this?"

Laozi said, "When first undertaking the Way, endeavor to be clear and endeavor to be calm. Do not force it, do not lengthen it." (*The Manifest Dao* 4a)

The assumption appears to be that a seasoned practitioner will breathe long, relaxed breaths; thus novices might be inclined to purposely make themselves breathe in such a way, and this proves to be difficult. Laozi's answer to the problem is that you should just be serene and relaxed, and should not make any deliberate effort to slow, deepen, or lengthen your breathing. Apparently, your breathing is supposed to naturally become deep and long as your mind and body enter into deeper states of concentration, serenity, and equilibrium.

In the course of each day you are recommended to practice the reclining meditation three or four times; to practice it an excessive number of times is undesirable, because, as Laozi states, "The Way takes away the breath of people" 道奪人氣息, meaning that somehow the method can put stress on the body if not practiced in moderation. However, after the regimen has been continued for 100 days, somehow "the Way is accomplished" (*daocheng* 道成); from this point onward you can engage in as many meditation sessions as you please, without incurring stress or damage. Also, you may practice it outdoors, which is something strictly forbidden prior to the crucial 100-day juncture (6a).

During the 100 days (or more) of the regimen there are also various protocols to be observed in regard to eating. You must not eat immediately after a session of meditation, but should first at least get up and walk around for a while. Otherwise, "the *qi* will combine with and envelop your food and drink, and become dissipated" 氣合含飲食則消矣; this apparently means that the primal *qi* that you had activated from the lower Elixir Field through the exercise ends up getting expended in digesting your food, and becomes excreted along with it, instead of properly circulating and nurturing the body. When you do eat, you are allowed to eat only dry and light foods such as "parched rice, roasted wheat, dried meat, dates and chestnuts" 粳糧麥麨脯腊棗栗—preferably in small amounts—so as to "enable your breaths to be long" 令息條長. You should not eat until you are full, for doing so causes the five viscera to "mingle and conflict" 交格, making it difficult for the *qi* to circulate. You can thus consume both meat and starches, but in a dried, nonperishable form. The assumption seems to be that moist, perishable foods can more seriously impede the circulation of *qi*; there also may be the underlying attitude here that "you are what you eat"—thus, by eating perishable foods you yourself remain perishable. One can surmise that the foods recommended here were the things that people typically included in their provisions when embarking on a journey or sojourn away from civilization. After the "Way is accomplished" (meaning perhaps that you have completed a 100-day meditation retreat with satisfactory results) you can return to eating ordinary heavy, cooked food if you desire; however, you must wait 100 days before doing so, and should even then take care to limit the volume of your intake (8a–b).

Regarding the possibility of "eliminating grains" (*juegu* 絕穀) we find the following exchange:

或問 道 常道氣 可絕穀不

老子曰 將欲度世離俗 急當絕之 以氣息久久 不飢不渴 道之大要

Someone asked, "In practicing the Way, if there is constant Dao-*qi*, can you eliminate grains or not?"

Laozi said, "If you want to transcend the world and separate from the worldly, it is urgent that you should eliminate them. By means of your *qi* and your breathing, after a long while, you do not hunger or thirst. This is the great essential of the Way." (*The Manifest Dao* 8b)

What the interlocutor is apparently asking is whether it is possible to stop eating entirely if a practitioner of the Plain Way has become adept to the point where the Dao-*qi* or primal *qi* is becoming activated on a constant basis. (If to "eliminate grains" here simply meant to avoid starches, this would presumably be something that anybody could undertake immediately by subduing hunger with other types of food.)[10] Laozi confirms that such is indeed the case, and that the attainment of such a condition is in fact necessary if one is to "transcend the world." At this level of attainment, apparently, your *qi* and your breathing alone are sufficient to sustain you. As discussed in chapter 2, such is indeed what *The Great Peace* describes as having been the condition of the first humans at the time of their creation.

In the subsequent exchange, the interlocutor asks whether it would be permissible if one wished only to engage in "refined contemplation" (*jingsi* 精思) without "eliminating grains." To this Laozi responds:

食穀滿腹 腐洿盛糞 神不居形 但道不止 久久自不飢

When you eat grain and fill the belly, the rotten filth piles up as feces, and the gods will not dwell in your body. Just practice the Way endlessly, and after a long while you will naturally not hunger. (*The Manifest Dao* 8b)

Solid food thus not only impedes the free flow of *qi* through the body, but also repels the corporeal deities by becoming so hideously malodorous during the digestion process. In any case, one is to be reassured that the sustained practice of the Plain Way will naturally eliminate hunger.

After the earlier exchange, we find the following one:

或問道 人生從小至大 以穀自長 何爲絕穀乎

老子曰 穀唯生人長大 不欲使人食之至老 老死皆由於穀矣

Someone asked about the Way, "People are born, and then from the time they are small until the time they are big, they grow by means of grains. Why should one eliminate grains?"

Laozi said, "Grains only produce growth in people. [I] (or grains?) do not want to have people eat them and bring forth decrepitude. Decrepitude and death are all caused by grains." (*The Manifest Dao* 9a)

What Laozi means to say here (if our interpretation is correct) is that the foods we eat, though they do indeed help us grow to maturity, also eventually become agents that cause decrepitude, and eventually death. (Actually, because the subject of the second sentence in Laozi's reply is omitted, it seems possible [but probably not accurate] to regard the "grains" themselves as the object of the sentence. If so, Laozi would seem to be saying that the foods we eat have some sort of conscious will of their own, by which they cause us to become old and die, so that we will not continue eating them.)

After this, we find the interlocutor asking, "By eliminating grains is it possible to transcend the world?" 絕穀可得度世不 To this, Laozi responds most affirmatively:

合無者自知 自然不食 但存氣鍊形 何憂不長存

Those who merge with nothingness naturally understand. Naturally they do not eat. They just preserve the *qi* and refine the body. Why should they worry about not existing perpetually? (*The Manifest Dao* 9a)

Thus he speaks of the most ideal condition where not eating comes about naturally while the mind understands something in a condition where it has "merged with nothingness"—what exactly is meant by this is unclear, but it would seem to denote a state of mind free of deluding thoughts and agitating feelings. In this condition the body is sustained and refined through *qi*.

Having said this, however, for somebody whose condition falls short of the ideal, "eliminating grains" is not the best idea. Thus we find the following exchange:

或問道 欲絕穀 五臟有微病 云何

老子曰 且勿絕穀 節食爲之 又百日之後斷穀 [餌]稻米粥及餌(?) 清物

Someone asked about the Way, "If I want to eliminate grains, but my five viscera have subtle ailments, what do you say about this?"

Laozi said, "For now, do not eliminate grains. Handle the situation by limiting your food. After 100 days you can cut off grains. Eat rice porridge as well as pure things." (*The Manifest Dao* 9a)

Unclear here is whether the interlocutor means to say that the "subtle ailments" are being caused by the rigors of fasting, or rather that this is a preexisting condition that is making the undertaking difficult. In any case, Laozi recommends reducing your food intake rather than complete fasting, but also believes that after 100 days of doing so, "cutting off grains" should become feasible. The final phrase here concerning rice porridge and "pure things" is perhaps corrupt, and would make much better sense if the verb "eat" (*er* 餌) was placed before "rice porridge" (*daomi zhou* 稻米粥). If such an emendation is correct, Laozi is here recommending the limited consumption of rice porridge and other bland or "pure foods" during the 100 days leading up to the complete fast.[11] However, if so, one does wonder why rice porridge would be recommended here despite the fact that in another passage (on 8a; discussed earlier) he had recommended dried grains for consumption. Perhaps he is addressing the specific condition of the visceral "subtle ailment," for which soft, bland porridge is considered best by virtue of being easiest to digest.

In the "Sudao jie" we find just one verbal exchange concerning sexual activity. It reads:

或問 道成後 可得入房室 不

老子曰 欲得飛仙度世 勿入房室 不欲度世者 百日之後可自恣矣

Someone asked, "After the Way is accomplished, can one enter the bedroom [for sexual intercourse], or not?"

Laozi said, "If you want to transcend the world as a Flying Transcendent, do not enter the bedroom. Those who do not want to transcend the world may do as they wish after a hundred days." (*The Manifest Dao* 6b–7a)

Thus the contemplative regimen required celibacy. Presumably this was for the preservation of essence. Celibacy for the remainder of your life is required for attaining immortality and the ability to fly. It is not necessary for those adepts who are less spiritually ambitious. What rewards, then, are available to those who resume sexual activity? Most likely they are supposed to be able to expect impeccable health and great longevity, but alas within an impermanent existence bound to the earthly realm with limited powers. What is not quite clear is whether "100 days" here means 100 days of practicing the regimen (during which the "Way is accomplished"), or rather a 100-day interval of abstinence that accrues after you stop practicing the regimen. In either case, a transgression of the 100-day prohibition was presumably thought to badly undermine the salubrious effects of the regimen. The very fact that the interlocutor would inquire about the resumption of sexual activity suggests that *The Manifest Dao* does *not* issue from a monastic *milieu*. Laozi is apparently speaking to an audience that considers sexual intercourse a normal part of life.

The actual meditation technique of the "Sudao jie" is indeed a "plain way." Essentially, while lying on your back, you are to focus attention on a region in the lower abdomen under the navel known as the Elixir Field (*dantian* 丹田); doing so is supposed to activate from there an internal surge of *qi* known as the "primal *qi*" (*yuanqi* 元氣) or "Dao-*qi*" (*daoqi* 道氣) that can circulate, nourish, strengthen, transform, and levitate the body. However, the meditation session does commence with the performance of a simple procedure of ritual invocation and active imagination. Our text reads:

或問 道時有所存呼

老子曰 先呼五神名 心神名呴呴 肝神名監監 肺神名嚴嚴 脾神名卑卑 腎神名撫撫 從次呼之以處丹田 氣則至矣

Someone asked, "When [practicing] the Dao, is there something that one should visualize and call upon?"

Laozi said, "First call out the names of the five spirits. The name of the spirit of the heart is Houhou. The name of the spirit of the liver is Jianjian. The name of the spirit of the lungs is Yanyan. The name of the spirit of the spleen is Beibei. The name of the spirit of the kidneys is Fufu. One after another call out to them in order make them reside in the Elixir Field. The *qi* will thereby arrive. (*The Manifest Dao* 10b)

Thus, in order to activate the primal *qi* from the Elixir Field in the belly, you are to concentrate all of your psycho-physical resources there. Thus you invoke the names of the resident spirits of the five viscera so as to gather them there.[12]

Another method mentioned in *The Manifest Dao* meant to aid your focus and facilitate the flow of *qi* toward the Elixir Field is that of "using a 3 *cun* long tally stick to prop up the Elixir Field" 以籌長三寸柱丹田 (5b). The exact meaning of this is unclear, although it would seem to mean that you somehow hold a stick vertically on top of or under the portion of the lower abdomen where the Elixir Field is supposed to lie.

The contemplation of the Elixir Field is thus the essential technique for the activation and circulation of the primal *qi* that forms the crux of the Plain Way. However, this contemplation is to be carried out only during the daylight hours. This is because the "night is [the time of] dead *qi*, when the wicked ghosts also roam about" 夜為死氣邪鬼並行. Daytime, contrarily is the time of living *qi*; dawn in particular is a time when the *qi* can circulate easily (7a). However, there is another sort of contemplation that is recommended for the nighttime. Laozi states:

晝存氣府 夜存神宮 氣府者 名曰丹田 神宮者 名曰明堂 晝不存氣府 元氣不行 夜不存神宮 目不覩神

In the daytime observe the Mansion of *Qi*. At night observe the Divine Palace. The Mansion of *Qi* is called the Elixir Field. The Divine Palace is called the Hall of Light. If you do not observe the Mansion of *Qi* in the daytime, the primal *qi* will not circulate. If you do not observe the Divine Palace at night, your eyes will not see the gods. (*The Manifest Dao* 4b–5a)

Thus, during the night you are to focus on the Divine Palace or Hall of Light, which—though not specifically indicated here—is most likely understood to be located in the head, in between the eyes.[13] Apparently, the object of this exercise is the fortification of vision—in particular an internal or mystical sort of vision by which you hope to be able to see gods/deities/spirits (*shen* 神), which exist inside your body as well as outside of it.[14]

Regarding the Elixir Field and the activation of the Dao-*qi*, we find the following verbal exchange:

或問 道氣出入 常從何來

老子曰 氣出丹田者 人之命門 元氣之本根 五臟得之以鮮明 元氣之所出入也

Someone asked, "When the Dao-*qi* emerges and enters,[15] where does it always come from?"

Laozi said, "The *qi* emerges from the Elixir Field, because [the Elixir Field] is a person's Gate of Destiny, and is the original root of the primal *qi*. The five viscera obtain this and become fresh and clear. This is where the primal *qi* emerges and enters." (*The Manifest Dao* 4b)

Thus, the Elixir Field is identified as the crucial location from which the *qi* (known variously as the primal *qi* or the Dao-*qi*) emerges. The Elixir Field in the belly[16] is thus the wellspring from which pristine, cosmic vitality emerges from within your very own being. When the primal *qi* enters the five viscera (liver, heart, spleen, lungs, kidneys) they become "fresh and clear," which perhaps simply means that they become purified and invigorated; however, the text here could also be alluding to a sort of inner X-ray-like vision by which you are supposed to actually see the inside of your anatomy.

*The Manifest Dao* then reads:

或問 道氣生丹田 出入何臟

老子曰 呼入肺心 吸入腎肝 呼吸相逢 交會太倉 三焦和引 拘制魂魄 自然之氣 道之命長 審而行之 必為真人

Someone asked, "The Dao-*qi* issues from the Elixir Field. What organs does it go in and out of?"

Laozi said, "When you exhale, it enters the lungs and heart. When you inhale, it enters the kidneys and liver. Exhalation and inhalation meet each other, mingling in the Great Storehouse (stomach). The Three Burners[17] harmonize and guide (?), taking under control the cloud-souls and white-souls. This is the *qi* of naturalness; the life of the Dao is long. If you clearly understand and practice this, you will definitely become a Genuine Person. (*The Manifest Dao* 4b)

Apparently, while you continue to breathe in and out in the ordinary manner, the inner primal *qi* undergoes its own circulation that is synchronized with the inhalations and exhalations of external air. By route of the lungs, heart, kidneys, and liver, the inner vital *qi* converges in the stomach. The essential consequence appears to be that the digestive system is replenished, leading to a state of satiation that is also conducive to psychological stability and well-being. The primal *qi* thus serves as nourishment, and you are eventually expected to be able to live off of it while abstaining from ordinary eating. Note here that the primal *qi* is also called the "*qi* of naturalness" (*ziran zhi qi* 自然之氣), which as we have seen in chapter 2 is a term used in the Taiping Group texts to denote the *qi* by which both fetuses and people at the beginning of creation are said to be or to have been nourished thoroughly without eating any food.

The initial activation of the primal *qi* from the Elixir Field is supposed to bring forth definite tangible symptoms:

或問 息得時 何爲驗

老子曰 氣初至時 腸鳴脉動 手足痛 氣之故也

Someone asked, "When the breathing is obtained, what will be the sign?"

Laozi said, "When the *qi* first arrives, your intestines will rumble and your pulse will quicken. Your hands and feet will ache. This is due to the *qi*." (*The Manifest Dao* 4a)

Here this decisive moment that is anticipated is referred to as the "obtaining of the breathing," or the "arrival of the *qi*." The primal *qi* that had been absent or dormant becomes activated and initiates a sort of internal "breathing" of its own. When thus activated, the primal *qi* causes very conspicuous physical symptoms—rumbling in the belly, rapid pulse, aching in the hands and feet—that may seem unpleasant, but which indicate a significant breakthrough and are thus to be regarded as highly auspicious and encouraging.

*The Manifest Dao* continues:

或問 氣至 身何如

老子曰 氣至身 身漸寒 欲驚 安心定志 無使之驚 聽氣之所為也

Someone asked, "When the *qi* arrives, what will happen to the body?"

Laozi said, "When the *qi* arrives in the body, the body will gradually get cold, and you will be on the verge of being frightened (shivering?). Calm your mind and stabilize your will; do not allow them to be frightened. Listen to what the *qi* does." (*The Manifest Dao* 4a–b)

Understandably, a drop in body temperature, especially when accompanied by rumbling intestines, quickened pulse and aching in the limbs, can be a frightening experience. It too, however, is an auspicious symptom brought on by the primal *qi*, and should be taken calmly in stride. You must simply stand by passively but attentively, and allow the *qi* to work its marvels.

*The Manifest Dao* makes it quite clear in the following passage that the "Plain Way" can be practiced by both men and women:

或問 道氣 男女同法 不

老子曰 丈夫精者 二三日得氣 婦人精者 四五日氣通 則有所聞見 道之證驗 精氣之大効

Someone asked, "[In activating and circulating] the Dao-*qi*, is the method the same for men and women, or not?"

Laozi said, "Gentlemen who are diligent can obtain the *qi* in two or three days. Women who are diligent can get the *qi* to penetrate in four or five days. Thereby, one will see and hear things. These are the signs of proof of the Dao—the great effects of the essence and *qi*." (*The Manifest Dao* 5a–b)

Thus, although a male body and mind is considered somewhat of an advantage, women are also deemed capable of "obtaining the *qi*" and benefiting from the results that can be subsequently brought about. We can surmise that the movement from which the text issued included people of both sexes within its fold. Visions and locutions are to be anticipated with hope, although you are not likely to have any for at least the first couple of days. The visions and locutions are "signs of proof" (*zhengyan* 證驗) indicating that your essence and *qi* are being mobilized in the desirable manner, and that the universal force of eternal life (the Dao) is present and active within.

Apparently, one type of vision that adepts anticipated was that of lights. The text reads:

或問 道 時丹田久晝明日 可因之 不 將更久乎

老子曰 數明久 田無發 絕久久 自見其田明如日光 氣到如涌雲

"Someone asked, "[In practicing] the Dao, at times the Elixir Field will for a long time [shine like] the bright daytime sun. Can I go along with this, or not? Can it [shine] even longer?"

Laozi said, "After shining lengthily for several times, the Field will stop emitting [light]. [The light will be] cut off for a long time, but then naturally you will see the Field become bright as sunlight, and the *qi* will arrive like gushing clouds." (*The Manifest Dao* 5b)

Apparently among the earliest signs of proof to be experienced is a radiance that emerges from the Elixir Field. How and in what sense you are supposed to "see" this radiance is unclear, at least to those who have not experienced it. Is it a radiance that is visible from outside with the naked eye? More likely, perhaps, it is experienced through a more subtle, internal form of "vision" that you are supposed to come to possess. The vision of the radiance can linger for long periods, and disappear for long periods. But even after lengthy absences it will reappear, and will be accompanied by the arrival of gushing clouds of *qi*; whether this cloud-like *qi* is also a vision, or something more like an invigorating, buoyant sensation, is unclear.

As you progress further into the practice of the Plain Way, yet another, more eerie sort of vision is to occur:

或問 道 所見怪何物乎

老子曰 道數十日 有白頭老嫗從一女子 常侍左右 有頃去 忽不知所在 是其怪也

Someone asked, "[When practicing] the Dao, what are the specters that one will see?"

Laozi said, "After [practicing] the Dao for some multiples of ten days, there will be a white-headed old woman, always attended on her left and right by a girl. After a while they will leave, and suddenly you will not know where they are. This is the apparition." (*The Manifest Dao* 7a–b)

After twenty, thirty, forty or more days of practice, you have presumably long since activated the primal *qi* and are likely to experience visions and other strange phenomena that can be rather eerie and disturbing in nature. One might perhaps surmise that the extended period of seclusion is causing some degree of stress and anxiety, or that contents of your subconscious are somehow caused to emerge upon the horizons of your awareness.[18]

Perhaps even more eerie and disturbing than the visions are the symptoms that can manifest themselves in your bodily movements and speech:

或問道 見怪 手足擾 口妄言 瞑目顧念田 不

老子曰 專心一意 瞑目念田 行氣如故 勿醒勿疑 久久怪自休

Someone asked, "If, when I see the specters, my hands and feet shake, and I utter senseless words, should I then close my eyes and contemplate upon my [Elixir] Field?"

Laozi said, "Concentrate your mind and single-mindedly close your eyes and contemplate upon the [Elixir] Field. Circulate the *qi* as before. Do not give up, and do not entertain doubts. After a long while, the specters will cease." (*The Manifest Dao* 7b)

It would appear that the interlocutor is a practitioner with some experience who has seen the visions spoken of by Laozi and who has on such occasions manifested involuntary shaking and babbling speech. Though these symptoms may seem suggestive of a mental or neurological disorder, Laozi regards them as typical occurrences that need not be cause for alarm. You must simply continue to calmly concentrate on the Elixir Field.

The text continues:

或問 道 常瞑目念田 何容見怪

老子曰 意未專 志未定 則見怪 無自是 無恐起為他事 無與之語 與之語 則將人俱去矣

Someone asked, "If in [practicing] the Dao, you constantly close the eyes and contemplate upon the [Elixir] Field, how can you end up seeing specters?"

Laozi said, "If your mind is not yet concentrated and your will is not yet stable, you will see specters. Do not be self-satisfied, and do not give rise to fear and take on other tasks. Do not converse with it (the specter). If [a person] converses with it, it will take the person away with it." (*The Manifest Dao* 7b)

If you are perfect in your calmness and concentration, we are told, specters cannot appear. However, Laozi here apparently recognizes that even the most capable and earnest people tend to fall short of perfection, meaning that encounters with specters are to be expected. You must not, however, become fearful or discouraged—much less give up the contemplation. The situation indeed appears to be dangerous, however. You are liable to become "self-satisfied" or to be drawn into conversation with the specters; in the worst case scenario you will be "taken away." The precise meaning of all of this is rather ambiguous, but perhaps at the stage where they see the specters, adepts are liable to fall into self-delusion or insanity.

The text continues:

或問道 未至時 手足擾 口妄言 豈故為之 將自然乎

老子曰 是自然 氣之所為 非邪所教

Someone asked, "When it (the *qi*? the apparitions?) has not yet arrived, my hands and feet shake and I utter senseless words. I am not doing this on purpose. Is this due to something natural?"

Laozi said, "This is natural. It is the doing of the *qi*. It is not caused by anything wicked." (*The Manifest Dao* 7b)

This interlocutor sounds very worried about the involuntary shaking and babbling, which furthermore seems to be coming about prematurely. The realization that you are not in control of your movements and speech would certainly be very disturbing. Yet, Laozi reassures the interlocutor that the shaking and babbling is a natural phenomenon, the source of which is not malignant or demonic. It is being caused by the very *qi* that promises to be the agent of the great transformation toward eternal life. Thus, though the shaking and babbling may seem even stranger and scarier than the visions, we are told that they are in fact quite benign and much less dangerous.

The text continues:

或問 道 手足擾口妄言不止 云何

老子曰 遠者二時 近者一時 氣定意專 則自休矣

Someone asked, "[In practicing] the Dao, what if the shaking of the hands and feet and the senseless utterances do not stop?"

Laozi said, "Within two hours at most, or in just one hour, if the *qi* is stable and the mind is concentrated, [the shaking and babbling] will naturally cease." (*The Manifest Dao* 7b–8a)

This segment, if I have understood it correctly, indicates that the involuntary shaking and babbling, when it does occur, usually persists for an hour or more. Again, though this may sound like a very worrisome situation, Laozi reassures the interlocutor that the shaking and babbling will cease naturally within two hours at most—if you can maintain a proper degree of inner composure through all of it.

The text continues:

或問 道 見怪者 告人 已 不

老子曰 告人者 神後不復來 怪者真人之媒驛 勿罵呵 跫為善

Someone asked, "If I see specters, will they stop [coming if I] tell [other] people about them, or not?"

Laozi said, "If you tell other people, the spirits will no longer come. Specters are the intermediaries of the Genuine Persons. Do not yell insults at them. The sound of their footsteps is good." (*The Manifest Dao* 8a)

In Laozi's view, although the specters appear due to lack of composure and concentration, and can be very harmful, they are also the "intermediaries" of benevolent, holy immortals known as Genuine Persons (*zhenren* 真人).[19] Thus, their source is not from within your own mind. It appears that they are regarded as external, low-ranking spirits that are dispatched by more exalted beings, who wish to test you. By maintaining composure you pass the test, and become more likely to at some point personally encounter a Genuine Person, who is likely to bestow lofty teachings or great blessings. Going public with your mystical experiences violates the protocol between you and the divine beings.

The text continues:

或問 道已解 得講諸繆惡 不

老子曰 講諸不祥 則致凶傷 惡夢恍惚 眾邪合同 正氣難致 邪氣往從

Someone asked, "Once you have disengaged from the [practice] of the Way, can you speak of false and wicked things, or not?"

Laozi said, "Speaking of inauspicious things brings about misfortune and injury. Bad dreams will hazily appear, and the multitude of evils will converge. Proper *qi* will be difficult to bring forth, while wicked *qi* will come following along." (*The Manifest Dao* 8a)

The interlocutor here is asking about a situation where you are still in retreat in the mountains for the practice of the 100-plus day regimen, but at the particular moment are not actually in the act of reclining supine and concentrating on the Elixir Field. It should be recalled here that you are not all alone, but have at least one attendant with you. You apparently do have some opportunities for conversation when not actually meditating. However, the content of the conversation must be about proper, good, and positive things, so as not to attract malignant forces and spirits, while repelling auspicious forces and spirits. Thoughts and words have a power and life of their own, which must be taken seriously into account when you are undertaking the highly sensitive regimen of the Dao. Thus, further on in our text we find the following exchange:

或問道 意常不樂 惆悵不安 何所存思

老子曰 常念善 則善氣來 若嘗思念惡 邪來傷人 但專心守道 邪無以干

Someone asked, "If my mind is always unhappy, melancholy and uneasy, what should I think about?"

Laozi said, "Always think of good things, and thereby good *qi* will come. If you constantly ponder and think of bad things, wickedness will come and do harm. Just guard the Dao single-mindedly, and wickedness will be unable to do anything." (*The Manifest Dao* 10a–b)

Thus Laozi endorses the power of positive thinking, which elicits positive *qi*.

Another effect that the Plain Way is said to bring about is something referred to as *ascending lightly* (*qingju* 輕舉):

或問 道有輕舉 何等輕舉 意將夢之 其形自舉乎

老子曰 道氣久 精神振之 其形自舉 此道將欲成之

Someone asked, "In the Way there are those who ascend lightly. How does one ascend lightly? By dreaming of it with one's mind, will the body naturally rise up?"

Laozi said, "After [activating and circulating] the Dao-*qi* for a long time, the essence and spirit will arouse it, and the body will rise up. This means that the Dao is about to bring it to completion." (*The Manifest Dao* 6b)

The meaning of ascending lightly (*qingju* 輕舉) here is not clear. This term usually refers to the ultimate ascension to heaven undergone by the Daoist Transcendent at the end of his or her worldly career. Here, however, the interlocutor and Laozi perhaps are talking about a sensation of levitation experienced occasionally by seasoned practitioners, which constitutes but one of the many "signs of proof" along the way to immortality. Laozi seems to describe it not as the climactic soteriological attainment, but rather as a sign of progress toward the goal.

Regarding some more of the glorious results that come about from lengthy perseverance and lofty attainment, one finds the following exchange:

或問 道氣成積年 以何爲證

老子曰 積年道日久 洞浸萬里 日月星辰 明鏡炬火 輝輝日光 來照形兆 諸神營衛 不召自來 是道之證 慎勿妄語

Someone asked, "When the [activation and circulation] of the Dao-*qi* has been accomplished over many years, what can one take as proof?"

Laozi said, "After you have practiced the Way for many days and years, you will penetrate and permeate a myriad *li*. The sun, moon, stars and planets will appear bright as a luminous mirror illuminated by torch fire. The brilliant radiance of the sun will come and illuminate your body. The various gods will come to guard you. They will come of their own accord, even without being summoned. This is proof of the Dao. Be careful not to speak to others about [these things]." (*The Manifest Dao* 10b–11a)

Laozi thus states that there are signs of proof that can be expected to occur after you have diligently carried out the contemplative practice over many years. These include vision or psychic power that can perceive distant things, along with visions of radiant lights and of guardian deities. However, if you experience these things, you must not speak of them to others. Laozi earlier in the text warned that the gods have a way of distancing themselves from adepts who are not discreet. Also, one can surmise that speaking outwardly about mystical experiences can tend to attract attention from the wrong types of people, and may cause you to develop harmful pride and vanity.

The text further reads:

或問 道成時有限度 不

老子曰 六十日爲中度 百日爲大度 其已道成 身不復老 數有日久 氣行如風雨

Someone asked, "Is there a time period during which the Way is to be accomplished, or not?'

Laozi answered, "It is 60 days for the intermediate degree, and 100 days for the great degree. Once the Dao is accomplished, the body no longer ages. As the days accumulate, the *qi* goes about like wind and rain." (*The Manifest Dao* 11a)

It would appear that the point where the aging process is brought to a halt is the point where one can say that "the Dao has been accomplished." The more you practice, the more vigorous the primal *qi* becomes. Presumably, the "intermediate degree" and "great degree" would be distinguishable also based on the magnitude of benefits or "signs of proof" that accrue, but Laozi does not say what these are.

The conversation on the Plain Way is brought to a close by directions from Laozi pertaining to the discretion involved in transmitting the method. Laozi declares that his Way is not something that should be sold for financial profit, nor should it be flaunted to gain attention from powerful, influential people. You must not damage the Way by sharing it with liars and flatterers. The Way is a secret and serious matter on which no price can be placed. It is to be brought out if there is a Sage 聖 worthy of receiving it, but should be concealed otherwise. Transmitting it to the right person will make the Way "clear and bright" 清明, but transmitting it to the wrong person will bring disaster upon you. Thus, you must guard and conceal the Way under a blood oath (*xuemeng* 血盟) proclaimed before the Primal Predecessor (Yuanxian 元先) residing up above (11a–b).

These proclamations are followed by a brief exposition on another meditation method by Laozi that seems to be distinct from the Plain Way, but perhaps could have been practiced in tandem with it. The method involves visualizing your spirit as bearing a bright, white form resembling a pearl. In the early morning around sunrise you visualize it under your nose at your philtrum (*renzhong* 人中). At breakfast time you visualize it amidst the hair on your head, at high noon you visualize it above your head, and in the late afternoon you visualize it at your nape. You can also visualize it at your lower back in the late afternoon, and then at the "turtle rump" (*guikao* 龜尻 the perineum?) at sundown. At midnight you visualize it at "the head of the jade flower" (*yuyingtou* 玉英頭), after which over the course of the night it travels through the stomach and spleen. By the moments before dawn ("when the roosters are calling" 雞鳴) it reaches the lungs, after which it passes through the throat and is back under the nose by sunrise. Laozi concludes that to visualize in this manner amidst all activities—even when drinking, eating, or walking about—is what is called "preserving the spirit" and that this conduces to long life and "plants the roots for Dao Virtue" 種道德之根 (11b–12a).

The "Juegu shiqi fa," the fasting manual at the end of *The Manifest Dao*, starts out by stating:

凡欲絕食昇虛求仙之道 當安處靜室 先呼三神之名 然後服氣

If you wish for the Way to eliminate foods, ascend to the void and seek Transcendence, you must reside peacefully in a quiet room. First you call out the names of the three gods, and after this you imbibe *qi*. (*The Manifest Dao* 12a)

The three gods to be invoked at the beginning are the gods of the upper, middle, and lower Elixir Fields. They respectively bear the names Primal Predecessor-Imperial Chamberlain (Yuanxian Diqing 元先帝卿), Cinnabar Radiance-Firm Protection (Zidan Guangjian 子丹光堅), and Primal Yang-Valley Mystery (Yuanyang Guxuan 元陽谷玄). Each of these is implored to guard their proper Elixir Field, and to "enable me to seek and obtain the movable feast brought by your serving [spirits], and make my *qi* sufficient" 使我求得 所從送給行廚 令氣充足 (12a).

Here we may have evidence that the "Juegu shiqi fa" dates later than the "Sudao jie," because there we were concerned with just one Elixir Field—the lower one in the belly. The notion of middle and upper Elixir Fields in the chest and head respectively is not mentioned in the aforementioned *Taishang laojun zhongjing* or *Taishang huangting waijing yujing* (pre-fourth-century texts featuring elaborate descriptions of the inner anatomy and pantheon), but had come to be known by the early fourth century, for it is mentioned at the beginning of chapter 18 of Ge Hong's 葛洪 (283–343) *Baopuzi neipian* 抱朴子內篇,[20] and also figures prominently in the Shangqing scriptures of the latter half of that century. The names given to the three gods here in fact closely resemble names given to them in the Shangqing scriptures.[21] Thus one might speculate that the "Sudao jie" predates the fourth century while the "Juegu shiqi fa" does not, and perhaps consider these two sections of *The Manifest Dao* as issuing from originally unrelated parties. However, it is highly significant to note here that the name of the deity (Primal Predecessor) to whom you swear your oath when having the Plain Way transmitted to you matches with the first part of the name of the god of the Upper Elixir Field. This would seem to suggest some link between the parties that produced the two different sections, and might also suggest that practitioners of the Plain Way actually were familiar with the notion of three Elixir Fields with their resident gods.

After the invocations of the three gods follows the eating of *qi* or imbibing of *qi* (*fuqi* 服氣), which here consists not only of swallowing air, but saliva as well, while lying down. To stimulate the flow of saliva you are to place one peppercorn in your mouth. A total of 360 mouthfuls of swallowed *qi* constitutes "a meal" (*yidun* 一頓), although you are supposed to divide the meal into four segments of 90 mouthfuls, with breaks in between. Such a *qi* meal is to be eaten three times a day, at sunrise, high noon, and sunset. If you get thirsty, you are allowed to drink water or "honey juice" (*mijiang* 蜜漿). After 100 days of this, "the medicinal strength for the first time becomes sufficient" 藥力始備—meaning perhaps that you come to internally possess *qi* that has optimal nourishing and transforming power (12b–13a).

The text then goes on to describe in vivid terms the effects that you will experience over the course of the 100 days. After three days and again after fourteen days you will experience a minor crisis in which the head feels dizzy; however, you must not think it strange, nor become scared. Also, by the 10-day juncture you will begin to feel weak and your complexion will become sallow. At the 20-day juncture your bodily movements will become dizzy and staggered, and there will be swelling in your limbs and joints. Your large bowel movements will be "slightly difficult" 微難 and your urine will be a reddish-yellow color. In some cases there may also be diarrhea. At the 30-day juncture your body becomes gaunt and has trouble moving about (13a–b).

However, at the 40-day juncture a healthy color will begin to return to your complexion, and you begin to feel joyful and relaxed. At the 50-day juncture your five viscera become harmonious and "your essence and *qi* are inwardly nourished" 精氣內養. By the 60-day juncture the condition of your body is fully restored to what it had been prior to the rigors of the fast. At the 70-day juncture you begin to loathe noise and clamor, as you yearn to fly up high. At the 80-day juncture you feel placidly detached and serene. At the 90-day juncture your appearance and complexion become glorious and lustrous, and your voice becomes strong and clear. At the 100-day juncture "the essence and *qi* all arrive" 精氣皆至, so that henceforth if you continue the practice your destined life span gets extended and more and more auspicious transformations occur. After three years all scars and blemishes disappear; after six years you possess clairvoyant powers; and by the end of nine years you become an immortal Genuine Person who commands ghosts and spirits and is attended by Jade Maidens, and who assists the Supreme August One (Shanghuang 上皇) up above (13b).

Thus, the "Juegu shiqi fa" provides us with descriptions of physical effects that rival those of the "Sudao jie" in their concreteness and vividness. However, the respective methods that bring the effects about are very different, and one wonders what the relationship between the two sections and their methods could have been. It seems fairly likely that the "Juegu shiqi fa" was placed alongside the "Sudao jie" with the intention that the reader might practice its method as a means of preparing for or facilitating the Plain Way of the "Sudao jie." Ideally, perhaps, one was supposed to be able to overcome hunger and thirst and gain immortality just by calmly awaiting the coming forth of primal *qi* from the lower Elixir Field; in practice, the hunger could get severe enough that the swallowing of air and saliva would become an appealing option.

The most noteworthy feature of the "Sudao jie" for us is its vivid descriptions of drastic and alarming physical sensations (rumbling of the intestines, quickening of pulse, pain in the hands and feet, drop in bodily temperature) and involuntary movement and speech (shaking of hands and feet, babbling speech) that occur as the result of the mobilization of primal *qi* induced through the simple, sustained concentration upon the Elixir Field in the lower abdomen. Such descriptions of physical sensations and involuntary shaking and babbling cannot be found in the Taiping Group texts or the *Laozi-Xiang'er*, and are in fact quite rare within the entirety of Daoist literature; however, similar descriptions eventually do emerge within Neidan literature—most notably in a discourse entitled *Jindan zhengyan* 金丹證驗, included in the Yuan 元 period anthology *Zhuzhen neidan jiyao* 諸真內丹集要 (ca. 1300).[22]

The "Sudao jie" does resemble the Taiping Group texts in how it lays emphasis on visions of inner lights and spirit beings. The specific vision described most concretely, however, seems quite eerie and peculiar, and bears no clear counterpart in the Taiping Group texts. The vision is of an old woman attended by a young woman, and tends to be accompanied by rather disturbing involuntary shaking and babbling. You are liable to become drawn into conversations with the apparitions, and this can apparently bring very dire consequences. The encounter with these apparitions is a hazard but also a test, which if passed (by ignoring the apparitions and maintaining your calm and focus), can lead to much more auspicious interactions with holy immortal beings. In the sense that it features an elderly woman and constitutes a test preliminary to loftier epiphanies this vision described in *The Manifest Dao* is rather reminiscent of a sort of vision sequence—featuring a fiery red snake and the Queen Mother of the West—that gets described in at least six different Daoist texts ranging in date from the early medieval period up to the modern period (and which we discuss in the next two sections of this chapter).

A feature that the *Xiandao jing* has in common with both the Taiping Group texts and the *Laozi-Xiang'er* is its assertion that total abstention from food is possible, and is indeed a definitive trait of immortals of the highest order. Its prescription of temporary sexual abstinence—or even better, permanent celibacy—is a feature not to be found in the Taiping Group texts. However, as we have mentioned already, the *Laozi-Xiang'er* does strongly emphasize sexual restraint (even though it can be somewhat plausibly read as prescribing intercourse with the context of early Heavenly Masters School Merging of *Qi* rites).

The "Sudao jie" in *The Manifest Dao*, it should also be noted, emphasizes not only the proper performance of the meditation technique, but also the quality of your thoughts and words at times when you are not meditating. The activation of the salubrious *qi* within you requires constant purity of mind and good moral conduct. In this feature, one could say that *The Manifest Dao* holds an affinity to the basic teaching of the *Laozi-Xiang'er* pertaining to how to keep the body filled with the *qi* of the Dao. Finally, it is probably worth noting the emphasis that *The Manifest Dao* puts on 100 days as a significant milestone within the meditation regimen. In *GP Instructions* 100 days is regarded as the "minor calm" in the regimen of Guarding the One.

### THE *RUSHI SI CHIZI FA* 入室思赤子法 (*CONTEMPLATING THE BABY*)

*Contemplating the Baby*[23] (*Rushi si chizi fa* 入室思赤子法; Method for Entering the Room and Contemplating upon the Baby) is one among at least six texts that describe a particular sort of vision sequence featuring a fiery red snake and the Queen Mother of the West.[24] It is a short text and is included in the 55th *juan* (9b–14a) of the important Northern Song period Daoist anthology, the *Yunji qiqian* 雲笈七籤.[25] *Contemplating the Baby* bears no colophon or any references to names, dates, or events by which a precise dating is possible, though it can obviously date no later than circa 1025, when the *Yunji qiqian* was compiled. The *Yunji qiqian* incorporates a considerable amount of material that is datable to the early part of the Six Dynasties (220–618), and it is possible that *Contemplating the Baby* is among these earlier materials. With the exception of one ambiguous phrase, there is no Buddhist influence apparent in its contents.

# Dramatic Physical and Sensory Effects    105

*Contemplating the Baby* takes the form of a discourse uttered by Laozi 老子. It commences with Laozi describing the attributes of "his" Dao 道. Laozi first points out that his Dao eludes our ordinary senses. He states:

吾道生於恍惚而無形 視之不可見 聽之不可聞 隨之不見其後 迎之不見其首

My Dao emerges from obscurity and is formless. Look at it and it cannot be seen. Listen to it and it cannot be heard. Follow it and you cannot see its rear. Beckon it and you cannot see its head. (*Yunji qiqian* 55/9b)

The Dao, Laozi also states, is vast enough to envelop the universe, and yet is also small enough to fit inside a single thin hair. It is the creative force that emanates and integrates through the functioning of the *yin* 陰 and *yang* 陽, sun and moon, sky and earth, husband and wife, the eight trigrams, and the like.

Laozi then speaks of the processes of conception and gestation (which are also the workings of the Dao), and goes into a complex and abstruse description of the human anatomy and its inner processes that is full of terms referring to special bodily locations and deities. Among these descriptions we find what appear to be directions pertaining to meditation, and among these directions we find the following statements:

甲癸邀辰巳 子午都集會 吾道自索子 邀之於南極 真人自告子 安之令審諦 枯木不煩擾 乙壬於寅卯 午申亦相須 丙辛於亥酉 未戌邀中野 吾道已見矣 忽然無所有 丁庚子與午 戊己卯與酉 失候不相覿 吾道去萬里 周旋天地間 傷命還害子 觀吾陰與陽 交精相哺乳 此謂養赤子 勿失其時矣

On *jia* and *gui* days meet [my Dao] at the *chen* and *si* hours. At the *zi* and *wu* hours all gather and meet. My Dao on its own comes looking for you. Come and meet it at the Southern Extreme. The Genuine Person himself will tell you to pacify it and make you clearly observe. The withered tree should not be disturbed. On *yi* and *ren* days you should [meet my Dao] at the *yin* and *mao* hours; at the *wu* and *shen* hours you need to as well. On *bing* and *xin* days, at the *hai*, *you*, *wei* and *xu* hours, meet [my Dao] at the Central Plain. My Dao will have already appeared. Suddenly, nothing exists. On *ding* and *geng* days [meet my Dao] at the *zi* and *wu* hours. On *wu* and *ji* days [meet my Dao] at the *mao* and *you* hours. If you miss the times, you will not see [my Dao]. My Dao will depart to 10,000 miles away,[26] to circulate between heaven and earth. This will injure your life and bring harm to you. Observe how my *yin* and *yang* merge their essences and together feed milk. This is called "nurturing the Baby." Do not miss the proper times. (*Yunji qiqian* 55/10b)

Much of the meaning of the previous passage will become clearer when we look at what comes later in the text. However, we can now note that Laozi's Dao—that had at the outset been described as something so elusive to the senses—is here said to be something that will come to you and appear on its own, provided that you go and "meet" it at the proper place at the proper time. Doing so requires that you "pacify it," "clearly observe," and make sure not to let your "withered tree" get disturbed; withered tree here probably refers to the mind's calm composure, and is an allusion to the anecdote about Nanguo Ziqi in the second chapter of the *Zhuangzi* (see chapter 1). The Dao will appear when it does, not when you make it or wish it to. However, when it does appear, suddenly "nothing exists" (*wu suoyou* 無所有). This perhaps means that it disappears almost as soon as it appears, or that when it is manifesting itself there is no sensory data of the ordinary sort. Another possible—but perhaps less likely—interpretation here, if the term *wu suoyou* is to be understood in its Buddhist sense, is that you arrive at the ontological realization that all phenomena lack inherent existence.[27] In any case, if you miss the proper times you will not get to see the Dao—a serious failure, because this causes the Dao, which is the very source and sustainer of your life, to distance itself remotely from you. To observe the Dao means to observe within your own person the psycho-physiological processes that take the shape of the interplay of the bipolar *yin* and *yang* forces and that serve to nourish an inner "Baby."

In sum, it appears that the object of the exercise is to calmly, in a timely manner, observe the phenomena that the Dao brings about naturally in your mind and body, rather than to make things happen at your own volition and initiative. The volitional mental activity that you do engage in—which involves directing attention to particular locations in the body, and possibly some degree of visualization—is largely meant to help you maintain your focus so that the phenomena that the Dao spontaneously brings about can be clearly witnessed and responded to appropriately.

The earlier passage is followed by seven lines of anonymous annotation (*zhu* 注) in which the proper times and days for meditation practice are sorted out. It states that on *jia* 甲 (#1)[28] and *gui* 癸 (#10) days you must practice during the *chen* 辰 (7–9 A.M.), *si* 巳 (9–11 A.M.), *zi* 子 (11 P.M.–1 A.M.) and *chou* 丑 (1–3 A.M.) hours. On *yi* 乙 (#2) and *ren* 壬 (#9) days you must practice during the *yin* 寅 (3–5 A.M.), *mao* 卯 (5–7 A.M.), *wu* 午 (11 A.M.–12 P.M.) and *shen* 申 (3–5 P.M.) hours. On *bing* 丙 (#3) and *xin* 辛 (#8) days, you must practice during the *hai* 亥 (9–11 P.M.), *you* 酉 (5–7 P.M.), *wei* 未 (1–3 P.M.), and *xu* 戌 (7–9 P.M.) hours. On *ding* 丁 (#4) and *geng* 庚 (#7) days, you must practice during the *zi* 子 (11 P.M.–1 A.M.) and *wu* 午 (11 A.M.–1 P.M.) hours. On *wu* 戊 (#5) and *ji* 己 (#6) days, you must practice during the *mao* 卯 (5–7 A.M.) and *you* 酉 (5–7 P.M.) hours. In sum, then, you are told to meditate for eight hours per day during six out of every ten days (days #1–3, 8–10), and four hours per day on the other four days (days #4–7). (See *Yunji qiqian* 55/10b–11a.) The annotation also indicates that it is the inner observation carried out on the *ding*, *geng*, *wu*, and *ji* days that is particularly crucial; failing to carry out the practice on these particular days is what causes the Dao to distance itself 10,000 miles from you. Also, after enumerating the correct hours for practice on *bing* and *xin* days, the annotation states:

爲老公 見之勿驚也 道之化見矣

If it becomes an elderly gentleman, do not be startled when you see it.
A transformation of the Dao will have appeared. (*Yunji qiqian* 55/11a)

Thus, it is indicated that while the Dao itself may be of an ineffable nature, it does have the propensity to appear in different "transformations" (*hua* 化). The problem is that you are also likely during the course of practice to encounter various other spontaneous visions that are of quite a different sort.

Near the end of *Contemplating the Baby* we find some instructions, presented as direct utterances by Laozi, regarding some further protocols for undertaking the exercise. You are to "enter the room" (*rushi* 入室) to commence the regimen on the *wuzi* 戊子 day (#25) of the sexegenary cycle.[29] Presumably the choice of day for commencing the undertaking is crucial, because the specifications as to which hours you should meditate on each day are based on the assumption that you have commenced the regimen on the *wuzi* day. It would appear that the proper synchronization of your activities (mental and physical) with the rhythms of the universe is essential. The total duration of the regimen is to be 100 days, or until the "divine radiances" (*shenming* 神明) become visible. The regimen also requires certain protocols pertaining to hygiene and diet, although these are not described in detail. Laozi simply states, "Completely sincere, you shall eat little, in order to observe purifications and precepts. Clean your heart; bathe your head and body" 精之畢熟 少食 為有齋戒 洗心沐浴 (13b).

The meditation method itself and the experiences it evokes are described in a series of passages (11a–13a) that begin with the phrase, "Laozi said . . ." 老子曰. The first of these reads:

老子曰 爲吾道者 當先安牝牡 牝牡者腎也 腎門（閒？）元氣也 元氣氣常下行 元常上昇 元者赤 氣者白 元上到心中 心中當動 動即元下矣

Laozi said, "To practice my Way, you should first pacify the Female and Male. The Female and Male are the kidneys. They are the primal *qi* at the gate of the kidneys (or perhaps, ". . . between the kidneys"). Of the primal *qi* (*yuanqi*), the *qi* constantly goes downward, and the *yuan* (the "primal") always ascends upward. The *yuan* is red, and the *qi* is white. When the *yuan* ascends and reaches the middle of the heart, the heart is likely to move. If it moves, the *yuan* will go down." (*Yunji qiqian* 55/11a–b)

To "pacify" the kidneys or the primal *qi* that exists between them probably means to calmly focus your mind on the region of your kidneys. Quite unique here (not found in other Daoist texts to my knowledge) is the notion that the primal *qi*, or *yuanqi* 元氣, bifurcates into an ascending *yuan*, and a descending *qi*. Also rather surprising is the seeming subsequent lack of concern with the descending *qi* of the kidneys, because this sounds like something that could be taken as connoting the expending of *qi* or essence through the genitals that occurs in sexual activity—something that can be perceived as depleting to one's vitality, as we have seen in *Laozi-Xiang'er*. Our text here instead focuses its concern on the ascending *yuan* that is likely to cause movement in the heart or agitation in the mind. This agitation is said to cause the *yuan* to go back down again. The implication here is that you must therefore take care not to become agitated when the *yuan* rises to the heart, for all subsequent progress is contingent on the *yuan* lodging in the heart, from where it will subsequently move on to the head. By stating that the *yuan* is red and the *qi* is white, the idea is perhaps that you should be visualizing these colors. Or, the idea could be that the *yuan* and *qi* become somehow "visible" to you—spontaneously, whether you visualize them or not—as they go into motion, and by knowing what to anticipate you are less likely to become startled. In any case, when the *yuan* rises to the heart, you apparently feel or perceive something that is likely to agitate you.

The text continues:

老子曰 元者安雌雄 雌雄者心也 一名明堂 得元因共養 合成赤子 赤子自然也 念令上昇 昇於真人 真人者宿衛之臣 赤子到則因安心定意 泊然安意洞房中矣

Laozi said, "The *yuan* pacifies the Feminine and Masculine. The Feminine and Masculine are the heart. It is also called the Hall of Light. Having obtained the *yuan*, [the Feminine and Masculine] together nurture it, and combine to complete the Baby. The Baby is natural. Contemplate and cause it to ascend. It will ascend to the Genuine Person. The Genuine Person is the official minister who keeps guard [over the Baby]. When the Baby arrives you thereby pacify the mind and stabilize your attention. Placidly ease your mind inside the Cavern Chamber." (*Yunji qiqian* 55/11b)

After the *yuan* rises to the heart, the heart becomes for the next while the locus of attention and activity. The heart, as was the case with the kidneys, is also described as a male-female pair that gets "pacified." Oddly, whereas the previous passage said that the arrival of the *yuan* agitated the heart, here it seems to say that the *yuan* pacifies the heart. Perhaps the idea is that once you have managed to maintain composure when witnessing the arrival of the *yuan* in the heart, you are able to settle into a calm state of mind with your attention now focused on the heart. In this condition somehow a Baby takes shape. The Baby is said to be "natural" (*ziran* 自然)—perhaps meaning that it emerges through natural processes that occur as you just calmly focus your attention on the region of your heart. Once the Baby has come into being you are to somehow contemplate in a manner that will make the Baby ascend to the Cavern Chamber (in the head, between the eyes [see later]), where it is met and taken into the care of a Genuine Person.

This leaves us with some important questions. How do you know when the Baby is present and is ready to ascend? Exactly what sort of contemplation is supposed to cause the Baby to ascend? Some clues to answering these questions emerge in the subsequent passages describing the vivid visions that are to occur. However, further questions come to mind regarding the nature of these internal personages known as the Female, the Male, the Feminine, the Masculine, the Baby, and the Genuine Person. Can these be understood as representations of various components and functions of your mind or personality? Does the Baby, which develops after the impersonal *yuan* is calmly nurtured and transmuted, perhaps represent a new core of your consciousness that freshly evolves out of your organic existence or from your subconscious mind?

Regarding the relationship between the Baby and the Genuine Person, the text further states:

老子曰 赤子到 因還意於洞房 洞房者兩目間 有真人不衣而到住 下視赤子 赤子到 真人乃立 真人所以到住 何也 欲令赤子得昇耳 赤子昇 真人復 赤子不昇 真人不復 不復早已

Laozi said, "When the Baby arrives, you thereby turn your attention toward the Cavern Chamber. The Cavern Chamber is the space between your two eyes. There will be a Genuine Person, unclothed, who will arrive and stay. He/she will be looking downward at the Baby. The Genuine Person will thereby stand. Why is it that the Genuine Person comes and stays? It is only because he/she wants the Baby to get to ascend. If the Baby ascends, the Genuine Person returns. If the Baby does not ascend, the Genuine Person does not return. If he/she does not return, it is over with early." (*Yunji qiqian* 55/11b)

So what exactly is this Genuine Person? (And why is he or she naked?) Is he or she the personification of your inner composure or wisdom, or is he or she some sort of benevolent being who comes from outside of your mind and body? Where does he or she come from or return to? In any case, his or her presence is essential for your progress, and is contingent on whether the Baby ascends.

Also, how do you know when the Baby is present and is ready to ascend? How do you make him or her ascend? The answers to these questions begin to emerge from the following striking statements:

老子曰 夫赤子初欲昇時也 形似丹蛇 其光照人 忽然到著人面 若炬火聲矣 此即赤子到矣

老子曰 夫赤子之欲昇時 形似丹蛇 安意如故 須臾當忽然不見矣

老子曰 丹蛇者 日之精也 日精作火形 來著人 欲來著人 人心動 人心動 即赤子不得昇 遂令後難致 難致則冥冥絕矣

Laozi said, "When the Baby is first about to ascend, his/her form resembles a red snake, and his/her radiance illuminates people. Suddenly he/she arrives and attaches to a person's face, with the sound of a torch fire. Thus, the Baby will have arrived."

Laozi said, "When the Baby is about to ascend, his/her form resembles a red snake. Pacify your mind as before. After a while you will suddenly not see it."

Laozi said, "The red snake is the essence of the sun. The essence of the sun takes on the form of fire and comes to attach itself to the person. As it is about to come and attach to a person, the person's heart moves. If the person's heart moves, the Baby cannot ascend. Ultimately this makes it difficult to bring about [what is supposed be brought about] later. When it becomes difficult to bring about, it will darkly become cut off." (*Yunji qiqian*, 55/12a)

Thus the Baby, when it is ready to ascend, becomes visible in a form that looks nothing at all like a baby, and which is likely to alarm you. Whether this is the first time the Baby appears to you in any form, the text does not say. Regarding what you are supposed to do with your mind before, during, and after the Baby's serpentine epiphany, the text merely says to "pacify it," and reassures you that the scary image will naturally disappear. It is also simply by remaining calm that you enable the Baby to ascend to the Cavern Chamber in the head. Although perhaps there was also understood to be some sort of visualization occurring (of the Baby, its "parents" [the Feminine and Masculine], the Genuine Person, or the red snake?) such is not specifically indicated. As far as we can tell, it seems perhaps that the fiery red snake is supposed to appear spontaneously before you, while all you are purposely doing is calmly directing the mind inward toward the region of the heart. It would appear that it is not a vision wrought by auto-suggestion, but perhaps rather the result of subconscious mental contents emerging to the surface of the conscious mind. The text itself, however, says that the red snake that you encounter is the "essence of the sun," and thus seems to attribute the surprising vision to an infusion of energy from the cosmos outside you that coincides with the Baby's emergence and ascension from the heart.

Once the Baby has been enabled to safely lodge in the Cavern Chamber, the following is what is supposed to happen:

老子曰 丹蛇來到 心不驚不恐者 當與真人共語 時目中忽然見正黃 浩浩而無形兆身體 因變化見西王母乘鳳凰之車 後駕六赤龍 車前三朱雀 見之忽驚也 有頃忽然去矣

Laozi said, "When the red snake arrives, if your mind does not get startled or scared, you will be able to converse with the Genuine Person. At times, your eyes will suddenly see a proper yellowness, vast and with no form or body. Due to its transformations you will see the Queen Mother of the West (Xiwangmu 西王母)[30] riding on a phoenix chariot, with six red dragons harnessed behind, and with three vermilion sparrows in front. If you see this, do not be startled. After a while it will abruptly leave. (*Yunji qiqian* 55/12a–b)

What seems to perhaps happen at this point is that you become the Baby. You see things and hear things from the perspective of the Baby, and thus now dwell in the Cavern Chamber in the head between the eyes. You now assume tutelage under this mysterious Genuine Person who has come to meet, guard, and mentor you. From this point you encounter more visions that you must not become startled by, and that will dissipate on their own. The vision of the Queen Mother of the West mentioned here, however, does constitute something of a trial:

老子曰 當見西王母之時 與人語 慎勿答也 不答當復有所告問於人 慎勿答 不答恚怒勿恐怖也 恚不止真人自代子與語 畢自去矣

Laozi said, "When you see the Queen Mother of the West, and she starts to talk to people, be careful not to answer. If you do not answer she will again say things and ask things from people. Be careful not to answer. If you do not answer and she gets angry, do not be scared. If her anger does not stop, the Genuine Person will himself speak to her on your behalf. When done [talking], she will leave. (*Yunji qiqian* 55/12b)

So why does the Queen Mother of the West want to talk to you, and why must you not answer her? Why does she get so cranky? Although no definite explanation is given here, the idea seems to be that she has come to distract you and undermine your practice, and is perhaps an imposter. The text later describes subsequent visions that it clearly explains as illusions generated by the resident spirits of the body's internal organs. Whoever this "Queen Mother of the West" actually is, it would appear that your silence and composure angers her because her purpose is to disturb and distract you, though her motive for wanting to do so is unclear. One wonders also what the consequences might be if you do engage her in conversation. Is it simply the case that you will make no further progress in your training, or is there some sort of mental or physical damage that might result? In any case, you can take comfort in the fact that the Genuine Person has your best interests in mind and will help you, though his or her nature and provenance are also mysterious.

The text then continues:

老子曰 西王母去後 大道來見矣 當大道見時 身形乃曠然 昭浩而無形兆 上見日月星宿 若有若無 當有天師與真人來見 倡樂萬端 慎勿視也 仙人玉女 慎勿觀也 龍虎禽獸 慎勿驚也

老子曰 此倡樂天師仙人玉女禽獸 皆非真也 但自子形中五藏六府 都精神耳 非真道也

老子曰 天師真人來見子之時 安心定意 善與人語言 吾見子信 告子道 張羅其網 具見子矣

Laozi said, "After the Queen Mother of the West leaves, the Great Dao will come and appear. When the Great Dao appears, the body will be vast and vacant, bright and without form. Above you will see the sun, moon and constellations, which will seem to be, and seem not to be. There will be Heavenly Masters and Genuine Persons who will come to see you, [accompanied by] myriad sorts of entertainers and musicians. Be careful not to look at them. [There will be] Transcendents and Jade Maidens. Be careful not to look at them. [There will be] dragons, tigers, birds and beasts. Be careful not to be startled."

Laozi said, "These entertainers, musicians, Heavenly Masters, Transcendents, Jade Maidens, birds and beasts are all not real. It is just the subtle spirits of the five viscera and six bowels inside your body. It is not the real Dao."

Laozi said, "When the Heavenly Masters and Genuine Persons come to see you, calm your mind and focus your attention. Speak well with the people. I will see that you are faithful. I will proclaim the Dao to you. I will spread out its net and show it all to you." (*Yunji qiqian* 55/12b–13a)

Thus, once you have survived the encounter with the Queen Mother of the West (with the help of the Genuine Person), you can proceed to the stage where you encounter the "Great Dao." This encounter involves both being told something and shown something by Laozi. In the end you get to know a Truth that is ordinarily unknowable, and perceive a Reality that is ordinarily imperceptible. However, even while the final revelation is occurring or is about to occur, you encounter many distractions and temptations.

Unfortunately for us, there are certain ambiguities in the text (perhaps intentional?) that make it difficult to discern what is supposed to be the actual nature of each phenomenon being described. In stating, "When the Great Dao appears, the body will be vast and vacant, bright and without form" it is unclear whether the "body" referred to is the Dao's, yours, or both. Laozi seems to be saying that the Dao, even in its epiphany, bears no form or appearance of the sort that can be described by words or even seen in the conventional sense. Perhaps, however, Laozi is speaking of a state of contemplative oblivion where you lose awareness of your own body. It should also be noted that this description resembles in wording the passage (*Yunji qiqian* 55/12a–b; discussed earlier) describing what you witness right before you see the Queen Mother of the West. Perhaps the idea is that at that point also you had briefly glimpsed at the Great Dao, or that you were in a state of mind where you were becoming oblivious of your own body and the distinction between yourself and other things was dissolving. The presence of such a mode of experience might perhaps also explain how the fiery, serpentine Baby rising from your heart can also be the essence of the sun.

In any case, what then emerges out of the formlessness is various divine, anthropomorphic, and zoomorphic beings that are but illusions wrought by the mischievous resident spirits of your bodily organs. The text states that these are therefore "not the real Dao" and should be calmly disregarded. What, then, was this vast, formless Great Dao (if such is the proper interpretation of the passage) that you had just encountered? Was this also an illusion that was actually not the real Dao?

Whatever the case, Laozi then goes on to say that when the Heavenly Master(s) and Genuine Person(s) come to see you, you should "speak well." This seems contradictory because in the previous portion of the passage Laozi had just included Heavenly Master(s) and Genuine Person(s) in the list of beings who were mere hallucinations wrought by mischievous corporeal spirits. Perhaps these are different Heavenly Master(s) and Genuine Person(s) who are actual sacred beings who have come to your aid, or have somehow been dispatched by the Dao to converse with you and test your "faithfulness." If so, one wonders what their relationship might be with the Genuine Person who had met the Baby in the Cavern Chamber, and had conversed with the Queen Mother of the West for you. One also wonders if, where, and how the "elderly gentleman" who is "the Dao's transformation," mentioned in the annotation earlier in the text (*Yunji qiqian* 55/11a; discussed earlier), figures into these final visions; strangely, he is not specifically mentioned at this point in Laozi's discourse. In any case, it is after your faithfulness has been verified that Laozi reveals to you the Dao in its fullness, apparently with no more distractions or illusions.

After concluding his descriptions of the visions and the culminating revelations, Laozi states that "the divine radiances will become visible" 神明相睹 within 100 days of commencing the regimen, after which you are to quit (13b). Thus it appears that the visual and auditory epiphanies should come about in 100 days if your practice is carried out properly and diligently. Why you should quit the regimen at this point is not stated. Was there perceived to be some sort of problem or danger that might occur if you were to persist longer in the regimen in hope of greater blessings and revelations? Were such deeper blessings and revelations considered impossible?

At any rate, the tangible benefits said to accrue as a result of the 100-day regimen are by no means slight. Laozi states that "your refined spirit will be pervasive and penetrating, and you will be able to walk 10,000 miles at a time" 精神通洞 舉足萬里, and that "your going and coming will be swift and rapid, like that of the wind and rain" 往來急疾 狀若風雨 (13b). However, Laozi stops short of promising immortality or heavenly ascension. In all likelihood, practitioners who had completed and benefited from this enlightening and invigorating regimen hoped to graduate to even more sophisticated methods that did carry the promise of earthly or celestial immortality. What such methods might have consisted of we cannot know, although one might conjecture that they involved more intensive contemplative and dietary regimens, or perhaps laboratory alchemy.

*Contemplating the Baby* concludes with a discussion of the human head, its vital importance, and its mystical anatomy. The discussion starts out with Laozi stating, "The human head is where the Dao comes and goes and takes it repose" 人頭者 道之所往來解止處也 (13b). We can surmise that it is for this reason that the meditation method culminates with the focus of attention in the head. It seems that initially you have to generate a fresh, innocent awareness out of the calm depths of your organic being; thus you first pacify the kidneys and then the heart—or the Hall of Light—in order to generate the Baby out of the *yuan*. However, it is in the head that the Dao can be encountered, and thus the Baby must be enabled to ascend up there.

In any case, Laozi goes on to further state that the two eyes—the *yin* and *yang* 陰陽— are "the official ministers of the One of the Dao" 道一

之臣人 and are also "the instruments esteemed by the Dao" 道之所尊器. He also states that in between the eyebrows there exists a one inch-square area called the Hall of Light. One inch behind it into the head is the Cavern Chamber, which is also one inch-square, and another inch behind it is the Elixir Field, which is also one inch-square (13b–14a; these three areas within the head are also mentioned in the text's highly abstruse opening section [10a]). *Contemplating the Baby* elsewhere (*Yunji qiqian* 55/11b) refers to the heart as the Hall of Light. As we saw in the case of *The Manifest Dao* (and will also seem to be the case in *The Inscription* and *Embryonic Breathing* [see chapter 7]) Daoist texts often lay emphasis upon an Elixir Field that is in the lower abdomen, and that in the *Taishang Laojun zhongjing* is said to be "the root of the two kidneys."[31] One might therefore expect *Contemplating the Baby* to also refer to the region of the kidneys that constitutes the locus of attention and activity in the first phase of the meditation sequence as the Elixir Field. It does not, for whatever reason. In any case, this degree of emphasis on the head and its complex cranial mystical anatomy is a feature of *Contemplating the Baby* that is not found in the *Taishang Laojun zhongjing* or the *Taishang huangting waijing jing*, and which perhaps indicates that it is not as early as those texts. Its description of the three areas in the head does closely match that of Bai Lüzhong's 白履忠 (aka, Liangqiuzi 梁丘子; fl. 722–729) commentary to the *Huangting waijing jing*.[32]

In sum, *Contemplating the Baby* describes vividly at some length a vision sequence that spontaneously unfolds during meditation. At all junctures of this meditation the prime emphasis is on observing calmly and maintaining your composure. It is probably because you are largely observing phenomena that emerge on their own—rather than voluntarily instigating them—that keeping the correct days and hours is so crucial; the Dao works on its own time and not yours. Having said this, it is also true that you exercise some degree of initiative by directing the mind to the proper bodily location at the proper time; there also may be some degree of visualization involved, though indication of this is vague.

Lacking in *Contemplating the Baby* are descriptions of physical sensations and involuntary movement and speech such what we find in *The Manifest Dao*. However, *Contemplating the Baby* does seem to suggest that prior to the commencement of the dramatic visions, the vital force in the body (the *yuan* that rises from the kidneys to the heart) moves in ways that are somehow sensed or felt, and that can tend to cause feelings of agitation. More so than *The Manifest Dao* (or the Taiping Group texts or *Laozi-Xiang'er*), *Contemplating the Baby* emphasizes the correspondence between the workings of the body and the universe. Although *The Manifest Dao*, in apparent awareness of such a correspondence, ordains that the contemplation of the Elixir Field occur only during daylight hours, *Contemplating the Baby* conceives in much more subtle detail how bodily forces ebb and flow during specific hours on specific days, and thus prescribes the days and times for meditation accordingly. Regarding what causes the various apparitions, *Contemplating the Baby* offers the explanation that they are by and large the mischief of deities that inhabit the body's inner organs—an explanation that does not occur in *The Manifest Dao*. The vision of the red snake, however, is caused by mobilization of vital force that generates a new core consciousness; yet, it is at the same time the radiant solar force that arrives from outside to empower you. Perhaps this is tantamount to saying that the pristine consciousness and vital force at the depth of your being is identical to the consciousness and force—the Dao—that enlivens the whole world. Perhaps, also, these paradoxical insights result from the author's having experienced a state of consciousness where distinctions between inner and outer (or self and object) were blurred or irrelevant. Finally, it is perhaps again worth noting that 100 days is regarded also in *Contemplating the Baby* as a crucial milestone at which the desired effects are hoped to occur.

## THE *TAISHANG HUNYUAN ZHENLU* 太上混元真錄 (*THE TRUE RECORD*)

As already noted, a vision sequence featuring a red snake and the Queen Mother of the West is described not only in *Contemplating the Baby*, but in at least five other texts that vary widely in date. From among these texts we now focus our discussion primarily on *The True Record*[33] (*Taishang hunyuan zhenlu* 太上混元真錄; The True Record of the Chaotic Origin),[34] which is the text that gives the most extended and detailed description of the Red Snake-Queen Mother vision sequence (as we call it). *The True*

*Record* as a whole is a work of the Tang dynasty (618–907)³⁵ that embeds various teachings within a hagiographic narrative framework in which the sage-god Lord Lao (Laojun 老君; i.e., the deified Laozi) encounters Yin Xi 尹喜 and confers scriptures and teachings to him, first at the Hangu Pass 函谷關 (near Lingbao 靈寶 County, Henan), and then at Yin Xi's home in the Zhongnan mountains 終南山, at the site where the famous Louguan 樓觀 monastery (Zhouzhi 盩厔, Shaanxi 陝西) still exists. Kusuyama Haruki 楠山春樹 has speculated that the author of *The True Record* was probably Yin Wencao 尹文操 (622–688) or somebody associated with him. Yin Wencao was an eminent Daoist monk who at one time lived at the Louguan monastery, performed rituals at the court of Emperor Gaozong 高宗 (r. 650–684), and wrote various works including a lengthy and highly influential (but now lost) collection of Lord Lao lore entitled *Xuanyuan huangdi shengji* 玄元皇帝聖紀 (Holy Chronicle of the August Emperor of the Mysterious Origin).³⁶ Kusuyama has also noted the considerable overlap in the scriptures that we find Lord Lao conferring on Yin Xi in *The True Record* and those that are known to have been ritually transmitted along with the *Laozi* to Daoist initiates during the late Six Dynasties and Tang periods; he thus conjectures that *The True Record* may have been written with the purpose of describing such rituals through the medium of hagiography (presumably in order to justify and endorse them by showing ancient precedent for them).³⁷

Also among the texts we have that describe the Red Snake-Queen Mother vision sequence are two others that present it as part of the teachings that Lord Lao conferred upon Yin Xi; these two texts also contain further material that matches with *The True Record*. These two texts are *The Way of Transcendence* (*Xiantian Xuanmiao Yunü Taishang Shengmu zichuan xiandao* 先天玄妙玉女太上聖母資傳仙道; Way of Transcendence Conferred by the Most High Holy Mother, the Mysterious and Marvelous Jade Woman of the Prior Heaven),³⁸ and *The Holy Chronicle* (*Hunyuan shengji* 混元聖紀; Holy Chronicle of the Chaotic Origin).³⁹ *The Holy Chronicle* is a massive 9-*juan* compendium of Lord Lao lore compiled by Xie Shouhao 謝守灝 around 1191. The dating of *The Way of Transcendence* poses a greater problem. While Schipper assigns this text to the Tang period,⁴⁰ there is one reference to "internal alchemy" in it that is also found in *The Holy Chronicle* but not in *The True Record*, and which perhaps suggests an early Song period date (tenth or eleventh century?). In the course of our discussion both *The Way of Transcendence* and *The Holy Chronicle* are consulted for clarification on some of the material in *The True Record*.

Laozi legends started to take shape during the last several centuries BCE, as is evidenced most clearly in the *Zhuangzi* 莊子 and in Sima Qian's 司馬遷 (145–86 BCE) *Shiji* 史記 (Record of the Historian). According to what might be called the classical account as established by the *Shiji*, Laozi—whose actual name, we are told, was Li Er 李耳—was a wise old archivist at the royal library who rebuked and baffled Confucius, and later bestowed the famous wisdom treatise in 5,000 characters (i.e., the *Laozi*) on the Guardian of the Pass (*guanling* 關令) while departing from the Zhou 周 realm.[41] By the Latter Han period (25–220 CE) traditions came to develop maintaining variously that Laozi had attained immortality, that he was an eternal deity identical to the Dao itself, that he incarnates in various bodies and identities in various historical periods, that he appears before worthy persons (such as the first Heavenly Master Zhang Daoling 張道陵) to reveal the way to salvation, or that he had traveled westward to convert the "barbarians" and was identical to the Buddha, or was somehow responsible for the founding of Buddhism. Laozi/Lord Lao lore would continue to develop in medieval times, with the Daoists connected to the Louguan 樓觀 monastery and later the Tang royal court playing particularly prominent roles in its propagation.[42]

While the number of exploits attributed to Laozi/Lord Lao thus piled up over the centuries, so did the number of doctrines and practices that he allegedly taught, as is apparent from our examination of *Laozi-Xiang'er*, *The Manifest Dao*, and *Contemplating the Baby*. The difficulty in properly understanding *The True Record*, (as well as *The Way of Transcendence* and *The Holy Chronicle*, for that matter) is that the doctrines and practices embedded in or tacked on to the hagiographic narrative issue from diverse Daoist *milieus* with different views and priorities, and thus are difficult to integrate into one coherent system. Although *The True Record* is itself most likely a seventh-century compilation, the Daoist beliefs and practices it conveys are earlier—often much earlier, as is clearly the case in passages that quote sources such as the *Taishang Laojun zhongjing* (second century?) or *The Western Ascension* (fifth century). It is reasonable to surmise that some or much of the less readily traceable material—such as the passages that most concern us—could be quite early as well.

We proceed to examine the form and meaning that the Red Snake-Queen Mother vision sequence takes on in *The True Record*, and also speculate as to how the vision sequence was supposed to be brought about, according to the view of the author or of the source tradition he drew upon. This in fact becomes a great challenge, because *The True Record* describes a number of different meditation methods that could plausibly be understood as constituting the method that invokes the Red Snake-Queen Mother vision sequence. The method described in *Contemplating the Baby* cannot be found in *The True Record* (or in *The Way of Transcendence* or *The Holy Chronicle*), though we do find a method involving much similar imagery and terminology. We also find in *The True Record* a method of simply being "clear and calm" 清靜, and according to what is indicated in *The Way of Transcendence* and *The Holy Chronicle* (as well as the much later Neidan anthology, the *Zhuzhen neidan jiyao* 諸真內丹集要) this in fact is the specific method that brings about the vision sequence.

*The True Record* consists principally of a main narrative that is interspersed occasionally with passages of commentary that commence with the phrase "the discourse says" (*lun yue* 論曰). Both the narrative and the commentary are anonymous, although the first segment of narrative quotes poems by prominent literati poets Qian Chengshu 牽成叔 (d. 304)[43] and Xue Daoheng 薛道衡 (540–609).[44] Embedded throughout the narrative are numerous discourses on doctrine and praxis presented as the teachings spoken by Lord Lao to Yin Xi. Tacked on after the conclusion of the narrative are four additional segments of discourse, each commencing with the phrase "Lord Lao said" (*Laozi yue* 老子曰); these are followed by a passage of commentary, after which *The True Record* comes to an end.

The narrative of *The True Record* begins with the "times of Yin and Zhou" 殷周之時, during which we are told that Lord Lao had been living amid the world for 200-plus years, sometimes serving in the king's government, and sometimes living in retirement among common folk. However, during the reign of King Zhao 昭王 (ca. 995–977) Lord Lao came to be aware that the virtue of the Zhou dynasty was in inevitable decline. At the same time he was decreed by "the Most High" (*taishang* 太上) to journey to the lands of the west, for the purpose of preaching and converting people (1a). Lord Lao thus traveled westward, riding on a white carriage pulled by a black ox, floating amid a purple vapor. Awaiting Lord Lao at the Hangu Pass was the government official Yin Xi, a lifelong seeker of the Dao who, having seen the purple vapor from afar, knew that a great sage was on route, and had for the specific purpose of meeting the great saint requested assignment as Guardian of the Pass.

Yin Xi persistently begged Lord Lao to take him on as a disciple and teach him the Great Dao. Lord Lao feigned ignorance, claiming to be just a poor ignorant old man on his way to fetch some firewood. Yin Xi was not deceived, and persisted in his pleas for instruction. Lord Lao then told Yin Xi that was he traveling to the western regions because he had heard of an "ancient master" (*gu xiansheng* 古先生) in Zhuqian 竺乾 (India; or according to some accounts, the text tells us, in Daqin 大秦 [the Roman Empire, Palestine, or the far west])[45] who was "good at entering into nonaction that is without end or beginning" 善入無爲 不終不始, and wished to go and learn from him. Yin Xi did not fall for this story either, for he knew that Lord Lao himself was a great sage who certainly did not require instruction from anybody in barbarian lands. Lord Lao then had Yin Xi describe the omens by which he had become so certain that he (Lord Lao) was a great sage. After hearing Yin Xi's descriptions of the omens he agreed to teach him. However, he then tested his new disciple's character by killing—right before his eyes—a servant named Xu Jia 徐甲 by removing from his body the Taixuan Life Talisman (Taixuan shengfu 太玄生符) that had been keeping him alive for 200 years (Xu Jia had insolently demanded the 7.2 million cash in back wages that Lord Lao owed him). Yin Xi, heart filled with pity, and with the desire to see Lord Lao work the miracle of resurrection, prepared the sum of money owed to Xu Jia and asked Lord Lao to resurrect him. Lord Lao complied by resurrecting Xu Jia, after which he gave Xu Jia the money and sent him on his way. Yin Xi, through his display of compassion and generosity, thus qualified for full instruction from Lord Lao (see 4b–7a).

The narrative then goes on to describe how Yin Xi went on to receive a great variety of teachings. One of the first things that Lord Lao told Yin Xi was that if he wanted to ascend as a Transcendent, he had to "shut off emotions and desires, enter a deep chamber, refine metals, and eat *qi*" 閉塞情欲 入奧室 鍊金食氣 (7a). After this follows a discussion pertaining to laboratory alchemy (7a–9a), followed by a discussion on "eating *qi*" (9a–11a). In the course of the narrative and discussions, as well as in the accompanying commentary passages, various scriptures are mentioned. The teachings on laboratory alchemy were contained in the *Taiqing bafujing* 太清八符經, the *Taiqing guantian jing* 太清觀天經, the *Jiudu jing* 九都經, the *Shendan jing* 神丹經, the *Jinye jing* 金液經, and the "Lesson on Entering and Refining the Nine Cycle Reverted Cinnabar and the Subduing of Fire" 入鍊九轉還丹伏火之訣, all of which Lord Lao transmitted to Yin Xi.[46] In discussing the "eating of *qi*," Laozi first enjoined the cherishing of essence and *qi* by keeping the body calm and not over-using one's eyesight (9b; roughly five lines of the text here match with a portion of *The Manifest Dao* [2a–b]). He then proceeded to describe methods entailing the slowing and controlling of breathing and the swallowing of air and saliva. These included the method for invoking and swallowing the "five sprouts" (*wuya* 五牙) of the five directional heavens (north, south, east, west, and center). After describing these methods, Lord Lao wrote down and transmitted to Yin Xi the "*Yuli zhongjing* 玉曆中經 (Jade Calendar Central Scripture) in three volumes and 55 chapters,"[47] which likely refers to the *Taishang Laojun zhongjing*. The commentary here adds that Lord Lao subsequently also transmitted to Yin Xi the *Ziran jing* 自然經,[48] the *Lizang jing* 歷藏經,[49] and the *Huangting jing* 黃庭經,[50] along with "the inner secret Way of swallowing *qi*, gulping essence, preserving authenticity and solidifying longevity" 內祕嚥氣吞精存真固齡之道 (11a).

After this, Yin Xi mustered up the nerve to ask Lord Lao to teach him "the Great Dao," and Lord Lao agreed to do so. Yin Xi then feigned illness, resigned from his government position, and together with Lord Lao retired to his home located on the site that would become the Louguan monastery. There Lord Lao transmitted to Yin Xi the "5,000 words" of the *Laozi* and expounded upon their meaning and significance (11a–13b). He also, for Yin Xi's further benefit, wrote a commentary which provided "analysis by section" (*jiejie* 節解). This, as Kusuyama has noted, apparently refers to the *Laozi jiejie* 老子節解, an important but now lost commentary to the *Laozi* that is mentioned in the *Jingdian shiwen* 經典

釋文 (Lu Deming 陸德明 [556–627] ed.) and listed in the bibliographies of Sui, Tang, and Song standard histories.[51] The narrative of *The True Record* then gives a "summary" (*yao* 要) of this "analysis by section" commentary, which pertains largely to the inner anatomy, bodily deities, and their visualization (13b–15a). Kusuyama here points out that this "summary" actually consists of passages of the *Laozi jiejie* commentary that explain the first three chapters of the *Laozi*, and which are valuable because they significantly supplement the other *Laozi jiejie* fragments that have survived in other sources. (These other sources consist of two other Laozi commentaries[52] and one Buddhist polemical text, Falin's 法琳 [572–640] *Bianzheng lun* 辯正論.)[53]

The narrative then describes how Lord Lao proceeded to further expound on the "essentials of the *Daode jing.*" This discourse, which extends over almost four folios (15b–19a) is actually a synopsis of *The Western Ascension* (*Xisheng jing* 西昇經), the text that is the focus of the first section of our next chapter.

After bestowing all of these teachings, Lord Lao reveals that the "ancient master" in India that he had previously mentioned was actually "my body" 吾之身 in long past days, and that he had back then transformed and ascended to heaven from India, chagrined over the evil and cruelty that prevailed there. Since then he had been sent down from the heavens to serve as a teacher of the Chinese Zhou realm, and now intended to go again to the western nations to provide guidance for the people there. However, he would first ascend to heaven before descending again. Yin Xi proclaimed that he intended to follow Lord Lao wherever he would go. Lord Lao told him that he first had to train himself to the optimal level of attainment by studying the scriptures he had given to him. Thus, the two agreed to meet three years later at the "tavern of the black goat" (*qingyang zhi si* 青羊之肆) in Chengdu, and Lord Lao disappeared into the sky. Already missing his master, Yin Xi kowtowed and pleaded for one more look at Lord Lao's countenance, whereupon Lord Lao reappeared before him in full splendor in mid-air, and bestowed on him final words of wisdom. The narrative concludes by stating that Yin Xi diligently devoted himself to his studies, and over the course of four days saw auspicious dreams portending his future great attainments (19a–22a).

The hagiographic narrative that forms the setting of Lord Lao's numerous discourses in *The True Record* is very much a composite of lore that had accumulated and undergone embellishment over the centuries. Similarly, the teachings and training methods embedded in it prove to be highly eclectic so as to suggest provenance from diverse periods and schools. It would appear that the editor of the text took care to faithfully preserve in the narrative the various teachings that had come to be attributed to Lord Lao by different Daoist schools, without presuming to modify their contents in the interests of compliance to a singular doctrinal vision. The commentary passages do to some degree reflect the editor's personal leanings. However, they do not adequately clarify whether or how the various methods complement each other, or how they rank in priority.

In any case, as it turns out, it is the four segments of discourse tacked on after the conclusion of the narrative that are of greatest interest to us, because the description of the Red Snake-Queen Mother vision sequence is found in one of these. For convenience of discussion we refer to this segment as "LLS#4," because it is the fourth in a series of segments (LLS#1–LLS#4) that each begin with the phrase "Lord Lao said . . ." 老君曰. A puzzling question here is why these four segments are disembodied from the narrative and tacked on to the end of the *The True Record*; in both the *The Way of Transcendence* and *The Holy Chronicle* the corresponding passages are integrated into the narrative. Another problem is the relationship between the four LLS segments. Do they originate from a common textual or factional *milieu*? In trying to determine which practice was supposed bring forth the Red Snake-Queen Mother vision sequence, would it be correct to focus our attention on the methods described in LLS#1–LLS#4?

LLS#1 is noteworthy because it contains a description of something somewhat similar to the method of *Contemplating the Baby*. There Lord Lao states that in order to visualize the Three Ones you must first visualize the inside of the head. One inch (*cun* 寸)[54] into the space between the eyebrows is the Hall of Light (*mingtang* 明堂). Another inch beyond it is the Cavern Chamber (*dongfang* 洞房), and another inch deeper is the Muddy Pellet (*niwan* 泥丸), which is also known as the Upper Elixir

Field. Inside the Upper Elixir Field is the Baby (*chizi* 赤子), whose style name (*zi* 字) is Yuanxian 元先, and personal name (*ming* 名) is Diqing 帝卿. Three inches in height, he wears a red (*chi* 赤) turban, red robe, and red shoes. Next, you are to visualize the inside of the heart, which is known as the Crimson Palace (*jianggong* 絳宮), and which is the Middle Elixir Field. There dwells the Genuine Person (*zhenren* 真人), whose style name is Zidan 子丹 and personal name is Guangjian 光堅. He also is three inches tall and is clad in red. Next, you should visualize the Gate of Life (*mingmen* 命門) Palace located three inches under the navel; this is the Lower Elixir Field. In there is the Infant (*ying'er* 嬰兒), whose style name is Yuanyang 元陽 and personal name is Guxuan 谷玄; he also is three inches tall and clad in red. Then, you should visualize the Lower One (Infant) seated on a golden couch with a jade armrest stirring essence (*jing* 精) in a golden cauldron with a jade spoon. After this you should visualize the Upper One (Baby) coming down, along with the Middle One (Genuine Person) at its left. The Lower One, who is holding the cauldron and spoon and is standing at the right of the Middle One, first feeds the essence to the Upper One, and then to the Middle One. After you have thus drunk ten mouthfuls (apparently you are supposed to swallow saliva as you visualize the feeding of the Ones), you are to visualize the Upper One returning to its dwelling. Then you are to feed the Lower One and visualize it returning to its dwelling. Next, you should visualize a white vapor (*qi* 氣) the size of a cartwheel coming over you, and then visualize a red vapor coming to cover over the white vapor. After this you can lie down. Also, inside the Cavern Chamber there is a white vapor the size of a chicken egg and shining like the moon. These visualizations should be carried out day and night (23a–b).

In some ways, the technique and physiology (physio-theology?) described here are reminiscent of *Contemplating the Baby*. In LLS#1 the Baby and the Genuine Person figure prominently, there is interaction between the indwelling forces/spirits of the head, chest and lower abdomen, and there is "feeding" involved. The most important difference is that LLS#1 calls for constant conscious manipulation of the inner spirits and forces by means of active imagination, whereas *Contemplating the Baby* seems to emphasize primarily that one stay calm, so that the desirable physiological and sensory phenomena can unfold naturally as they are supposed to. Also, LLS#1 tells you to practice the method day and night; apparently the maximum benefit is to come by practicing as long and frequently as possible. In the case of *Contemplating the Baby*, the meditation is only to occur at specific hours on each day, and the duration of the entire regimen is limited to 100 days.

In LLS#1 Lord Lao goes on to describe the benefits of "guarding the One" (*shouyi* 守一). Lord Lao states that if your mind is on the One (the Dao) in all situations and activities, the One will protect you, provide for your needs, and fulfill your wishes. Essence must be retained within because "essence is" the river flow of the blood vessels and the numinous spirit that guards the bones. If [essence] leaves, the bones dry up, and if the bones dry up, you die" 夫精血脈之川流 守骨之靈神 精去則骨枯 骨枯則死 (24a). He further explains that *qi* transmutes into essence, which transmutes into spirit, which transmutes into the Infant, which transmutes into the Genuine Person, which transmutes into the Baby. This is the True One (*zhenyi* 真一). If you guard the One you can travel anywhere within Heaven and Earth and have nothing to fear. After guarding the One for a long time, the One will become visible, and once it is visible, the 36,000 gods in the body will propel the body upward, and you will ascend to Heaven in broad daylight. Such is the outcome for superior gentlemen (*shangshi* 上士). Middling gentlemen (*zhongshi* 中士) will at least be able to avoid disease and live long. Even inferior gentlemen (*xiashi* 下士), by having their minds on the One, can survive calamities when they occur (23b–24b).

Thus, the divine physiological personages of Infant, Genuine Person, and Baby are actually progressive transmutations of *qi*, essence, and spirit. The most refined transmutation is the Baby or the True One, which actually is supposed to manifest itself (it is no longer merely imagined) to you if you persevere. When your inner divinity manifests, your inner spirit-forces converge with a potency that brings about immortal ascension; this, at least, is the case if you prove to be among the most prodigious practitioners. Thus, the benefits promised surpass considerably what is promised in *Contemplating the Baby*.

Interestingly, Lord Lao also acknowledges that "guarding the One" can bring about frightening experiences. He states:

守一之道 得惡夢及見怪 勿以告人 但正心念一則不為災害

If in practicing the Way of Guarding the One you have bad dreams or see apparitions, you should never tell others about it. Just rectify the mind and continue to contemplate the One, and you will not be harmed. (*The True Record* 24b)

Thus, the regimen—especially if pursued with persistence and rigor—can wear on one's mind and nerves. However, we are reassured that this, too, is something that the One—the eternal, universal Dao that dwells and acts in you—will protect you from if you maintain faith, composure, and rectitude. Why you should not tell others about the bad dreams and apparitions is not made clear. Perhaps telling others constitutes a violation of trust with the Dao, which may hinder your prospects of further progress. (As we have seen, *The Manifest Dao* contains similar enjoinders for keeping discreet about the apparitions you have seen.)

In LLS#2, Lord Lao speaks of the wonders and benefits that unfold through sheer serenity:

夫 人欲修身養性 行道化形 求福致願 結氣成神 延年益壽 終始無窮者 要當清靜 故天靜以為政 地靜以爲定 神靜以為變 人靜以為生 故清則感 靜則應也 將靜之時 反聽內觀 還念形中 心不妄念 口不妄言 形不妄動 然後乃 無色之色 為之見 無聲之聲 為之聞 無味之味 為之甘 不言之言 為之崇 神景為之降 福德為之臻 和氣為之應 心則聖 意則明 好夢善隱 能覩求於徵夢 則正觀於未然 如未覩者 由精誠未至 至則通矣

If people want to cultivate their persons and nurture their innate natures, practice the Way and transform their bodies, seek blessings and realize their wishes, bind together their *qi* to complete their spirits, prolong their years and increase their life spans, and become endless and beginning-less without limit, it is essential that they be clear and calm. Earth is calm, and is thereby stable. The gods are calm, and thereby work their marvels. People are calm, and thereby are able to live. Therefore, if you are clear, there will be [inter-]feeling. If you are calm, there will be responses. As you are about to become calm, turn back your hearing and observe what is inside. Turn your attention back onto the inside of your body. In your mind, do not think foolish thoughts. With your mouth, do not speak foolish words. Do not move your body foolishly. Once you have done so, the colorless color will thereby be seen. The soundless sound will thereby be heard. The flavorless flavor will thereby be savored. The wordless utterances will thereby be revered. Divine radiances will thereby descend. Blessings and merits will thereby come forth. Harmonious *qi* will hereby respond to you. Your mind will thus be sagely, and your awareness will thus be clear. Good dreams will nicely await in hiding. You will be able to see portending dreams, and accurately see things that have not yet occurred. If you do not see them, your pure sincerity is still insufficient. Once it is sufficient, you will communicate. (*The True Record* 24b–25a)

Thus we are told that keeping the mind clear and calm is the very thing that keeps us alive, and is what is most important both in the process of transformation into an immortal being, as well as in the communications with sacred forces that bring forth guidance and blessings. The immortal transformation comes about because the serenity enables you to harness your *qi* in a way that enhances and fortifies your spirit, or perhaps your spirits. It is difficult to determine here whether "spirit" is to be understood as a singular entity that the entire body transforms into once all of its *qi* has been refined to the utmost, or whether it is to be understood as the numerous spirits that inhabit the body, and which in LLS#1 are described as propelling the body up toward the heavens. In any case, regarding the reason why serenity brings forth helpful communications and blessings from the spiritual realm, Lord Lao explains that it is because inner clarity brings forth "feeling" (*gan* 感), by which is apparently meant a sort of sympathetic inter-feeling or resonance that occurs between human beings and spiritual and cosmic forces. The "responses" (*ying* 應) are the tangible good or negative results that can come about according to the nature of the sympathetic resonance occurring. Lord Lao then describes a method of meditation in which you turn your senses and attention inward, and begin to passively observe and experience things that are so subtle as to defy description in terms of form, sound, taste and meaning in the ordinary sense. After describing this most subtle state of mystical consciousness, Lord Lao speaks of the sympathetic responses from the divine realm, which can come in the form of gods appearing before you and bringing their blessings, or in the form of prophetic dreams that enable you to see the future in beneficial ways. The ability to see such dreams appears to be regarded here as particularly important, and the inability to see the dreams is blamed on lack of the "pure sincerity" (*jingcheng* 精誠) that holds the key to establishing the "communication" (*tong* 通) with the divine. Thus while serenity is the pervading theme of LLS#2, it would appear that along with keeping the mind free of deluding thoughts and agitating emotions, you also need to possess a single-minded focus on your religious goals that is free of other concerns and motives.

A crucial issue for our understanding of *The True Record* and what it has to say regarding serenity and the effects that it can bring about is whether we can regard LLS#2, LLS#3, and LLS#4 (the segment describing the Red Snake-Queen Mother vision sequence) as constituting a natural cohesive unit, even though they are each preceded by the phrase "Lord Lao said," which could be taken to suggest that the three segments are to be regarded as having been spoken on separate, unrelated occasions, or which may cause us to surmise that they may come from separate textual sources. If they are a natural coherent unit it would seem that the serene, passive meditation described in LLS#2 was perhaps indeed what was supposed to bring forth the Red Snake-Queen Mother vision sequence.

In fact, in both *The Way of Transcendence* (7b–8a) and *The Holy Chronicle* (3/16b–17a) the three segments are seamlessly conjoined. A passage nearly identical to LLS#2 (excluding the last 35 characters) appears, and is conjoined with a few phrases concerning ritual purification and the commencement of confined contemplation (corresponding to part of LLS#3), and a description of the Red Snake-Queen Mother vision sequence (corresponding to LLS#4). According to these two texts, the Red Snake-Queen Mother vision sequence seems to come about directly as a result of the meditation technique of serene passive inner observation described in LLS#2. In *The Holy Chronicle* it is indicated that this discourse combining LLS#2 with the Red Snake-Queen Mother vision sequence was conferred upon Yin Xi by Lord Lao at Yin Xi's mansion in the Zhongnan mountains, after Yin Xi had resigned his government post. Interestingly, this combined discourse appears virtually word for word in *Zhuzhen neidan jiyao*,[55] a Neidan anthology of ca. 1300, compiled by a certain Xuanquanzi 玄全子, who probably belonged to the Quanzhen tradition. There the discourse is attributed (apparently)[56] to the semi-legendary Neidan master/Immortal Lü Dongbin 呂洞賓, rather than to Lord Lao.⁵⁷ As for why this combined discourse would be adopted by the Quanzhen Neidan tradition, it is perhaps because it was highly compatible to the Quanzhen tradition's emphasis on the habitual cultivation of serenity and its meditation methods. It would be interesting to know whether in fact Quanzhen Neidan practitioners actually did (or do?) experience the same sort of vision sequence of which their medieval predecessors spoke.

In any case, in light of this unanimity in three different texts, it is tempting to conclude that LLS#2 and the Red Snake-Queen Mother vision sequence really did originally belong together. However, in *Contemplating the Baby* we have already seen an instance where the Red Snake-Queen Mother vision sequence is linked to a different meditation technique—albeit a technique that is also of a considerably passive nature. Also, in these three other texts the last 35 characters of LLS#2—the portion pertaining to prophetic dreams—are missing, giving the impression that they may even have been purposely chopped off by some editor who wanted the discourse on serenity to interflow more seamlessly into a discourse on isolated contemplation and the visions it brings forth, without digressing into the matter of prophetic dreams.

Turning our attention back to *The True Record*, in LLS#3 Lord Lao describes how to "enter the quiet room" (*ru jingshi* 入靜室 or "enter the room" [*rushi* 入室]). He states that the regimen must always commence on the final day of the year (*xuri* 除日), and that prior to this you must prepare yourself through bathing and 25 days of ritual abstention and discipline 先沐浴齋戒二十五日. The quiet room should be entered only after "the cloud-souls and white-souls are harmonious inside the body" 身中魂魄和平. If the spirit is disharmonious, this will lead to confusion, commotion, and unease. Thus, Lord Lao states, "For the sake of worthies of later times, I shall now describe the prodigies" 故為後賢敘說變事焉 (25a–b).

LLS#4, if we can regard it as a continuous unit with LLS#3, perhaps constitutes that description of prodigies. There Lord Lao states that when you "enter the room," the red snake will come and attach to your heart. If you manage to not be frightened by this, you will be able to converse with the Genuine Person. Or, you may see the Queen Mother of the West riding in a phoenix carriage, attended by six red dragons in back, and three vermilion sparrows in front. You must remain calm, and be careful not to converse with her, even if she gets angry. If her anger does not subside, the Genuine Person will speak to her for you. After the Queen Mother leaves, the Great Dao will come and manifest itself (25b).

What we have here is thus strikingly similar to what we saw in *Contemplating the Baby*. However, Lord Lao here does not say that the red snake is the Baby, nor does he link the coming of the red snake to the ascension of the Baby; indeed, he makes no mention of any Baby in LLS#4 (although he does in LLS#1). He also does not say that the red snake is the essence of the sun. Is this because the meditation method that evokes the vision sequence in this case is significantly different from that of *Contemplating the Baby*, and simply does not involve any Baby or sun or observation thereof? The Genuine Person does, however, enter into the picture here as your mentor and protector, and by maintaining composure and silence in the face of the red snake and Queen Mother, you partake in an epiphany of the Dao.

Lord Lao in LLS#4 goes on to state that when the Great Dao appears, you will see the sun, moon, and stars up above. Perhaps you will be visited by Heavenly Masters and Genuine Persons who are accompanied by singers and musicians, or by Transcendents and Jade Maidens; you must not pay any attention to these. Dragons, tigers, birds, or beasts may come to attack you, but you must not be scared. As Lord Lao states, "These are all the doing of the subtle spirits in your body; they are not real" 此並子形中精神所為非真也 (25b). As we have seen, all of these illusory apparitions wrought by corporeal deities are also mentioned by Laozi in *Contemplating the Baby*.

However, in LLS#4, Lord Lao goes on to describe many additional apparitions. He mentions that you may encounter "an old woman and a person of strange form" 老婦及異形者, whom you must neither speak to nor associate with. (Here one is somewhat reminded of the vision of the old woman mentioned in *The Manifest Dao* 7a–b; discussed earlier.) After 25 days in the quiet room, "two women" 兩女 will come wishing to converse, but you must not speak with them, nor with the "academy student" 書生 who will come calling at the 45-day juncture. At the 60-day juncture "two bright stars will come and linger above the room for three days" 室上有兩明星躊躇 經三日, but you need not feel that this is strange (25b–26a).

At the 85-day juncture, Lord Lao states, "a white-haired elderly gentleman riding on a white deer will come to beckon you" 有白首老公乘白鹿來呼子. It is at this point that you are to finally break your silence. You should say to the white-haired elderly gentleman, "I am still burdened with the transgressions of my forebears. I am still unable to bring forth worthies" 吾有先人罪負未能致賢也 (26a).

The reason why you are not supposed ignore this white-haired elderly gentleman would seem to be because he is no mere illusory apparition, but is an authentic epiphany of the Dao. One can indeed recall here the passage of commentary in *Contemplating the Baby* (*Yunji qiqian* 55/11a) that mentions such a vision of an elderly gentleman and explains that you need not be startled by it, since it is a "transformation of the Dao." While the elderly gentleman strangely fails to receive specific mention in Laozi's description of the vision sequence that we find further on in that text, we do find him in the vision sequence in *The True Record*. One can further surmise that this white-haired elder is Lord Lao himself, and this connotation is further strengthened by the fact that he is said here to ride on a white deer. One can find instances within Lord Lao lore in which he is said to have ridden on a white deer. One source, Cui Xuanshan's 崔玄山 *Laixiang ji* 瀨鄉記 (Record of Lai Village), quoted in the *Taiping yulan* 太平御覽, cites a stele stating that Lord Lao, mounted on a white deer, entered Mother Li's 李母 womb, and was born 72 years later in Quren Hamlet, Lai Village in Ku County 苦縣瀨鄉曲仁里.[58] *The Holy Chronicle* describes an episode in which Lord Lao, at the end of a prior earthly sojourn, ascended to heaven on a white deer (*The Holy Chronicle* 2/45a–b).[59]

Lord Lao in LLS#4 goes on to state that at the 105-day juncture "a Heavenly Master will come to examine the merits and virtues of your ancestors" 有天師來考子祖宗功德. Hereupon, you should humbly say to the Heavenly Master, "The transgressions and faults from past generations have not been exhausted. It is simply for this reason that I diligently train myself in this room" 先代以來罪過未盡 是以故於室中精鍊耳. Thus, as we can see, the undertaking of isolated contemplation constituted at least in part an exercise for the purgation of hereditary guilt (*The True Record* 26a).

Humble statements of the sort to be uttered here toward the white-haired elder and the Heavenly Master are perhaps what Laozi in *Contemplating the Baby* (*Yunji qiqian* 55/13a) is referring to when he says that if you "speak well with the people" 善與人語言 you will be deemed "faithful" 信, and consequently have the Dao proclaimed to you (see earlier). One should note, however, that at this point in LLS#4, the regimen has continued past the 100-day juncture, which in *Contemplating the Baby* was the point of termination. Lord Lao in LLS#4 prescribes a much longer regimen that is to bring much more wondrous results.

By speaking humbly and appropriately to the epiphanies (white-haired elder and Heavenly Master), you open further the door of opportunity for greater wonders. However, you still have considerable hurdles to overcome. At the 125-day juncture, Lord Lao states, "there will be one thousand battle chariots and ten thousand cavalry standing 300 steps away from your room" 去室三百步有千乘萬騎, which you should not consider strange (26a). It appears here that you are to be confronted again with illusory apparitions that perhaps embody your deep-seated, instinctual fears of harm and death. Or, perhaps, the understanding is supposed to be that the troops are genuine, auspicious epiphanies of divine envoys that arrive for your protection.

At the 150-day juncture, Lord Lao states, "evil spirits claiming to be your father, mother, wife and children will come to test you" 邪神稱子父母妻子來試子; however, you must simply maintain your composure (26a). Confronting apparitions of your parents, wife (or wives?), and children is a trying experience, albeit perhaps for different reasons for different people. In what way these apparitions are supposed to be a "test" is unclear, although everybody certainly carries a great deal of complex, deep feelings toward those closest to them. This far into your seclusion, you would understandably be liable to feeling lonely and nostalgic toward your closest of kin, but might also harbor feelings of guilt, envy, or resentment that can be unsettling and which perhaps can emerge from your subconscious mind and confront you in the form of visions.

Whatever the actual specific nature of the peril imposed by the familial apparitions may be, it is the final hazard specifically mentioned. After this, you begin to reap the benefits. At the 180-day juncture, Lord Lao states, "in your room, you will naturally clearly know about all matters pertaining to safety, danger, survival and perishing throughout the nation" 室內自明知國中安危存亡; furthermore, "all lined up in the body, the palaces and mansions will appear before you" 具列身中宮府顯見. In other words, you obtain wide-ranging clairvoyant powers and can also see the inside of your body with all its organs. At the 280-day juncture, "all malignant diseases will be eradicated from your body, and wicked *qi* will not come upon your body" 形中惡病皆除 邪氣不加身. Finally, after 1,000 days, "all wounds, scars, blemishes, burns and bruises will disappear, and you will become a Genuine Person" 金瘡痍瘢灸斫自滅 遂為真人矣 (26a–b).

Thus the description of the Red Snake-Queen Mother vision sequence comes to an end. However, LLS#4 is not finished. Lord Lao continues on in LLS#4 by enumerating the "Nine Rooms" (*jiushi* 九室), which are nine types of contemplation that you are supposed to successively, progressively undertake. It would seem logical to surmise that these nine contemplation methods were supposed to be practiced one after another during the 1,000 days in the quiet room, during which the Red Snake-Queen Mother vision sequence occurs, as they are described within LLS#4.

Such, however, is not what the authors of *The Way of Transcendence* and *The Holy Chronicle* would have you think. In both of these texts we find Lord Lao stating:

修道之士得內丹者 可以延年 得外丹者 可以昇天 三一九思者內修之要也 九丹金液者外丹之極也 合而修之道成決矣

Gentlemen who cultivate the Dao and obtain the inner elixir can extend their years. Those who obtain the outer elixir can ascend to Heaven. The Three Ones and the Nine Contemplations are the essentials of inner cultivation. The Nine Cinnabars and the Golden Liquid are the ultimate among Outer Elixirs. If you practice these in tandem you will certainly accomplish the Dao. (*The Way of Transcendence* 5a–b; *The Holy Chronicle* 3/13a)

Interesting here is the usage of the term *neidan* 內丹 or "inner elixir." This term is uncommon in Daoist literature prior to the late Tang period, and perhaps indicates that *The Way of Transcendence* was compiled at a date closer to that of *The Holy Chronicle* (1191) than to that of *The True Record* (ca. seventh century). It should also be noted, though, that the manner of usage of the term *neidan* is an archaic one, or is at least incongruous with its usage within prominent Neidan traditions such as the Quanzhen or Nanzong 南宗,[60] particularly in that the "inner elixir" is presented as something to complement the "outer elixir" of laboratory alchemy.

In any case, both *The Way of Transcendence* and *The Holy Chronicle* shortly later on have Lord Lao describing the Way of the Three Ones and the method for Guarding the One in words closely matching LLS#1, and also enumerating the Nine Contemplations (*jiusi* 九思) by names that closely match those given to the Nine Rooms in LLS#4 (see *The Holy Chronicle* 3/14b–16a; *The Way of Transcendence* 6a–7a).[61] *The Holy Chronicle* indicates that these discourses were among the teachings conferred by Lord Lao upon Yin Xi at the guard station at Hangu Pass. After this we are told that Yin Xi resigned his government post and retired to his mansion in the Zhongnan mountains, bringing Lord Lao with him as his guest, and it was then that the teachings corresponding to LLS#2 and the first part of LLS#4 (the Red Snake-Queen Mother vision sequence) were conferred. Thus *The Way of Transcendence* and *The Holy Chronicle* give the impression that the meditations of the Nine Rooms/Nine Contemplations belonged to a set of teachings separate from those directly pertaining to the Red Snake-Queen Mother vision sequence.

Now, as is discussed in chapter 2, a concept of "Nine Rooms" as a regimen of secluded contemplation by which you bodily transform into a Divine Person (*shenren* 神人) or a "Sagely Person of the upper heavens" (*shangtian shengren* 上天聖人) is mentioned within the Taiping Group texts—in *GP Synopsis* 5/13b–14a—but without distinct descriptions of the nine successive meditation techniques. *The True Record*, in the latter part of LLS#4, however, gives us such descriptions, and in doing so perhaps preserves some information that may have once been part of a more complete *Taiping jing*. Unfortunately, the descriptions are not particularly straightforward. Nonetheless we try to make some sense of them.

The First Room, according to Lord Lao in the LLS#4, is the Contemplation for the Expulsion of Wickedness (*quxie si* 去邪思). In this contemplation, we are told:

三神為其守 太陽居左教之 太陰居右與之 太和居內利之

Three Spirits serve as its guard. Great Yang resides at its left and instructs it. Great Yin dwells at its right and keeps it company. Great Harmony dwells inside and benefits it. (*The True Record* 26b)

What are the three spirits of Great Yang, Great Yin, and Great Harmony guarding? Are they perhaps guarding a "Baby" 赤子 of the sort that figures so prominently in *Contemplating the Baby* or in LLS#1? What exactly are these Three Spirits anyway? Are they the three cloud-souls? Or, are they perhaps the spirits of the Three Ones that inhabit the three Elixir Fields, also featured in LLS#1?

From the brief descriptions of the remaining eight "rooms" that follow, it remains difficult to reconstruct the specific methods employed and the overall underlying theory.[62] From the second through sixth "rooms" Lord Lao describes how you are to observe the functions, movements, and interactions of your essence 精, *qi* 氣 and spirit 神, as well as the "ghosts and specters" (*guiwu* 鬼物) that dwell and intermingle with them. Progressively, your essence, *qi* and spirit move toward harmony, while the ghosts and specters are forced into a marginal position. At the end there emerges a completely rectified and unified spirit, integrated with the body and at total ease. During the seventh "room," you are to witness the arrival of a Great Genuine Spirit (*dazhenshen* 大真神), which perhaps is understood as a product of the merging of essence, *qi* and spirit; whatever the case, the ghosts and specters, in deference to this Great Genuine Spirit, all leave. During the eighth "room" your body (*shen* 身) merges fully with the Great Spirit to "become a person" (*weiren* 爲人); the implication here would seem to be that mind and body are in full harmony, integrated in the eternal, universal life and consciousness—the Dao—and also that the body has transformed into a deathless state. Also, throughout the day and night, you are no longer inclined to give any thought to earthly, secular matters. By the ninth "room" you have become a Genuine Person (*zhenren* 真人), and thus need to do nothing more than "accord with *qi* and lie down" 隨氣而臥 (26b–27a).

After enumerating the Nine Rooms, Lord Lao explains that because you are no longer supposed to have any knowledge of human affairs while in the quiet room, the door to the room should be firmly closed so that you do not see any other person. If you need food, your attendant should prepare the food for you and place it outside by the door, so that you can retrieve it for yourself. If the attendant notices that you are no longer taking food, he or she need not worry nor panic. This is because you "are changing your appearance, and naturally the time will come for you to leave" 當易其形容 自有去時矣 (27a–b).

Thus, in order to be free of any need to deal with other people or to occupy yourself with any matter other than contemplation, you are assumed to have an attendant who assists you with the provision and preparation of food, and other needs. Eventually, we are told, a time will come when you will not partake of the food given, which might ordinarily lead others to think that you are ill, starving, or dead. However, no such concern is in order, for you are undergoing the transformations that will result in your "leaving" as a Genuine Transcendent. Apparently, the body of a Genuine Transcendent does not require food.

The correspondence or intimate relationship between this portion of LLS#4 and the *Taiping jing*—or at least *GP Synopsis*—is quite apparent, particularly in their common terminology that includes not only the term Nine Rooms, but also the expressions "change their appearance" 易其形容 and "accord with *qi*" 隨氣. It can be recalled (see chapter 2) that in *GP Synopsis* (5/14a) it is stated that people who undergo the successive practice of the Nine Rooms "change their appearance" 易其形容. It also states that diligent, steadfast adepts "transform in accordance with the *qi*" 隨氣而化. It is also noteworthy in this regard that LLS#4 describes how the person who is transforming his or her appearance in the meditation room might stop eating. As we have seen, the Taiping Group texts emphasize not eating as a definitive characteristic of an immortal or a person of extremely high attainment.

It should also be noted, however, that in LLS#4 the meditation of the Ninth Room is designated as "the Contemplation of the Great Cavern" 大洞思 and is described as a stage at which "the Way of the Great Cavern is fully complete" 大洞道備. The term "Great Cavern" (*dadong* 大洞) bears strong connotations of Shangqing Daoism, for the scripture regarded as supreme within that tradition was the *Dadong zhenjing* 大洞真經 (Genuine Scripture of the Great Cavern). The appearance of the term "Great

Cavern" thus appears anachronistic to the second-century setting of the original 170-*juan Taiping jing*. However, it is not too unlikely that the term could have existed within the version of the *Taiping jing* that had been summarized to form *GP Synopsis*, because that was quite likely Zhou Zhixiang's reconstituted 170-*juan* version of the late sixth century.

*The True Record* concludes with one last portion of anonymous commentary. There it states:

夫人入室者 意在清齋誦經 或服藥行氣 或思真鍊神 志唯求道 精懇愈切 專想不二 則能洞感變形易顏 以至仙飛

As for people who enter the room, their intention can be [any of the following things: They can] recite scriptures while observing a pure retreat, ingest medicines and circulate the *qi*, or contemplate what is genuine and refine the spirit(s). Their aspiration should only be to seek the Dao, with their pure dedication ever steadfast. If your thoughts are single-mindedly focused, you can penetratingly [inter-]feel [with divine forces], transform your body and change your face, and progress to where you fly off as a Transcendent. (*The True Record* 27b)

The message here, then, is that the specific method that you employ while in seclusion does not matter so much, and may not necessarily be meditation per se. What matters is whether you are sincere, focused, and diligent in whatever approach you choose. In the view of this commentator, then, our exhausting quest for the method specifically intended for the generation of the Red Snake-Queen Mother vision sequence is a rather silly one, for that also is brought about by sheer sincere, single-minded determination regardless of your specific technique.

The commentary concludes *The True Record* by saying that Yin Xi, after training for three years as directed by Lord Lao, was rejuvenated in countenance, and his visage became golden. After this he went to Chengdu 成都 (in Sichuan 四川). This, the commentator explains, is symbolic of the fact that his "study of the Dao was totally (*dou* [*du*] 都) completed (*cheng* 成)" 學道都成 (27b).

In sum, unlike *Contemplating the Baby*, which describes with relative clarity the specific meditation technique and regimen that is to bring forth the Red Snake-Queen Mother vision sequence, *The True Record* leaves the reader uncertain. Although the editor gives the impression that it is the diligence of your practice, not the specifics of the method pursued (which does not necessarily even have to be meditation) that matters, such was perhaps not the attitude of whoever composed the original source text describing the Red Snake-Queen Mother vision sequence. We are left to consider various methods and approaches as candidates for recognition as the prime vision-inducing method; these include the Eating of *Qi*, recitation of scriptures (especially the *Laozi*), the Visualization of the Three Ones, the Guarding of the One, the simple maintaining of inner clarity and calmness, the method of the Nine Rooms, and the ingestion of medicines (alchemical or otherwise).

In fact, laboratory alchemy cannot be excluded as a candidate either. As was mentioned, two full folios of discourse in *The True Record* are devoted to the topic of laboratory alchemy. Within this discourse we can find a passage in which Lord Lao goes so far as to state:

汝當欲神仙 當先服還丹金液 乃存其神 即時昇仙 上為真人 汝不服還丹金液 虛自苦耳

If you desire Divine Transcendence, you must first ingest the Reverted Cinnabar and Golden Liquid. Thereupon if you preserve your spirit you can ascend as a Transcendent and become a Genuine Person on high. If you do not ingest the Reverted Cinnabar and Golden Liquid, you are just tormenting yourself in vain. (*The True Record* 8b; cognate passage in *The Holy Chronicle* 3/12b)[63]

Thus, if one were to regard all the teachings set forth by Lord Lao in *The True Record* as conforming to a coherent system, one would have to conclude that the practitioner who sees the Red Snake-Queen Mother vision sequence is supposed to be practicing laboratory alchemy.

One might then also speculate that in instances where adepts actually did see the hallucinations or epiphanies, this may have had something to do with the effects of alchemical drugs. However, one should note that *Contemplating the Baby* says nothing about ingesting drugs (although it is possible that you were supposed to do so after the completion of your 100 days in the meditation room, if you desired the highest levels of immortality). The topic of alchemy is never brought up again in any of the discourses in the remaining seventeen pages of *The True Record*. There one finds numerous discussions on contemplative and physical practices, each of which seem to promise supreme immortality if carried out faithfully and exclusively. Perhaps there was a tacit understanding that Golden Liquid and Reverted Cinnabar are to be ingested before any of these methods are carried out. However, it seems more likely that the incongruence is real, owing to the fact the editor has intermixed material originating among proponents of alchemy with material issuing from nonalchemists.

While *The True Record* thus leaves us with no clear solution to our problem, the authors of *The Way of Transcendence* and *The Holy Chronicle* for some reason were content with the understanding that it is the passive observation method of clarity and calmness (that described in LLS#2) that leads to the Red Snake-Queen Mother vision sequence. Their understanding is adopted in a Neidan text of around 1300. If indeed it is the case that methods such as those of *Contemplating the Baby* and LLS#2 are what best bring forth the dramatic vision sequences, this could perhaps be because the contents of the subconscious surface more readily in a mind that is clear and calm, and is not having too many thoughts, feelings, and images willfully imposed upon it.

FOUR

# Integrating Buddhism

*Earlier Phase*

In this chapter we discuss *The Western Ascension* and *The Original Arising*, two texts that betray a significant degree of Buddhist influence, but which do not engage in the ontological discourse on Emptiness in the manner that would become common in texts of the Sui (581–618) and Tang periods (618–907). While the key Mahāyāna Buddhist concept of Emptiness is lacking in these two texts, it is nonetheless clear that other essential elements of Buddhism—especially the doctrine of *karma* and rebirth, and the ideal of limitless compassion—have profoundly impacted their worldview and their soteriological ideals. This left a great impact on their understanding as to why serenity should be cultivated, and on the approaches to meditation they endorse.

### THE *XISHENG JING* 西昇經 (*THE WESTERN ASCENSION*)

*The Western Ascension* (*Xisheng jing* 西昇經; Scripture of the Western Ascension), which is quoted extensively in *The True Record*, is itself a text bearing the format of oral instructions bestowed by Laozi upon Yin Xi, embedded in a narrative concerning his journey toward the western regions. Two versions of *The Western Ascension* are found in the *Daoist*

*Canon*, each of which are accompanied by commentary and were edited during the Northern Song 北宋 (960–1127) period. The somewhat earlier version—which we refer to as "version A"[1]—is entitled *Xisheng jing jizhu* 西昇經集註 (Scripture of the Western Ascension with Assembled Commentaries), and was edited by Chen Jingyuan 陳景元 (1025–1094). Attached to the scripture's main text in this version are explanatory passages drawn from commentaries by four different medieval authors, namely, Wei Jie 韋節 (496–569), Xu Daomiao 徐道邈 (fl. seventh century), Chongxuanzi 沖玄子 (dates unknown), Li Rong 李榮 (fl. 658–663), and Liu Renhui 劉仁會 (sixth or seventh century?). The other version—which we refer to as "version B"[2]—though entitled simply *Xisheng jing* (Scripture of the Western Ascension), bears a commentary written around 1117 by Northern Song Emperor Huizong 徽宗 (r. 1100–1126). While the scripture text in the two versions is essentially the same, there occasionally are discrepancies, and in at least one place, as we shall see, there is a discrepancy that presents us with some difficulty in arriving at a proper interpretation. Also, for some reason, the sacred personage who expounds the scripture is referred to as "Laozi" in version A, and "Lord Lao" in version B.

Livia Kohn, who has written a fine monograph on *The Western Ascension* (with English translation of the entire text) estimates that it appeared sometime in the fifth century. As she points out, *The Western Ascension* is mentioned or quoted by several Buddhist anti-Daoist polemical works of the sixth century, as well as in the Daoist encyclopedia, the *Wushang biyao* 無上秘要 of the same century; furthermore, as noted earlier, version A includes commentary by Wei Jie (who was an eminent Daoist cleric of Mt. Hua 華山 [Shaanxi]), who flourished during the sixth century. The fact that the text was this well known in the sixth century would suggest that it had already appeared in the preceding century.[3] A date even earlier than the fifth century, however, does not seem so likely, in light of the significant degree of Buddhist influence that is discernible in the text.

The main text of *The Western Ascension*, in both of the *Daoist Canon* versions, is divided into thirty-nine chapters (*zhang* 章). The first chapter, much like *The True Record*, describes how Lord Lao, who was heading toward the land of Zhuqian 竺乾 (India) in the west to "open up the Way" (*kaidao* 開道), was met at the Hangu Pass by Yin Xi. Lord Lao thereupon, for Yin Xi, "expounded the Way and the Virtue, laid out in two volumes" 説道德列以二篇 (namely, the *Laozi*). He then proclaimed to him "the essentials of the Dao" (*daoyao* 道要). Those essentials are the teachings that we find expounded over the remainder of the thirty-nine chapters of *The Western Ascension*. *The Western Ascension*, it would appear, is meant to be understood as something of a companion volume to the *Laozi*. Indeed, much of the content of *The Western Ascension* reinforces the main teachings of the *Laozi*. Naturally then, mental serenity and its benefits is one of the important themes of the text. As we shall see, *The Western Ascension* in a few places does discuss meditation practice more specifically and concretely than does the *Laozi*, and in doing so mentions meditation techniques and theories that had become prominent by the medieval period. However, unlike *The True Record*, *The Western Ascension* contains no references to or endorsements of laboratory alchemy, and offers no dramatic descriptions of sensory or physical phenomena comparable to the Red Snake-Queen Mother vision sequence. Both *The True Record* and *The Western Ascension*, set as they are within the context of a narrative related to Lord Lao's so-called conversion of the barbarians (*huahu* 化胡), betray an awareness of the existence of Buddhism, and imply a polemical stance toward it. However, in the case of *The Western Ascension*, Buddhist doctrines have clearly been incorporated into its own teachings. Buddhist influence is quite apparent, as we see when we examine the manner in which *The Western Ascension* addresses issues such as the relative worth of the mind and the body, and the nature of their interrelationship.

In the first four chapters of *The Western Ascension* Lord Lao talks about the ineffable, profound nature of the Dao, the apprehension of which requires diligence and dedication, but also an attitude of nonaction (*wuwei* 無爲) that is devoid of artifice and selfish attachments. After hearing these initial teachings, Yin Xi, we are told, feigned illness to resign from his government post and went into seclusion. There:

恬淡思道 臻/歸⁴ 志守一 極虛本无 剖析乙密

[Yin Xi] contemplated the Dao in placid detachment. He concentrated his will on Guarding the One. [Apprehending] the utmost emptiness and the original nothingness, he dissected and analyzed the single secret. (A 1/10a–b; B 1/7a)

Thus, we are told, a calm and concentrated mind apprehends a great secret that normally eludes the intellect. We are then further told that Yin Xi recited the text (namely, the *Laozi*) ten-thousand times, and that "through this pure diligence, his contemplation penetrated" 精誠思徹. (A 1/11a; B 1/7b).

It is in the fifth and sixth chapters that we begin to see the impact of Buddhism. In chapter 5 Lord Lao discusses how even though the Dao itself is without perceivable form, the world generated out of it is full of perceivable multiplicity in which the four elements (earth 地, water 水, fire 火, and wind 風; this is an Indian concept borrowed from Buddhism) and four seasons interplay and alternate. The things of creation vary greatly in their qualities despite their common single source. Living beings, each in their own way "receive their bodies" 受形身 due to the differences in their characters and actions. While their spirits originate from empty nothingness, they bring about through their thoughts, words, and actions the grim reality that there are the "paths of birth and death" 生死道 that they must travel on (A 1/12a–17b; B 1/8b–11b). What Lord Lao is apparently speaking of here is the principle of rebirth that Daoists had begun to incorporate from Buddhism by at least the fourth century (as evident in the Shangqing scriptures), and had fully integrated into their worldview by the fifth century (as is evident here, as well as in the Lingbao scriptures).[5] In the sixth chapter the reference to rebirth is unmistakable. There Lord Lao speaks of how the myriad creatures, through "the intertwining of their emotions and actions" 情行相結連, bring it about that "if they are destroyed, they take shape again, and if they perish, they are born again" 如壞復成 如滅復生 (A 2/1a–b; B 1/12a).

In the seventh chapter Lord Lao carries out a discourse on the relative worth of the body and the spirit. He states:

偽道養形 真道養神 真神通道 能亡能存 神能飛形 并能移山 形為灰土 其何識焉

The false way is to nurture the body and the True Way is to nurture the spirit. The Genuine Spirit corresponds with the Dao. It can perish and it can survive [as it pleases]. The spirit can make the body fly, and it can move mountains. The body is ashes and dirt. What does it know? (A 2/8b–9b; B 1/16a)

It would appear that Lord Lao is saying that the spirit is worth a great deal more than the body, and is the only one of the two worth "nurturing" (*yang* 養). The spirit is of an altogether different order because it is conscious, and can—at least potentially—do great things. Such is not the case with the body, and the "ashes and dirt" (*huitu* 灰土) out of which it is composed. Here, right after Buddhist concepts such as the four elements and the principle of rebirth had been brought into play in the prior two chapters, Lord Lao puts forth a categorical distinction between spirit and body that is rather incongruous with other materials we have examined so far, that had spoken of how essence, *qi* and spirit can transmute into each other, or of how the body can be transformed into spirit. To say that "the false way is to nurture the body" could—it would seem—easily be taken to mean that physical longevity practices of the sort that were being pursued in medieval Daoist religion ought to be abandoned, perhaps in favor of psychologically oriented practices (such as those of Buddhism) that focus on eradicating ignorance in a manner that would erase the *karma* that binds you to the cycle of successive rebirths.

However, Lord Lao's statements need not necessarily be taken as a condemnation of longevity practices. The nurturing of the body referred to here could also be understood as meaning the way that worldly people, in the pursuit of material abundance and pleasure, feed and indulge the body and its senses in a way that is actually detrimental both to it and to the mind. One should also note that one of the powers of the spirit mentioned here is that of making the body fly. What this seems to mean is that it is possible for the body to ascend into the heavens; however, this comes about through the wondrous power of the spirit, if the spirit is nurtured to the point where it can exercise such power. Lord Lao also says that a "Genuine Spirit" (*zhenshen* 真神) that corresponds with the Dao can perish or survive at will. Here one might say that Lord Lao is describing himself, for he is a being that has appeared, disappeared, and reappeared bodily in the world numerous times, not due to the laws of *karma* and *saṃsāra*, but rather by his own free will, for he is himself the embodiment of the Dao that kindly comes to guide humanity.

Lord Lao then goes on to speak of the harm that comes about through the sounds, sights, odors, and flavors that the body's senses encounter, and points out that the very fact that one has a body is what makes one suffer from stress, pain, itching, cold, and heat. He then states:

觀古視今 誰能形完 吾尚白首 衰老孰/熟年

> Observing matters from ancient times until present, who has ever been able to keep the body complete? Even I have white hair, and have become decrepit and ripe in years. (A 2/10a–b; B 1/17a)

Thus, not only does the body present you with much stress and discomfort, it is not something that can ever be made free of defects or impervious to old age. This, perhaps even more than the prior statement denigrating the nurturing of the body, could be interpreted as a call to give up all physical longevity practices in favor of focusing on the perfection of the spirit. Apparently, even though Lord Lao is able to incarnate into the world whenever and as often as he pleases, even he cannot keep the physical body alive and youthful forever. This is if Lord Lao's words are to be taken as a sincere admission, and not as some sort of expedient didactic ploy. (If it is to be understood as a didactic ploy, one could say that it is one that resembles—purposely or not—the ploy of the Buddha of the *Lotus Sūtra* [more on this later in the discussion of *The Original Arising*] who appears to undergo births and deaths while concealing the fact that he abides eternally.) One further wonders here, in light of the prior statements regarding how "the spirit can make the body fly," whether even a body that has triumphantly mounted the heavens must alas suffer old age and death.

The theme of rebirth reappears several times over the remainder of the text, as does the notion that one ought to not care too much about the body. In the ninth chapter Lord Lao discusses how the attainment of wisdom is not something that can come about solely as a result of one's own efforts and abilities in the present life, but is always conditioned by the "causes and connections" (*yinyuan* 因緣) that are your actions from past lives, as well as the personal influences (such as good or bad teachers) that you encounter (A 2/15b–17b; B 1/20a–21a).

In the eleventh chapter Lord Lao states:

以是生死有 不如無爲安 無爲無所行 何緣有咎愆 子不貪身形 不與有爲怨

Therefore the existence of birth and death, is not as good as the ease of non-action. If in non-action you have nothing that you do, by what causes could you have transgressions? Do not crave the body. Do not partake in the enmities [that come about through] action. (A 3/7a; B 2/5a)

Thus, nonaction is proposed here as a way of preventing the generation of *karma* that perpetuates the cycle of rebirth. One is to drop all craving for embodied existence, so as to seek the condition of perpetual ease of nonaction. The classical Daoist term "nonaction" (*wuwei* 無爲), by being contrasted here directly to "birth and death," seems to get used in a sense synonymous to the Buddhist term *nirvāṇa* (*nieban* 涅般), which describes the condition of the enlightened one who has no more suffering and rebirth. Such a usage of the term *wuwei* was in fact current among Buddhists, as is evident from various instances in early Chinese Buddhist scripture translations where the word *wuwei* is employed to translate *nirvāṇa*, or in other cases *asaṃskṛta* (not formed by causes; without birth and annihilation).[6]

Further on, in the thirteenth chapter, we find Lord Lao stating,

能知無知 道之樞機 空滅成無 何用飛仙 / 空虛滅無 何用仙飛

To be able to know [how to be] without knowledge is the pivotal mechanism of the Dao. If you can disappear into empty space and become nothing, what need is there to fly away as a Transcendent? (A 3/15b–16a; B 2/10b–11a)

In speaking of disappearing into empty space and becoming nothing, Lord Lao again seems to be speaking of *nirvāṇa*. He seems to be saying that *nirvāṇa* is a higher attainment than ascending the heavens as a Transcendent. Regarding what is meant here by being "without knowledge" there is a passage in the twentieth chapter that seems to provide an explanation. There Lord Lao states:

道者虛無之物也 若虛而爲實 無而爲有也 天者受一氣 蕩蕩而致清也 氣下化生於萬物 而形各異焉 是以聖人者 知道德混沌玄<u>妙/x</u>同也 亦知天地清靜 皆守一也 故與天同心而無知 與道同身而無體 而後天道盛矣

The Dao is a thing of empty nothingness. It seems to be empty, and yet it makes fullness. It is nothingness, and yet it makes being. Heaven receives the one *qi*, and vastly brings forth clarity. The *qi* comes down to produce the myriad creatures, each of whom differs in their forms. Hereby the Sage knows that the Dao's virtue, the primordial chaos and the mysterious marvels are all the same thing. He also knows that the clarity and calmness of heaven and earth is due to the fact that they both guard the One. Therefore, he is of the same mind as heaven, and is *without knowledge* (emphasis added), and is of the same body with the Dao, and has no body. Thereby, the Way of Heaven flourishes. (A 4/9a–10b; B 2/21a–b)

From this passage we can perhaps surmise that when Lord Lao spoke of "disappearing into empty space and becoming nothing," he was perhaps referring more to a state of mind that has transcended all egotistical thoughts and desires, and that magnanimously identifies with the Dao and all that it pervades, becoming oblivious to one's own body in the process. If so, it is equivalent to *nirvāṇa* in the sense of full enlightenment, rather than in the sense of the condition of the fully enlightened person after death. Now, it can be noted here that the Sage, while transcending his ego and identifying with the universal Dao, also emulates heaven and earth by Guarding the One in a state of clarity and calmness. The One is the one *qi* of the Dao that creates and sustains all things. Thus, the disregarding of one's own body paradoxically results in the successful harnessing of the vital force that sustains you. The final phrase "the Way of Heaven flourishes" seems to refer not only to how his body is thus made to flourish, but to how the Sage's activities and/or governance (that are characterized by nonaction) meet with auspicious outcomes. (The theme of sagely governance is found most prominently in chapters 24, 25, and 27 of *The Western Ascension*.)

The seventeenth chapter of *The Western Ascension* contains a particularly important discussion on the relationship between mind and body. To start out it states:

生我者神 殺我者心 夫心意者 我之所患也 我即無心 我何知乎 念
我未生時 無有身也 直以積氣聚血 成我身耳

> That which gives life to me is my spirit. That which kills me is my mind. Generally speaking, my mind's intentions are what afflict me. If I was of no mind, what would I know? When I think of the time prior to my birth, [it occurs to me that] I had no body. Only because of the accumulation of *qi* and blood was my body completed. (A 4/3b–4a; B 2/17a–b)

Actually, this passage, before even bringing the body into discussion, begins by setting out yet another dichotomy within one's mental aspect. It contrasts the life-giving spirit (*shen* 神) to the death-bringing mind (*xin* 心). It is the mind—not the spirit—that generates the sort of knowledge that is ego-laden and which leads to strife and self-destruction. The spirit, then, seems to be a form of consciousness that is of itself blessedly free of such knowledge, and which has the capacity to sustain life. In this capacity to sustain life it is the same as the earlier mentioned single *qi* of the Dao. Perhaps the spirit and the Dao-*qi* are to be regarded as the same entity. Lord Lao then points out that this physical body that forms so much of the focus of our selfish concerns is something that did not even exist prior to the time of birth. Perhaps the spirit, by implication here, does exist prior to birth and is thus a more rightful object for your concern.

Lord Lao then states:

我身乃神之車也 神之舍也 神之主人也 主人安靜 神即居之 躁動
神即去之

> My body is my spirit's carriage. It is my spirit's lodging. It is my spirit's host. If the host is peaceful and calm, the spirit will dwell there. If [the host] is restless, the spirit will leave it. (A 4/4b; B 2/17b)

Thus the metaphors of carriage/passenger, house/resident and host/guest are used here to describe the relationship of body and mind. The point being made is that by keeping the body calm you ensure that the spirit will stay in it and keep it alive. Thus, although the text elsewhere says that you should disregard your body, here we find advice on how to keep the body alive. To keep the body calm apparently means to practice nonaction—to simplify or limit your activity to only that which is of natural necessity—as well perhaps to cultivate states of deep calm through meditation. Maintaining such calm requires the absence of ego-laden knowledge of the sort that the mind generates, and which causes the body to act out in self-destructive ways.

Continuing on, Lord Lao states:

是以聖人 無常心者 欲歸初始 反未生也 人未生時 豈有身乎 無身當何憂乎 當何欲哉 故外其身 存其神者 精耀留也 道德一合 與道通

Hereby, the reason why the Sage has no constant mind is because he wishes to return to the beginnings and revert to the condition prior to birth. When people have not yet been born, they certainly do not have bodies! If you have no body, what shall you worry about? What shall you desire? Thus, by disowning your body (lit., "regarding your body as outside"), you preserve your spirit. Those who preserve their spirits, retain the refined brilliance. Dao and virtue combine into one, and you correspond with the Dao. (A 4/5a–6a; B 2/18a–b)

To "have no constant mind" here most likely means to not have any set notions or agendas of a self-centered sort. A noteworthy precedent for this usage of "constant" (*chang* 常), which the author seems to be following, is to be found in the episode in the *Zhuangzi*'s sixth chapter (see chapter 1) where Yan Hui reports on how he is able to "sit and forget," and Confucius praises him for "having no constants" (*wuchang* 無常). Here also this state of mind comes about by being oblivious to one's body, and this oblivion is here equated to a return to the condition prior to birth. This mind of the Sage is also described here as one that disowns the body; yet, it is by doing so that you retain the spirit and keep the body alive. Paradoxically, the disregarding of the body is the most effective way of caring for the body.

A similar, related paradox is stated in most audacious terms in the twenty-sixth chapter, where Lord Lao proclaims:

我命在我 不属天地 我不視不聽不知 神不出身 與道同久

My destiny is in my own hands, not in those of heaven and earth. I do not look, do not listen and do not know. My spirit does not exit my body, and I live as long as the Dao. (A 5/8a; B 3/6a–b)

Thus, the best way to take your destiny into your own hands is by seeing, hearing, and knowing nothing.

In the twenty-first chapter, Lord Lao makes statements encouraging the care of the body that sound, at least on the surface, quite selfish:

人哀人不如哀身 哀身不如愛神 愛神不如含神 含神不如守身 守身長久長存也

For a person to pity other people, is not as good as to pity one's own body. To pity your body is not as good as cherishing your spirit. Cherishing the spirit is not as good as containing the spirit. Containing the spirit is not as good as guarding the body. If you guard the body for a long time you will survive for a long time. (A 4/13a–14a; B 2/24b)

To say that self-pity is better than compassion seems like a rather uninspiring sort of moral exhortation. However, the point here would seem to be that we are too often oblivious to the fact that we ourselves are in a pitiable condition because we habitually afflict ourselves with our unnecessary thoughts, desires, and actions. Though caring for others is in itself probably not a bad thing, we need to first recognize the need to take better care of ourselves by changing our own ways; maybe then we are better equipped to care for others (though the text admittedly does not quite go as far as to say this). In any case, pitying and caring for yourself consists of "cherishing the spirit," "containing the spirit," and "guarding the body," in ascending order of priority. As for what the difference is between "cherishing" and "containing" the spirit, and why the latter is deemed even better than the former, is difficult to say. One might surmise that containing is preferable in that it is a condition lacking in emotion and conscious volition, and is thus better than consciously and purposely cherishing the spirit. Such an interpretation at least seems to be confirmed by the commentator Li Rong, who explains that when you cherish the spirit you still "do not avoid belaboring [yourself] and you still afflict harm upon yourself" 未免勞役 猶嬰患害. However, when you contain the spirit, this means that "externally you are unattached and undefiled, and internally you do not think and worry" 外則不執不染 內則無思無慮. This makes you "clear and pure inside and out" 內外清淨, causing the spirit to stay within your body (A 4/13b).

As for why guarding the body is even more important than containing the spirit, Li Rong explains that the spirit, despite being so marvelous, somehow "does not stand on its own" 不自立 and must entrust itself to a body in order to perform its functions. Its dwelling must be therefore taken care of. But what does it actually mean to "guard the body"? Quite plausibly, it would seem, this could mean that you should, alongside maintaining inner serenity, take care to regulate your diet or your mundane activities in a way that avoids harm or danger to your body. Li Rong, however, understands the guarding of the body in terms of mental states and meditative practice. As he explains:

必淨必清 同道同德 通幽通徹 則與虛極不二 存三守一 乃共真神合契也

You must be clear, you must be pure. Be in unity with the Dao and with the virtue. Penetrate the darkness thoroughly, and become non-dual with the extreme of emptiness. Preserve the Three and guard the One, to merge and tally together with the Genuine Spirit. (A 4/13b–14a)

What he perhaps means to say is that before you can enjoy a habitual state of serenity and partake of the benefits thereof, you need to undertake meditative practice in which you enter into trance states of profound mystical consciousness. Meditation practice can be regarded as a guarding of the body in that in undertaking it you indeed turn your attention on your inward bodily locations and forces such as the three Elixir Fields and their indwelling deities (if these are indeed the "Three" that Li Rong has in mind for you to "preserve"). In doing so, you somehow "merge and tally" (*heqi* 合契) with the Genuine Spirit. As we have seen, the seventh chapter of *The Western Ascension* describes the Genuine Spirit as something that corresponds with the Dao, and which can survive or perish at will. It seems to be a sort of spirit that the adept is supposed to strive to ultimately attain, but also seems like an apt description of Lord Lao himself, as an embodiment of the Dao that incarnates or departs from the world at will. Li Rong, by saying that you "merge and tally" with the Genuine Spirit perhaps means that you unite your multiple bodily spirits into one Genuine Spirit, or that you integrate and control them with your Great Spirit. Or perhaps Li Rong means you achieve a union with the Great Spirit of the eternal Dao that is from time to time embodied as Lord Lao himself.

In the twenty-second chapter of *The Western Ascension*, Lord Lao makes one more significant pronouncement regarding the relationship between body and spirit:

神生形 形成神 形不得神 不能自生 神不得形 不能自成 形神合同 更相生 更相成

The spirit gives life to the body, and the body completes the spirit. If the body does not obtain a spirit, it cannot give life to itself. If the spirit does not obtain a body, it cannot complete itself. Body and spirit combine together to further give life to each other and further complete each other. (A 4/14b–15a; B 3/1a)

The notion that the body needs the spirit to be alive and stay alive was stated in some of the passages of *The Western Ascension* that we have already examined. What is noteworthy here is the notion that the spirit needs the body in to be "completed" (*cheng* 成). The spirit being spoken of here that needs to be completed is apparently not the Genuine Spirit that corresponds with the Dao and which can survive or perish at will. The process of becoming completed is the process by which the not-yet-genuine spirit becomes the Genuine Spirit. This process requires successive incarnations during which the embodied spirit can undertake the sort of self-cultivation by which spiritual perfection can come about. Such cultivation requires a physical body.

As for what this self-cultivation ought to consist of, that would primarily appear to be meditation. In the fourteenth chapter of *The Western Ascension* Lord Lao states:

先損諸欲 無令意逸 閑居靜處 精思齋室 丹書萬卷 不如守一

First lose all of your desires, and do not allow your attention to be lax. Dwell in solitude in a quiet place. Carry out refined contemplation in a room of retreat. Ten thousand scrolls of elixir books are not as good as Guarding the One. (A 3/19a–b; B 2/13a)

Regarding the sorts of meditation techniques you should employ, Lord Lao, in the twelfth chapter, states:

觀諸次為道 存神於想思 道氣與/和三光 念身中所治 彷彿/髣髴象夢寤 神明忽往來 惔/淡泊志無爲 念思有想意 自謂定無欲 不知持念異

Observe in the various stages to practice the Dao. Visualize the gods in your contemplations; [also visualize] the Dao-*qi* and the Three Radiances (or "guide your *qi* and the Three Radiances"). Contemplate the parts of the body where they govern. You will see their forms vaguely as though you were waking from a dream. The gods will suddenly come and go. [Then,] be without concern and aspire to non-action. If you [still] have thoughts within your contemplations, and [yet] say of yourself that you are in stability and are free of desires, you do not understand that maintaining [the mind of stability and non-desire] and thinking are [two] different [things]. (A 3/8a–9a; B 2/6a–7a)

Here we are told that contemplative practice proceeds in stages, and that prior to proceeding to the highest stage you are to first carry out visualizations of gods and of the locations within your body in which they reside. According to the commentary here by Li Rong, the character *dao* 道 in the compound *daoqi* 道氣 (that we tentatively rendered as "Dao-*qi*") should be understood in the sense of the verb *dao* 導 (to lead or guide), and thus *daoqi* should be understood as meaning *daoyin* 導引, which denotes light bodily movements and stretches meant to enhance and harmonize the flow of *qi* in the body. The "Three Radiances" (*sanguang* 三光; which in ordinary cosmological terms denotes the sun, moon, and stars) in the human body, according to Li Rong, are the gods of the Three Ones (of the three Elixir Fields) (A 3/8b). According to the commentary of Song Emperor Huizong, the Three Radiances are spirit, *qi*, and essence (B 2/6b).

In any case, the visualization of bodily deities (perhaps accompanied by *daoyin* exercises) is here also said to be efficacious in summoning gods to your presence, and in bringing about visions—albeit murky—of them. However, once some such degree of positive effect is brought about through the visualization of deities, you need to advance to the next stage, which means doing away with visualizations. Such at least is the interpretation of the earliest commentator Wei Jie:

次當遣存神之心 惔泊志於無爲 此存神之思 猶有相有意 故當又遣之 以定于無欲 亦乃忘其思念 故不知我之持心念神之異也

Next, you must rid yourself of the mind that visualizes the gods, so as to be free of concerns and to aspire to non-action. This contemplation that visualizes the gods still involves forms and intentions. Thus you must rid yourself of this in order to stabilize yourself in non-desire, and thereby forget those thoughts. Thus [people] do not understand my distinction between maintaining the mind and thinking of the spirits. (A 3/9a–b)

Though the visualization of deities has its benefits and is an effective way of focusing the mind on subtle inner things, it alas involves the formations of thoughts that can become attachments. Thus you need to move beyond it. To "maintain the mind" (*chixin* 持心) apparently means to maintain the condition of clarity, purity, and nonaction; one needs to understand the difference between this and the visualization of gods.

The most concrete description of how you should foster inner serenity, and of the results that are to be thus wrought, is found in the text's twentieth chapter, which bears the title "The Void of the Dao" (Daoxu 道虛). There Lord Lao states:

是以君子 終日不視不聽不言不食 內知而抱玄 夫欲視亦無所見 欲聽亦無所聞 欲言亦無所道 欲食亦無所味 惔/淡泊寂哉 不可得而味也 復歸於無物 若常能清靜無爲 無/氣自復也 反/返於未生而無身也 無爲養身 形體全也 天地充實 長保年也

Hereby the gentleman to the end of the day does not look, does not listen, does not speak and does not eat. On the inside he knows and thereby embraces the mysteries. If he wanted to look, he would see nothing. If he wanted to listen, he would hear nothing. If he wanted to speak, he would say nothing. If he wanted to eat, he would taste nothing. How unconcerned and calm he is! It cannot be acquired so as to be tasted. He returns to [the condition where] there are no things. If you can always maintain [a condition of] clarity, calmness and non-action, *non-being/qi* (emphasis added) will return. You will return to the condition prior to birth when you did not have a body. Nourish your body by doing nothing, and your shape and body will be complete. Heaven and earth will fill you to plenitude, and you will lengthily maintain your years. (A 4/11b–12b; B 2/22b–24a)

Thus, you are to at all times throughout the day maintain a state of total disengagement from external sensory stimuli while concentrating inwardly; in doing so you somehow know and embrace something mysterious (the Dao, presumably). One naturally wonders how literally one is to follow these directions. Should one eat nothing at all, observe constant silence, and deprive the senses entirely? The commentator Li Rong does soften the injunction by explaining here that you should "take care in your speech not to be flowery and elegant" 慎言語不華綺 and should "limit your drinking and eating, and cut out delicious flavors [from your diet]" 節飲食斷滋味 (A 4/11b). Whether the author of the main text would have accepted such a modified understanding is unclear; perhaps one could begin with moderation, and ultimately advance toward complete silence and fasting.

Whatever the case, while disengaging from outward things, your mind is supposed to become utterly indifferent to them, to the point where what you do happen to see, hear, say, or taste leaves no lingering impression that would undermine your inner calm and clarity. As Li Rong explains it, "When you understand that the myriad surroundings are all Empty (*kong* 空; *śūnyatā* in Sanskrit), your mind becomes entirely still" 悟萬境皆空 心即俱靜 (A 4/11b–12a). Here Li Rong is drawing on an essential Mahāyāna Buddhist doctrine that the main text's author may or may not have had in mind. "Empty" here means that a thing or concept lacks any independent, self-sufficient existence; Li Rong means to say that all things are conditioned (and hence impermanent), and that all concepts, values, and labels are relative—hence nothing is worth clinging to. (In the main text of *The Western Ascension* the word *kong* [empty] is found eight different times, but denotes a condition of vacancy or of empty space; it is never employed in the sense of the Mahāyāna concept of *śūnyatā*.) Putting things into such a perspective so as to engender a state of detachment can be said to constitute a new technique that became available to Daoists from the fifth century onward for the cultivation of clarity and stillness.⁷ However, *The Western Ascension*, which itself probably appeared in that century, does not resort to that technique.

The abiding detached calmness, the main text goes on to tell us, is a condition constituting a return to that prior to creation and all differentiation ("no things" [*wuwu* 無物]), and cannot be acquired (*de* 得) or tasted (*wei* 味) in any conventional sense. The text in its two versions then presents us with a conundrum. Version A states that by constantly maintaining a mental condition of clarity, stillness, and nonaction, "nonbeing" (*wu* 無) will return, whereas version B states that it is *qi* 氣 that will return. To say that nonbeing returns would seem to convey the notion of a return to a condition prior to creation and differentiation, and would fit well with the ensuing phrase stating that you will return to the state prior to birth and prior to when you possessed your own body. All of this could be taken as referring to a state of mind where you have transcended ego-hood and the stressful attachments that come with it. With such an ego-less, detached mind you are—paradoxically—enabled to nourish your body in the best possible way, which is through nonaction.

Interestingly, though, it is in the comments of the earliest commentator Wei Jie—which are found in version A—where we find a reading suggesting that it is indeed *qi* that returns to you when you constantly maintain clarity, calmness, and nonaction:

道氣復歸其身 則忘身 忘身則德合天地矣 夫天地不自生 故能長生 若然者身不保而自全 年不保而自生也

When Dao-*qi* returns again to the body, you forget your body. When you forget your body, your virtue matches that of heaven and earth. Heaven and earth do not regard themselves as living, and are therefore able to live long. If you are like this, your body will be complete though you do not preserve it, and you will naturally stay alive even though you do not [purposely] maintain your longevity. (A 4/12b)

According to this statement, the ego-transcending mental state is accompanied, or rather caused, by an infusion of the Dao-*qi* 道氣. Wei Jie is not clear here as to how and from where the *qi* "returns," but to say that it returns would suggest that you had once possessed it, but had lost it, perhaps due to too much self-centered desire and activity. It would appear, anyway then, that the positive change brought about through serenity and nonaction is not only psychological, but also pertains to the quality or quantity of *qi* that animates the body. Another one of the commentators Xu Daomiao (fl. seventh century) states, "The refined *qi* (or essence and *qi* [?]) of heaven and earth fills up my body, and my lifespan equals that of the two forms (heaven and earth)" 天地精氣充實我身 壽同二儀 (A 4/12b). The idea seems to be that salubrious, nurturing cosmic *qi* naturally gravitates toward you when your mind is clear and still, thus bestowing you with long life, even though you make no conscious effort toward that end.

*The Western Ascension* is an important, influential (as attested to by the presence of commentaries) text that addresses key soteriological issues pertaining to body, mind, and spirit that were arising in medieval times in large part due to the influence of Buddhism. The text addresses these issues in ways that ultimately affirm the body for its role in harboring the spirit and enabling its perfection. It also proclaims the importance of maintaining the body, although it paradoxically proposes the disregarding of the body as the best means of doing this. As for how one is to go about one's religious self-cultivation, the text and its medieval commentators endorse meditation of the various types that existed in medieval times, but also convey the understanding that proactive, visualization-based methods belong to a more rudimentary stage of practice, from which one should eventually graduate to the level of pure, serene contemplation where no intentional conjuring of images is involved.

In sum, even though *The Western Ascension* sets forth the cultivation of spirit by means of serene, passive meditation as the highest practice, it also affirms the validity of proactive meditation methods (and *daoyin* exercises, according to Li Rong), as well as the possibility of great longevity and bodily ascension. However, as perhaps an inevitable result of its incorporation of the notion of *saṃsāra*, it discusses the relationship of spirit and body in quite strongly dualistic terms. (Although its notion of a transmigrating spirit is also incongruent with Buddhist doctrine, this is a sort of notion that was common within the early Chinese Buddhist fold.)[8] Its exposition is concerned far more with states of mind than with physiological processes, and many of its statements taken out of context could be construed as a rejection of the quest for physical longevity and immortality.

### THE *XUWU ZIRAN BENQIJING* 虛無自然本起經 (*THE ORIGINAL ARISING*)

*The Original Arising*[9] (*Taishang laojun xuwu ziran benqi jing* 太上老君虛無自然本起經; The Most High Lord Lao's Scripture on the Original Arising from the Naturalness of Empty Nothingness) can be found in two versions. One version constitutes the 10th *juan* of the early eleventh-century Daoist compendium, the *Yunji qiqian* 雲笈七籤.[10] The other version[11] is found individually in the *Xu Daozang* 續道藏, the 1607 supplement portion of the *Daoist Canon*. The version in the *Yunji qiqian* bears the slightly different title, *Laojun Taishang xuwu ziran benqi jing* 老君太上虛無自然本起經; this seems rather odd, because in scripture titles or any other context, when the words "Laojun" and "Taishang" appear together, they almost always appear in the sequence of "Taishang Laojun" (Most High Lord Lao). However, otherwise, when one does find variations (all quite minor) between the two versions of *The Original Arising*, the *Yunji qiqian* version's wording is more coherent. Thus, when citing or quoting *The Original Arising* in our ensuing discussion, we refer to the *Yunji qiqian* version.

*The Original Arising* bears no colophon, nor any references to events, places, or people that would betray its provenance. It can at the very least be said with certainty that it predates the compilation of the *Yunji qiqian*. John Lagerwey, regarding *The Original Arising*, has observed, "This is a philosophical treatise typical of eighth-century Daoism. The vocabulary—from the dialectical as well as from the conceptual point of view, especially terms like *biru* 譬如 (or *biruo* 譬若) and the phrase *suoyi zhe he* 所以者何—is reminiscent of Buddhist-influenced texts of the seventh-century."[12] As we shall see, the "Buddhist-influenced" nature of *The Original Arising* is indeed unmistakable. The doctrine of rebirth and the various levels thereof is integral to its worldview. Equally or even more Buddhistic is its emphasis on the compassion toward all sentient beings that is exhibited by the supremely holy person who perpetually "*shows* (emphasis added) deaths and births" 見死生 in the *samsaric* realm in order to guide and aid those who suffer. This notion of a supremely holy person seems almost certainly to draw its inspiration from the Mahāyāna Buddhist conception of what the true, eternal Buddha is like.

However, one particularly important Buddhistic concept is conspicuously missing in *The Original Arising* (and was also missing in the main text of *The Western Ascension*)—namely, the concept of Emptiness. While *The Original Arising* uses the word *kong* 空 (which can variously mean "Empty"; "Emptiness"; "empty space"; "sky"; "in vain"), it uses it in a cosmological sense (as empty space) that is not congruent with the ontological concept of Emptiness (*śūnyatā*; lack of inherent existence) as employed in Mahāyāna philosophy or in the Daoist Twofold Mystery (*chongxuan* 重玄) discourse that emerged by the late sixth century, and is represented in works such as *The Original Juncture* that we examine in our next chapter. One gets the sense that the author of *The Original Arising* may have been under some degree of Buddhist influence in his propensity to use the word *kong*, but was not fully aware of its Buddhist ontological meaning. Such a manner of appropriating the word *kong* perhaps suggests a date of authorship nearer to that of *The Western Ascension* (fifth century), which is also a text that is attributed to Laozi/Lord Lao and employs the word *kong* similarly.

Also noteworthy is the term *xuwu ziran* 虛無自然 or "Naturalness of Empty Nothingness" that appears in the full title of *The Original Arising*, and is employed repeatedly within the text to denote certain levels of meditation practice. We can note here (see chapter 2) that the same term is employed similarly in the Taiping Group texts, where it denotes a meditation technique that is ranked second highest among a set of practices known as the Nine Degrees. We may also recall (see chapter 3) that *The True Record* describes a series of meditations called the Nine Rooms that perhaps correspond or bear some relation to the meditations of Nine Rooms mentioned in *GP Synopsis*. From this we might surmise the existence of a medieval group or groups devoted to Lord Lao that incorporated the doctrine and praxis of the old *Taiping jing* into their own system. Or perhaps such Daoist groups were related to those who undertook the embellishment and reconstitution of the *Taiping jing*. One might also speculate that such groups were somehow connected with the early Heavenly Masters tradition because that tradition is known for having revered Lord Lao, embraced the *Taiping jing* and the lore of its revelation to Gan Ji, and produced its own version of the *Taiping jing*—the *Taiping dongji jing* in 144 *juan*.

The cosmological usage of the word *kong* as denoting empty space appears near the beginning of *The Original Arising*. There we find described a series of cosmic emanations in which the Dao, at the stage of the Great Beginning (*taichu* 太初), was an essence (*jing* 精) imbued with radiant red *qi* (*chiqi* 赤炁). This red *qi* "flourished" (*sheng* 盛) and became a radiance known as the Great Yang (*taiyang* 太陽; the sun?), or Zidan of the Original Yang (Yuanyang Zidan 元陽子丹), a deity whose name is reminiscent of corporeal deities we have encountered in *The Manifest Dao* and *The True Record*. This radiant red *qi* then transformed into a yellow *qi* (*huangqi* 黃氣) known as the Central Harmony (*zhonghe* 中和), which in turn transformed into Lord Lao (Laojun 老君), who is also known as the Spirit Lord (Shenjun 神君), or the Yellow Spirit (Huangshen 黃神) of the Great Simplicity (*taisu* 太素). This spirit then entered into bodies of bones and flesh to bring about human beings. Subsequently, at the stage known as the Great Commencement (*taishi* 太始), the yellow *qi* transformed into the white *qi* that is the essence of water (*shui zhi jing* 水之精) and is known as the Great Yin (*taiyin* 太陰); the Great Yin then transformed into the Lord of Great Harmony (Taihejun 太和君). Because the water thereby emits a white *qi*, this is known as "the beginning of *qi*" (*qi zhi shi* 氣之始). The text then goes on to state that *qi* (white *qi*) contains spirit (yellow *qi*), which in turn contains essence (red *qi*); collectively, the triad is referred to as the Three Ones. These Three Ones merged together, we are told, are what is called Hundun 混沌—the primordial chaos out of which all of creation emanates. These Three Ones are also contained in the human body, and thus this triad is also known as the "Three Life-Givers" (*sansheng* 三生), the "Three Essences" (*sanjing* 三精) or the "Three Shapes" (*sanxing* 三形) (1a–b).

The text then goes on to further state that the Three Ones are the "void" (*xu* 虛), the "nothingness" (*wu* 無) and the "empty space" (*kong*

空). The empty space, which is white, contains the nothingness, which is yellow; the nothingness in turn contains the void, which is red. As for what exactly is meant by the empty space (*kong* 空), the text states:

空者 未有天地山川 左顧右視 蕩蕩溿溿 無所障礙 無有邊際 但洞白無所見無以聞 道自然從其中生

[As for] "empty space," [it refers to the condition that existed] when there still was no heaven, earth, mountains and rivers. You could look left and right clearly and vastly without hindrance and without limit. There was only transparency with nothing to see or hear. The Dao spontaneously emerges from there. (*The Original Arising* 2a)

What is thus described by the word *kong* is not the Buddhist ontological concept of Emptiness. Rather, it is empty space that is utterly free of content, and is yet paradoxically endowed with unlimited creative capacity; it alludes to how the Dao, which in and of itself is utterly lacking in any perceivable form, sound, smell, taste, or texture, nonetheless brings about all tangible natural phenomena.

The theme within the cosmological prologue of *The Original Arising* that appears most germane to the principal subject matter of the remainder of the text is the idea of an original condition of "void," "nothingness," or "empty space." What the remainder of *The Original Arising* sets forth as its principal assertion (and thus making the text relevant to our inquiry) is the necessity, possibility, and supreme soteriological benefit of bringing the human mind to a condition described as the "Naturalness of Empty Nothingness" (*xuwu ziran* 虛無自然), and thereby fully embodying the Dao and its sublime attributes. Directly following on the cosmological prologue, *The Original Arising* states:

是以聖人作經誡 後賢者欲使守道 空虛其心 關閉其耳目 不復有所念 若有所念思想者 不能得自然之道也

Hereby the sages produced the scriptures and precepts. Worthies of later times want to make you guard the Dao. Empty out your mind. Shut your ears and eyes. Do not have any more thoughts. If you still have something that you are thinking about, you will be unable to attain the Way of Naturalness. (*The Original Arising* 2a–b)

Thus, we are told, the teachings of the Daoist religion were written down and expounded specifically so that people could attain a state of mind that is empty of any thoughts and thus endowed with the attribute of naturalness akin to that of the Dao itself. We need guidance in how to properly attain this Naturalness of Empty Nothingness because we are, sad to say, remotely distant from such an ideal condition at present. As for how we got to be the way we are, *The Original Arising* explains:

道未變爲神時 無端無緒 無心無意 都無諸欲 澹泊不動不搖 及變爲神明 神者外其光明 多所照見 使有心意 諸欲因生 更亂本真 或曰思想 不能復還于道 便入五道 無有休息時

> When the Dao was not yet transformed into spirit, it had no source, no origin, no mind and no intention. It had no desires whatsoever. It was placid, unmoving and unwavering. [But] when it changed into spiritual light [the following is what happened]: Spirit emitted its radiance outwardly, [thereby] illuminating and seeing many things. This caused it to have thoughts and intentions, and the various desires arose. When the original authenticity is further disturbed, it is sometimes referred to as "thought." Unable to return to the Dao, it thereby enters the five paths [of *saṃsāra*], and has no moment of respite. (*The Original Arising* 2b)

The text goes on to explain that the "five paths" into which the spirit is degraded include that of celestial deity, human being, beast, hungry ghost, or denizen of purgatory. This is in keeping with the standard Buddhist notion of the "five paths." However, an even profounder and quite unusual degree of Buddhist—more specifically Mahāyāna Buddhist—influence can be seen when the text proceeds to state:

是以賢者學道當曉知虛無自然守虛無者得自然之道不復上天也常在世間變化見死生為世人師守神者能練骨肉形為真人屬天官當飛上天此為中自然也守氣者能含陰陽之氣以生毛羽得飛仙道名曰小自然故神有廣狹知有淺深明有大小

> Hereby, those who are wise, in studying the Dao, should get to know the Naturalness of Empty Nothingness. Those who guard the empty nothingness attain the way of naturalness. They no longer ascend to Heaven. They remain perpetually amidst the world, changing their form

and *showing* (emphasis added) deaths and births, while serving as teachers of the people of the world.

Those who guard the spirit are able to refine their bodies of bone and flesh to become Genuine Persons. They assume posts as heavenly officials and fly up to heaven. This is known as the Intermediate Naturalness.

Those who guard the *qi* are able to contain the *qi* of the *yin* 陰 and *yang* 陽, and can thereby grow fur and feathers, and attain the way of the Flying Transcendents. This is called the Small Naturalness.

Therefore, among the spirits there are the vast and narrow; in knowledge there is the shallow and the deep; in illumination there is the great and the small. (*The Original Arising* 3a)

Presented here is a graded hierarchy of religious attainment where the highest attainment (referred to elsewhere in the text as the Great Naturalness of Empty Nothingness [*da xuwu ziran* 大虛無自然])[13] is that where you altruistically, for the sake of the world, choose not to dwell in heaven (though capable of doing so), but rather to stay in the company of mortals and appear to die and be reborn continuously in different forms. The proper understanding here is probably that you merely "appear" to die and be reborn because you in fact knowingly partake in the life of the universal Dao; also, you are not bound to the dictates of the laws of *karma*, but nevertheless choose to abide in *saṃsāra* in a form of your own choosing. This, according to Mahāyāna doctrine, is precisely what the Buddha is and does. Famously, in the sixteenth chapter ("The Lifespan of the Tathagata" 如來壽量品) of the *Lotus Sūtra* (*Miaofa lianhua jing* 妙法蓮華經 [or *Fahua jing* 法華經]; *Saddharma-pundarika sūtra* in Sanskrit), the Śākyamuni Buddha declares that he (by manifesting what would come to be known as a Transformation Body [*nirmanakaya*; *yingshen* 應身/ *huashen* 化身]) only appears to undergo birth and death, even though he is in fact eternally among us (this eternal, ineffable body is what would come to be known as the Dharma Body [*dharmakaya*; *fashen* 法身]).[14] Here, quite surprisingly, in this Daoist scripture that is *The Original Arising*, this Mahāyāna Buddha-like state is considered a level of attainment higher than that of the Genuine Persons (*zhenren* 真人) who ascend to heaven in a refined immortal body and the Flying Transcendents (*feixian* 飛仙) who possesses immortal life and the power of flight, albeit on the earthly plane.[15]

Now, it should be recalled that *The Western Ascension* (A 2/8b–9b; B 1/16a) posited that the Genuine Spirit can "exist or perish" at will, and led us to speculate that Lord Lao himself was to be regarded as just such a being. The supreme ideal described in *The Original Arising* is similar to this, but is even more compassionate, because you are to choose to remain perpetually in *saṃsāra*, without indulging any whims to leave it. Because the full title of *The Original Arising* would seem to indicate that it is supposed to be a discourse uttered by Lord Lao it is probably meant to be understood that Lord Lao himself is just such a being of supreme compassion. (Oddly, though, there are some places in the text where the *Laozi* is quoted, preceded by the phrase, "Lord Lao said. . . ." Is Lord Lao quoting himself?)

This highest attainment, according to *The Original Arising*, comes about by "guarding" the empty nothingness, which is a condition or entity more pristine than the spirit and the *qi* that are guarded respectively by the Genuine Persons and the Flying Transcendents. You should be mindful of your pristine unity with the Dao that preceded the emergence of your spirit; this way you can reunite with the Dao and partake in its ubiquity. As the text states,

夫守道之法當熟讀諸經還自思惟我身神本從道生道者清靜都無所有...

是故當熟自思此意其神本自清淨無此情欲但思念此意諸欲便自然斷止斷止便垢濁盡索便為清靜便明見道與道合便能聽視無方變化無常

The way to guard the Dao is to thoroughly read the various scriptures and then reflect [as follows]: "My body and spirit originally emerged from the Dao. The Dao is clear and still, and has nothing whatsoever." (*The Original Arising* 3a) . . .

(A description follows here of how the workings of the mind, senses, emotions and desire lead to corruption and entrapment in *saṃsāra*.)

Therefore you should thoroughly contemplate what this means. The spirit is originally clear and pure, and does not have these emotions and desires. If you can just be mindful of what this means, your desires will naturally come to cease. Thereby all your defilements will be eliminated. If all your defilements are eliminated, you will be clear and pure. Thereby you can clearly see the Dao and unite with the Dao. Thereby you will be able to hear and see without limit, and transform without a constant [tangible shape]. (*The Original Arising* 4a)

Thus we are told that if the mind can be made completely clear and pure, the ineffable Dao can somehow be "seen" and "united" with; this is said to endow you with supernatural, limitless powers of perception, as well as the powers to change your physical form and condition at will—hence, perhaps, the ability to "appear to undergo births and deaths" in the same manner as the eternal Buddha or Lord Lao.

*The Original Arising* then proceeds to claim that this awareness of your original state of purity is fundamental and indispensible if you are to have any hope of subduing and overcoming your desires. In doing so it criticizes meditation practitioners of "the school(s) of the outside way(s)" (*waidao jia* 外道家; the author may have Buddhists specifically in mind here, ironic though this is given the fact that *waidao* is the term used in Buddhist literature to denote non-Buddhists) who "do not understand that the human spirit is originally clear and pure, and yet enter into the [meditation] room to try to force themselves to close their ears and eyes and cut off their emotions and desires" 不曉人神本清淨 而反入室 強塞耳目斷情欲 (5b). Such misguided practitioners do not understand that emotions and desires emerge from the mind itself, rather than from external sensory stimuli. Because they are internal, psychic phenomena, their manner of emerging is subtle and intangible ("formless"; *wuxing* 無形), and is virtually unceasing, without any fixed times ("timeless"; *wushi* 無時). To prevent and control them by force is impossible. However, eliminating them is definitely possible if your manner of religious self-cultivation is grounded in a basic awareness of the fact that the mind is originally clear and pure (4b–5b).

*The Original Arising* does maintain that mystical experience cultivated in meditation is instrumental in bringing about a direct awareness of the mind's original purity. However, before discussing this, *The Original Arising* emphasizes that the proper spiritual grounding also requires the careful study of the Daoist scriptures and the performance of good deeds ("the meritorious virtues of doing good" 爲善之功德) (5b–6b). The logic here is that the scriptures provide an accurate rational understanding of the nature of the mind with its feelings and emotions, and the performance of good deeds fosters a humble, unselfish, and righteous disposition that makes you less vulnerable to temptation.

The need for performing good deeds gets explained in more depth further on in *The Original Arising* in an interesting piece of psychological analysis that divides the human psyche into Three Ones that are situated respectively in the center, on the left, and on the right. In the center is the core of your awareness and personality; this One is known as Lord of the Dao (Daojun 道君) or Zidan of the Primal Yang (Yuanyang Zidan 元陽子丹), who is also described as the Noble Person (*guiren* 貴人) or the Divine Person (Shenren 神人). On the left is the One that gets described variously as Heaven (*tian* 天), Sun (*ri* 日), Father (*fu* 父), Yang 陽, Virtue (*de* 得 [understood as corresponding to *de* 德]), Teacher (*shi* 師), and Cloud-Soul (*hun* 魂). The role of this One is to govern (*zuozheng* 作政) you properly. On the right is the One that gets described variously as Earth (*di* 地), Moon (*yue* 月), Mother (*mu* 母), Yin 陰, Body (or Form; *xing* 形), and Demon who Controls Destinies (Siminggui 司命鬼). This spirit is wicked, and is a devil whose role is to carry out evil deeds (7b–8a).

If you understand this tripartite nature of your makeup, and see to it that you—that is, the One in the Center who is also known as "the Child of the Dao" (Daozi 道子)—always follow the directions given to you by the righteous One on the Left, you will become less and less vulnerable to the wicked temptations that are always being provided to you by the One on the Right. If, on the other hand, you do not habitually perform the good deeds recommended to you by the One on the Left, you become susceptible to the wicked suggestions coming from the One on the Right, and thus fall into habitual evil behavior (8a–b). We are somewhat reminded of how in *Contemplating the Baby* you (whose core consciousness at some point comes to be personified as the Baby) are told to entrust yourself to the mentoring of the Genuine Person, and to disregard the verbal approaches and reproaches of the Queen Mother of the West.

Based on this principle, the text then explains why in practicing the Way it is not sufficient to merely understand the Dao without performing good deeds. If you do not perform good deeds you inevitably become "affiliated with the wicked" 屬邪; this causes you to be prone to anger and to deluded outbursts, and to be surrounded by wicked demons and spirits. If, furthermore, in this condition you attempt to practice "calmness" (*jing* 靜; meaning here meditation), wicked demons will certainly incessantly arouse wicked thoughts within you. If, on the other hand, you have performed ample good deeds and have fully entrusted yourself to the guidance of the One on the Left, you cannot be brought to disorder by demonic temptations (8b).

Once the proper grounding in scripture study and habitual good works has been established, you can get down to the business of practicing meditation, or "stillness" (*jing* 靜). The best way of doing this is described as:

其靜守道時當少食正閉耳目還神光明著絳宮絕去諸念不得強有所視思想也久久喘息稍微從是以往不復自覺喘息泊然不自知有身無身從是以往為得定道之門道者虛也當爾之時神在天上虛無中左顧右視但皓然正白中無所見有狀如雨雪時四向樹亦白山亦白地亦白一切都白皆無所見所以者何神出天上前向視不復見日月星宿山川河海如此為復命返道還入虛無也若得是當下視乃見天下諸事便當迴心念師言為道當濟度天下但見是念故便止前所見白更冥神便來還形中不如此者神便入道中散形與道合便為天下骨肉便蹌踕故老君曰知白守黑為天下式見白者為見空守黑者發心下視念天下以有之故便冥是謂守黑為天下式謂神還形中長在天下為人道師是謂大虛無之自然也

When guarding the Dao in silence, eat little food. You should close your eyes and ears and send back the radiance of your spirit, keeping it on your Crimson Palace (heart). Eliminate all your thoughts, and do not force yourself to see or imagine anything. After a long while your breathing will become very faint, and from this point on you will no longer be aware of any breathing. Placidly, you will no longer know whether you have a body or not. What occurs from here constitutes the gateway to obtaining the way of meditative trance. The Dao is the void. At this time your spirit will be amidst the empty nothingness above the heavens. Whether you look left or right, there will only be a blank whiteness, with nothing to be seen. There will be a condition resembling times of wind and rain, when in the four directions [surrounding you] the trees are white, the mountains are white, and the ground is white. Everything is white, and nothing can be seen. Why is this? Your spirit has gone out above the heavens; when you look before you, you no longer see the sun, moon, stars, mountains, rivers and seas. Such as this is to return to one's [original] life and to return to the Dao. [It is to] enter back into the empty nothingness. If you attain this you should look down below. Thereupon you will see the various affairs under the heavens. Thereby you should reflect back on the sayings of your teacher, [who taught you that] in practicing the Dao you must rescue [all the living beings] under the heavens. Only because you bring forth these reflections you then bring to an end what you had been seeing previously. The whiteness will become dark, and your spirit will then return to your body. Otherwise (if you remain in the whiteness), your spirit will enter into the Dao; [you will] scatter your form and merge with the Dao. For the sake of the bodies of bone and flesh under the heavens, [you should] tread carefully. Therefore Lord Lao said, "Know the white but guard the black, and become an example for all under heaven" (*Laozi*, ch. 28). To see the white means to see the empty space. To guard the black means to give rise to a mind that looks down and thinks about [the world] under the heavens. Because there is this (world), one darkens. This is what it means to guard the black and become an example for all under heaven. It refers to when the spirit returns to the body to remain perpetually under the heavens to serve people as a teacher of the Dao. This is what is known as the Naturalness of the Great Empty Nothingness. (*The Original Arising* 9a–10a)

Thus, when undertaking meditation, you need to decrease your food intake. No specific visualizations or incantations are to be employed; you are told simply to inwardly directly your attention toward your heart, clear your mind of all thoughts, and ultimately enter into self-oblivion. You are not told to hold your breath. Rather, the text states that the breathing will naturally become softer and softer as you fade into self-oblivion. Once in self-oblivion, you will no longer be aware of your respiration.

Although it is certainly possible here to surmise that at this point your respiration—and perhaps pulse (?)—goes into a state of suspension, such is not clearly stated.

Then, suddenly, we are told, you find that your spirit has already risen to a place above heaven. Looking around, there is nothing to see other than a bright, blank whiteness—at least not until you look down below and see how far you have come. At this point, you need to awaken your heart of compassion, "darken" the spirit (whatever this means), and return back down to your body. If you continue any further amid this sublime radiance, you will merge eternally with Dao, leaving the unenlightened masses to their misery. It would appear that the understanding here really is that if you do not return down to your body you will undergo physical death while in meditation; note here that the text does suggest that your breathing is severely retarded or suspended, and thus your physical condition already bears a resemblance to that of death.

The purpose of the ascent is clearly neither to attain nor to prepare your way for an eternal life of transcendence, for you are expressly told to opt out of such a thing. Rather, the purpose is to directly witness the source of your spirit, which is the realm of the Empty Nothingness of the Dao. This experience will provide the necessary grounding for your essential awareness of your pure origins, without which you cannot overcome the tyranny of your desires and senses, and cannot serve as a truly helpful guide for sentient beings. From this point on, even though you remain in *saṃsāra*, it is due to your own compassionate will; the mystical ascent, and the insight it bestows, frees you from bondage to the laws of *karma*, and imbues you with the power to abide in the form and existential plane of your choice (which presumably is this very realm of suffering, if you possess the compassion that you should).

While *The Original Arising* thus maintains that out-of-body experience and the celestial ascension of the spirit are valuable for the mystical perspective and insight they confer, but should most ideally not be taken as an avenue toward transcendent bliss, it is nonetheless highly significant that *The Original Arising* cites out-of-body experience and spiritual flight among the effects that can accrue from the sheer cultivation of inner clarity and stillness. This claim is one that is unique among the medieval Daoist data that we have examined so far, and which also anticipates claims of the sort that would come to be made much later within Neidan literature.[16] (Heavenly flight is a prominent theme in Shangqing Daoism, where, however, it is experienced or anticipated largely as a result of intensive visualizations accompanied by invocations.)[17]

At the very end of *The Original Arising* we find some additional instructions pertaining to the meditation method of the Great Naturalness of the Empty Nothingness. These instructions are of a cautionary nature:

夫 爲大虛無之道 得無象無聲教 無思想都無識念之欲 守時亦法 教道 不得取景夢候効也 或時神相見 尚不得與神共語言 所以者 何 或有邪神來試人 此處無象自然 求道不求神也 略小取大 故可 得自然 故老君曰 有光而不曜 謂欲養其光明至於徹視 不欲小電 曜光精 獨與一神相見也 如此不能悉見天下之事矣

> Now, when you practice the Way of the Great Empty Nothingness, you obtain the teaching that is formless and soundless. Because you engage in no thinking, there is no desire that arises from conscious thought. When guarding it you accord with the teaching and the Dao. You must not seize upon visions and dreams to gauge the effects. At times, forms of gods will appear. Yet, you must not converse with the gods. Why is this? It is because there may be [among them] wicked gods who have come to put the person to the test. Hereby reside in the naturalness of formlessness. Seek the Dao; do not seek the gods. Do without what is small and choose what is great. Thereby you can attain Naturalness. Therefore Lord Lao said, "[The sage] has radiance but does not shine" (*Laozi*, ch. 58).[18] What he meant by this was that you want to nurture your radiance to the point where you see [all things] clearly and thoroughly. You do not want [to see] a small flash or spark, and thereby only meet with a single god. If you are like this you will be unable to see all of the affairs under heaven. (*The Original Arising* 15a–b)

This passage starts out by reiterating that in the meditation method of the Great Naturalness you are to foster a state of mind that is utterly free of thoughts and desires, and in which there are no forms seen nor sounds heard; yet, within this there is the most profound insight (pertaining to the Dao and the originally pure mind) to be gained. Incidentally, visions of gods may indeed occur; however, these visions should be disregarded and should certainly not be sought out. The author is concerned here that you might get involved in conversations with the gods, and fears that this is dangerous, because a god that you converse with might in fact be one of a malignant character that is out to tempt and deceive you. Even if the god is not wicked, paying attention to it is not helpful, for it will impede your progress toward the greater, truer goal that is the attainment of omniscience that comes about through the direct encounter with the pristine Dao itself. Gods are but trivial entities, mere flashes and sparks, when compared against the mind of the Dao, the light of which illuminates all things.

*The Original Arising* also provides some discussion and description of the meditation methods of Intermediate Naturalness and Small Naturalness. Before describing the meditation method of the Intermediate Naturalness, the text points out that method's most significant shortcoming:

夫守中自然之法 不能曉知天地人物所從出 不能知道之根源 變化所由緣 不能及不能知 虛空之事 其所見聞心便疑惑 怪之且迥然不知道

When you carry out the method of Intermediate Naturalness, you are unable to understand and know about that from which heaven, earth, people and things emerge. You are unable to know the root and source of the Dao, and the causes by which it transforms. You cannot reach and cannot know of the things of empty, vacant space. Things that you do see and hear cause your mind to give rise to doubts and to be suspicious. Remote indeed are you from knowing the Dao. (*The Original Arising* 10a)

Thus, practicing the method of the Intermediate Naturalness cannot confer the crucial direct experience and understanding of the primordial Dao, without which it is impossible to attain the Dao's capacity for limitless transformation by which you could hope to yourself constantly manifest numerous and diverse incarnations amidst *saṃsāra* for the benefit of all sentient beings. The meditation method of Intermediate Naturalness itself is then described as follows:

當除情欲 閉塞耳目 邊神絳宮 下視崑崙山 或有教令將神升崑崙山 視其上 想見中黃道君 始時想見 久而見之 久久悉見諸神 與

神語言 講說天上事 無復有世俗之念 身中骨腦血日變成萬神盛
強共舉身而上天 受籙署 不得下在人間 此謂真人道也 名曰中虛
無之自然也

You must remove your emotions and desires. Shut and block your ears and eyes, and return your spirit to your Crimson Palace. See Mt. Kunlun below you. Perhaps there are Spirit Generals who Teach and Command ascending to Mt. Kunlun. Look above them and visualize the Dao Lord of the Central Yellow. At first you will be imagining seeing them. After a long while you will see them. After a very long while you will see all the various gods, and will converse with the gods. You will discuss with them the affairs up in heaven, and will no longer have any thoughts of worldly and secular things. The bones, brains and blood in your body will over the days transform into ten thousand gods, who will attain their full strength and will together lift your body and ascend to heaven. There you will receive registers and an official appointment. You will never again get to go down to the midst of humans. This is called the Way of the Genuine Persons. It is called the Naturalness of the Intermediate Empty Nothingness. (*The Original Arising* 10a–b)

The method of Intermediate Naturalness thus first of all requires you to empty the mind of emotions and desires, although strictly speaking this cannot be accomplished with optimal effectiveness and thoroughness unless you already possess an understanding of the Dao and the originally pure nature of consciousness—an understanding that can only come about through the method of the Great Naturalness. Apparently, though, you are to clear out the mind to the extent that such is possible. Then, similarly to what is described in the method of the Great Naturalness, you are to focus your attention on the Crimson Palace—that is, the heart. However, what gets described subsequently is a technique of active imagination. You are to intensively visualize Daoist deities converging on the sacred peak of Mt. Kunlun; intensive visualization is said to eventually make the deities actually appear before you and to enable you to have edifying conversations with them. As we have seen, all of this visualization and divine conversation is precisely what practitioners of the method of Great Spontaneity are told to refrain from. Although these conversations may edify you of celestial things and breed indifference toward worldly things, they still do not amount to the apprehension of the pure consciousness of the Dao itself. In any case, here we are told that further sustained practice of this visualization technique will ultimately result in the divine transformation and immortal ascension of the body into the heavens. Once you receive appointment within the immortal celestial bureaucracy, you are unable to return to the midst of ordinary humans, and thus cannot undertake the supremely compassionate activities of those who attain the Great Naturalness of Empty Nothingness. Thus, while this method of active imagination does bring forth attainments that seem quite lofty indeed by most standards, these attainments fall short of those realized when you engage in the method of the Great Naturalness, in which you engage in no thinking or visualization whatsoever.

The method of the Small Naturalness is described more briefly as follows:

夫守小虛無自然之法 亦當除去情欲 閉塞耳目 還神絳宮 下視崑崙山 和天地日月陰陽雌雄魂魄之精氣以養真人 以吾身陰陽氤凝精骨潤光 便生毛羽 飛上五山 時有奉使 按行民間 亦不得久止也 此謂小虛無自然也

As for guarding the method of the Small Naturalness of Empty Nothingness, you must also remove your emotions and desires. Close your ears and eyes, and return your spirit to your Crimson Palace. Look at Mt. Kunlun down below. Blend the essence and *qi* of heaven and earth, sun and moon, *yin* and *yang*, female and male, and cloud-soul and white-soul to thereby nourish the Genuine Person. Because your body's *yin* and *yang* breaths have congealed their essences and your bones bear a moist luster, you thereby grow fur and feathers and fly up to the five mountains. At the time there will be envoys walking about the midst of the people, and therefore you cannot dwell there long. This is called the Small Naturalness of Empty Nothingness. (*The Original Arising* 10b–11a)

This description is, unfortunately, rather vague. Similarly to the method of the Intermediate Naturalness you are to clear the mind of emotions and desires (to the extent possible) and turn your attention inward toward the heart (Crimson Palace); you are also supposed to somehow "see" (visualize) Mt. Kunlun. What exactly you are to do beyond this is not at all clear, but whatever it is, it effects a melding and blending of the bipolar *yin* and *yang qi* and essence that results in conferring upon you the power of flight. Although you cannot ascend to celestial immortal realms, you can travel at will to the peaks of high mountains. Doing so, among presumably other things, is to enable you to avoid contact with certain "envoys"—perhaps spirit officials of the celestial bureaucracy that record the merits and demerits of humans, and whose actions can conceivably lead to the bringing of limitations to the extent of one's longevity.

*The Original Arising* goes on to state:

夫從此大虛無中虛無小虛無以下 便有爲之法 不及虛無也

Beneath these [methods of] Great Empty Nothingness, Intermediate Empty Nothingness and Small Empty Nothingness, there are the methods that have action, and which do not attain to the Empty Nothingness. (*The Original Arising* 11a)

By implication, then, the three aforementioned meditation methods of the Naturalness of Empty Nothingness are collectively, in contrast to the methods that "have action" (*youwei* 有爲), methods of nonaction (*wuwei* 無爲). They are superior methods by virtue of the fact that they—in the spirit of the ancient enjoinders of the Daoist philosophical classics—abide by the principle that "less is more"—that it is preferable to minimize one's actions, and that this, paradoxically, allows more to be accomplished. As for what the methods that "have action" (*youwei* 有爲) entail, the text states:

夫有爲者 謂曆藏導引動作諸氣 飛丹合藥 吞符跪拜帶印禁忌隨日時王相 醮祭 名號精靈 使人解占候 此謂有爲 不能知道 何所謂也 亦有住年亦有尸解 從此已下 便爲鬼道 非得長生也

By "[methods that] have action" is meant [practices such as the following]: traversing the bodily organs, *daoyin* exercises that mobilize the various *qi*, making the cinnabar fly (alchemy), concocting medicines, swallowing talismans, kneeling and bowing, bearing insignia, observing taboos in conjunction with the ascendancies of days and hours, performing libations and offerings, calling out the names of spirits, having people prognosticate. These are called "[methods that] have action"; by means of them you cannot know the Dao. What do they refer to?

There are people who [by means of these methods that have action] attain Transcendence, or prolong their years, or attain Liberation by the Corpse (posthumous immortality, or immortality after feigning death).[19] Methods that are beneath these are the Ways of the Demons; with them you cannot obtain long life. (*The Original Arising* 11a)

Thus we can see that the "has action" category includes the visualization of the resident gods of the various bodily organs, along with practically every other sort of practice other than meditation that medieval Daoists are known to have practiced as a means of enhancing their well-being. All of these are acknowledged as bearing the potential for facilitating immortality (immediate or posthumous) or longevity; methods of the "demonic" variety do not have this capacity.

However, in the view of *The Original Arising*, while Daoism offers a wide variety of immortality methods that vary in the degree to which they entail action, the greatest of its methods that confers the highest level of attainment is that which entails the least action of them all—the meditation method of the Great Naturalness of Empty Nothingness, in which one simply sits still and does not purposely think of or visualize anything. The text goes on to further explain that when you attain the Way of the Great Naturalness of Empty Nothingness, you affiliate yourself only with "Lord Dao" (Daojun 道君), and not with heaven. Because of this you are able to variously disperse your form to merge with the Dao, transform at will into any shape, be in any place, and see and hear things without any limitations. However, again, reaching this level of attainment also requires that you obey the precepts, perform good deeds, and carry out evangelism. You must also maintain an equitable, magnanimous state of mind that neither covets nor harbors preferences or biases. You must not kill any form of living being; that is, you must maintain a vegetarian diet and refrain from blood sacrifices. This is because even the most seemingly lowly of creatures—such as flying and squirming insects—were given their forms by the Dao; to do harm to them is to do harm to the Dao. Interestingly, the text then mentions that among those who practice the Intermediate Naturalness there are still many who do engage in the taking of life "because they guard intermediate gods/spirits" 爲守中神. The text goes on to further explain,

神有虛無 所以有虛形 故有食有殺生祀祭 道無有故無祭祀不殺生

Gods have empty nothingness, and therefore have forms of emptiness. Therefore there is eating and there is the ritual worship wherein living things are killed. The Dao does not have anything (not even a form of nothingness!); thus for it there is no ritual worship and no killing of living things. (*The Original Arising* 11b)

Essentially, then, adepts of the Great Naturalness do not take life and do not perform sacrificial rituals because they serve and belong to a power (the Dao) more sublime and selfless than any of the gods served by adepts of the Intermediate Naturalness. Thus, while the author of *The Original Arising* does, as we just saw, try to take a conciliatory attitude by acknowledging as legitimate and efficacious the practices of Daoists other than the adepts of the Great Naturalness, he nonetheless leaves us with the sense that a fairly significant rift had developed with the Daoist fold in regard to basic issues of ethics, diet, and ritual praxis.

FIVE

# Integrating Buddhism

*Emptiness and the Twofold Mystery*

In this chapter we examine three texts—*The Original Juncture, The Five Kitchens,* and *The Clarity and Calmness*—that in content pertain greatly or primarily to the cultivation of insight and detachment that both facilitates and is facilitated by serenity. The insight here is grounded on the Mahāyāna Buddhist ontological discourse on Emptiness. Regarding the cultivation of bodily longevity/immortality and related physiological phenomena the three texts seem to have little to say, though more body-related interpretations and applications were conceived for *The Five Kitchens* and *The Clarity and Calmness.*

### THE *BENJI JING* 本際經 (*THE ORIGINAL JUNCTURE*)

*The Original Juncture* (full title, *Taixuan zhenyi benji miaojing* 太玄真一本際妙經; The Great Mystery Wondrous Scripture of the Original Juncture of the Genuine Unity) is a lengthy scripture written around the beginning of the seventh century, which became quite widely read during that century. For some reason, of its original 10 *juan*, only the 2nd and 9th *juan* are found in the *Daoist Canon*, where they appear as separate texts bearing different titles. Two versions of the 2nd *juan* are found in the

*Daoist Canon*. One of them bears the title *Taixuan zhenyi benji miaojing*, and also has the subheading, "Chapter on the Entrustment" (Fuzhu pin 付囑品).¹ The other version, however, bears the title *Yuanshi dongzhen jueyi jing* 元始洞真決疑經 (The Primordial Cavern-Truth Scripture that Resolves Doubts),² and does not bear any subheading suggesting that it was part of a larger work. This reflects the fact that the 2nd *juan* of *The Original Juncture* also circulated under this other title as an individual text by at least the eighth century, as is evident from quotations in other texts of that period (the *Yiqie daojing yinyi miaomen youqi* 一切道經音義妙門由起³ and the *Chuxue ji* 初學記⁴). Aside from the differences in their titles, the *Daoist Canon*'s two versions of the 2nd *juan* of *The Original Juncture* largely match each other in content, although the version entitled *Yuanshi dongzhen jueyi jing* contains some significant textual corruptions and lacunae.⁵ The 9th *juan* of *The Original Juncture* is found in the *Daoist Canon* bearing the title *Taishang dongxuan lingbao kaiyan bimi zang jing* 太上洞玄靈寶開演祕密藏經 (The Most High Cavern-Mystery Numinous Treasure Scripture that Expounds upon the Secret Repository).⁶ It would thus appear likely that it also circulated both as an individual scripture, and as a chapter of *The Original Juncture*.

However, despite its sparse presence in the *Daoist Canon*, almost the entire original text of *The Original Juncture* can be reconstructed from manuscripts recovered from the famous caves of Dunhuang 敦煌. This has been done by Wu Chi-yu 吳其昱 in his *Pen-tsi king: Livre de terme originel*.⁷ From the sheer volume of material that the caves provided Wu for his worthy project we can see how well known and influential *The Original Juncture* was during the seventh century; nearly a quarter of the Daoist manuscripts recovered from Dunhuang were chapters or fragments of *The Original Juncture*.⁸

*The Original Juncture* was apparently written jointly by Liu Jinxi 劉進喜 and Li Zhongqing 李仲卿. Both of these men were Daoist clerics who resided at the Qingxuguan 清虛觀 Daoist Monastery in Chang'an 長安 (Xi'an 西安) and were involved in the highly contentious Buddhist-Daoist debates of the early Tang.⁹ The source that specifically names these two men as the authors of *The Original Juncture* is Xuanyi's 玄嶷 (fl. 684–704) *Zhenzheng lun* 甄正論,¹⁰ a polemical treatise written from the

Buddhist perspective; its author had himself once been a Daoist, but had converted to Buddhism. There we find the following statement:

至如本際五卷 乃是隋道士劉進喜造 道士李仲卿續成十卷 並模寫佛經潛偷罪 搆架因果參亂佛法

> As for the *Benji* [*jing*] (*The Original Juncture*) in five *juan*, this is the creation of the Daoist cleric Liu Jinxi of the Sui period (581–617). The Daoist cleric Li Zhongqing subsequently expanded it into ten *juan*. Both of them imitated Buddhist *sūtras* in order to covertly steal [Buddhist teachings on] transgressions and blessings. They fabricated [tales regarding] cause and effect, thus confusing the Buddha Dharma. (*Zhenzheng lun* 569c)

The fact that *The Original Juncture* would attract the hostile attention of a Buddhist polemicist is further testimony to the fame that the text enjoyed at the time. In any case, just by naming ordinary human authors for *The Original Juncture*, Xuanyi impugns its dignity. *The Original Juncture* and most other Daoist and Buddhist texts that describe themselves as a *jing* 經 (classic; *sūtra*) claim to record the direct authentic teachings of gods, Transcendents or Buddhas. Thus, by naming ordinary human authors, Xuanyi is already calling out the text as a fraud. At the same time Xuanyi criticizes the text for being a mere imitation of Buddhist *sūtras* that co-opts basic Buddhist moral teachings pertaining to cause and effect. This, in his view, "confuses the Buddha Dharma," perhaps because by attributing the revelation of the doctrines to Daoist deities rather than to Śākyamuni Buddha, Liu Jinxi and Li Zhongqing are diverting people's devotion toward the wrong savior, and thus undermining their chances of attaining genuine religious merits through devotion.

In *The Original Juncture* the deity who appears in the role of the preacher varies by chapter. In the 1st, 2nd, and 10th *juan*, the preacher is the Primordial Heavenly Worthy (Yuanshi Tianzun 元始天尊). In the 3rd, 4th, 6th, 7th, and 9th *juan* the preacher is the Most High Lord Dao (Taishang Daojun 太上道君). Both the Primordial Heavenly Worthy and the Most High Lord Dao preach in the 8th *juan*, and in the 5th *juan* alone the preacher is the Most High Lord Lao. This reflects major changes and developments that were occurring in the Daoist pantheon, and which had caused Lord Lao to become relegated to presiding over the realm of Great Purity (Taiqing 太清), a heavenly realm positioned beneath the Most High Lord Dao's realm of Upper Purity (Shangqing 上清), which was in turn beneath the Primordial Heavenly Worthy's realm of Jade Purity (Yuqing 玉清). These developments appear to have primarily been spurred by the Shangqing and Lingbao revelations that had occurred in southern China in the fourth and fifth centuries, and which had glorified previously unknown heavens and deities as sources of revelation. The Shangqing and Lingbao scriptures and the new sort of pantheon inspired by them seems not to have penetrated much into the north until the second half of the sixth century. It was then that Emperor Wu 武帝 (r. 561–578) of the Northern Zhou 北周 dynasty promoted Daoism as a state ideology, and in doing so sponsored a form of Daoism that emphasized the southern scriptures and upheld the pantheon that was based on them.[11]

When one examines the content of *The Original Juncture*, one certainly finds that it draws heavily on Buddhist doctrines on *karma* and *saṃsāra*, and attributes to the Primordial Heavenly Worthy a revelatory and soteriological role resembling that of Śākyamuni as portrayed in Mahāyāna Buddhist *sūtras*. Much of the same can be said about so many other Daoist scriptures that emerged from the early fifth century onward, starting with the Lingbao scriptures. The very format of these texts, in which the Primordial Heavenly Worthy (or some other lofty deity) sits before a large audience of deities and worthies in some splendid venue, responding to questions by figures such as the Most High Lord Dao or Zhang Daoling 張道陵—whose interlocutory role parallels that of major disciples and Bodhisattvas in the Mahāyāna sutras—seems to be inspired by that of Buddhist *sūtras*. This being the case, one may wonder why *The Original Juncture*, among the great multitude of Daoist scriptures of this genre, attracted so much attention in its day.

*The Original Juncture* can in fact be said to be of unique importance for a number of reasons. First of all, as has been pointed out by Frederike Assandri, it "is one of the first texts to present mature Twofold Mystery teaching."[12] "Twofold Mystery" (Chongxuan 重玄), as we discuss further on, refers to a certain mode of philosophical discourse that became popular in the seventh century, and was based simultaneously on

Mahāyāna Buddhist Mādhyamika philosophy and the *Laozi*. Whereas the other main early texts featuring Twofold Mystery discourse are commentaries to the *Laozi*, *The Original Juncture* presents Twofold Mystery discourse as revelations by celestial deities, proclaimed in wondrous and vivid settings alongside other pronouncements involving a wider range of religious concerns. Assandri also points out that *The Original Juncture*, unlike some other medieval Daoist scriptures, was not an esoteric text meant for internal circulation among initiates, but was rather an exoteric scripture meant for widespread proselytizing—certainly another factor that would have contributed to its fame and influence.[13]

As we shall see in our discussion, *The Original Juncture* sets forth lucidly and cogently doctrines—highly Buddhistic, no doubt—that constituted significant innovations in Daoist cosmology, soteriology, and praxis. These teachings on cosmology and soteriology, as we shall see, follow along similar lines with what is articulated in *The Original Arising*, but are formulated around a theory regarding the nature and role of the Primordial Heavenly Worthy. The teachings on praxis revolve around the themes of devotion, along with the cultivation of correct insight based on mental clarity—thus, the relevance of *The Original Juncture* for our study.

In the 2nd *juan* of *The Original Juncture*, the Primordial Heavenly Worthy declares to an assembly of gods and worthies, "I shall now return my spirit and revert to the place of perpetual stillness in the calmness of non-action" 今當反神還乎无爲湛寂常恒不動之處 (*The Original Juncture*[*14] 1b; Wu 1960, 23). Upon leaving, he entrusts the care and guidance of the faithful to his disciple, the Most High Lord Dao. But before he can depart, he has much that he needs to tell his distraught audience. In order to reassure them, the Primordial Heavenly Worthy proclaims as follows, regarding his own eternal nature and role as a savior:

元始天尊抗手告眾 汝等當知 我之真身清淨无礙 猶如虛空 不生不滅 常住善寂 大智慧源 雖復窈冥 其精甚信 无量劫來 證此真體 恒安不動 超絕无倫 非聖所知 非凡所解 爲眾生故 應見受身 遊入五道 稱緣開度 隨宜方便 皆使悟入 應物根性 權示色相 故名應身 而此應身 亦无生滅 无有去來 常住不變 爲利一切 隱顯不同

The Primordial Heavenly Worthy raised his hand and proclaimed to the audience, "You must know that my True Body is clear and pure, and without obstruction. It is like empty space. Never born and never dying, it perpetually abides in blissful calm. It is the source of great wisdom. Although it reverts to darkness and obscurity, its essence is very much to be trusted. Over countless *kalpas* I have apprehended this true substance and have been in perpetual, unwavering peace. Remotely transcendent and without peer, I [in my True Body] am not known by the sages, and am not understood by ordinary people. For the sake of sentient beings, I manifest myself by taking on a [visible] body. I wander into the five paths (the realms of gods, humans, beasts, hungry ghosts and hell denizens) to proclaim [teaching regarding karmic] causes and thus open the way to deliverance. Accordingly employing skilful means, I make all of them enter into enlightenment. Responding to mental capacities of creatures, I expediently show them a form. Thus it is called the 'Body of Response.' Furthermore, this body of response is also without birth and death. It neither goes nor comes; it abides perpetually without changing. In order to bring benefit to all, it hides and manifests variously." (*The Original Juncture\** 16b; Wu 1960, 30)

Here, from the mouth of the Primordial Heavenly Worthy, *The Original Juncture* articulates in its own Daoist religious terms the doctrine that constitutes the core revelation of that most influential of all Mahāyāna scriptures—the *Lotus Sūtra*. As mentioned in the last chapter, the key moment in the *Lotus Sūtra* occurs when Śākyamuni Buddha, in response to his baffled disciples who have just seen millions of Bodhisattvas emerge from the earth, reveals that he in fact attained Buddha-hood countless *kalpas* (an inconceivably, virtually limitlessly long time) ago; he never dies and is never reborn—he only makes it seem as though he undergoes births and deaths. Though eternally present, he does not allow ordinary people and creatures to see his eternal form for fear that they might become complacent. However, people "who practice meritorious ways, who are gentle, peaceful, honest and upright," can see Śākyamuni "in person, preaching the Law."[15] Similarly here in *The Original Juncture*, the Primordial Heavenly Worthy reveals that he is an eternal being that is forever present, but whose "True Body" (*zhenshen* 真身) is not visible to the eyes of ordinary sentient beings. However, for their sake he also eternally possesses a "Body of Response" (*yingshen* 應身; *nirmanakaya* in Sanskrit) that can appear before them in the various realms of *saṃsāra* to guide them in the most appropriate, effective way possible. *The Original*

*Arising*, as we have seen, without ever mentioning the Primordial Heavenly Worthy, ascribes this sort of astounding capacity to any Daoist adept who can successfully practice the Way of the Great Naturalness of the Empty Nothingness.

The Primordial Heavenly Worthy's True Body, as he describes it, is like empty space, in that it is "clear and pure" (*qingjing* 清淨; a homophone of *qingjing* 清靜 [clear and calm; serene] that is often used interchangeably with it) and "without obstruction" (*wuai* 无礙)—that is, without any false distinctions or attachments that hinder a clear apprehension of reality as it is. Because it is so utterly clear and pure, it is the source of great wisdom. In the phrase, "although it reverts to darkness and obscurity, its essence is very much to be trusted," the Primordial Heavenly Worthy does use terminology that is specifically Daoist. This is an allusion to the twenty-first chapter of the *Laozi*, where, in describing the Dao, it states rather cryptically, "Obscure! Dark! Within it there is an essence. That essence is very genuine, and within it there is trust" 窈兮冥兮其中有精 其精甚真 其中有信 (2/4b). The gist of the passage would seem to be that while the Dao itself is imperceptible, it contains the latent force—described as "essence"—that brings about all creation and natural phenomena; in the natural phenomena brought about by this force one can find trustworthy evidence that the Dao is indeed very real. Here in *The Original Juncture* the Primordial Heavenly Worthy perhaps means to say that although he will now revert to his True Body and conceal his countenance from the eyes of sentient beings, he continues to possess and manifest the power that bears testimony to his Truth. In the much later Quanzhen Neidan tradition, this essence would come to be understood as denoting a latent vital force that becomes activated within one's own person amid the depths of serenity in meditation.[16] Whether such an internalized, psychophysiological interpretation would have occurred to the minds of the author(s) of *The Original Juncture* is uncertain.

In any case, the Primordial Heavenly Worthy's invisible True Body can be said to be equivalent to the eternal Dao, or, in Buddhist terms, to the Dharma Body (*fashen* 法身; *dharmakāya* in Sanskrit). The ability to somehow, in a higher state of consciousness transcending the rational intellect, apprehend this True Body, is what enables the Primordial Heavenly Worthy to reside in total peace; here he declares that he has in fact possessed this total peace wrought through transcendent apprehension "for countless *kalpas*." A further implication here is that ordinary mortals, if they can similarly apprehend the True Body/Dao/Dharma Body, can also attain the eternal life and wondrous powers of the Primordial Heavenly Worthy.

Leaving aside for now the matter of directly apprehending the Dharma Body and becoming like the Primordial Heavenly Worthy, how can one go about gaining the opportunity to gaze upon the Primordial Heavenly Worthy's Body of Response, and receiving blessings through his active, compassionate power? Regarding this matter, the Primordial Heavenly Worthy offers the following explanation:

我今昇玄入妙 汝等肉眼不見我真實之身 謂言滅盡 但修正觀 自當見我 與今无異 若於空相 未能明審 猶憑圖像 係錄其心 當鑄紫金 寫我真相 禮拜供養如對真形 想念丹禱 功德齊等

I will now ascend to the mysterious and enter the wondrous. You with your eyes of flesh cannot see my actual body, and will thus say that I have become extinct. Only if you practice correct insight can you see me no differently as you do now. If you cannot clearly make it out in its form in Emptiness, you can still rely on pictures and statues to record it in your minds. You should cast and depict my true form in purple and gold. Worship and make offerings as though facing my true form. Whether you visualize my true form or pray sincerely [to a statue or picture], the merit gained is the same. (*The Original Juncture** 3a; Wu 1960, 24])

Thus, for his anxious audience that is about to witness his departure, the Primordial Heavenly Worthy recommends from here on either cultivating "correct insight" (*zhengguan* 正觀) or worshipping an image (painted or sculpted) of his visible body. As we discuss in more detail shortly, correct insight refers to the wisdom that views things properly in a manner most conducive to inner purity. This wisdom and purity can enable you to obtain a vivid, concrete vision of the Primordial Heavenly Worthy's Body of Response, identical to the countenance with which he spoke while still in the midst of the holy assembly. This vision is not attainable to most people, however, because the requisite wisdom and mental purity is a highly elusive thing. However, even though you may lack in the capacity for such sublime spiritual attainment, you have nothing to fear. Somewhat surprisingly, perhaps, the Primordial Heavenly Worthy declares that the simple pious act of praying toward a painting or statue of him grants an equal degree of merit and blessing. Such is the wondrous compassion of the Primordial Heavenly Worthy. Here again, in how it grandly—seemingly even extravagantly—extols the merits of a most simple act of piety, *The Original Juncture* can be said to resemble the *Lotus Sūtra*, which promises the greatest of blessings and attainments to those who simply revere the *sūtra*.

Further on in the 2nd *juan* of *The Original Juncture* we find the Primordial Heavenly Worthy giving instructions on two ways of "contemplating the Dao":

> 夫念道者 道能制滅一切惡根 猶金剛刀 无所不斷 猶如猛火 无所不燒 念有二種 一念生身七十二相八十一好 具足微妙 人中天上 三界特尊 是我歸依覆護之處 一念法身猶如虛空圓滿清淨 即是真道 亦名道身 亦名道性 常以正念 不間餘心 是名念道

> In regard to contemplating the Dao: The Dao can subdue and eliminate all the roots of evil. Like a diamond sword, it has nothing that it cannot sever. Like a ferocious fire, there is nothing that it does not burn. In its contemplation there are two types. One is to contemplate the living body that is subtle and wondrous, complete with the 72 marks and 81 signs. It is uniquely revered among humans and up in the heavens. It is one's place of refuge and cover. One [other type of contemplation] is to contemplate the Dharma Body that is like empty space that is complete and pervasive and is clear and pure. This is the True Dao that is also called "the Dao Body," and also called the "Dao Nature." Always contemplate it properly without extraneous thoughts; this is what is called "contemplating the Dao." (*The Original Juncture*\* 15b; Wu 1960, 29)

The purpose of contemplating the Dao is to purge the mind of all deluded thoughts and emotions that form the causes of evil actions. The idea conveyed here is that if you intently contemplate the Dao, the Dao will exercise its power on you to swiftly remove the impurities from your mind.

The first of the two methods recommended for contemplating the Dao is the visualization of the Primordial Heavenly Worthy's glorious

Body of Response, adorned with all of its extraordinary physical features (marks [*xiang* 相] and signs [好]) that distinguish him above any other living being anywhere. This method, then, is clearly one of active imagination, and can be said to be similar to the various indigenous medieval Daoist methods of visualizing deities inside and outside the body. However, this particular method of visualization is clearly one that draws its inspiration from Buddhism. The visualization of a Buddha's (be it Śākyamuni, Amitābha, or some other) glorious body with its 32 marks and 80 signs (here the Primordial Heavenly Worthy is given forty additional marks!), in the hope of generating a vision or gaining the Buddha's blessing or empowerment, is a well-known practice in Buddhism.[17]

The second recommended method for contemplating the Dao involves imagining no tangible forms of any kind; yet, it would ultimately have to be categorized as a method of active imagination, rather than passive observation. What one actively imagines is, oddly, something that is formless and intangible. (As may be recalled [see chapter 2], techniques similar in this regard are described in the Taiping Group texts.) How this is even possible, the text does not even state, although one would imagine that you would need to begin by removing from your mind all sensible, tangible things of the world. Whatever the case, it should be pointed out that the Primordial Heavenly Worthy here, in speaking of his invisible True Body, refers to it specifically by the standard Buddhist term, Dharma Body. The Primordial Heavenly Worthy also states that this body of his is equivalent to the Dao, and can be alternatively referred to as the Dao Body or Dao Nature.

As it turns out, actually, all sentient beings—unknowingly in most cases—partake of this very same eternal body and life. In the 4th *juan* of *The Original Juncture* we find the following statements uttered from the mouths of a holy assembly:

衆生根本相 畢竟如虛空 道性衆生性 皆與自然同 忘相入生死 夢幻无始終 隨倒淪五道 漂流轉未窮 明師勝善友 開示教愚蒙 發生大道意 正觀啓六通

... The original basic countenance of sentient beings,
Is ultimately the same as empty space.
The Dao Nature is the nature of sentient beings.

All are identical to the naturalness [of the Dao].
Forgetting their [original] countenance, they entered life and death.
The dreams and mirages are without beginning and end.
Respectively they fall and sink into the Five Roads.
They drift and rotate endlessly.
A bright master is better than a good friend.
He opens up and reveals the teachings to the ignorant.
[The ignorant] give rise to the mind of the great Dao,
And through correct insight open the Six Penetrations (*liutong*).[18] (Wu 1960, 101)

Here it is proclaimed that all sentient beings in fact possess an "original basic countenance" (*genbenxiang* 根本相) that is "like empty space" (*ru xukong* 如虛空), and which by forgetting about, they have fallen into *saṃsāra*. The Primordial Heavenly Worthy, we shall recall, possesses a True Body, which by apprehending he is able to possess eternal life and wondrous power. It would appear indeed that this original countenance of sentient beings is identical to the True Body of the Primordial Heavenly Worthy; after all, the Primordial Heavenly Worthy's True Body is also called the Dao Nature, and here we are told that the Dao Nature is the nature of sentient beings. When sentient beings had not yet forgotten about their original countenance or True Body that they share in common, they were in perfect accordance with the spontaneous workings of the Dao that underlies the natural world. What sentient beings now need to do is find a good teacher and undertake the effort of attaining "correct insight" (*zhengguan* 正觀); this will ultimately enable them to attain wondrous powers of the sort wielded by the Primordial Heavenly Worthy; here these powers are designated by the standard Buddhist term (Six Penetrations [*liutong* 六通]) used to denote the full range of supernormal powers gained by those who attain the enlightenment of *nirvāṇa*.

As for what this correct insight is, and how one might go about attaining it, an explanation is offered from the mouth of the Genuine Man of the Great Ultimate (Taiji Zhenren 太極真人) in the 8th *juan* of *The Original Juncture*:

太極真人曰 正觀之人 前空諸有 於有无着 次遣於空 空心亦淨 乃曰兼忘 而有既遣 遣空有 故心未能淨 有對治 故所言玄者 四方无

着乃盡玄義 如是行者 於空於有 无所滯着 名之為玄 又遣此玄 都无所得 故名重玄 眾妙之門

The Genuine Man of the Great Ultimate said, "People of proper insight first regard all being as Empty, and thus have no attachment to being. Then they abandon Emptiness, and the mind of Emptiness is also purified. This is called Twofold Forgetfulness. Once you have discarded being, you should discard Emptiness and being. Therefore when the mind is not pure, there is a [way to] remedy it. Therefore what is called the 'mystery' refers to when one has no attachments in all four directions. This exhausts the meaning of the 'mystery.' In this way the practitioner has no attachments to Emptiness or to being. This is what is called the 'mystery.' Furthermore, [one] discards this 'mystery' and has nothing whatsoever to obtain (transcends the dichotomy of subject and object). Therefore this is called the Twofold Mystery, the Gate of all Wonders." (Wu 1960, 164)

In other words, to possess the correct insight means to have a mind that is pure. This can be brought about by first recognizing that all things and concepts lack inherent existence (are Empty [*kong* 空; *śūnyatā* in Sanskrit]) and are not worthy of attachment; all things depend on certain conditions for their origination and perpetuation, and are thus fleeting and impermanent; all concepts and value judgments are formed out of a mind that is limited to its own capacity and viewpoint, and thus are only valid within the framework of those limitations. While thus seeing all as Empty is a great help in enabling you to detach from things and concepts, it can also breed yet another harmful, egotistical attachment—namely, attachment to the concept of Emptiness and to the detachment that it brings. One danger here is that you will fall into the notion that you somehow gain or attain something of a transcendent nature through your detachment from things; yet this is false, for you yourself are also Empty, and there is no transcendent anything anywhere that has inherent existence. Another danger is that you will fail to recognize that all things and concepts, despite lacking inherent existence, do hold a provisional existence that is valid temporarily under the requisite conditions or within the limitations of a particular cognitive framework. Inability to recognize this provisional existence that intertwines inextricably with their lack of inherent existence causes you to be unable to skillfully and compassionately respond to the needs of sentient beings (including your own provisional "self") who suffer in a way that is all too real to them. For example, out of preoccupation with the notion that all concepts and value judgments are relative, one may fail to recognize that the moral precepts taught within the religion are, within the conditions common to most humans, valid and necessary for remedying the cognitive and behavioral patterns that cause and perpetuate our suffering. All of this is essential Mahāyāna Buddhist Mādhyamika (Middle Way) philosophy.[19]

However, *The Original Juncture* gives a Daoist complexion to this philosophy by saying that the detachment from both being and emptiness is "the mystery" (*xuan* 玄), and that the detachment from this very detachment is the Twofold Mystery (*chongxuan* 重玄). This is an allusion to the end of the first chapter of the *Laozi* that reads, "the mystery of mysteries, the gate of all marvels" 玄之又玄 眾妙之門 (1/2a). To allude to the *Laozi* in this manner is to imply that the Mahāyāna Mādhyamika philosophy as just described is what the author(s) of that ancient Daoist classic had in mind. *The Original Juncture*, in thus employing Mādhyamika philosophy and linking it with the *Laozi*, goes along with a mode of philosophical discourse that can be identified in a significant number of Daoist texts of the Sui and early Tang periods, and has caused some modern scholars to speak of a "Chongxuan Faction."[20]

In sum, *The Original Juncture* holds a significant place in the evolution of Daoist methods for fostering serenity because it incorporates and compellingly articulates key concepts that pertain to the pristine, transpersonal nature of the mind, and also proposes several approaches by which one can go about fostering optimal serenity and reclaiming one's rightful participation in the eternal life of the Dao—or the Primordial Heavenly Worthy's Dharma Body. Having said this, it should also be noted that none of the contemplative techniques proposed in *The Original Juncture* can be said to be passive in the strict sense; the methods rather consist of active imagination (though the object of imagination may be a formless one), and the cultivation of insights (Emptiness, the Twofold Mystery) that foster calm detachment.

One should also note that undoubtedly due in large part to Buddhist influence, the doctrines and practices described in *The Original Juncture* are lopsidedly metaphysical and psychological. Matters pertaining to human physiology and longevity hardly enter into the discussion at all. Indeed, one begins to wonder whether *The Original Juncture*, despite its adoration of the Primordial Heavenly Worthy and its allusions to the *Laozi*, is little more than a Buddhist text in disguise, and whether the Daoist religion was relinquishing most or all of what substantively distinguished it from Buddhism. As we shall see, there emerged Daoists who bemoaned this very problem, and thus worked effectively to reestablish the quintessential Daoist emphasis on the body and its inextricable link to the mind. Nonetheless, the key Mahāyāna Buddhist themes borrowed and set forth in *The Original Juncture* would subsequently remain as an important part of the Daoist worldview.

## THE *WUCHU JING* 五廚經 (*THE FIVE KITCHENS*)

*The Five Kitchens* (*Wuchu jing* 五廚經; Scripture of the Five Kitchens) is a Tang period text ascribed to Laozi, which is preserved in the *Daoist Canon* in two slightly varying versions accompanied by a preface (bearing the date of 735 in one of the versions) and commentary by the prominent Daoist abbot Yin Yin 尹愔 (these two versions shall subsequently be referred to as versions A[21] and B[22]). The scripture's short main text in twenty verses, along with the preface and commentary by Yin Yin 尹愔, has been fully translated by Livia Kohn.[23] The main text of *The Five Kitchens* can also be found quoted in full in the version of Sima Chengzhen's *Fuqi jingyi lun* 服氣精義論 (Treatise on the Subtle Meanings of the Imbibing of Energy) contained in the *Yunji qiqian*.[24] There its twenty verses, which are divided into five sets of four verses each, are referred to by the alternative title *Wuling xindan zhang* 五靈心丹章 (Chapter of the Five Holy Heart Elixirs), and are accompanied by a description of a method by which you can recite the verses in a manner that can variously enable you to harmonize your *qi*, satisfy your hunger, cool yourself off, warm yourself up and quench your thirst.[25] The twenty verses of *The Five Kitchens* can also be found incorporated into an eighth-century Buddhist scripture entitled *Foshuo sanchu jing* 佛說三廚經 (*The Scripture of the Three Kitchens Preached by the Buddha*).[26] There the verses are embedded within a much more elaborate description of a technique of recitation and visualization—allegedly preached by Śākyamuni Buddha—by which you are supposed to be able to overcome hunger.[27] In his well-known collection of Daoist miracle stories, the *Daojiao lingyan ji* 道教靈驗記 (Record of Daoist Miracles), the eminent late Tang Daoist cleric Du Guangting 杜光庭 (850–933) tells the story of how a Buddhist monk named Xingduan 行端 plagiarized *The Five Kitchens* to produce this text, and then received his bloody and fatal comeuppance at the hands of a Divine Person (*shenren* 神人).[28] This fascinating Buddhist apocrypha and the controversy surrounding it and *The Five Kitchens* have been discussed masterfully by Christine Mollier.[29]

Yin Yin's commentary to *The Five Kitchens* starts off by glossing the scripture's title with the following statement:

夫存一炁和泰和 則五藏充滿五神靜正 五藏充則滋味足 五神靜則嗜欲除 此經是五藏之所取給 如求食於厨 故云五厨爾

If you can preserve the harmony of the *qi* of the One [that brings about] peaceful harmony, your five viscera will be completely full and your five spirits will be calm and rectified. If the five viscera are full, flavors will be sufficient. If the five spirits are calm, your cravings will be eliminated. This scripture is what is taken and supplied by (or to?) the five viscera, in the manner in which one seeks food in a kitchen. Thus [this scripture] is called the "five kitchens." (A 1a; B 6b [i.e., *Yunji qiqian* 61/6b])

What Yin Yin alludes to in the first sentence here is the first five-character line of the main text of *The Five Kitchens*, which reads, "If the *qi* of the One is harmonious, there is peaceful harmony" 一氣和泰和. The "*qi* of the One" (*yiqi* 一氣/一炁) is probably to be understood as meaning the pristine, undivided cosmic *qi* of the Dao that creates and sustains all; this, later on in the text gets contrasted favorably to the *qi* that you acquire through eating (*zhushiqi* 諸食氣). By simply maintaining this peaceful harmony that somehow comes from the harmony of the one *qi*, Yin Yin assures us, you will need no more "flavors" (*ziwei* 滋味), and you will have no more cravings. This, he explains, is because the five viscera (liver, heart, spleen, lungs, and kidneys) become full, and the spirits residing in each of them become calm. An important question here is what Yin Yin specifically means by flavors. Does he mean food of any and all sorts, or does he just mean food of the particularly tasty, fancy variety? In saying that "flavors are sufficient," does Yin Yin mean to say that you no longer crave tasty foods and can settle for bland fare, or does he mean that you are sufficiently satiated and nourished without taking in any food at all? The fact that he ascribes this "sufficiency of flavors" to the "fullness" of the five viscera would seem to suggest that he has in mind more of the physical quantity of nutrition required by body. One might further deduce, then, that in speaking of the calming of the five visceral spirits and the elimination of "cravings" (*shiyu* 嗜欲), Yin Yin has in mind primarily the mental craving for food. It is also possible, however, that the cravings that Yin Yin refers to here are those of the senses more generally, and perhaps more specifically, those of the sexual variety. In other words, it is also possible that Yin Yin saw the teachings of *The Five Kitchens* as being conducive to the reduction and elimination of desires and attachments more generally, rather than as a way of subduing hunger specifically. However, it is certainly beyond doubt that *The Five Kitchens* was a text favored and employed by adepts (Daoist and Buddhist) undertaking intensive fasting.

Interestingly, Du Guangting, in his aforementioned account regarding the Buddhist plagiarism of the *Wuchu jing*, briefly quotes "Yin Yin's commentary" 尹愔注:

蓋五神之祕言 五藏之真氣 持之百遍 則五氣自和 可以不食

[The verses of *The Five Kitchens*] are the secret sayings of the five spirits and the genuine *qi* of the five viscera. If you can hold them 100 times, the five *qi* will naturally be harmonious, and you can do without eating. (*Daojiao lingyan ji* 12/2b)

This passage is not to be found in either version of Yin Yin's commentary preserved in the Daoist Canon. Du Guangting either had access to a different or longer version of Yin Yin's commentary to *The Five Kitchens*, or he was quoting imprecisely from memory, while unintentionally adding some of his own interpretation in the process. In fact, one is even led to suspect that he may be citing—very loosely—the very same gloss to the scripture's title by Yin Yin (from *The Five Kitchens* A and B) that we just reviewed. By quoting Yin Yin as saying that the five sets of verses constituting *The Five Kitchens* "are the secret sayings of the five spirits and the genuine *qi* of the five viscera," Du Guangting seems to help us better understand Yin Yin's rather ambiguous statement (in versions A and B), "this scripture is what is taken and supplied by (or to?) the five viscera." The idea seems to be that the twenty verses in five sets were revealed to Laozi by the spirits of his five viscera, and that the verses, when recited or contemplated, somehow divinely embody the visceral *qi* and/or serve to supplement them. To "hold" (*chi* 持) the verses probably means to recite them vocally or mentally; doing so 100 times enables one to withstand hunger and survive without food, according to "Yin Yin's commentary" as quoted by Du Guangting.

Considering the immense stature of Du Guangting within Tang Daoist circles, there is little reason to doubt that his view regarding *The Five Kitchens* as a text to be recited or contemplated for the overcoming of hunger was a standard one among his Daoist contemporaries. It is also highly possible that both Yin Yin himself and the author of the twenty verses of *The Five Kitchens* would have approved of this means and purpose for employing *The Five Kitchens*. In medieval Daoist religion, techniques for subduing hunger and radically decreasing the volume of one's food intake were various and numerous; doing so was widely thought to be conducive to transforming the body and becoming immortal. Prominent among such methods were those that sought to nourish and transform the body with the subtle energies of the five directions and/or the five viscera—the so-called five sprouts (*wuya* 五芽/五牙). Such methods could entail visualizations (of the five directional heavens, of the five viscera, and of the five-color directional/visceral energies), recitations and the swallowing of saliva or air. Given this fact, one might fully expect to find in *The Five Kitchens* and in Yin Yin's commentary an exposition of such techniques and theories.[30]

Curiously, though, when one examines the main text of *The Five Kitchens* itself, along with the remainder of the full commentary of Yin Yin, there is no explicit mention of recitation, nor of fasting, nor—for that matter—of the five viscera. Of the two versions, only version B divides the main text's twenty five-character-line verses into five sets and assigns them respectively to the five directions (which would correlate to the five viscera and might imply some location or direction to which one should face or direct one's concentration). The actual teaching to be found throughout *The Five Kitchens* (versions A and B) pertains entirely to the fostering and maintenance of a clear, calm, utterly detached mental state, and to the harmony of the *qi* of the One that accompanies it. Yin Yin's commentary sticks faithfully to these themes, while simultaneously quoting passages from the *Laozi* and employing Buddhist terminology for illumination.

Though the state attained when preserving the *qi* of the One is one of peaceful harmony, the main text of *The Five Kitchens* also states, "It is harmonious, yet not a single thing is harmonious" 和乃無一和 (A 1b; B, 7b). What this means, as Yin Yin explains, is that when you are in the state of peaceful harmony you eventually progress to where you have moved beyond any awareness of or attachment to the *qi* of the One or to the harmony.[31]

Further on, the main text makes statements such as the following:

不以意思意 亦不求無思 意而無有意

Do not intentionally think or intend, but also do not seek to not think. Be conscious, but do not have thoughts. (A 2a–b; B 7b–8a)

莫將心緣心 還莫住絕緣 心在莫存心

Do not use your mind to bind the mind with [karmic] connections; but do not abide in the severing of [karmic] connections. The mind is there, but do not preserve the mind. (A 3a–4a; B 8b–9a)

The gist of such statements is along the lines of the doctrine of the Twofold Mystery. The essential idea here is that you must eliminate thoughts, feelings, and desires, and then proceed to let go of the endeavor to eliminate thoughts, feelings, and desires.

The fifth and final set of verses of the main text of *The Five Kitchens* reads as follows:

諸食氣結氣 非諸久定結 氣歸諸本氣 隨取當隨洩

The *qi* that you eat congeals its *qi*, but does not hereby stay congealed for long. *Qi* returns to its original *qi*; as you take, you shall consequently leak. (A 5a–6a; B 10a–b)

Finally, here the text does bring up the topic of eating. It is stating matter-of-factly that the nourishment that we take in through eating does not nourish and sustain us permanently. Our physical bodies consist of matter and energy that is consumed and incorporated, only to be abandoned and to dissipate after a while. Although this passage perhaps could be read as an endorsement of fasting (food cannot sustain you permanently anyway, so who needs it?), it seems to work better as an articulation of the very Buddhistic insight that the body is impermanent and devoid of any intrinsic, independent essence that can be deemed as a "self," and is thus not worth being attached to.

In his commentary to this final section Yin Yin starts out by stating that when the *qi* of the One congeals within to bring about peaceful harmony, your "wisdom shines in constant tranquility" 慧照常湛 (A 5a–b; B 10a). He then states:

今（令）口納滋味 以充五藏 身聚泡沫 以載其形 生者受骸於地 凝濕於水 稟熱於火 持息於風 四緣結漏 皆非妙質 故淄（緇）涅 一氣 昏汩泰和 令生想受識動之弊穢矣[32]

Now your mouth takes in flavors and thereby fills the five viscera. The body assembles like a soap bubble, and with it carries its form.[33] When you are born, you receive your bones from the earth; you form your moisture from water; you are endowed with heat from fire; and possess breath from wind. The four causes congeal and leak; none of them are wondrous substances. Therefore they pollute the *qi* of the One and drown away the peaceful harmony. They make you give rise to the evil defilements of thoughts, feelings, consciousness and movement.[34] (A 5b; B 10a)

Here Yin Yin is lamenting the condition of the human body, which depends on food for nourishment, and is as fragile and fleeting as a soap bubble.[35] The body is formed of the material elements (earth, water, wind, and fire),[36] which inherently lack the "marvelous" quality of the *qi* of the

One and the luminous wisdom consciousness. Sadly, these marvelous entities, dwelling in the body as they are, are at constant risk of pollution and corruption at the hands of the material elements.

Further on, Yin Yin states:

慧照湛常 一無所有 則出入無間矣 不（一）者 則食氣歸諸四緣 業成淪於六趣[37]

If your wisdom illuminates tranquilly and constantly, you will not claim possession of a single thing, and you will freely go in and out of the space of non-being. If not,[38] then the *qi* that you eat will return to the four causes (earth, water, fire and wind). *Karma* will be generated and you will sink into one of the six destinations [of *saṃsāra*] (purgatory, hungry ghost, beast, human, *asura*, *deva*).[39] (A 6a; B 10b)

Here Yin Yin extols the mind of luminous wisdom that is utterly unattached to anything, and which freely participates in the realm of transcendent, eternal nonbeing. He then warns that if one does not attain this level of higher consciousness, the physical body composed of the material energy procured from food will die and return to the elements; furthermore, the *karma* generated by the unenlightened mind will cause yet another blighted body to take form within one of the realms of *saṃsāra*.

In sum, it can be said that the main text of *The Five Kitchens* simply enjoins the maintenance of inner calmness and harmony, which entails keeping the "single *qi*" harmonious and simultaneously involves the elimination of all desires and attachments—including even the desire to eliminate desire, and the attachment to detachment. It concludes with the observation that the body is a mere composite of fleeting *qi* accumulated through eating—implying thus that it does not merit attachment. Yin Yin's commentary extols the luminous, transcendent wisdom that results from the calmness, harmony, and detachment, and which brings about liberation from *saṃsāra*. It is only in his gloss to the scripture's title that he appears to (most likely) specifically mention the overcoming of hunger as a benefit to be obtained from the maintenance of the harmony of the *qi* of the One. But if the *qi* of the One is able to eliminate the body's need for food, is it perhaps able also to prevent its dissolution back into the four elements and confer upon it great longevity or even immortality? It would not be surprising to see such a claim upheld by Yin Yin; yet, he never explicitly makes such a claim in his commentary to *The Five Kitchens*.

### THE *QINGJING JING* 清靜經 (*THE CLARITY AND CALMNESS*)

Among the medieval texts attributed to Lord Lao extolling the virtues and benefits of serenity, the one that has enjoyed the greatest, longest-lasting influence and popularity has probably been *The Clarity and Calmness* (*Qingjing jing* 清靜經; the Scripture of Clarity and Calmness).[40] This short scripture appears to have been in existence by the eighth century. As has been pointed out by Hans-Hermann Schmidt, extant sources indicate that there had at one time existed commentaries to it written by Sima Chengzhen 司馬承禎 (647–735) and Li Simu 李思慕 (d. 756), as well a manuscript by the hand of the famous Buddhist monk-calligrapher Huaisu 懷素 dated 785.[41]

Wang Zhe 王嚞 (1113–1170), the founder of the influential Quanzhen school—which is to this day the predominant school of monastic Daoism—is said to have encouraged people to recite *The Clarity and Calmness* and the *Laozi*, along with the Buddhist *Heart Sūtra* (*Bore xinjing* 般若心經)[42] and the Confucian *Classic of Filial Piety* (*Xiao jing* 孝經).[43] *The Clarity and Calmness* is today still recited regularly by Daoist clerics as part of their morning liturgy. In our current *Daoist Canon*, the organization of which was overseen by the 43rd Heavenly Master Zhang Yuchu 張宇初 (1361–1410), *The Clarity and Calmness* is given quite a prominent place—at the very beginning of the "main texts" (*benwen* 本文) division of the Dongshen 洞神 (Cavern Spirit) section. The *Daoist Canon* contains seven different commentaries to *The Clarity and Calmness*, most of which issue from the hands of Neidan authors of the Song and Yuan Periods. It also contains another text (likely of Tang authorship) that in the majority of its content matches *The Clarity and Calmness*, and is entitled *Taishang Laojun qingjing xin jing* 太上老君清靜心經, or "the *Heart Sūtra of Clarity and Calmness Spoken by the Most High Lord Lao*."[44] This title seems to betray intentions of presenting itself as a Daoist counterpart to the *Heart Sūtra*. Indeed, one could say that *The Clarity and Calmness* itself, in the central gist of its teachings, is somewhat like the *Heart Sūtra* in that it uses paradoxical wording to instill insight into the Empty nature of things, and thereby breed detachment. Perhaps Wang Zhe recommended the recitation of both *The Clarity and Calmness* and the *Heart Sūtra* because he saw them as cross-faith counterparts that conveyed a fundamental, common truth.

*The Clarity and Calmness* starts off by speaking of the paradoxical subtleties and wonders of the Dao—how it is formless, nameless, emotionless, and ineffable, yet it creates, nurtures, and animates the world with all its creatures and phenomena. It then moves on to talk about how the Dao brings forth the world and its phenomena through the interplay of complementary dualities such as clarity (*qing* 清) and turbidity (*zhuo* 濁), motion (*dong* 動) and stillness (*jing* 靜), and man (*nan* 男) and woman (*nü* 女).

*The Clarity and Calmness* then makes a statement that appears to be most pregnant with meaning, but is yet most difficult to interpret. It reads (tentatively), "If a person can always be clear and calm, heaven and earth will all return" 人能常清靜 天地悉皆歸 (1b). What, exactly, does this mean? Do heaven and earth return to you? How, and in what sense, is this possible? Or, if they do not return to you, where do they return to? And where do they return from?

One possible solution might be to understand the passage as meaning not that heaven and earth themselves return, but that their *qi* does. In other words, the *qi* of the Dao (which pervades and animates the entire universe), which you had previously possessed but had squandered as a result of mental agitation and excessive desire, returns to nourish you if your mind is clear and calm. This would match well with the fundamental message we saw conveyed in *Laozi-Xiang'er*.

Although "to return" is perhaps the most basic and frequent meaning of the character *gui* 歸, this character does have other possible meanings, some of which could apply to our difficult passage. It can also mean to go to some place (where you have not necessarily been before); to take up dwelling or refuge in some place; or to entrust, surrender, ally, or affiliate with something or somebody. *The Clarity and Calmness* might thus be variously read as saying that if you are constantly clear and calm, heaven and earth will come together to ally themselves with you, or will become your possession, or will become your responsibility, or will faithfully come to your aid.

The Yuan period Neidan virtuoso Li Daochun 李道純 (fl. 1288–1292) comments on the passage in question by saying, "When you have been clear and calm for a long time, your spirit comes together with the Dao, and you become one with heaven and earth" 清靜久久 神與道俱 與天地爲一 (*Taishang Laojun shuo chang qingjing jing zhu* 2b).[45] Thus, to him *gui* seems to mean that heaven and earth become one with you. In this condition you identify sympathetically with the Dao and all between heaven and earth that it imbues and animates (i.e., everything); you attain a magnanimous state of mind that cares equally for all beings and has risen above petty, egocentric hostilities and anxieties. Essentially, then, the effect said to be brought about by constant clarity and calmness is wisdom and moral perfection.

Another Yuan dynasty (most likely) commentator to *The Clarity and Calmness*,[46] who refers to himself merely as "Mr. Anonymous" (Wuming shi 無名氏), explains the effects of constant clarity and calmness as:

太上言 人能禀大道之祖氣 使身心之虛靈 神氣之清靜 如此能體其大道也 與天地合德 故天地自然而從順 悉皆歸依也

> The Most High says that if people can be bestowed with the ancestral *qi* of the great Dao, this will bring about emptiness and holiness in the body and mind, along with clarity and calmness in the spirit and *qi*. In this way they can embody the great Dao. They will unite in virtue with heaven and earth. Thus heaven and earth will naturally be obedient to them, and everything will come to their allegiance. (*Taishang Laojun shuo chang qingjing zhu* 15a–b)[47]

Here the condition of clarity and purity is said to prevail over both spirit and *qi*, and both mind and body attain a blessed state. All of this is brought about by an infusion of the "ancestral *qi* of the Dao." The result is not only a drastic improvement in your mental and physical condition, but also the power to control all the phenomena in the world that surrounds you. The fact that Mr. Anonymous has such a power in mind here becomes clear from the incident that he proceeds to narrate in illustration of his point. The incident is said to have taken place in the Qingli 慶曆 reign era of the Tang dynasty (?).[48] Ms. Han 韓氏, the pregnant, 26-year-old wife of a high government official named Wang Gui 王珪, we are told, was cruelly murdered by the ghost of a certain General Wei of the

Jin dynasty 晉朝韋將軍. Ms. Han's ghost appeared before her husband Wang Gui to reveal to him the identity of her ghostly assailant. She also uttered the words:

> 我聞此鎮有田先生 自小念太上老君清靜經 行此之清靜无爲者也 此能剪㦸鬼神 有通天之德 故曰 人能常清靜 天地悉皆歸 斯其以報妾之冤

I have heard that in this township there is a certain Mr. Tian who since his childhood has recited *The Clarity and Calmness* and has practiced its [teachings on] clarity, calmness and non-action. He is able to slay demons and spirits, and possesses virtue that penetrates the heavens. Thus it is said, "If people are able to always be clear and calm, heaven and earth will all come to them." You should employ him to take revenge for me. (*Taishang Laojun shuo chang qingjing zhu* 17a–b)

Wang Gui thereupon took her advice and went to see Mr. Tian 田先生 to ask for his help. Mr. Tian complied by performing a midnight ritual in which he donned his vestments, wielded his ritual implements, burned incense and lighted lamps, closed his eyes and recited incantations to address the deities of heaven and earth. As a result of his efforts, the Emperor of Heaven (Tiandi 天帝) sentenced the ghost of General Wei to 300 strokes of the iron rod, and banished him to the Northern Mountain of the Shadows (Beiyinshan 北陰山) to endure 1,000 years of torment. At the same time it was determined that the spirit of Ms. Han would return to life in the human world by entering the body of a young woman who had just died, whose name was Wang Shou 王壽; this was because Ms. Han's own corpse had already been buried. Sure enough, Wang Shou, three days after having been declared dead, revived and declared—in a voice identical to that of Ms. Han prior to her tragedy—that she was Ms. Han, the wife of the official Wang Gui. However, rather than resume their prior conjugal relationship, Wang Gui and the resurrected Ms. Han entered the Daoist clergy to become a monk and nun respectively. Both of them lived to the ripe old age of 120 (15b–20b).

The point of the story is that constant clarity and calmness—along with the habitual recitation of *The Clarity and Calmness* itself—imbues you with a great virtue that makes all the forces of the universe sympathetic or compliant toward you; in this case it meant that Mr. Tian possessed the ritual power to mobilize the divine agents of justice in the afterlife. Thus, the attainment of supreme ritual power could constitute yet another reason why a person—in particular a Daoist cleric—ought to aspire to constant clarity and calmness (and study and recite *The Clarity and Calmness*).

The statement in *The Clarity and Calmness* that reads, "If a person can always be clear and calm, heaven and earth will all return," was given yet another sort of interpretation by Ma Yu 馬鈺 (1123–1184), the second Patriarch of the Quanzhen School. This interpretation can be found in a passage in the *Danyang zhenren yulu* 丹陽真人語錄 (Record of Sayings by the Perfected Man Danyang),[49] which reads:

清靜之道 人能辨之 則盡善盡美矣 故經云 人能常清淨 天地悉皆歸 言天地者 非外指覆載之天地也 蓋指身中之天地也 人之膈已上爲天 膈以下爲地 若天氣降 地脉通 上下沖和 精氣自固矣 此小任仙所說也

The way of clarity and calmness—if people could understand it, all would be well and all would be beautiful. Therefore the scripture says, "If a person can always be clear and pure, heaven and earth will all come [together]." In speaking of heaven and earth, it does not point externally toward the heaven and earth that cover and carry. It is actually speaking of the heaven and earth that are inside the body. The area above a person's diaphragm is heaven; the area beneath the diaphragm is the earth. If the *qi* of heaven descends, the arteries of the earth will inter-flow. Above and below will be harmonious, and the essence and *qi* will naturally solidify. This is what was spoken by the little Transcendent Ren. (*Danyang zhenren yulu* 6a)

Thus, drawing on what was said by a certain Daoist surnamed Ren (who is otherwise unknown), Ma Yu claims that the passage of *The Clarity and Calmness* in question speaks entirely of internal, psychophysiological phenomena—of how constant clarity and purity causes your essence and *qi* to gather together from the upper and lower ends of the body. According to Neidan theory of the sort subscribed to by Ma Yu and others, combining and solidifying your essence and *qi* in such a manner not only ensures good health, but can lead ultimately to the creation of an inner

Radiant Spirit (*yangshen* 陽神) that can a enjoy a complete immortality and freedom.⁵⁰

In sum, interpretations can and have varied greatly as to what exactly "heaven and earth will all return" means. *The Clarity and Calmness* itself, without any further clarification on this matter, goes on to discuss why and how serenity is possible to attain. It states:

夫人神好清 而心擾之 人心好靜 而慾牽之 常能遣其欲 而心自靜 澄其心 而神自清

The human spirit is fond of clarity, but the mind disturbs it. The human mind is fond of calmness, but desires pull at it. If you can always dismiss your desires, your mind will naturally be calm. If you can make your mind clear, your spirit will naturally be clear. (*The Clarity and Calmness* 1b)

The main point here would seem to be that serenity is possible because we have a natural propensity toward it. States of confusion and agitation are aberrations and deviations imposed upon the higher inner faculties by the lower ones. The highest inner faculty is "spirit," below it is "mind," and below that is "desires." As may be recalled (see chapter 4), a similar contrast between spirit and mind (which favored the former and disparaged the latter in much starker terms) was made in *The Western Ascension* (A 4/3b–4a; B 2/17a–b). Here and in *The Western Ascension* "spirit" appears to constitute our faculty for pure awareness that can observe things for what they are only if left free of skewed and biased input imposed by thoughts and desires. The "mind" is the faculty that generates thoughts, and while it is the agent that unwittingly obstructs the proper functioning of the spirit, it actually would like to stay calm and thereby form only good and proper thoughts. However, the mind loses its calm due to the influence of emotions. But in any case, because both spirit and mind actually are innately inclined toward clarity and calmness, the endeavors to eliminate desires and bring about serenity can most certainly succeed.

*The Clarity and Calmness* goes on to describe the mental condition and experience of one who has done away with desires:

內觀於心 心無其心 外觀於形 形無其形 遠觀於物 物無其物 三者

既悟 唯見於空 觀空以空 空無所空 所空既無 無無亦無 無無既無
湛然常寂 寂無所寂 慾豈能生 慾既不生 即是真靜 真靜應物 真常
得性 常應常靜 常清靜矣

> Inwardly observe the mind; in the mind there is no such mind. Outwardly observe the body; in the body there is no such body. In the distance observe the things; in the things there are no such things. Once you have understood these three facts, you only see Emptiness. But when you observe Emptiness by means of Emptiness, [you see that] Emptiness has nothing that is to be deemed Empty. Since there is nothing that can be deemed as Empty, the non-existence of nothing also does not exist. Since the non-existence of nothing does not exist, you are always tranquil, like a deep pool of water. Though tranquil, there is nothing to be regarded as tranquil. How can desires possibly arise? Since desires do not arise, this is true calmness. In true calmness you respond to things, and true calmness obtains the innate nature. Always responding, always calm, [you are] always clear and calm. (*The Clarity and Calmness* 1b–2a)

Thus, when you have managed to set aside your desires, you can and should be able to see and understand that you (both as a self-conscious mind and a physical body) and all the things around you lack inherent existence; you and they are Empty. But it is also to be understood that even this Emptiness is a concept that stands valid only on the basis of a particular way of viewing things, because viewed from another angle, all that is Empty also has a temporary, provisional existence. With this total, unbiased perspective on things, it becomes possible to be detached from everything, including the even concept of Emptiness and the tranquillity of detachment itself. Thus, we are told, the mind that is free of desires is also immune from the danger of engendering new desires. Because you are unattached to the tranquillity of detachment, you are willing and able to respond to things, but in doing so you never lose the inner calm that is most basic to your nature. Such a condition is the "constant clarity and calmness."

The text then continues:

如此清靜 漸入真道 既入真道 名為得道 雖名得道 實無所得 為化
眾生 名為得道 能悟之者 可傳聖道

If you are clear and calm like this, you will gradually enter the true Dao. When you have entered the Dao, this is called "obtaining the Dao." Even though it is called "obtaining the Dao," there is actually nothing that you obtain. For the sake of converting sentient beings, it is called "obtaining the Dao." Those who are able to understand this can be transmitted the sacred Dao. (*The Clarity and Calmness* 2a)

Thus here we have presented the ultimate religious paradox, namely, that the highest religious attainment involves understanding that there is nothing to be gained through religious striving. Any notion that there is something to be gained is merely a ploy devised by compassionate beings to appeal to people who are unable to think in terms other than those of gain.

After thus taking much recourse to Mahāyāna Buddhist terminology and metaphysics, the text briefly reverts to the language of the *Laozi*, stating:

上士無爭 下士好爭 上德不德 下德執德 執著之者 不名道德

Superior gentlemen do not compete. Inferior gentlemen are fond of competing. Superior virtue is not virtuous. Inferior virtue is that which is attached to virtue. To be attached to it is not what is called "the virtue of the Dao." (*The Clarity and Purity* 2a)

Refraining from competition is something that is enjoined in seven different chapters (3, 8, 22, 66, 68, 73, and 81) of the *Laozi*, while "superior virtue" that is not "virtuous" (in any pretentious way) is mentioned in its 38th chapter. Here these themes and terms are drawn on apparently to expand on the paradox put forth in the previous passage. The point seems to be that you must not hold any pride in or pretensions of having acquired any sort of laudable virtue as a result of your religious cultivation; much less should you ever compete with others in gaining recognition for them.

The text then goes on to describe how "depraved thoughts" 妄心 "startle" 驚 the spirit and cause you to be attached to the myriad things. This attachment leads to cravings, which leads to confused thoughts (*fannao* 煩惱), which leads to endless agony and suffering as you remain endlessly trapped in *saṃsāra* ("drift about through births and deaths" 流

浪生死). Thus the text once again reverts to largely Buddhist terminology and doctrine, although the choice of the verb "startle" is probably inspired by the thirteenth chapter of the *Laozi*, where it describes how thoughts of favor and disgrace startle the minds of people who are not able to disregard the self (*Laozi* 1/10a–b).

*The Clarity and Calmness* then concludes by stating:

真常之道 悟者自得 得吾道者 常清靜矣

The Dao of true constancy is something that those who understand obtain by themselves. Those who obtain my Dao are always clear and calm. (*The Clarity and Calmness* 2a)

Note here that clarity and calmness—namely, serenity—figures in this last phrase not as something expected to bring forth certain favorable outcomes, but rather as the goal that is to be desired in and of itself. One might perhaps also add, based on what the text stated earlier, that in gaining this serenity you really gain nothing at all, for serenity is a propensity that you possessed all along.

In sum, *The Clarity and Calmness* is a concise, strongly Mahāyāna Buddhist-inspired exposition along the lines of the Twofold Mystery doctrine. It makes use of certain terms and themes from the *Laozi*, among which "clarity and calmness" (*qingjing* 清靜) is itself one. Much like *The Original Juncture* and the main text of *The Five Kitchens*, its teaching seems to pertain entirely to spiritual enlightenment and liberation from *saṃsāra*, and has nothing to say about physical health and longevity, and the forces (such as *qi* or essence) underlying it, unless one is to apply a creative interpretation of the sort conceived by Ma Yu in regard to the phrase, "heaven and earth will all return." It seems doubtful that such an interpretation would have occurred to the author of *The Clarity and Calmness*. However, as we see in our next chapter, there were voices within the Daoist fold of the same period (mid-Tang; ca. eighth century) that objected to theories of self-cultivation and salvation that left the body and its immortality out of the discussion.

# SIX

# Serenity and the Reaffirmation of Physical Transformation

*Sitting and Forgetting* and *Stability and Observation* are two texts that object to any notion that enlightenment alone—without physical longevity, transformation, and immortality—can constitute supreme attainment or salvation. However, both texts nonetheless describe primarily psychological approaches to self-cultivation. While they assert that serene mental cultivation can and must lead to a blessed physical transformation, they do not describe or explain with any concreteness or detail the actual physiological processes related to the inner anatomy and vital *qi* that are supposed accrue in this transformation.

## THE *ZUOWANG LUN* 坐忘論 (*SITTING AND FORGETTING*)

*Sitting and Forgetting* (*Zuowang lun* 坐忘論; The Treatise on Sitting and Forgetting) has been attributed to Sima Chengzhen 司馬承禎 (647–735), one of the most eminent Daoists of the Tang. However, the veracity of this attribution is uncertain. Whatever the case it is a substantial and influential work that deals in depth with the cultivation of serenity, both as a habitual state fostered throughout mundane activities, as well as in the form of trance states experienced in meditation. The treatise concludes with some harsh criticisms of those who would maintain that spiritual enlightenment alone, without the immortal transformation, is a worthy and adequate goal for one's religious cultivation.

The *Daoist Canon* contains two versions of *Sitting and Forgetting*, which we shall refer to as versions A[1] and B.[2] Version A bears a colophon stating that it was authored by Sima Chengzhen, as well as a preface authored by a certain "lay devotee (or hermit-scholar?) Zhenjing" 真靜居士.[3] This preface mentions that the edition was printed in the *dingwei* 丁未 year of the sexegenary cycle. Version A also bears an appendix entitled *Zuowang shuyi* 坐忘樞翼 (Wings of the Pivot of Sitting and Forgetting), which in content mostly corresponds to the main text (without the commentary) of *Stability and Observation*, the scripture that is the topic of the next section of this chapter. The last portion of this *Zuowang shuyi* is a discussion of the phases of mental and physical transformation known as the Five Stages and Seven Phases (*wushi qihou* 五時七候), which matches considerably (but not entirely) with that found in *The Inscription*—the text that is the focus of the first section of our next chapter. (*Stability and Observation* describes the Seven Phases, but not the Five Stages.)

*Sitting and Forgetting* version B, on the other hand, does not indicate the name of its author. It also lacks Zhenjing's preface, and the *Zuowang shuyi* has come to be omitted from it.[4] Its content mostly matches version A. However, there are numerous variations in wording, and the author's preface in version B is about three times as long as that in version A. Most significantly, the two versions bear different concluding statements (the last 51 characters of version A versus the last 92 characters of version B) that convey what could be regarded as conflicting messages. Version B seems to say that serene mental cultivation can or perhaps even must be complemented by the Divine Elixir (*shendan* 神丹)—likely meaning laboratory alchemy—for the immortality of both body and spirit to be brought about. No such thing is mentioned in version A.

It is also noted that in the second *juan* of the Daoist anthology *Daoshu* 道樞 (compiled by Zeng Zao 曾慥 around 1151)[5] there is a section called the "Zuowang pian" 坐忘篇 (Chapter on Sitting and Forgetting), which is divided into three distinct parts. "Part One" (*shang* 上; 1a–4a) is a synopsis of *Sitting and Forgetting* and the appendix (*Zuowang shuyi*), but the identity of the author of the text being summarized is not indicated. "Part Two" (*zhong* 中; 2/4a–6b) and "Part Three" (*xia* 下; 2/6b–8a) do not correspond to *Sitting and Forgetting*. Part Two is presented as the utterances of Tianyinzi 天隱子 (Master Recluse of Heaven), and is a somewhat abbreviated version of a text called the *Tianyinzi* that is found separately in the *Daoist Canon* with a colophon stating that it was "spoken" (*shu* 述) by Sima Chengzhen.[6] Part Three contains what *Daoshu* compiler Zeng Zao considered the best among the three parts of his "Zuowang pian" section. Zeng Zao expressly presents it as the utterances of Sima Chengzhen. In its content Part Three turns out to be almost identical to a short discourse that was inscribed on a stele on Mt. Wangwu 王屋山 (Henan) in 829 by Liu Ningran 劉凝然 and Zhao Jingyuan 趙景元, and which is preserved in the *Jigu lumu* 集古錄目 (Catalog of Collected Ancient Inscriptions; compiled in 1069 by Ouyang Fei 歐陽棐).[7] In this stele inscription the author of the discourse is not named, but there are hints that it is indeed Sima Chengzhen, because it states that the text of the discourse had been obtained from Mt. Tongbai 桐柏山 in the Tiantai 天台 mountains (Zhejiang), which happens to be where Sima Chengzhen spent most of his career.

Sima Chengzhen was the twelfth patriarch of the influential Shangqing school of Daoism. His reputation enabled him to receive the summons of Emperors Wu Zetian 武則天 (624–705), Ruizong 睿宗 (662–716), and Xuanzong 玄宗 (685–762). Xuanzong revered him so much that he personally received Shangqing Daoist initiation from him and entrusted one of his daughters to him as a disciple. Sima Chengzhen also persuaded Xuanzong to establish altars of worship to the gods and immortals of the Shangqing pantheon at all of the Five Peaks,[8] thus further enhancing the prestige of his school. Along with *Sitting and Forgetting*, various other works in the *Daoist Canon* were authored by or attributed to Sima Chengzhen, including the *Fuqi jingyi lun* 服氣精義論 (*Treatise on the Subtle Meanings of the Ingesting of Breath*), a substantial treatise on various longevity techniques such as the holding of breath, swallowing of air and/or saliva, fasting, ingestion of medicines, and light gymnastics.[9] Because he was the patriarch of the Shangqing school, one would also surmise that he possessed thorough knowledge and mastery of the sorts of intensely visual and choreographed meditation methods prescribed in the Shangqing scriptures. Thus, if Sima Chengzhen did indeed esteem the cultivation of mental serenity in the manner expounded in *Sitting and Forgetting*, it would appear that he certainly did not do so to the exclusion of proactive meditation and longevity practices.

Now, in regard to whether we actually ought to accept Sima Chengzhen's ascribed authorship of *Sitting and Forgetting*, matters are rather complex. Zhenjing's preface to version A, which (like the colophon) attributes the authorship of *Sitting and Forgetting* to Sima Chengzhen, unfortunately bears only the sexegenary cyclical date *dingwei* 丁未 (44th segenary year). However, one can surmise that this *dingwei* year must be one that falls some time after the Tang period (618–907), because Zhenjing mentions the text's being printed (printing only became common during the Song [960–1279]); Zhenjing also refers to Sima Chengzhen as "Master Zhenyi *of the Tang* (emphasis added)" 唐貞一先生, which suggests that Zhenjing lived under a different dynasty. All of this, added to the fact that neither version B nor Part One of "Zuowang pian" in the *Daoshu* indicate the name of an author, makes it possible to suspect that perhaps *Sitting and Forgetting* was actually not composed by Sima Chengzhen, and only came to be attributed to him long after his lifetime.

The bibliographical chapter of the *Xin Tangshu* 新唐書 (Official History of the Tang) does mention a book authored by Sima Chengzhen entitled *Zuowang lun*, and similar confirmation is to be found in bibliographies from the Song and Yuan periods.[10] However, there turns out to be significant doubt as to whether the *Zuowang lun* being referred to in those sources actually corresponds to *Sitting and Forgetting*. In the aforementioned Part Three of the "Zuowang pian" section of the *Daoshu*, as well as the 829 stele inscription to which it corresponds, the author—who, according to Zeng Zao, *is* Sima Chengzhen—states that he had recently seen "the *Zuowang lun* in seven chapters" 坐忘論七篇 that was written by the Daoist cleric Zhao Jian 趙堅. He then goes on to criticize Zhao Jian's work, claiming that "its subject matter is broad and its wording is complicated; its meaning is simple and its wording is eloquent" 其事廣 其文繁 其意簡 其詞辯; consequently it would better fit the title, "sit and hurry" 坐馳 (i.e., it causes thoughts to race through the mind even while one sits; an apparent allusion to a passage from the fourth chapter of the *Zhuangzi* that we have discussed [see chapter 1]).[11] It is significant here to note that *Sitting and Forgetting* in fact bears the format of seven sections, and is quite wide-ranging—perhaps at times wordy—in its exposition. It should also be recalled that Zeng Zao, while summarizing what corresponds to *Sitting and Forgetting* and its appendix (*Zuowang shuyi*) in Part One of his "Zuowang pian" section, does not name an author; he seems to regard Part Three alone as the work of Sima Chengzhen. This seriously makes one wonder whether *Sitting and Forgetting* is actually the treatise of Zhao Jian. On the other hand, though, it should be noted that Zeng Zao himself does not identify Part One as being the work of Zhao Jian.

*Sitting and Forgetting* has been thoroughly studied and translated into English by Livia Kohn.[12] Here we highlight and discuss the points in the text that are most pertinent to our study. *Sitting and Forgetting* consists of an author's preface (A 1a; B 1a–2a), followed by seven sections entitled as follows:[13]

1. "Reverence and Faith/Faith and Reverence" 敬信/信敬[14] (A 1a–2a; B 2a–b)
2. "Severing Connections" 斷緣 (A 2a–b; B 2b–3b)
3. "Recollecting the Mind" 收心 (A 2b–7a; B 3b–7b)
4. "Simplifying Affairs" 簡事 (A 7a–8a; B 7b–9a)
5. "True Observation" 真觀 (A 8a–12a; B 9a–12b)
6. "Peaceful Stability" 泰定 (A 12a–14a; B 13a–15a)
7. "Obtaining the Dao" 得道 (A 14a–15b; B 15a–16b)

The "Reverence and Faith" section argues for the fundamental importance of believing and respecting Daoism and its teachings. It asserts that the Dao can most certainly be obtained if you can just believe in the Daoist teachings and take them seriously—difficult though this indeed is, because the Dao is something that eludes the senses of those whose minds still have desires. Having made this observation, *Sitting and Forgetting* directs our attention to one specific passage in Daoist literature, and claims that this passage is most worthy of our reverence and faith. The passage comes from the *Zhuangzi*, and is in fact one that we examined in chapter 1. As is recalled, the *Zhuangzi*'s sixth chapter has Yan Hui declaring to Confucius, "I destroy my limbs and body and I eliminate my intelligence. I separate from my body and I do away with knowledge. I become identical with the Great Pervader. This is called 'sitting and forgetting'." Regarding what these words mean, *Sitting and Forgetting* lucidly explains:

夫坐忘者 何所不忘哉 內不覺其一身 外不知乎宇宙 與道冥一 萬慮皆遺

When you sit and forget, what is there that you do not forget? Internally you are not aware of your entire body, and externally you do not know that there is a universe. Mysteriously united with the Dao, the ten thousand thoughts are all left aside. (*Zuowang* A 1b; B 2b)

*Sitting and Forgetting* then laments that because the phrasing of the *Zhuangzi* seems "shallow" (*qian* 淺), this causes people to fail to heed what it teaches, which is in fact profound. Thus in the first section of *Sitting and Forgetting* the paramount importance of clearing the mind of all thoughts—sitting and forgetting—is set forth as fundamental in the endeavor of "obtaining the Dao." A classic passage from the *Zhuangzi* is endorsed as embodying a truth that must be believed and revered.

The second section of *Sitting and Forgetting*, "Severing Connections," enjoins us to disengage from worldly activities and involvements, so as to acquire the degree of calm and leisure in which the proper cultivation of the Dao is possible. Particularly to be avoided are actions of various sorts that people do in the hope of gaining social recognition and advancement; ironically, one of these regrettable behaviors is that of pretentious pseudo-hermits who feign worldly detachment so as to gain a virtuous reputation and acquire high status.

The third section, "Recollecting the Mind" is significantly longer than the first two sections, and discusses meditation and mental discipline. In describing how to embark on meditation, it states:

學道之初 要須安坐 收心離境 住無所有 <u>因住無所有</u>/xxxxx 不著一物 自入虛無 心乃合道

When you begin to study the Dao, you need to sit peacefully, recollect your mind and detach from your surroundings (or "mental projections"). Dwell [mentally] where there is nothing to be regarded as existing. *Because you dwell where there is nothing to be regarded as existing /xxxxx*, you will not become attached to a single thing, and you will naturally enter into empty nothingness. Your mind will thus unite with the Dao. (*Sitting and Forgetting* A 3a; B 3b–4a)

The description of the meditation method here is so terse as to lead one to wonder whether a significant amount of detail has been left out. Could there or should there not be some sort of mental technique for better enabling you to disengage mentally from things? Actually, in stating that you are to mentally "dwell where there is nothing to be regarded as existing" (*wu suoyou* 無所有; a Buddhist term),[15] the text is telling you to ground your meditation upon a particular ontological insight. In your mind you understand that nothing exists in and of itself without being contingent upon or relative to something else (namely, everything is Empty). Thus you can become completely detached from all things, and this nonattachment makes the union with the Dao in empty nothingness possible.

Further on, the text states:

若x/能淨除心垢 開識/釋神本 名曰修道 無復流浪 與道冥合 安在道中 名曰歸根 守根不離 名曰靜定 靜定日久 病消命復 復而又續

If you cleanse away the filth in your mind, you will open up your consciousness to the origins of the spirit. This is called "cultivating the Dao." No longer wandering aimlessly [in *saṃsāra*], you will mysteriously unite with the Dao. To be at peace inside the Dao is what is called "returning to the root." To guard the root without relent, is what is called "calm stability." If you remain in calm stability for many days, your ailments will disappear and your vitality will be restored. Once restored, it will continue on. (*Sitting and Forgetting* A 3a–b; B 4a)

Here the process leading to the union with the Dao is described as a cleansing process where the "filth" of deluding thoughts is cleared away to reveal the spirit in its original condition, which is a condition of union with the Dao that transcends *saṃsāra*. This union and consequent liberation from *saṃsāra* is apparently, in the view of the author of *Sitting and Forgetting*, what is meant in the *Laozi*'s sixteenth chapter by the term "return to the roots" (*guigen* 歸根). The same chapter of the *Laozi* also says that the return to the roots is also called "stillness" (*jing* 靜) and referred to as *fuming* 復命. As we noted in chapter 1, this word *fuming* could quite plausibly be translated as "return to destiny." However, according to the interpretation of the author of *Sitting and Forgetting* it is best translated as "restore vitality." In his view, the state of mental stillness that unites with the Dao to transcend *saṃsāra* also has the effect of restoring your physical health and prolonging your life, and thus he uses the term *fuming* in this sense.

Further on the text states:

若執心住空 還是有所 非謂無所 凡住有所 則x/自令心勞xx/氣發 既不合理 又反成病/疾 但心不著物又得不動 此是真定正基 用此 爲定 心氣調和 久益清/輕爽 以此爲驗 則邪正可知矣/x

If your mind becomes attached to abiding in Emptiness, this is also a place of [perceiving and attaching to] existence. It cannot be said to be a place of non-being. Whenever you dwell in a place of existence, you belabor your mind *xx/and your qi discharges*. Since you do not unite with the Principle (the underlying order of the universe; the Dao), you contrarily become ill. For the mind to not attach to things and to not waver—this is the proper foundation of true stability. If mind and *qi* are controlled and harmonious, after a long while they will be enhanced in their *clarity/lightness* and vigor. With this you can verify [your progress], and know whether [your method of training] is perverse or proper. (*Sitting and Forgetting* A 3b; B4b)

Thus, although insight into the Empty nature of all things does aid in facilitating detachment from them, the idea of Emptiness itself poses the threat of becoming a hindrance to enlightenment, for you can easily fall into the error of regarding Emptiness as inherently real and making it an object of attachment. Any sort of attachment—even attachment to Emptiness and to detachment itself—exhausts the mind and can lead to illness. Version B here also mentions the discharge of *qi* as the pathological consequence of mental exhaustion. On the other hand, when the mind attains a genuine state of stillness and detachment, this leads to harmony of mind and body, and ultimately a feeling of refreshed vigor that is most definitely a favorable sign. Thus, *Sitting and Forgetting*, similarly to *The Original Juncture* and other Tang Daoist texts, holds to the doctrine of the Twofold Mystery and advocates the approach of Dual-Forgetting. However, it also links the consequent mental detachment intricately with the improvement of the physical condition, which is inextricably linked to one's spiritual progress.

Although any sort of mental attachment to anything needs to be eliminated from the mind, does this mean that one is to seek to eliminate all mental activity? Apparently not, according to *Sitting and Forgetting*, which further on states:

若心起皆滅 不簡是非 則/x永斷覺知 入於盲定 若任心所起 一無收制 則與凡夫/人元來不別

> If all arising of the mind is annihilated regardless of whether it is good or bad, you will forever be cut off from conscious knowledge, and will enter into blind stability. If you give free reign to all mental activity, without any recollection or control, you are then no different to begin with from ordinary folk. (*Sitting and Forgetting* A 3b–4a; B 4b)

Here the reader is first warned against entering into a mental condition known as "blind stability." What this perhaps denotes is a state of unconsciousness akin to that of inanimate objects, or a lack of higher intelligence akin to that of nonhuman animals. When in such a state of mind one may be immune to confusion, but one is also incapable of developing higher states of consciousness and genuine wisdom. Although thoughts and feelings that involve attachments to things must be eliminated, there are apparently certain sorts of mental functioning that ought to remain. Unfortunately, the text is not specific as to what these are, but one can surmise that they might include the mystical apprehension of the ineffable Dao, supernormal psychic and perceptive powers, and perhaps compassionate impulses to aid fellow sentient beings. In any case, while the text thus maintains that you must not eliminate all mental functioning, it also warns that you certainly must not indulge indiscriminately in mental activity either, since doing so makes you no different from heedless, ego-ridden worldly people.

The text further on states:

今則息亂而不滅照 守靜而不著空 行之有常 自得真見

> If you now put an end to all disorder while not extinguishing your illumination; if you guard your calmness while not attaching to Emptiness;

and if you practice this constantly, you will naturally obtain the true view. (*Sitting and Forgetting* A 4a; B 4b–5a)

Thus, although you need to constantly clear the mind of its attachments and delusions (including the attachment to the idea of Emptiness), the mind must always continue to "illuminate"; that is, it is to continue to calmly observe reality, so that one day genuine insight might come.

Further on, the text admonishes the reader against paying heed to both praise and criticism. If, upon being praised or criticized, you are to "receive it in your heart" 將心受, it will cause your heart to be "full" 滿, and "if your heart is full, the Dao has no place [in it] to dwell" 心滿則道無所居 (A 4b; B 5a). On the other hand, when you are unconcerned with your reputation ("external name" 外名) you abide in the condition known as the "peaceful mind" (*anxin* 安心). Thereby, "if your mind is at peace and is empty, the Dao will on its own come to assume its dwelling [in it]" 心安而虛 道自來居/止 (A 4b; B 5a). Then the text further states, quoting a certain scripture (which it does not identify, but which is apparently *The Western Ascension*),[16] "If people are able to empty their minds and practice non-action, even if they have no desire for the Dao, the Dao will come to them on its own" 人能虛心無爲 非欲於道 道自歸之 (A 4b; B 5a). Thus, a mind that is free of attachments and desires can become infused with the Dao itself. As we shall see, according to *Sitting and Forgetting*, this infusion of the Dao is supremely empowering, and constitutes the primary means by which the spiritual and physical transformation into an immortal becomes possible.

The fourth section of *Sitting and Forgetting*, "Simplifying Affairs," preaches the need to simplify your way of living by refraining from frivolous activity and extravagant consumption. The fifth section, "True Observation," pertains to maintaining the proper perspective on problems and temptations that you are likely to encounter in life. Here, notably, among other things, we find some very strong admonitions against sexual desires—even those between husband and wife—which are said to most certainly land a person in purgatory.

In the sixth section, "Peaceful Stability," the topic of meditation finally comes up again. Here we are told that "stability" 定 (meditative absorption; *samādhi* in Sanskrit) is "the ultimate ground for *exiting from/cutting off* worldliness, and the initial foundation for bringing forth the

Dao" 出/盡俗之極地 致道之初基 (A 12a; B 13a). The text gives the following description of the cultivation of "peaceful stability" 泰定:

> 形如槁木心若死灰 無感無求 寂泊之至 無心於定而無所不定 故曰泰定 莊x/子云 宇泰定者發乎天光 宇則心也 天光則發慧也 心爲道之器 宇虛靜至極 則道居而慧生 慧出本性 非適今有 故曰天光

Make your body like a withered tree and your mind like dead ashes. Without feeling and without seeking, [abide in] the utmost quietude and stillness. Without giving any thought to stability, there is nonetheless nothing that is not stabilized. Zhuang[zi] said, "He whose house is peaceful and stable will emit the heavenly light." The "house" is the mind. The "heavenly light" is the emergence of wisdom. The mind is the vessel of the Dao. If the "house" is empty and calm to the utmost, the Dao will reside there and wisdom will emerge. Wisdom comes from your original nature. It is not something that comes to exist just now. This is why it is called the "heavenly (natural, as originally created) light." (*Sitting and Forgetting* A 12a; B 13a)

Thus we are told that by sitting still and utterly calming and clearing the mind, without making any conscious effort to enter any state of meditative trance, you naturally enter into a trance of the most profound kind, wherein the Dao enters the empty space in the mind, and causes it to give rise to "wisdom." This wisdom is an innate capacity that you thus restore; it is not some sort of knowledge or cleverness that you newly acquire.

As has already been discussed in chapter 1, the expression "the body like a withered tree and the mind like dead ashes" is one that is found more than once in the *Zhuangzi*. Most famously, at the beginning of the *Zhuangzi*'s second chapter this description is applied to the entranced condition of Nanguo Ziqi. The expression is also found in an anecdote in the *Zhuangzi*'s twenty-third chapter where it is used—by the wise old master Laozi—to describe the natural condition of a baby, who is completely unaware of what he or she is doing. Laozi there explains that a person whose mind is in such a condition experiences neither misery nor pleasure, and is immune from the calamities that afflict ordinary people. This observation is then directly followed by the very passage quoted earlier, pertaining to the "heavenly light" that issues from the "peaceful and stable house." The Laozi of the *Zhuangzi*'s twenty-third chapter goes on to remark that such a person whose mind is so clear and calm as to "emit heavenly light" will be aided and favored by Heaven. In the view of the author of *Sitting and Forgetting*, it would appear that this aid and favor comes about through the Dao entering the human heart and restoring its natural wisdom; and, though not stated specifically in the *Sitting and Forgetting* passage quoted earlier, the Dao also heals, revives, and transforms the body.

The "Peaceful Stability" section of *Sitting and Forgetting* goes on to warn the reader that this innate wisdom is a treasure that can be easily damaged or squandered. Once it has been restored and made to emerge, it must be guarded and hidden secretly within you. Pursuing worldly ends or accumulating worldly knowledge can quickly cause you to lose your wisdom all over again. Flaunting your wisdom will embroil you in public recognition and its consequent temptations, and will thus also quickly squander away your wisdom.

The seventh and final section of *Sitting and Forgetting*, "Obtaining the Dao," discusses the numerous benefits that come about when the Dao is made to enter you and empower you. It states:

上士純心/信 克己謹/勤行 虛/空心谷神 唯道來集 道有深/至力 徐/染易形神 形隧/隨道通 與神合/爲一 謂之神人 神性虛融 體無 變滅 形與道/之同 故無生死 隱則形同與/於神 顯則神同於氣/形 所以蹈水火而無害 對日月而無影 存亡在己 出入無間 身爲滓質 猶至虛妙 況其靈智 益深益遠乎

Superior gentlemen are of pure *heart/faith*. Conquering themselves, they diligently practice. They empty their minds to form a valley for the spirit. The Dao alone comes and gathers [there]. The Dao *has profound/ utmost* power, which *gradually/infiltrates and* transforms the body and spirit. The body follows the Dao and penetrates, and unites with the spirit. This is what is called a Divine Person. The divine nature vacantly relaxes, its substance never changing or becoming extinct. The body becomes identical to *the Dao/it*, and thus it has no birth or death. When hidden, the body is the same as the spirit. When manifested, the spirit is the same as *qi/the body*. Thus [such superior gentlemen] can tread upon water and fire and be unharmed, and do not cast a shadow when facing the sun or moon. Existing and perishing is in their own hands, and they can exit and enter the space of nothingness. The body is but the dregs, yet even it attains the marvel of emptiness. Much more so then does the numinous wisdom, which is even more profound and far-reaching. (*Sitting and Forgetting* A 14a–b; B 15a–b)

Thus, by clearing out the mind you enable the Dao to enter in. The Dao then has the power to transform both the body and the mind. The transformation of body and mind is a fusion of body and mind, which means that the two are never to be separated by the phenomenon of physical death, and form an immortal spirit-body that can make itself invisible or visible at will, and which is no longer bound to *karma* and *saṃsāra*.

However, the text further on also states:

虛無/心之道 力有淺深 深則兼被於形 淺則唯及於/其心 被形者x/
則神人也 及心者 但得慧覺而x/已 身不免謝

The Way of empty *nothingness/mind*, in its power can be shallow or profound. If profound, it will also cover the body. If shallow, it will only reach the mind. Those whose bodies have been covered [by the power of the Dao] are Divine Persons. Those whose minds [alone] are reached [by the power of the Dao] only obtain wisdom and enlightenment, while their bodies cannot avoid dismissal. (*Sitting and Forgetting* A 14b; B 15b)

Thus, depending on the diligence and thoroughness of your practice, the degree to which the power of the Dao transforms you will vary. Although the highest ideal is to be transformed both physically and spiritually into a Divine Person, it is also possible that you might manage only to be transformed spiritually; the result, then, is "only" wisdom and enlightenment, with no immunity from physical death. Thus, while spiritual enlightenment or wisdom may be a worthy and necessary thing, it does not constitute the ultimate goal.

One typical problem with such practitioners who only manage to attain the spiritual transformation has to do with their failure to properly treasure the wisdom that is awakening in them. When they become aware that their practice is making them wise, they become delighted and "very talkative" (*duobian* 多辯). Consequently, we are told:

神氣漏/散洩 無靈潤身光/x 遂/生致早終 道故難備 經云尸/屍解
此之謂也

Their spirit and *qi* leak out, and thus there is no holy entity to moisten the body's *radiance/x*. Finally this brings about an early end. The Dao thus becomes difficult to be equipped with. What the scriptures refer to as "Liberation by the Corpse" is this. (*Sitting and Forgetting* A 14b–15a; B 15b)

The flaunting of your spiritual attainment thus not only causes the mind to relapse into egoism and delusion, but also somehow (through the babbling mouth?) squanders your precious store of spirit and *qi* and brings about death. This, we are told, is what happens in scenarios described in Daoist literature as Liberation by the Corpse (*shijie* 尸解).[17] When one examines how this term gets used in Daoist texts one will find that its meanings and connotations are not consistent. Generally, though, it refers to a scenario where a person of some degree of virtue or attainment dies or seems to die, but ultimately ends up becoming some sort of immortal being after all, either because some miraculous posthumous transformation has occurred, or because the "death" had merely been feigned (by means such as magically transforming a sword or a bamboo cane into the semblance of a corpse). Immortality gained in such ways tends to be regarded as something less than the highest immortality. Here in *Sitting and Forgetting* Liberation by the Corpse appears to be regarded as something even less, which is to be held in even lower esteem. It is apparently understood as denoting a scenario where a practitioner dies due to an inability to become thoroughly transformed in both mind and body by the power of the Dao. What exactly awaits such a person after death is not made clear, but it seems doubtful that any sort of resurrection or posthumous transformation awaits the body. At best perhaps, the spirit, after its separation from the corpse, does undergo some sort of favorable rebirth.

*Sitting and Forgetting* goes on to explain that therefore, rather than flaunt his wisdom in such a manner that depletes spirit and *qi* and leads to Liberation by the Corpse or something even worse, "the great man contains his light and hides his brilliance" 大人含光藏輝. By concentrating the mind, treasuring the *qi* and cultivating a condition of "no mind" (*wuxin* 無心), the spirit can unite with the Dao, and this is what is known as "obtaining the Dao" (*dedao* 得道). The text then states:

經云 同於道者道亦得之 又云 古之所以貴此道者何 不日求以得 有罪以免邪/耶 山有玉 草木以/因之不彫 人懷道 形骸以/體得之 永固 資薰日久 變質同神 鍊形/練神入微 與道冥一 散一身爲萬法 混萬法爲一身

> The scripture (*Laozi*, ch. 23) states, "As for those who are the same as the Dao, the Dao also obtains them." It also says (*Laozi*, ch. 62), "Why did the ancients treasure this Dao? It is because without seeking it for days, you can obtain it. Those who have transgressions can by means of it avoid evil." When mountains have jade in them, grasses and trees thereby do not wither. When people embosom the Dao, their bodies are forever firm. Through lengthy infusion over many days they can transform their substance to be the same as spirit. *Refining their form/refining their spirit*, they enter into the subtle and darkly unite with the Dao. They can disperse the one body to become the myriad phenomena, and can mingle the myriad phenomena into a single body. (*Sitting and Forgetting* A 15a; B 15b–16a)

The proper understanding of this passage is made difficult because of the two quotes from the *Laozi*. These passages in and of themselves, even in their original context within the *Laozi*, are rather ambiguous in meaning and are worded differently in different received versions of the *Laozi*.[18] Here we have the further problem of trying to determine what they would mean to a Tang period adherent of Daoist religion. What *Sitting and Forgetting* is trying to help illustrate by quoting them is the notion that the Dao, when accorded with, united with or obtained, becomes an agent of a most wondrous and beneficial transformation. The passage from *Laozi*, chapter 23 could perhaps be read as saying that the Dao itself somehow consciously and actively affirms, reaches out to and embraces the good Daoist, particularly because we are in this case dealing with a Daoist religion wherein the Dao frequently does get personified as a savior-deity such as Lord Lao or the Primordial Heavenly Worthy. In quoting the passage from *Laozi*, chapter 62, the author of *Sitting and*

*Forgetting* perhaps understands it as meaning that by obtaining the Dao and receiving the infusion of its power, your bad *karma* from the past is eliminated, and you consequently avoid bad rebirths.[19]

*Sitting and Forgetting* shortly further on quotes the passage of *The Western Ascension* (A 4/10b; B 2/21b) that reads, "[The Sage] is of the same mind as heaven, and is without knowledge, and is of the same body with the Dao, and has no body. Thereby, the Way of Heaven flourishes." As we have discussed in chapter 4, this passage describes the state of mind that has transcended all egotistical thoughts and desires, and that magnanimously identifies with the Dao and all that it pervades, becoming oblivious to one's own body in the process. *Sitting and Forgetting* then quotes another passage familiar to us (see chapter 4) from *The Western Ascension* (A 5/8a; B 3/6b) that reads, "My spirit does not exit my body, and I live as long as the Dao." It then comments:

且身與道同 則無時而不存 心與道同 則無法而不通 耳與/則道同/x 則/耳無聲而不聞 眼與/則道同/x 則/眼無色而不見 六根洞達 良由於此

Also, if the body identifies with the Dao, there will be no time during which it will not exist. If the mind identifies with the Dao, there will be no phenomena that you will not penetrate. If your ears identify with the Dao, there will be no sounds that you will not hear. If your eyes identify with the Dao, there will be no forms that you will not see. The thorough penetration of the six senses hereby comes about. (*Sitting and Forgetting* A 15b; B 16a–b)

In sum, then, we are told that if you, through the serene practice of sitting and forgetting, can become fully transformed by the power of the Dao, you will never die and your spirit and body will never separate. Furthermore, the six senses (mind-knowledge, eyes-sight, ears-hearing, nose-smell, mouth-taste, body-touch) of your eternal mind and body will be limitless in their knowledge and perception. The condition attained is something far greater than mere wisdom, and is something that the body fully participates in along with the mind or spirit.

It is after the earlier passage that *Sitting and Forgetting* versions A and B part ways, and each wrap up with their own concluding remarks. Version A concludes by stating:

近代常流 識不及遠 唯聞捨形之道 未達即身之妙 無慙己短 有効
人非 其猶夏蟲不信冰霜 醯雞斷無天地 其愚不可及 何可誨焉

As for the common ilk of recent times, their knowledge does not reach far. They have only heard of the way of abandoning the body, and have not attained to the wonders that occur here immediately in the body. With no shame of their own shortcomings they emulate the mistakes of others. They are like summer insects that do not believe in the existence of ice and frost, or like gnats in the vinegar pot that are sure that there is no heaven and earth. In their ignorance they are unreachable; how can one teach them? (*Sitting and Forgetting* A 15b)

The author thus laments the preponderance of religious practitioners who do not know and understand that the power of Dao can transform both body and spirit, and instead are attracted to what is known as the "way of abandoning the body" (*shexing zhi dao* 捨形之道). So what and who exactly is he criticizing here? To "abandon the body" could perhaps merely mean to focus one's attention lopsidedly on the cultivation of the mind alone, with no concern for the body and its longevity. However, the author may have very well had in mind practitioners—Buddhist and Daoist—who actually resorted to acts of self-immolation and suicide, out of the belief that the body was of no worth, and that its intentional destruction could expedite the enlightenment and liberation of the spirit. As has been brought to light particularly vividly and cogently by James Benn, these sorts of actions were well known and fairly widely esteemed (though also controversial) within Buddhist circles in medieval China.[20] Also, in the *Taishang dadao yuqing jing* 太上大道玉清經 (The Most High Great Dao Scripture of Jade Purity),[21] a lengthy Daoist scripture of the late Six Dynasties or Tang, one can find various vivid and virulent passages that portray and rebuke self-immolators. The *Taishang dadao yuqing jing* bemoans the fact that such ignorant practitioners are to be found even "within the Great Way"; suggesting apparently that the author was aware of the presence of self-immolators not only among Buddhists, but within the Daoist fold as well. The error of such self-immolators, according to the *Taishang dadao yuqing jing*, lies in their failure to realize that they first must "complete" their bodies, and that it is "immediately within this body" (*ji ci shen* 即此身) that you "obtain the Dharma Body" (*de fashen* 得法身).[22] The phrasing we find here in *Sitting and Forgetting* pertaining to "the wonders that occur here immediately in the body" (*ji shen zhi miao* 即身之妙) tends to give the impression that the authors of *Sitting and Forgetting* and the *Taishang dadao yuqing jing* were upholding the same viewpoint and addressing the same problem.

The concluding portion unique to *Sitting and Forgetting* version B is less harshly critical in tone, but it specifically names the targets of its polemics. It starts out speaking of "the hidden secrets of the Upper Purity (Shangqing)" 上清隱秘 and of the feeling or sympathetic resonance that comes about through pure cultivation. (Speaking in such terms seems fitting for a Shangqing School Patriarch such as Sima Chengzhen, though these statements strangely appear only in the version of *Sitting and Forgetting* that does *not* name Sima Chengzhen [or anybody else] as its author.) It then speaks of how "by taking recourse to the Divine Elixir to refine your substance, your wisdom and knowledge are because of this thoroughly forgotten" 假神丹以鍊質 智識爲之洞忘. It also points out, on the other hand, that "by the accumulation of empty-mindedness you wash away your burdens, and your body by means of this loses its shadow" 蘊虛心以滌累 形骸得之絕影. (As can be seen in a passage we quoted earlier from *Sitting and Forgetting* [A 14a–b; B 15a–b], to "not cast a shadow when facing the sun or moon" is one of the traits of the marvelously transformed body of the Divine Person.) In this way, the methods for cultivating body and mind complement each other, and thus the text concludes that "the marvel of the two is not something that Confucianism and Buddhism are able to come near to" 二者之妙 非孔釋之所能隣 (see B 16b).

Whereas the rest of *Sitting and Forgetting* seems to be claiming that deep inner serenity, with the infusion of the Dao and its power that it brings forth, is sufficient to bring about the most marvelous transformations of the body, these final statements found only in version B make it sound as though the deep serenity must be accompanied by the ingestion of a "Divine Elixir" that is for the "transformation of substance," but which also has the auxiliary effect of helping the mind reach the desirable state of oblivion (if this is indeed what is meant by the somewhat curious compound *dongwang* 洞忘 that I rendered as "thoroughly forgotten"). This also raises the question of whether the "elixir" meant here is one of the sort concocted in a laboratory, or whether meditative "internal" alchemy—Neidan—is what is meant here. And, if Neidan is what is meant, one wonders what sort of meditation the author would have had in mind, and how this would have differed from the cultivation of "empty-mindedness."

While the final comments of version B seem incongruous with the rest of *Sitting and Forgetting*, they seem rather similar in gist to the concluding portions of Part Three of the *Zuowang pian* section of the *Daoshu* and of its corresponding stele text. There it states that even when you have attained the supreme wisdom that comes about from "sitting and forgetting," you are still a physical being subject to the "molding and smelting of *yin* and *yang*" 陰陽之陶鑄. Thus:

必藉夫金丹以羽化 入于無形 出乎化機之表 然後陰陽爲我所制矣

You must rely on the Golden Elixir in order to grow wings, enter into the formlessness, and emerge upon the surface of the mechanisms of transformation. After this, *yin* and *yang* will come under your control. (*Daoshu* 2/8a–b)

In other words, the serene, passive meditation by which you "sit and forget" needs to be supplemented by alchemy if the full immortal bodily transformation is to come about. One certainly wonders whether the author of the previous words was also the author of the final portion of *Sitting and Forgetting* version B, and if he was in fact Sima Chengzhen.

In any case, it would appear that *Sitting and Forgetting*, in the process of coming down to us in its two *Daoist Canon* versions, underwent editing by the hands of persons or factions who differed in opinion as to whether "sitting and forgetting" could by itself make both spirit and body immortal, or whether alchemy was also necessary for the supreme transformation. What both versions do agree on is that both spirit and body ought to be cultivated and made immortal.

*Sitting and Forgetting* incorporates the same sort of Buddhistic discourse on Emptiness and the Twofold Mystery that in *The Original Juncture* seemed to virtually obviate any concern over the physical body and its cultivation. However, *Sitting and Forgetting* is at the same time a treatise deeply concerned with reestablishing the importance of physical immortality as a soteriological goal. Yet, while reaffirming that the body can and should be made immortal, *Sitting and Forgetting* is nonetheless rather heavily psychological in its thematic emphasis. Without developing any sort of detailed theory on how the body's essence, *qi* and various organs function in the process, *Sitting and Forgetting* (with the exception of the concluding comments of version B) attributes the immortal transformation entirely to the wondrous, mysterious power of the Dao that lodges in the person whose mind has been thoroughly calmed and emptied. Although some of the other texts we have looked at affirm the usefulness of more proactive meditation techniques at least as auxiliary or preparatory measures, such things are never even mentioned in *Sitting and Forgetting*.

### THE *DINGGUAN JING* 定觀經 (*STABILITY AND OBSERVATION*)

*Stability and Observation* (*Dingguan jing* 定觀經; Scripture on Stability and Observation) is found in the *Daoist Canon* in two virtually identical versions. Version A is entitled *Dongxuan lingbao dingguan jing zhu* 洞玄靈寶定觀經註 (Cavern Mystery Numinous Treasure Scripture on Stability and Observation, with Commentary).[23] Version B is entitled *Dongxuan lingbao dingguan jing* 洞玄靈寶定觀經 (Cavern Mystery Numinous Treasure Scripture on Stability and Observation).[24] Contrarily to what their titles may seem to suggest, *both* versions have the same anonymous commentary attached to the scripture's main text. The only important difference between the two versions is that version A alone has a postface by a certain Lengxuzi 冷虛子 (Master of Cold Emptiness) that was written on the third month of a certain sexegenary *renshen* 壬申 year. (In the ensuing discussion, citations of the *Dingguan jing* refer to version A.)

As has been mentioned, the *Zuowang shuyi* (the appendix to *Sitting and Forgetting* version A) mostly corresponds to the main text (without the commentary) of *Stability and Observation*. Toward the end of the main text of *Stability and Observation* we find a discussion on phases of physical transformation called the Seven Phases, which in the *Zuowang shuyi* are a preceded by a description of Five Stages of mental progress. *The Inscription*, as we shall see in the next chapter, also has a description of Five Stages and Seven Phases that is very similar, but not quite the same. It would appear that *Stability and Observation* was authored, edited, and circulated within the same circles as *Sitting and Forgetting* and *The Inscription* and can thus be plausibly dated to around the eighth century. *Stability and Observation* has been previously studied and fully translated into English by Livia Kohn.[25] It is of particular interest to us due to its thoughtful discussion on the cultivation of mental serenity and wisdom, which addresses some of the problems and detrimental effects that can arise when one's way of practice is anxious and unbalanced.

The main text of *Stability and Observation* bears the format of a discourse proclaimed by "the Heavenly Worthy" (Tianzun 天尊) to his disciple, the Genuine Man of the Mystery of the Left (Zuoxuan Zhenren 左玄真人). Exactly which Heavenly Worthy is supposed to be speaking here is unclear, but it seems most likely to be the Primordial Heavenly Worthy (Yuanshi Tianzun 元始天尊) or perhaps the Heavenly Worthy of the Numinous Treasure (Lingbao Tianzun 靈寶天尊). Judging from this format, along with the fact that the text's full title bears the heading "Dongxuan Lingbao," the text's author perhaps saw his work as following in the legacy of the influential Lingbao scriptures of the fifth century.

The main text begins by proclaiming that you should first abandon all involvement in worldly affairs, so that disorder will not be brought to the mind. After doing so, you can "sit peacefully" 安坐 and "inwardly observe the arising of the mind" 內觀心起. However, as soon as you witness the arising of a single thought, you must eliminate (*chumie* 除滅) it so that you can be peaceful and calm. Even if the thought is not one that evokes any particular feelings of greed or attachment, it should be eliminated. All of your random, wandering thoughts need to be eliminated. The commentary explains that this is because if all thoughts—even those of the most random, indifferent nature—are eliminated, this will preclude the possibility that you will develop feelings of greed and attachment[26] (see 1a–2b).

*Stability and Observation* then goes on to state that this attentive observation and clearing of the mind is to be carried out diligently day and night. However, in doing so you must "only eliminate the moving mind; do not eliminate the illuminating mind" 唯滅動心 不滅照心 (2b). The commentary explains here that "the moving mind" refers to what the mind does when it gives rise to deluded thoughts or discriminates between things (which leads to preferences and dislikes, which leads to attachments), while the "illuminating mind" refers to the mind's capacity to recognize and effectively eliminate such thoughts and discriminations. Thus to say that the mind should be kept clear of thoughts does not mean that it should be allowed to become idle or unaware.

After thus describing how to meditate, the main text moves on to acknowledge the fact that the ordinary human mind is prone to restlessness, and that for novices it is truly difficult to calm the mind and keep it calm for any sustained duration. The solution to this problem is simply to continue the practice of "refined contemplation" (*jingsi* 精思; i.e., meditation). You must not get discouraged and abandon the practice of meditation, since the practice will eventually bring the mind under control if continued long enough. Once a significant degree of calm is thus attained, you must also train yourself to be able to foster peace of mind during all activities ("whether walking, standing, sitting or lying down" 行立坐臥), even when tending to affairs or when placed in the midst of clamor and noise (3a–4a).

Although sustained practice is of the essence, it is apparently also possible to try too hard. The main text states:

若束心太急 又則成病 氣發狂顛 是其候也

If you constrict your mind too hurriedly, you will become ill, or your *qi* will discharge and bring about insanity. These are signs of this [constriction of the mind]. (*Stability and Observation* 4a)

The commentary here explains that "constricting the mind" refers to when you "with a biased mind, obsess upon being calm" 偏心執靜. It also explains that when "you see forms outside the mind" 心外見相, this is what is called insanity. Apparently, in faithfully sustaining your practice you must at the same time remain relaxed and patient (without being lazy and careless), as opposed to being tense and anxious. Calmness itself can constitute an idea or a preference (wrought by discrimination) that becomes an attachment and ironically makes genuine serenity impossible. When serenity is purposely sought, it is never attained, and this leads to tension and anxiety. The mounting tension can lead to illness or to insanity. The insanity—which the main text interestingly links to a "discharge of *qi*"—is primarily understood or known of by the commentator as a sort of psychosis that entails visual hallucinations (4a).

Thus, the main text goes on to explain that moderation is of the essence. It states,

心若不動 又須放任 寬急得所 自恒調適

If the mind is not moving, you should let it go and leave it alone. If ease and effort are in proper proportion, you will always be properly regulated. (*Stability and Observation* 4a–b)

In other words, if it so happens that the mind is not currently giving rise to discriminating thoughts, it can and ought to be left alone; you need not assert any conscious effort to calm it down, because it already is calm.

The commentary explains that "letting go and leaving alone" (*fangren* 放任) refers to what happens when wisdom (*hui* 慧; *prajñā* in Sanskrit) emerges out of the state of "stability" (*ding* 定; meditative trance; *samādhi* in Sanskrit). "Wisdom" here denotes the capacity to perceive and understand things as they really are (lacking inherent existence [Empty], while possessing provisional existence), without giving rise to the sorts of discriminating thoughts that breed attachment. Wisdom can emerge from a calm mind, but you need to allow it to do so; at some point you need to relinquish conscious effort so that the wisdom can emerge naturally (4a–b).

The commentary then further states, "If there is [too] much stability, you become stupid. If there is [too] much wisdom, you become crazy" 定多即愚 慧多即狂 (4b). This is certainly a provocative statement, although it does not seem to make sense unless one is to understand both the terms "stability" and "wisdom" in a looser sense. The stability that you can have too much of is presumably a false stability where you needlessly continue to strive for calmness, even though the mind had ceased giving rise to discriminating thoughts; at this point the conscious effort to be calm prevents the emergence of wisdom and keeps you "stupid." The wisdom that you can have too much of is presumably a false wisdom; the commentator seems to have in mind a scenario where you have come under the impression that you possess wisdom, and this engenders self-satisfaction that completely undermines whatever wisdom you may have at any point actually had. This self-satisfaction further breeds feelings of grandiosity that when expressed or flaunted outwardly will make it apparent to others (or at least to those of some discernment) that you have gone crazy.

The main text then moves on to discuss "true stability" (*zhending* 真定), which is something that must be maintained in all of life's situations, not just meditation. It states that true stability has been attained when you can "be in the midst of clamor without loathing anything, and manage your affairs without becoming worried" 處喧無惡 涉事無惱 (4b). In other words, your well-honed propensity for solitude and quietude can tend to make you a person who is easily irritated and annoyed by human company. Habitual disengagement from the world can cause you to easily feel stressed when you are required to tend to the business of living in the world. If such is the case, your serenity is not genuine. However, the main text also states that when you have gotten to the point where you feel as though you can maintain your serenity in the midst of loud and busy circumstances, you should by no means seek out such circumstances on purpose. You are to only get involved and act in the world when the circumstances dictate that such is necessary.

The main text then returns to the topic of the importance of maintaining a patient and relaxed approach to meditation. It states:

慧發遲速 則不由人 無令定中 急急求定 急則傷性 傷則無慧

The slowness or speediness of the emergence of wisdom does not come from the person. Do not make yourself hectically seek wisdom in the midst of stability. If you hurry, you will harm your innate nature; if it is harmed, there will be no wisdom. (*Stability and Observation* 5a–b)

In other words, there is nothing you can do out of your own effort to make the wisdom emerge out of your stability; it will emerge naturally in its own due time. To try to consciously aid or accelerate its emergence is not only unhelpful, but is actually harmful. It can harm your state of consciousness in a way that makes the emergence of wisdom impossible.

The main text then goes on to state that "true wisdom" (*zhenhui* 真慧) only emerges out of stability when it is not purposely sought, and that once it emerges it should not be "used" (*yong* 用). Though you are now "actually wise" (*shizhi* 實智), you should act "as if stupid" (*ruoyu* 若愚); in other words, you should never try to display your wisdom to others. The commentary here explains that to "not use" your wisdom means to "be thoroughly without discrimination" 了無分別, and that to be "as if stupid" means to "sheath your brilliance and conceal your traces" 韜光晦跡. In other words, when wisdom emerges and you realize that you see and understand things clearly as never before, you need to avoid the temptation to use that clear perception to start making distinctions and forming preferences all over again. This temptation is accompanied by the equally pernicious temptation to flaunt your wisdom to others (5b).

After this, the main text raises the issue of visions that occur in meditation. It states:

若定中念想 多感衆邪 妖精百魅 隨心應見 所見天尊 諸仙真人 是其祥也

If you have thoughts during your stability, this will evoke responses from the many wicked beings. Evil sprites and a hundred specters will show themselves in response to your mind. The Heavenly Worthies and the various Transcendents and Genuine Persons that you see are the auspicious of them. (*Stability and Observation* 5b–6a)

Thus, if you harbor thoughts during meditation—which you are not supposed to do—this can cause you to have visions of spirits and beings of both the evil and holy variety. The explanation given for this is that your thoughts provoke the mischief of evil spirits who appear before you and distract you. As the commentary explains:

爲心取相 諸相應生 一切邪魔 競來撓亂

Because the mind grasps forms, various forms are produced in response. All the wicked devils compete at coming to confuse and distract you. (*Stability and Observation* 5b)

The understanding here, then, is not that the visions are hallucinations. Although your own mental activity plays an initial role in causing them, actual spirits do come and appear before you.

Quite troublesome and difficult to understand and translate here is the sentence in the main text concerning the appearance of the Heavenly Worthies, Transcendents, and Genuine Persons. The preceding sentence would seem to indicate that visions are an undesirable effect caused by the presence of superfluous thoughts, and that it is demonic beings that come and appear before you. Perhaps, then, the Heavenly Worthies, Transcendents, and Genuine Persons are to be understood to be demons that are in disguise and are trying to mislead you. The notion that demons (internal or external) can and do indeed resort to this devious tactic is something that also appears in *Contemplating the Baby* (*Yunji qiqian* 55/13a) and *The True Record* (25b), as we have seen in chapter 3. Regarding the visions of the holy beings, the commentator states, "These are the various forms. Do not grasp and hold on to them" 此爲諸相 不可取著 (6a). Thus, in the commentator's view, the visions of the holy beings belong within the category of the "various forms" (*zhuxiang* 諸相) that appear in response to the thoughts that you harbor; for this reason you must make sure not to become attached to them. Whether the commentator thinks that the holy beings are in fact the evil beings in disguise is not clear, but such could be the case.

However, what remains most unclear is what the author of the main text thinks of the visions of the holy beings. This is due to the ambiguity—and hence my awkward translation—of the phrase "the auspicious of them" (*qi xiang* 其祥). The character *xiang* 祥 that is used here is rather difficult to associate with negative connotations, because it usually means something like "lucky" or "auspicious" as an adjective, or as a noun it can mean "a lucky omen." Although one might here suspect a textual corruption, that suspicion is not corroborated in the matching portion of the *Zuowang shuyi* where this character is also found. Perhaps, then, the author of the main text did regard the visions of the holy beings as genuine holy epiphanies that are a sign of spiritual progress or of good things to come.

After this the main text goes on to state that by maintaining the mind of stability you can erase past *karma,* put an end to the generation of new *karma*, eliminate all impediments to your wisdom, free yourself from the world, and obtain the Dao.

If the text were to come to an end right here, we would have a text on meditation and mental discipline that has nothing to say about physical longevity and immortality or about the cultivation of the body and its *qi* (although in speaking of insanity it is worded in a way suggesting that insanity is connected with an unhealthy "discharge of *qi*"). The text could easily be accused of being Buddhism in Daoist clothing. However, the text as we have it does not end here, but proceeds to enumerate Seven Phases of transformation that are to be undergone when you "obtain the Dao."

In the first phase "the mind gains stability, and you become easily aware of your dust and outflowings" 心得定 易覺諸塵漏 (6b). The commentary here explains, "When the mind gains clarity and calmness, your dusty thoughts are all known by you" 心得清靜 塵念盡知 (6b). In other words, the transformation of the first Phase is still a mental one. When the mind is not serene, it gives rise to discriminating, attachment-breeding thoughts ("dust" [*chen* 塵; *rajas* in Sanskrit] or "outflowings" [*lou* 漏; āsrava in Sanskrit]) and is not even aware that it is doing so. Only when the mind is serene can it recognize such thoughts for what they are, and remove them when they arise. Dust and outflowings are both standard Buddhist terms that are used here in a manner consistent with their standard Buddhist usage. In Neidan literature of the Song onward it would be common to employ the term "outflowing" in a much more physiological manner to denote the emission of vital energies—"essence" (semen) in particular—from the body; however, such does not seem to be the case here.[27]

The transformations said to occur during the subsequent Phases are of a more physical nature. In the second Phase, the main text states, "chronic ailments all disappear, and your body and mind feel light and vigorous" 宿疾普銷 身心輕爽 (6b). Here the commentary explains that the elimination of chronic ailments is due to the fact that "the genuine *qi* carries out embryonic breathing" 真氣胎息 (6b). Thus, here we find an improvement in physical health linked to the meditation practice, and the commentary further offers the explanation that this is because the mental serenity is complemented by the simultaneous salubrious activity of *qi* that is concentrated in the Elixir Field in the lower abdomen (or such, anyway, seems to be the best interpretation of the explanation).

In the third Phase, "you fill and replenish what had been lost prematurely, reverting your years and restoring your life" 填補夭損 還年復命 (6b). In other words, your once-depleted vital forces get replenished, and you are rejuvenated. In the fourth Phase you gain longevity of tens of thousands of years, and thus become a Transcendent. In the fifth Phase, you "refine your body into $qi$" 鍊形爲氣 and become a Genuine Person. The commentary here explains that to "refine body into $qi$" means that you "acquire the $qi$ of the original prime" 得本元氣, and that the designation "Genuine Person" is based on the fact that "your innate nature is rectified and has no artificiality" 正性無僞. Perhaps the commentator here has in mind a transformation that is not quite as dramatic as what the author of the main text had in mind; perhaps in his mind it is not quite the case that the entire solid body dissolves into thin air (7a).

Whatever the case, the main text states that in the sixth Phase you "refine $qi$ into spirit" 鍊氣成神 to become a Divine Person. In the seventh Phase you "refine your spirit and unite with the Dao" 鍊神合道. The main text goes on to state that as you undergo the transformations of each Phase, your "perceptive powers" (*jianli* 鑒力) become "increasingly bright" (*yiming* 益明) (7a–b).

In closing, the main text remarks:

若乃久學定 心身無一候 促齡穢質 色謝方空 自云慧覺 又稱成道 求道之理 實所未然

If you practice stability for a long time and yet do not undergo a single one of the Phases in your mind and body; if you advance in age and the form of your impure substance vainly declines; and yet you say of yourself that you are wise and awakened and that you have accomplished the Dao; the principle of seeking the Dao is certainly not like this. (*Stability and Observation* 7b)

In other words, any presumption of being enlightened or having "obtained the Dao" is false if positive effects are not manifested in both body and mind. The decline and death of the body is certainly a sign of insufficient attainment. The author in saying this apparently is remonstrating against people (Buddhists or Daoists?) in his midst who think otherwise.

While *Stability and Observation* thus concludes with a rebuke of practitioners who disregard the need for physical transformation and longevity, *Stability and Observation* itself does not concern itself at all with such things until it enters into its exposition on the Seven Phases. It could perhaps be that the exposition on the Seven Phases was tacked onto *Stability and Observation* at some point after it had begun to circulate, by somebody who felt dissatisfied by its lopsidedly mental emphasis.

SEVEN

# Serenity, Primal *Qi*, and Embryonic Breathing

The two texts discussed in the previous chapter make a plea for a renewed emphasis on physical transformation, health, and longevity, and yet describe almost entirely psychological approaches to meditation and actually say very little about physiology and vital forces. In this chapter we focus on two texts of the same period (Tang dynasty), which describe or allude to certain physiological processes and effects that accrue in conjunction with serene, internally focused states of mind. *The Inscription* is a text that makes the same plea for renewed physical emphasis found in *Sitting and Forgetting* and *Stability and Observation*, but which unlike those texts speaks of processes and effects related to the Lower Elixir Field and to primal *qi*, and in one place refers to its method as "embryonic breathing." *Embryonic Breathing* describes a method and processes highly similar to those in *The Inscription*, but also describes or seems to allude to additional, even more wondrous processes and effects that accrue once the inner "embryo" actually begins to "breathe."

## THE *CUNSHEN LIANQI MING* 存神鍊氣銘 (*THE INSCRIPTION*)

*The Inscription* is a short treatise of which two versions—which we refer to as versions A and B—are to be found in the *Daoist Canon*. Version A is entitled *Cunshen lianqi ming* 存神鍊氣銘 (Inscription on the Preservation of the Spirit and the Refining of *Qi*)[1] and bears a colophon stating that it was "uttered by Simiao, the Genuine Man Sun of the Tang" 唐思邈孫真人述. It is thus attributed to the prolific physician and Daoist master Sun Simiao 孫思邈 (581–682),[2] whom posterity has deified and still worships by the title of Yaowang 藥王 (King of Medicine). Version B bears the longer title *Taiqing cunshen lianqi wushi qihou jue* 太清存神鍊氣五時七候訣 (The Great Purity Lesson on the Preserving of the Spirit, the Refining of the Breath, the Five Stages and the Seven Phases)[3] and is found in the 33rd *juan* of the *Yunji qiqian*. Version B itself bears no colophon identifying Sun Simiao as its author, but is preceded in the same *juan* of the *Yunji qiqian* by Sun Simiao's *Sheyang zhenzhong fang* 攝養枕中方; whether this is based on the editor's assumption that *The Inscription* version B is also Sun Simiao's work, is hard to say.[4] In content the two versions of *The Inscription* are essentially the same, although there are a fair number of textual discrepancies owing to scribal errors.

Some doubt has been raised as to whether Sun Simiao is the actual author of *The Inscription*. Jean Lévi has pointed out that library catalogs of the Song dynasty list the work as anonymous, and has estimated that *The Inscription* is a work of the latter part of the Tang or the Five Dynasties (907–960).[5] In light of this it is significant to note that the colophon to version A refers to Sun Simiao as "Simiao, the Genuine Man Sun *of the Tang*"; the colophon would thus appear to come from the hands of somebody living after the Tang, and does not much help allay the doubts raised by Lévi.

*The Inscription* is a treatise that describes and discusses the salubrious and wondrous effects of a very simple, serenity-based meditation method that does not entail visualization or any complicated procedures for manipulating psychic and physiological processes. As we shall see, the treatise claims that by simply making the mind serene by focusing it on the Elixir Field in the belly, you can overcome hunger, eliminate all diseases, attain perfect health and immortality, and transform into a divine being with limitless powers. Although this point of view might seem to make all other more complicated Daoist methods of meditation and longevity cultivation obsolete, we cannot necessarily conclude that such was the view of the author—especially if the author was in fact Sun

Simiao. Sun Simiao studied, practiced, and wrote about virtually every sort of hygienic, therapeutic, longevity, and immortality practice known during his time. As for why he might have regarded all of these practices as useful and worthwhile despite claiming that sheer serenity can by itself accomplish virtually everything, is perhaps because he recognized that many or most people lack the opportunity, resolve, or discipline to cultivate serenity with the degree of thoroughness necessary for bringing about its optimal effects; thus they need to employ, or to be helped with, other methods. As we have seen, *Sitting and Forgetting*, a treatise that similarly extols the far-reaching salubrious and soteriological effects of mental serenity, is attributed to the eminent Shangqing Daoist Patriarch Sima Chengzhen 司馬承禎, who undoubtedly also held an eclectic and all-embracing attitude regarding the various longevity and immortality practices. It is also possible that Sun Simiao did *not* author *The Inscription* (and Sima Chengzhen perhaps did not write *Sitting and Forgetting*), and one could cite the straight and simple content of *The Inscription* as evidence in favor of this skepticism.

A full English translation of *The Inscription* has already been published by Livia Kohn.[6] We summarize and discuss the text's teachings on why and how one should cultivate serenity, and on the effects this brings about.

*The Inscription* starts out by explaining that the body—which is "the cave-dwelling of spirit and *qi*" 神氣之窟宅 (1a)[7]—can stay healthy and strong only if spirit and *qi* are in it; death is caused when spirit and *qi* leave the body. Spirit (*shen* 神) is what endows a body with consciousness, and *qi* is what animates it. Thus, the key to preserving your body lies in being able to make your spirit and *qi* repose peacefully within you, without scattering out. As long as you can do this, you can live forever and never die.

The notion of keeping the spirit within your body seems not to pose much of a problem to our understanding; this most certainly means to disengage the mind's attention from external distractions by concentrating it inwardly on your own body. The notion of keeping the *qi* from leaving the body poses more of a problem, since *qi* could quite easily be construed as meaning the air that is inhaled and *exhaled* in ordinary respiration. There did exist, as we have seen in the Taiping Group texts (see chapter 2) a notion that the involuntary act of respiration ("breathing the *qi* of *yin* and *yang*") was responsible for making us mortal, and that therefore we perhaps ought to emulate our primitive ancestors who supposedly breathed very softly, or fetuses in the womb, who do not breathe the outer air at all. Consequently various Daoist texts enjoin holding the breath, or at least consciously slowing it down or inhaling air in volumes greater than what you exhale.

However, *The Inscription* does not seem to enjoin that you should stop breathing. What *The Inscription* has to say about *qi* tends to make more sense if we understand it as meaning what the Taiping Group texts referred to as the primal *qi* or the *qi* of naturalness. This *qi* is more subtle than the air we breathe, and is something that (hopefully) remains within the body to keep it alive all along while the air we breathe is constantly exiting and entering. The existence of such a subtle, vital *qi* appears to have been posited at least in part due to the observation (made as we have seen in *GP Synopsis* [4/1a; 8/19b–20a]; see chapter 2) that fetuses live and grow in their mothers' wombs despite the fact that they do not breathe outside air through their noses and mouths. As we have seen, *Laozi-Xiang'er* describes *qi* variously as the Dao or the One (which becomes the Most High Lord Lao on Mt. Kunlun when congealed), and maintains that *qi* will leave the body if the mind is full of evil thoughts; in other words, exhalation does not deplete this *qi*, at least as long as the mind is not impure. In *The Manifest Dao*, the vital *qi* is referred to as Dao-*qi* or primal *qi*, and is said to emerge from the Elixir Field and circulate through the various vital organs inside the body, in a manner that is synchronized with your inhalation and exhalation of air. *The Inscription* itself does in fact in one place use the term "primal *qi*," and like *The Manifest Dao* designates the Elixir Field as the bodily locus on which to focus your attention.

Another point of emphasis in *The Inscription* is that the spirit and the *qi* are in a relationship of close correspondence and mutual reliance. To convey this special relationship *The Inscription* states, "*Qi* is the mother of spirit, and spirit is the child of *qi*" 氣爲神母 神爲氣子 (1a). The metaphor of mother and child certainly conveys the intimate relationship between *qi* and spirit; at the same time it conveys perhaps the sense that while vitality and consciousness are closely linked, vitality is somehow primary. One premise here would seem to be that in the natural process of the generation of life, vitality precedes consciousness. Children begin to breathe and develop their abilities to move their bodies before they begin to fully develop their capacity to think and talk; our breathing and our ability to move are capacities we share with other animals, whereas our more sophisticated mental capacities are something unique to the human species. Because vitality is thus primary to consciousness, the text states that if you want to pacify your spirit, you should first "refine your primal *qi*" 鍊元氣 (1a). Unfortunately, it is not quite clear as to what exactly is meant by "refine." However, the text seems to be saying that before any attempt to calm the mind can be effective, the body, or the *qi* that animates it, needs to be trained somehow. The basic idea would seem to be that a calm mind is not possible without a calm body.

In any case, the text tells us, the "refining" of the primal *qi* keeps the *qi* inside your body, which in turn enables your spirit to repose in the "Sea of *Qi*," which is another name for the Elixir Field. It further states, "If the Sea of *Qi* is full, the mind will be peaceful and the spirit stabilized" 氣海充盈 心安神定 (1a). For the Sea of *Qi*/Elixir Field to be "full" mostly likely is supposed to mean that it is full of *qi*; whatever the "refining" practice entails, its resultant effect apparently is to activate *qi* from the Elixir Field, or to somehow redirect and concentrate *qi* that had spread out to various parts of the body, back toward the Elixir Field. Whatever the case, when the Elixir Field is thus replete with *qi*, the spirit can repose there snugly. Taking the natal metaphor further—the *qi* forms a womb in which the spirit can rest like a fetus. Indeed, later on *The Inscription* refers to its method as "the meditative stability observation that enters the womb" (*rutai dingguan* 入胎定觀; 1b). Near the very end of the text the method is referred to as "the meditative stability observation of embryonic breathing" (*taixi dingguan* 胎息定觀; 3b). If the spirit can thus remain stabilized, this will create a condition where body and mind are in total harmony and thus calm ("body and mind are congealed and calm" 身心凝靜; 1a). It should be duly noted here that the character translated as "meditative stability" (*ding* 定) is a character used in Buddhist literature to render the Sanskrit term *samādhi*, which denotes meditative absorption or trance in its various stages and levels. The author of *The Inscription* (Sun Simiao or whoever) would have almost certainly been well aware of this usage of the word; he quite possibly understood the mental condition entered into by the practitioner of the method of *The Inscription* to be something equivalent or similar to that aspired to by Buddhist meditation practitioners.

*The Inscription* goes on to say that when the state of calm (*jing* 靜) and stability (*ding* 定) is thorough and sufficient, your body will survive forever, as you "perpetually dwell at the source of the Dao" 常住道源 (1a). What this apparently means to say is that in the condition of calm, meditative absorption, you somehow apprehend, abide in, or partake of the pristine, eternal Dao. Consequently, the text tells us, you will become a "sage" (*sheng* 聖). It also states—in version A—that "the *qi* will penetrate the surroundings of the spirit" 氣通神境 and "the spirit will penetrate the life of wisdom" 神通慧命 (1a). We here encounter the most problematic portion of the text to interpret, due to the apparent presence of Buddhist technical terms, which by using the author may or may not have had the standard Buddhist definitions in mind. To further complicate matters, version B of *The Inscription* differs in its wording here, stating not that "the spirit will penetrate the life of wisdom" 神通慧命, but that "the spirit will penetrate, and the innate nature [personality; consciousness] will be wise" 神通性慧 (*Yunji qiqian* 33/12b).

The word *jing* 境 that is previously translated as "surroundings" is a term used in Buddhist scriptures to translate Sanskrit words such as *viṣaya*, *artha*, or *gocara* denoting the objects that the mind and senses conceive or perceive. In the sense that all such objects possess only a reality that is relative to the limited perspective of the mind and senses, they can be said to be projections; Livia Kohn thus plausibly enough translates *jing* 境 as "projected reality" (Kohn 2010, 174). But if so, what does it actually mean for *qi*—meaning most likely your own vital *qi* that is also the primal *qi* of the Dao—to penetrate these objects/projections of your mind and senses? If in our interpretation we are to abide fully by the Buddhistic connotations and place emphasis on the provisional nature of mental objects as projections, we might perhaps understand the phrase "the *qi* will penetrate the surroundings of the spirit" to mean that the *qi* will somehow affect your thoughts and experiences in a manner that eradicates delusive mental projections and is thus conducive to enlightenment. Other interpretations become more plausible if we leave the possible Buddhistic meaning and connotations aside. If *jing* 境 is to be understood as simply denoting the physical surroundings or circumstances that you with your spirit (mind) encounter, the phrase is perhaps best understood to mean that you become able to employ your *qi* in a manner that gives you special powers (healing or exorcism, for instance) over things that surround you. If *jing* 境 is interpreted as "territory" or "realm," and the word *shen* 神 (spirit[s]) is understood as referring not to your own spirit but rather to gods or divine things out there, the phrase might best be taken as meaning that the *qi* enables you to somehow enter into communication with divine beings or forces.

What, then, is meant by the phrase, "the spirit will penetrate the life of wisdom" 神通慧命, if we are indeed to trust the wording of version A over that of version B? The term *huiming* 慧命 ("life of wisdom") can be found in certain Chinese Buddhist texts as early as the sixth century where it refers to the eternal life of the Dharma Body that you can partake in as long as you possess the wisdom of enlightenment.[8] As we can recall, in *The Original Juncture* we find the Primordial Heavenly Worthy stating that he dwells eternally in a state of total peace by virtue of the fact that he apprehends his True Body, which is also known as the Dharma Body or the Dao Nature. *The Original Juncture* also conveys the notion that all sentient beings, if they come to possess the correct insight, can also apprehend their Dao Nature and partake in its eternal life. It would appear quite likely—considering the text's date and the presence of apparent Buddhist terminology elsewhere in it—that the author of *The Inscription* was himself conversant in this Buddho-Daoist metaphysical discourse of the early Tang. Thus, he quite possibly means to say here that when the spirit lies serene within the "womb" of *qi* in the Elixir Field, it comes to possess the enlightened wisdom that apprehends the Dharma Body and partakes of its eternal life.

If, on the other hand, we are to prefer the wording of version B ("the spirit will penetrate, and the innate nature [personality; consciousness] will be wise" 神通性慧), we encounter yet another Buddhist technical term that had become a part of the Daoist vocabulary by this time. To say that the "spirit penetrates" (*shentong* 神通) in this case would seem to mean that you come to possess supernormal psychic and physical powers, because the characters *shen* and *tong* together as a compound noun denote such powers, of which there are said to be six for those who attain the enlightenment of *nirvāṇa*.⁹

In any case, *The Inscription* after this moves on to state, "When the life stays, the body is preserved, and you merge with the Genuine Nature" 命住(注)¹⁰身存 合於真性 (1a). The question here is whether "life" (*ming* 命) refers to the "life of wisdom," or more concretely to your physical longevity. If it does refer to the life of wisdom, the phrase would mean to say that when you attain the wisdom by which you apprehend the Dharma Body, this also enables your physical body to survive; if not, it is just saying that your vital force will be retained, thus enabling you to stay alive. In either case, we are told, you unite with the Genuine Nature, which is both your own original pure consciousness and the eternal consciousness of the Dao shared originally by all sentient beings. While the calming and stabilizing of your own spirit and *qi* may play the primary role in keeping you alive, there is also, on a more abstract, metaphysical level perhaps a certain empowerment that comes from being in union with the Dao/Dharma Body that extends eternally and universally beyond your personal body and mind.

The text then proceeds to a succinct description on how to meditate:

欲學此術 先須絕粒 安心氣海 存神丹田 攝心靜/淨¹¹慮 氣海如具/俱自然飽矣 專心修者 百日小成 三年大成

If you want to study this technique, you should first eliminate kernels. Calm your mind in the Sea of *Qi*. Preserve your spirit in the Elixir Field. Recollect your mind and *calm/purify* your thoughts. If the Sea of *Qi is furnished/[contains spirit and qi] together*, you will naturally be satiated. Those who practice this with a devoted heart can attain a minor accomplishment in 100 days, and a great accomplishment in three years. (*The Inscription* 1b)

Undertaking the method, we are thus told, requires that you "eliminate kernels" (*jueli* 絕粒)—an expression that, along with similar terms such as "avoid grains" (*bigu* 辟穀) or "cut off grains" (*duangu* 斷穀), has since at least early medieval times received differing interpretations from both practitioners and scholars. Although terms such as these can and have been taken (by practitioners themselves in some cases) as meaning the avoidance specifically of grains such as rice, wheat, barley, millet, and soy beans, they are usually better understood as referring to a reduction or elimination of general food intake (that is often facilitated by respiratory or air/saliva-swallowing technique, or by the ingestion of drug potions).[12] In this latter interpretation it is a practice that requires great forbearance and ability to withstand hunger, for it is no mere matter of choosing to avoid specific foods in favor of others. The purpose of such fasting would presumably have to do with the process of "refining the primal *qi*" and filling the Elixir Field with it; eating is thought somehow to impede this process. The good news is, however, that the method itself, if done properly, actually has the effect of satiating hunger. The actual method appears to be most simple; you just calm the mind and concentrate your attention on the Elixir Field/Sea of *Qi*. The recommended duration for the practice is 100 days, but three years of sustained practice is recommended if you desire the greatest rewards. It is apparently because the Elixir Field—in the belly—is "furnished" 具 with the spirit and *qi* that you no longer feel hunger; if this phenomenon were not to take effect relatively soon, it would presumably be impossible to sustain the regimen for very long.

The satiation of hunger is but the first sign that the practice is having its desired effect. The text thus goes on to elaborate on how, because the Elixir Field is full of *qi* and the spirit rests within it, you regain your youth and transform into an immortal being who is able transform, hide, or manifest him- or herself at will; such a being is said to "transcend the world" (*dushi* 度世), and is known as a "Genuine Person" (*zhenren* 真人). The text then states,

此法不服氣 不嚥津 不辛苦 要喫但喫 須休即休 自在自由 <u>無阻/</u><u>xx無礙</u>

> In this method you do not imbibe *qi*, you do not swallow saliva, and you do not undergo hard suffering. If you want to eat, just eat. If you need to cease (eating?; the regimen?), just cease. You are free to do as you will, without obstacles and hindrances. (*The Inscription* 1b)

The text here advertises the simplicity of its method; it does not entail swallowing air or saliva. It also advertises the fact that its method is nonstrenuous and nonconstraining. Unfortunately, the wording also leaves us with some ambiguities in interpretation. How can a method that requires the "elimination of kernels" not be strenuous? Does the *qi* in the Elixir Field begin to satiate you more or less immediately, or is the dietary regimen described as eliminating kernels the mere avoidance of starches after all? When saying that you can eat when you feel like it and cease when you need to, is the text talking about your condition all along as you undertake the method, or is it talking about the condition that occurs once you have attained the "great accomplishment"? By "ceasing" (*xiu* 休) does it mean ceasing your practice of the regimen, or does it mean to cease eating? Is it saying that there are certain things that you can eat while continuing to observe the regimen? (As may be recalled from chapter 3, *The Manifest Dao* [8a], which describes a similar technique of focusing the mind on the Elixir Field, does allow you to eat certain things such as parched rice, roasted wheat, dried meat, dates, and chestnuts.) Or, is eating tantamount to ceasing the regimen, which you can do any time you need to, without restrictions (unlike, for instance the case of *The Manifest Dao* [8b] where if you cease or interrupt the regimen you must wait 100 days before eating ordinary cooked foods [or resuming sexual activity]; see chapter 3)? Or, is the text saying that by thoroughly practicing the method you can transform your physical constitution in such a manner that allows you to eat whenever you please, and yet be able to easily and effortlessly cease eating if necessary (in times of famine, for instance)?

The remaining two-thirds of *The Inscription* consists of an enumeration and discussion of Five Stages (*wushi* 五時) and Seven Phases (*qihou* 七候) that you are to progress through when you properly practice the "meditative stability observation that enters the womb" (*rutai dingguan* 入胎定觀)—that is, the technique of concentrating calmly on the Elixir Field. This part of the text resembles the *Zuowang shuyi* (the appendix to *Sitting and Forgetting*, version A) and *Stability and Observation*. The exposition on the Seven Phases introduces a theory on progressive refinement of the body, *qi* and spirit that would later come to be adapted and widely adopted in Neidan theory.

The Five Stages are successive stages of progress in your degree of mental calm, described in terms of the relative proportion of "motion" (*dong* 動) and "calm" (*jing* 靜) in the mind. At first the mind has much motion and little calm (the condition of ordinary nonpractitioners); then, little calm and much motion (the condition of a novice in practice); then, equal parts calm and motion; then, much calm and little motion; and finally, pure calm (1b–2a). It is only after the condition of pure calm has been attained that the Seven Phases can begin to be manifested in your body.

During the First Phase, all chronic ailments become cured while the body feels light, and the heart perpetually joyful. During the Second Phase you become rejuvenated in your looks and attain a lifespan that surpasses what is considered normal. You also come to "penetrate the numinous and see pervasively" 通靈徹視. At this point you need to relocate to a different county where there are no old acquaintances living nearby. Apparently, total disengagement from the world and its distractions becomes imperative from this point on. During the Third Phase you gain the longevity of 1,000 years and the ability to fly to the great mountains, attended by Green Youths 青童 and Jade Maidens. During the Fourth Phase you "refine your body into *qi*" 鍊身成氣, thus becoming a Genuine Person (*zhenren* 真人). With a body of bright, ever-luminous swirling vapor you can wander to the various cavern palaces, attended by Transcendents. During the Fifth Phase you "refine your *qi* into spirit" 鍊氣爲神 and become a "Divine Person" (*shenren* 神人) who possesses the power to "move mountains and dry out the seas" 移山竭海. During the Sixth Phase you "refine your spirit to merge with forms" 鍊神合色 and become an "Ultimate Person" (*zhiren* 至人). Because your spirit has "penetrated the numinous" (*tongling* 通靈), you are able to "administer conversion in accordance with opportunity, manifesting your form in response to creatures" 對機施化 應物現形. This appears to be something tantamount to the Buddha or the Primordial Heavenly Worthy's ability to manifest the Body of Response, as described in *The Original Juncture*, or the ability of the practitioners of the Great Spontaneity of Void Nothingness to "change their form and appear to undergo deaths and rebirths, while serving as teachers of the people of the world," as described in *The Original Arising*. At the Seventh Phase you rise to the realm "beyond forms" (*wuwai* 物外), where you live with the throngs of worthies in the presence of the Jade Emperor of the Great Dao (Dadao Yuhuang 大道玉皇) (see 2b–3a).

After thus enumerating the Seven Phases, the text laments that "people of these times" 今時之人 do not "study the Way" (*xuedao* 學道) for sufficiently long periods and never manage to even enter into the First Phase; thus there is no way that they can "penetrate the numinous." Instead they manage no more than to "guard their ignorant emotions and preserve their defiled physical constitutions" 守愚情保持穢質. Inevitably their bodies wither, decline, and die, and yet they claim to have "attained the Dao" (*dedao* 得道); such a view, according to our text, is "erroneous" (*miu* 謬) (3a–b).

In sum, *The Inscription* asserts that its meditation method, if practiced diligently and thoroughly for a sufficient duration, not only brings about spiritual enlightenment, but also bodily transformation of a most radical and miraculous sort. The solid, defiled mortal body becomes completely healthy and rejuvenated, after which it becomes progressively rarified—first into a bright, airy body of *qi*; and then into spirit, which is in itself formless, but possesses limitless power to assume any form it pleases. This wondrous transformation is what constitutes "attaining the Dao." Religious practitioners who avoid the effort to bring about the immortal physical transformation and think that attaining the Dao is possible when the body remains mortal and unrefined, are wrong.

But in making these criticisms, who did the author of *The Inscription* have in mind? It appears quite possible that he was primarily concerned with Daoists, who as a result of their adoption of Buddho-Daoist metaphysics of the sort conveyed in texts such as *The Original Juncture* had come to understand salvation to be a matter primarily or exclusively of spiritual illumination, and had come to disregard the physical body. The fact that the author was himself familiar and conversant in this Buddho-Daoist discourse of the early Tang is apparent from the terminology that he uses occasionally in the text. However, while *The Inscription* does thus claim that its meditation regimen enables you to possess the enlightened wisdom that apprehends the Dharma Body or True Nature in a state of mystical union, it also claims that this mystical union empowers and transforms the body. When in its discourse on the Seven Phases, the text speaks of a "penetration of the numinous" (*tongling* 通靈) that enables you to undergo the Phases, it is perhaps referring to this mystical union.

The successive transformations described as occurring from Phases Four through Six, in which the body is transformed into *qi*, *qi* is transformed into spirit, and then spirit "merges with forms" (*he se* 合色), anticipates the transformational scheme that occurs within Neidan theory from the Song onward. In this latter scheme, it is not the body but rather essence that gets transformed into *qi*. Also, at the end of the process, the spirit is said to "merge with the Dao" (*he dao* 合道) or "return to the void" (*huan xu* 還虛), rather than "merge with forms."[13] By redefining the first of the three transformations as a transformation of essence, Neidan theory conceives of it as an endeavor to harness and sublimate one's sex drive—an issue that is not specifically addressed in *The Inscription*. In describing the third transformation as a merging with the Dao rather than a merging with forms, Neidan texts follow suit with the *Zuowang shuyi* and *Stability and Observation*, which otherwise resemble the exposition on the Seven Phases in *The Inscription*. In uniquely thus describing the third transformation as a merging with forms, one might perhaps say that the author of *The Inscription*, compared to the authors of these other texts, was more beholden to the Mahayanistic compassion-oriented idea of the sort best articulated (among Daoist scriptures) in *The Original Arising*, regarding how the person of supreme attainment eschews transcendent solitude and willingly lingers in *saṃsāra* for the benefit of sentient beings. However, the compassion ethic of *The Inscription* is alas not as thoroughgoing as that of *The Original Arising*, because at the very end you are said to rise to the realm above forms to be with the Jade Emperor of the Great Dao.

*The Inscription*, despite its brevity, can be said to richly incorporate the concerns and tendencies of multiple genres and periods of Daoist literature. Its meditation technique itself is highly reminiscent of that of *The Manifest Dao*. Yet, in its underlying theory as to why and how that method is supposed to work, *The Inscription* incorporates Buddho-Daoist theories of the early Tang, while at the same time combining those theories with indigenous theories on *qi*, spirit and the Elixir Field, and seeks to provide a corrective to the apparent tendency among some to downplay the importance of the body and its longevity. For good measure, it sets forth a scheme of personal transformation that anticipates what would be put forth in the Neidan tradition.

## THE *TAIXI JING ZHU* 胎息經註 (*EMBRYONIC BREATHING*)

As we have seen, *The Inscription*, which enjoins calming the mind and focusing it inward upon the Elixir Field where the vital *qi* is assembled, refers to its method in one place as "embryonic breathing" (*taixi* 胎息). The origins of the term embryonic breathing go back at least to the early centuries of the Common Era. In the *Houhan shu* 後漢書 (Official History of the Latter Han; by Fan Ye 范曄 [398–445]) it is related that a certain Wang Zhen 王真 who was 100 years old, but looked no older than 50, claimed:

周流登五岳名山 悉能行胎息胎食之方 嗽舌下泉咽之 不絕房室

I have traveled about the Five Peaks and other famous mountains, and am able to practice all the methods of embryonic breathing and embryonic eating. I rinse my mouth with the water of the springs beneath the tongue and swallow it, and have not ceased my sexual activities. (*Houhan shu* [*juan* 82b], 10:2750–2751)

From this description it would appear as though the embryonic breathing method was perhaps not actually a breathing technique but rather a method of swallowing saliva. However, it could be that the swallowing technique described here constitutes only "embryonic eating," and that there was an accompanying breathing technique that constituted embryonic breathing but is not described. Whatever the case, Wang Zhen here claims that his regimen has enabled him to remain sexually active even in old age.

Ge Hong 葛洪 (283–343), whose expertise covered virtually all matters related to the quest of immortality, explains in the eighth chapter ("Shizhi" 釋滯 [Releasing Impediments]) of his *Baopuzi neipian* 抱朴子內篇[14] that embryonic breathing is the optimal condition attained when one masters the method of "circulating the *qi*" (*xingqi* 行氣). As he explains:

得胎息者 能不以鼻口噓吸 如在胞胎之中 則道成

Those who attain embryonic breathing are able to not inhale and exhale with their noses and mouths. They are the way they were when they were still in the womb. Thereby, the Way is accomplished. (*Baopuzi neipian* 8/3a)

Ge Hong then describes as follows the method of "circulating the *qi*" (*xingqi* 行氣) by which embryonic breathing was supposed to be brought about: you are supposed to inhale a breath through the nose and hold it in while you count to the number 120, and then exhale it through the mouth. Both the inhaling and exhaling should be done as softly as possible, and to help ensure this you are to place a goose feather on top of your nose and mouth and try to let the feather move as little as possible as you lightly inhale, hold, and exhale. You are to also try to inhale more air than you exhale. As you gain experience in the practice you should increase the length of time you hold the *qi* up to the count of 1,000 and beyond and hopefully, ultimately, reach the condition of suspended breathing that Ge Hong regards as embryonic breathing.[15]

The condition of the fetus was considered worth reverting to because doing so was thought to constitute a reversal of the aging process and a restoration to the condition that existed when your vital forces had not yet begun to be expended. As may be recalled from chapter 2, *GP Synopsis* (4/1a; 8/19b–20a) extols fetuses for their ability to be sustained by the "*qi* of naturalness" and thereby survive and grow rapidly in both their physical and mental capacities without eating or breathing. It also maintains that once the baby is born and begins to inhale and exhale "the *qi* of *yin* and *yang*," the mortal condition begins. In the emulation of the fetus, the navel and the belly were frequently seen as playing a central role. Why this is so is explained most clearly in a passage (which has been quoted and discussed by both Henri Maspero[16] and Joseph Needham[17]) found in the preface to a short discourse dating most likely to the Tang (618–907) entitled *Taixi koujue* 胎息口訣 (Oral Lesson on Embryonic Breathing).[18] There it explains that when the fetus is in the mother's womb, there is "mud"[19] in the fetus's mouth, and breathing cannot occur through the nose and mouth. Instead, the fetus "swallows" (*yan* 嚥) *qi*, from the mother, through the navel and is able to develop to the proper form; from this one can "know that the navel is the Gate of Life" 知臍爲命門. This fact, we are told, becomes even more apparent in cases when a baby is just born, but is not able to independently initiate breathing through the nose and mouth; the problem can be solved by applying warm water to the umbilical cord and belly several times. By thus understanding the vital role played by the navel in the breathing of fetuses, it is said to be possible for you yourself to emulate their manner of breathing (see *Yunji qiqian* 58/13b).

However, when it comes to the matter of how exactly you should apply that understanding to re-creating the condition of the fetus, things got to be horribly varied and complicated. Methods described as embryonic breathing could entail one or more among various techniques such as the holding of breath, slowing of breathing, swallowing of air, swallowing of saliva, mental guiding of *qi*, and inner visualization of internal organs, colored *qi* or deities. Many of the embryonic breathing methods found in various texts are of the proactive sort that is not the intended focus of our study. A good case in point here is the method of the *Taiqing zhonghuang zhenjing* 太清中黃真經 (True Scripture of the Central Yellow of the Great Clarity).[20] According to this text, before even commencing embryonic breathing, you need to undertake a rigorous regimen of complete fasting and air-swallowing (*fuqi* 服氣; "ingesting *qi*") that purges the body of all impurities, makes you impervious to hunger, and makes the body's inner organs somehow "visible." After 90 days of this regimen you can begin to undertake embryonic breathing, which entails holding your breath and visualizing the colored *qi* of the five viscera. By holding your breath for the span of time normally required for taking 1,000 breaths, while visualizing the green *qi* of the liver, you cause the green *qi* of the liver to emerge and appear. The respective colored *qi* of the other viscera (heart-red, spleen-yellow, lungs-white, kidneys-black) are similarly actualized and mobilized, and the colored *qi* of the five viscera thus become the agents for your immortal transformation.[21] This approach by which very strenuous and active measures (fasting, air-swallowing and breath-holding) are used as catalysts for physical transformations and visions sharply contrasts that of *The Inscription*, which expressly states that it requires no swallowing of air or saliva, or any "hard suffering," and promises that you will become impervious to hunger as a natural result of clearing and calming the mind and directing it toward the Lower Elixir Field.

A method similar to that of *The Inscription* is also described (or at least appears to be) in the short scripture *Embryonic Breathing* (*Taixi jing* 胎息經; Scripture on Embryonic Breathing). *Embryonic Breathing* is found in three versions in the *Daoist Canon*, two of which are accompanied by a commentary. (As necessary, the two versions with commentary will be referred to as "version A" and "version B.")[22] The main text of the scripture itself is very short, and there is reason to think that it could date as early as the year 300 or so, because Ge Hong includes its title in his list of scriptures that he had seen in the possession of his own teacher Zheng Yin 鄭隱.[23] Unfortunately it is unclear whether the scripture that Ge Hong saw is actually the same in content as what we have now. The commentary (which is largely identical in versions A and B) dates no earlier than the eighth century, because it quotes statements by Wu Yun 吳筠 (d. 778), the famous Daoist and poet. Version A (but not version B) bears a colophon stating that the commentary is by a certain Mr. Huanzhen (Huanzhen xiansheng 幻真先生).[24]

In terms of its teachings, *Embryonic Breathing* presents us with some difficulties in interpretation. The first problem concerns the relationship between the author of the scripture proper and that of its commentary, and whether and to what degree the latter's interpretations match the former's intentions. The other problem is the brevity of both the scripture and the commentary, which results in their raising a number of questions that are difficult to resolve. In hope of clarification on these questions, we will later consult the input of the following four works related to embryonic breathing:

1. *The Embryonic Origins* (*Changsheng taiyuan shenyong jing* 長生胎元神用經; Scripture on the Divine Functions of the Embryonic Origin of Long Life).[25]
2. *The Embryonic Subtleties* (*Taixi jingwei lun* 胎息精微論; Treatise on the Essential Subtleties of Embryonic Breathing).[26]
3. *Holy Embryo* (*Zhuzhen shengtai shenyong jue* 諸真聖胎神用訣; Lessons from the Various Genuine Ones on the Divine Functions of the Holy Embryo).[27]
4. *Bodhidharma's Lesson* (*Damo dashi zhushi liuxing neizhen miaoyong jue* 達磨大師住世留形內真妙用訣; The Great Master Bodhidharma's Lesson on the Marvelous Functions of the Inner Authenticity for Living in the World and Remaining in Body).[28]

All of these texts contain passages that appear to be quotes from *Embryonic Breathing*. *Bodhidharma's Lesson*, interestingly or oddly, presents itself as secret teachings that the semi-legendary Chan Buddhist Patriarch

Bodhidharma (Damo 達磨; fl. ca. 500) had learned in the "western country" from his teacher Baoguan 寳冠 (Treasure Crown). However, in its content and much of its phrasing it matches what is found in the other three texts. Each of these four texts contain its own version of a discourse that we refer to as the "Marvelous Functions Discourse," which seems to provide clues for resolving some of the problems posed by the *Embryonic Breathing* scripture and commentary.

The *Embryonic Breathing* scripture in its entirety reads:

胎從伏氣中結 氣從有胎中息 氣入身來爲之生 神去離形爲之死 知神氣可以長生 固守虛無以養神氣 神行即氣行 神住即氣住 若欲長生神氣相注 心不動念無來無去 不去不入自然常住 勤而行之是真道路

> The womb is formed from within the subdued *qi*. The *qi* breathes from the inside of where there is a womb. When *qi* enters the body, you live because of this. When the spirit leaves the body, you die because of this. If you know the spirit and *qi*, you can live long. Firmly guard the empty nothingness and thereby nurture your spirit and *qi*. When the spirit goes, the *qi* goes. When the spirit stays, the *qi* stays. If you want to live long, spirit and *qi* must concentrate on one another. If your mind does not give rise to thoughts, it will not come and go. Not leaving and entering, it naturally constantly stays. To diligently practice this is the true road.

This short scripture preaches the need to keep the mind clear and calm while concentrating it inward. This, it states, enables you to keep the *qi* subdued within yourself, which enables you to stay alive. You must take care not to give rise to thoughts and not to let your attention get drawn away by external things, because this causes the spirit to leave the body, taking the *qi* with it—this is what leads ultimately to death.

The scripture, in speaking of *qi* 氣, is apparently not referring to the air breathed in ordinary respiration, but is referring to a subtler sort of *qi* that abides in the body and bestows it with its vitality. The *qi*, when properly subdued in the body, forms a "womb," and within this womb, the *qi* somehow, in its own way, "breathes" (*xi* 息); in effect it seems to become a new living body in and of itself. But when this occurs, how are you supposed to be able to recognize it? It would seem that there must be some inner sensation or physical symptom by which you are supposed to be able to verify this. One wonders whether there are supposed to occur sensations, visions, involuntary bodily movements, or babbling of the sort said to occur in *The Manifest Dao* (see chapter 3) when the primal *qi* emerges from the Elixir Field and "the breathing is obtained."

In any case, the subtle *qi*, we are told, does enter into the body from the outside (meaning probably that it is contained within the coarser *qi* that is the air that we breathe), but apparently does not exit it as long as the mind remains free of thoughts and is inwardly focused. If the *qi* that needed to be constantly retained were indeed the air that we breathe, *its* coming and going—not that of the spirit—would presumably be the more urgent problem, and the immediate task would be to hold your breath; that, apparently, is not the case here. The phrase, "not leaving and entering, it naturally constantly stays" perhaps has *qi* as its intended subject, and perhaps is meant to be read as meaning that your breathing becomes suspended. Perhaps this is the symptom by which you are supposed to be able to know that the *qi* itself is "breathing" inside you. In any case though, it would appear that this condition, if it does come about, does so not because you purposely stop inhaling and exhaling, but rather as a natural result of keeping the mind clear, calm, and inwardly focused.

We now turn our attention to the *Embryonic Breathing* commentary. The commentary states that you are to subdue the *qi* within the Sea of *Qi* or Lower Elixir Field located three inches under the navel; this place is also known as the Mysterious Female (*xuanpin* 玄牝). The commentary here is certainly alluding to the sixth chapter of the *Laozi*, and one can surmise that the commentator would interpret that chapter along the lines of the theory expounded in *Embryonic Breathing* and in his own commentary. The commentary also calls out for criticism here those who interpret Mysterious Female as referring to the mouth and nose (a position notably held in the influential Heshanggong Commentary to the *Laozi*, as well as in *The Embryonic Subtleties* and in *Bodhidharma's Lesson*),[29] which in the commentator's view are not the Mysterious Female itself, but rather its "gates for exiting and entering" (see version A 1a–b; B 1a).[30] Thus, while the commentary, like the *Embryonic Breathing* scripture, does primarily seem to have the subtle inner *qi*—not ordinary breath—in mind, and does not seem to prescribe the holding of breath, it does nonetheless seem to perceive a connection between the subtle *qi* that forms the "womb" and the coming and going of air through the nose and mouth. Unfortunately, it is hard to discern what this connection is and how it works.

In any case, the commentary states that when you subdue the *qi* (炁/氣)³¹ beneath the navel and guard the spirit within the body, spirit and *qi* merge to form the Mysterious Womb. Doing so, it claims most significantly, constitutes "Internal Alchemy (Neidan), the Way of Immortality" 內丹不死之道 (A 1b; B 1b). The commentary goes on to describe the intimate interconnection between spirit and *qi* by saying that "spirit is the child of *qi*, and *qi* is the mother of spirit" 神爲炁/氣³²子 炁/氣爲神母. It further explains that "when the womb-mother (the *qi* in the belly) has formed, the spirit-child can breathe on its own, and thereby the primal *qi* does not scatter" 胎母既結 即神子自息 即元炁/氣不散 (A 1b; B 1b). Thus, whereas the scripture text had suggested that the *qi* contained in the body could form a living, breathing entity in and of itself, here in the commentary that entity is more specifically located in the Lower Elixir Field, and is a conscious spirit. In sum, when you calmly concentrate inwardly upon the womb of *qi* accumulated in your belly, you conceive within the core of your being a fresh, innocent consciousness (spirit) that is endowed with pristine vitality. It should also be noted here that while the primal *qi* becomes the "mother" of its "child" that is the spirit, you yourself—your physical body as a whole—becomes a mother to this inner child that is the primal *qi* and spirit in union. But if it is the case that an inner spirit has just now been born, what is the relationship between it and the mind that has up to now been focusing inward so as to prevent the spirit from wandering outside? Does the location of the subjective core of your awareness shift from this point onward? Do you now think, perceive, and act from within your belly? If this is a fresh birth of spirit, do you now take on new spiritual capacities?

In any case, in elaborating further on why the spirit needs to be kept from wandering out of the body, the commentary uses the metaphor of a house (the body) and its master (the spirit), and in doing so quotes *The Western Ascension*. It explains that if you, as the master of your body are able to be peaceful and calm, your spirit will dwell in your body; if you are restless, your spirit leaves you, and your *qi* scatters. Your ears, eyes, hands, and feet cannot function or move on their own without a spirit to control them. Thus you must harness your spirit in you so that it can properly serve as the master of its house and prevent the body from falling apart (see A 1b–2a; B 1b).

After thus using yet another metaphor to enjoin serenity and inner concentration, the commentary brings up a whole other benefit of harnessing the spirit and *qi* that is not explicitly mentioned in the scripture. The commentary states:

神不離身炁/氣亦不散 自然內實 不飢不渴也

If the spirit does not separate from the body, the *qi* also will not scatter. Naturally, you will be full inside, and you will neither hunger nor thirst. (*Embryonic Breathing* A 2b; B 2a)

This is important in the view of the commentator because the "*qi* of foods" (食氣) are *yin qi* 陰炁/氣, while the primal *qi* is *yang qi* (*yang qi* 陽炁/氣). Citing a passage from Wu Yun's *Xuangang lun* 玄綱論,[33] the commentary explains that the body's constitution must be made completely *yang* if one is to become a Transcendent (*xian* 仙). This is why you must always decrease your food intake and limit your desires while making the primal *qi* "circulate inwardly" (*neiyun* 內運; note that this circulation of the subtle inner *qi* is also a topic not actually mentioned in the *Embryonic Breathing* scripture). The more the primal *qi* flourishes within you, the more the *yin qi* will dissipate, thus eradicating all diseases and bestowing you with peace of mind, health and long life (see A 2b; B 2a–b).

Returning our attention back to the relationship between spirit and *qi*, the commentary points out that when people are still fetuses in their mother's wombs, spirit and *qi* are of one substance, and laments that once they get born, they get distracted by external stimuli and desires, and consequently "not a single breath ever returns to the origin for even a moment" 未嘗一息暫歸于本 (A 3a; B 2b). What this statement could be taken to imply is that people after birth tend to lose their vitality not only because their minds are distracted and full of desires, but also because there is something wrong with their manner of breathing.

At the very end of the commentary in version A we find some additional comments that are not found version B. These additional comments—though difficult to fully understand—describe some interesting effects that embryonic breathing brings upon the body and the manner in which it can breathe:

凡胎息用功後 關節開通 毛髮踈暢 即但鼻中微微引氣 相從四支百毛孔中出 往而不返也 後氣續到 但引之而不吐也 切切於徐徐 雖云 引而不吐 所引亦不入於喉中 微微而散 如此内氣亦下(sic? 不?)流散

After you have carried out the exercise of embryonic breathing, your joints open up and interpenetrate, and the hair on your body and head flows smoothly. Thus you just lightly draw in the *qi* through your nose, and it exits through the hundred pores on your four limbs, and does not return. After this, *qi* continues to arrive as you just draw it in without expelling it, earnestly and slowly. Even though it can be said that you draw in but do not expel, what you draw in does not enter into your throat, but rather subtly disperses. In this way the inner *qi* also flows and scatters downward [into the body] (or, "does not flow and scatter [out of the body]"?). (*Embryonic Breathing* A 3a–b)

The idea here seems to be that the body's interior and surface become free of blockages that had been impeding the free flow of *qi* through the body's inner conduits and pores, and this enables the air that you breathe to flow unimpeded through your body and to escape through your pores, obviating any need to exhale it through the nose or mouth. You thus become able to constantly inhale (softly) without ever exhaling. The understanding apparently is that this manner of releasing the air you breathe through the pores rather than through the nose or mouth is somehow conducive to retaining the subtler primal *qi*—which is here referred as the "inner *qi*"—and nourishing the body with it. Somehow, the expulsion of breath through the throat (and subsequently through the nose or mouth) is considered to deplete the primal or inner *qi*, while expulsion through the pores is not. (As may be recalled from chapter 3, the "Plain Way" of *The Manifest Dao* was supposed to be practiced without clothes on, and we speculated that this might have to do with allowing air to go through the pores.) Interesting as they are, the earlier statements appear only in the commentary in version A, and unlike the rest of the commentary use the term inner *qi* rather than "primal *qi*." This does cause one to wonder whether the previous passage was tacked onto the commentary by someone other than the original commentator, and whether the original commentator (as well as the author of the *Embryonic Breathing* scripture) would have attested to the phenomenon it describes.

Also attached only to version A is the brief *Taixi ming* 胎息銘 (Inscription on Embryonic Breathing), which iterates the need to breathe softly and calmly while either sitting or lying down, and to be relaxed and at ease when walking or standing. It also states that you should avoid noise and clamor, and not eat meat and fish. It further states, "Though this is provisionally called 'embryonic breathing,' it is actually called 'Internal Alchemy'" 假名胎息 實曰內丹 (3b).

Having thus overviewed the contents of *Embryonic Breathing* and its commentary, we are left with some important unresolved questions. How does the subtle, vitality-bestowing primal *qi* enter the body, and how exactly does one, in the words of the scripture, "subdue" it? Is the entering of the primal *qi* something that occurs at conception or gestation, after which you hold on to a finite allotment of primal *qi*? Or, is the primal *qi* also something that is present in the air around us, and which can be replenished through a certain manner of breathing? Or can it be somehow ingested? Is there something flawed with the manner in which people normally breathe, which leads to the depletion of primal *qi*? And what is this "inner circulation" of the primal *qi* that only the commentary mentions, and at that only in passing? When and how is it to be carried out?

The character *fu* 伏 in the first sentence of the *Embryonic Breathing* scripture, which was translated earlier as "subdue," is homophonous to the character *fu* 服, which can mean to ingest or imbibe (as well as to subdue). The compound *fuqi* 服氣 is used in certain Daoist longevity texts—such as the aforementioned *Taiqing zhonghuang zhenjing*—to denote *qi*-swallowing techniques involving the gulping of saliva and/or air. This might seem to suggest that the author of *Embryonic Breathing* deemed such a method necessary.

Considerable clarification on this matter seems to come if we turn our attention to *The Embryonic Origins*. There we find what appears to be a quotation of the first two sentences of *Embryonic Breathing* (or at least of some common source) in which *fuqi* is indeed rendered as 服炁 instead of 伏氣; furthermore, this quotation is followed by a brief description of how to ingest/subdue the *qi*. The passage reads:

> 胎從服炁中結 炁從有胎中息 胎若內結 求死不得也 以鼻中納炁 以意送下元中 久習自然凝結成胎 胎因元炁結而成胎中元炁 而有息

> The womb forms from within the ingested *qi*. The *qi* breathes from inside of where there is the womb. If the womb forms on the inside, you could not die even if you wanted to. Take in the *qi* through your nose and use your mind to send it down to the inside of the Lower Origin (the Elixir Field). If you practice for a long time it will naturally congeal to form a womb. The womb forms because of the primal *qi*, and becomes the primal *qi* in the womb, and furthermore has respiration. (*The Embryonic Origins*, 4a)

Thus, according to *The Embryonic Origins*, the "ingesting" does not involve gulping air or saliva through the esophagus, but rather consists of inhaling the *qi* through the nose and mentally guiding it down toward your belly. The idea is perhaps that the air you inhale contains in it the more subtle primal *qi*, and that this *qi* gets distilled and deposited in the Elixir Field if your attention is focused there, even though the rest of the air that you inhaled does get exhaled. This perhaps is the method that the author of *Embryonic Breathing* had in mind.

*The Embryonic Subtleties*, in its first section—in a manner highly reminiscent of the opening lines of *Embryonic Breathing*—states, "Generally speaking, the womb is formed from within the *qi*. The *qi* is produced from the breathing of the womb. The womb gets completed from within the *qi*" 凡胎從炁中結 炁從胎息生 胎因炁中成 (*The Embryonic Subtleties* 2a). Affixed to this we find a gloss in small characters that reads, "If the *qi* is pure, it will congeal and bind together. If the *qi* is turbid, it will scatter and exit" 炁清則凝而結 炁濁則散而出 (*The Embryonic Subtleties* 2a). Somehow, then, the matter of whether the *qi* will stay inside to form a womb, or instead exit the body, is contingent upon the purity or turbidity of the *qi* itself. As for what it might be that causes the *qi* to be pure or turbid, the text unfortunately does not say. Perhaps it has something to do with keeping the mind pure, but such is not actually stated.

*The Embryonic Subtleties* goes on to state that by forming this womb it will be brought about that all diseases will be eliminated; the Three Ones 三一 and other Divine Spirits 神靈 will take up their rightful residence in the body, while the Corpses and Worms 尸蟲 all leave. The text then proceeds to rebuke all those misguided practitioners who "close their mouths and wrinkle up their noses in placing value upon making their breaths lengthy" 閉口縮鼻貴其炁長 (2a) or who "press down and block off their noses and mouths in trying to practice embryonic breathing" 仰塞鼻口擬習胎息 (2b). To do this, we are told, is to practice unnatural breathing that causes harmful blockages that do damage to the *qi* and the five viscera; it only belabors both mind and body with no benefit. Thus, if we are to surmise that the authors of *Embryonic Breathing* and *The Embryonic Subtleties* had in mind a common—or similar—method for forming a womb out of *qi*, the statements of *The Embryonic Subtleties* indicate that this method did *not* involve the holding of breath.

The second section of *The Embryonic Subtleties*, entitled *Neizhen miaoyong jue* 內真妙用訣 (Lesson on the Marvelous Functions of the Inner Genuineness), is its version of the aforementioned "Marvelous Functions Lesson," variant forms of which are found in *The Embyonic Origins* (1a–4b), *Holy Embryo* (1a–2b) and *Bodhidharma's Lesson* (entire text). The section starts out by stating that if you want to obtain long life, you ought to cultivate "the original basis by which you were born." 所生之本. It then goes into a description of the process of conception, gestation, and birth. As it explains, essence and *qi* (presumably of your father and mother) combined to form your initial shape (*xing* 形). You thus became endowed with primal *qi* and dwelled beneath your mother's navel. After being in a condition of "primordial chaos" (*hundun* 混沌) for three months you became equipped with a nose and mouth (your "mysterious" [*xuan* 玄] and your "female" [*pin* 牝]), and began to use them to inhale and exhale simultaneously with your mother. After ten months in the womb you became adequately equipped with *qi* and spirit, and were ready to be born. Your mother, the text surmises, at that time rejoiced and doted on you, ignorant of the fact that she had just been severely depleted of her own allotment of spirit and *qi* for your sake. (In *Bodhidharma's Lesson* it is here noted that it is for this reason that the Buddha taught us that we must cherish and respect our parents, and be mindful of the debt we owe them; see *Yunji qiqian* 59/15b.) Just seven days after birth, you began to express emotions outwardly by smiling, and this marked the beginning of the process by which the simplicity of the Dao got lost. By the time of adolescence and young adulthood your eyes, ears, and thoughts came to be preoccupied incessantly with external things, and the pristine simplicity was utterly lost.

So what should be done to mitigate and correct this problem? Regarding this, *The Embryonic Subtleties* pleads, quoting a certain *Zhongtai jing* 中胎經 (*Central Embryo Scripture*), "The child and mother inside the body—why do you not guard them?" 形中子母 何不守之 (*The Embryonic Subtleties*, 3b). It further explains that within the body the *qi* is the mother and the spirit is the child. In the corresponding portion of the "Marvelous Functions Lesson" in *The Embryonic Origins*, we do find a fairly detailed and concrete explanation of the method by which this guarding of the inner mother and child is to be carried out (something that is curiously lacking in *The Embryonic Subtleties*). There it explains that before you undertake the method proper, you first lightly inhale the "pure *qi*" (*qingqi* 清氣) through your nose and expel the turbid *qi* (*zhuoqi* 濁氣) through your mouth ten to twenty times. It then states:

閉口一任神炁 綿綿出入 鼻所納炁 以意想至下元玄珠 濛濛四合 即存玄珠為下元之主 不得生思 生思不成 積習之 自然凝結成珠 習為母也 既有其母 必有其子

> Close your mouth and leave matters to the spirit and *qi*. Softly [the breath] enters and exits. For the *qi* that the nose has taken in you should use your mind to direct it toward the Mysterious Pearl in the Lower Origin, which vaguely takes shape from the four directions (?). Thus preserve the Mysterious Pearl that is the master of the Lower Origin. Do not give rise to thoughts. If you give rise to thoughts it will not be accomplished. If you continue this practice, it will naturally congeal to form a pearl. Through practice it becomes the mother. Once there is a mother, there will definitely be a child. (*The Embryonic Origins*, 1b)

Here again is a description of the method of mentally directing the *qi* toward the Lower Elixir Field (here referred to as the Lower Origin), that as we have seen is also described more briefly elsewhere in *The Embryonic Origins*. This passage also speaks of a Mysterious Pearl that takes shape in the Elixir Field and which through further sustained practice becomes the mother, which can in turn produce the child. What is unclear here is whether by saying that you should "preserve" (*cun* 存) this "pearl" it is meant that you should visualize it. This perhaps is allowed or recommended as an aid toward keeping your attention focused on the Elixir Field, so that the primal *qi* can be channeled there. However, the passage also emphasizes that the mind should be kept free from thoughts. To say that you should "leave matters to the spirit and *qi*" would seem to mean that you should by and large calmly, nonintrusively, allow the inner phenomena of spirit and *qi* to unfold naturally. Again, it should be noted here that while a "mother and child" take shape in you, you are also a mother to them. Much in the same way that you as a fetus formerly "breathed" the *qi* that came down to you in the womb while your mother lived and breathed through her mouth and nose, now you breathe air through your mouth and nose, and send it down to your Elixir Field to nurture the fetus in you.

Once, through sustained, diligent practice you have come to possess this mother and child in your Lower Elixir Field, you enter into a new phase that entails a different mental technique, and which brings about more marvelous effects. *The Embryonic Origins* states:

夫神與炁相合 以意引之 循環臟腑之內 馭呼吸以上下 久習之後 則神自明 而炁自和 明照五臟 細功成後 內視見其真神矣 炁和而浹通於四肢 隨意而到 亦可治他人之病也

> Spirit and *qi* merge together. With your mind guide them and circulate them amidst your internal organs. Riding upon the exhalations and inhalations [the spirit and *qi*] ascend and descend. After lengthy practice the spirit naturally becomes bright, and the *qi* naturally becomes harmonious. They brightly illuminate the five viscera. After the meticulous exercise has been accomplished, you can internally see their genuine deities. When the *qi* is harmonious it can pervade your four limbs, and can arrive any place according to your will. You can also heal the illnesses of other people. (*The Embryonic Origins*, 2a)

Thus here we have described a method of circulating the primal *qi*, and it is explained that this is done by mentally guiding the *qi* on a circuit through the body; also, your ongoing inhalations and exhalations seem to play a role in propelling this circulating movement. Through the sustained practice of this method, your *qi* comes to possess healing power, and your spirit gains a new "brightness" by which it can direct the primal *qi* anywhere at will, even into the bodies of others. You come to fully perceive your inner landscape and the corporeal deities that inhabit it, and this is perhaps because the core of your awareness inhabits the inner child formed from the merged spirit and *qi*, and perceives the internal phenomena from his or her eyes.

Regarding how your respiration is coordinated with your inner spirit-*qi* circulation, it is explained as follows in *The Embryonic Subtleties*, in an interlinear comment:

至人以神為宰 御呼以下流 吸而上之 上至泥丸 下至莖端 二景相通 可為救老殘

Accomplished persons make their spirit the leader. Riding upon the exhalations they flow downward, and make it rise up as they inhale. Above, it reaches the Muddy Pellet (in the head), and below it reaches the tip of the stalk (penis). If the two radiances (spirit and *qi* [?]) interpenetrate, you can thereby rescue the decrepit and injured. (*The Embryonic Subtleties* 4b)

The idea here is perhaps that the downward movement of the air entering the nose and coming into the torso and abdomen elicits an opposing upward movement in the inner primal *qi*, while the upward movement of air being exhaled elicits a downward movement in the primal *qi*. By keeping spirit and *qi* together and constantly circulating them in this way, you gain the ability to rejuvenate and heal; it is unclear here, however, whether the text just means to say that you rejuvenate and heal yourself, or whether it is speaking of the ability to heal other people. It should be noted here that while *The Embryonic Subtleties* identifies the tip of the penis as the lower extremity of the internal circuit, in *The Embryonic Origins* and *Holy Embryo* the rout of the circuit gets described as "above it reaches the Muddy Pellet and below it reaches the Gate of Life" 上至泥丸 下至命門 (*The Embryonic Origin*, 3b; *Holy Embryo*, 2b). Regarding this "Gate of Life," the interlinear commentary to *The Embryonic Origins* explains that it is located "three inches under the navel" 臍下三寸 (3b); in other words, it is the Lower Elixir Field.

Actually, there is reason to think that the "exhalations and inhalations" meant here are not necessarily those of the normal sort that go through the nose, but are rather those of the spirit-*qi* fetus that are carried out while the ordinary sort of breathing at some point goes into suspension. Our four versions of the "Marvelous Functions Lesson" each contain a key statement that is worded slightly differently in each of them:

尹真人曰 若神能御炁 則鼻不失息

Genuine Man Yin said, "If the spirit can mount the *qi*, the nose will not lose breath." (*The Embryonic Subtleties*, 4b)

神能驅炁則鼻不失息

If the spirit can make the *qi* gallop, the nose will not lose breath. (*The Embryonic Origins*, 3a)

尹真人曰 若神能御炁 則鼻不息

Genuine Man Yin said, "If the spirit can mount the *qi*, the nose will not breathe." (*Holy Embryo*, 2b)

若住自然之息 神御氣 即鼻無出息 令為真胎息也

If you can make the natural breathing stay, your spirit will mount the *qi*, and the nose does not emit breath. [You thus] bring about true embryonic breathing. (*Bodhidharma's Lesson*, in *Yunji qiqian* 59/18a)

Three of the four passages, read in the most straightforward manner, seem to say that you enter a condition where no breath comes *out* of the nostrils. If one is to understand them as thus implying that air does still come into the nostrils, this would agree with the assertion that we found being made in the final comments that are unique to version A of the *Embryonic Breathing* commentary (though there is no mention of breath exiting through the pores). The passage from *Holy Embryo* says simply that the nose "does not breathe," though this could be because a character has been mistakenly omitted. In any case, it would appear that as you fixate your mind on the inner *qi* circuit that proceeds at a rhythm synchronized with your inhalations and exhalations, your breathing becomes soft or slow to the point where it at least seems as though there is no breath coming out of the nostrils. Nonetheless there persists this inner rhythm on which the circuit of primal *qi* is sustained, and this is experienced as an internal sort of breathing—"true embryonic breathing" (*zhen taixi* 真胎息), in the words of *Bodhidharma's Lesson*—that persists even when ordinary breathing seems to be somehow suspended. In *The Embryonic Origins*, in its interlinear comments to the passage, we find again a description of an accompanying visual technique:

神在玄珠之中 常與元炁 主一呼一吸 當內想見其真神 故稱爲之 主掌 令神炁混合 而鼻不失息

The spirit is in the Mysterious Pearl, always together with the primal *qi*. It is in charge of each exhalation and inhalation. You should visualize inwardly and see that Genuine Spirit. Thus this is referred to as the "person in charge." Make the spirit and *qi* merge together, and the nose will not lose any breath. (3a–b)

The idea here is perhaps that you make the core of your awareness inhabit the internal *qi*-embryo or Mysterious Pearl, and as the locus of mental activity shifts into that internal body, so does the locus of breathing activity. Thus you sustain the rhythmical breathing and circulation of that subtle inner body, even while there is no breath coming out from your nose.

The "Marvelous Functions Lesson" bemoans the fact that people generally do not guard their internal "child and mother," and instead simply allow spirit and *qi* to each go their own way. In other words, they pay no attention to the inside of the body and its *qi*. Consequently, it laments:

常使炁逐穢濁 而神不虛明 神不虛明 則元炁漸散

[People] always cause the *qi* to chase the filth, and their spirits are never empty and bright; if the spirit is not empty and bright, the primal *qi* gradually scatters. (*The Embryonic Subtleties* 4a)

What this perhaps means is that if the primal *qi* is neglected by the mind, the primal *qi* will end up being expelled from the body along with urine and feces; the mind also fails to attain its proper clarity and acuity. (As may be recalled [see chapter 3], *The Manifest Dao* (8a) states that you should not eat immediately after a meditation session, because this can cause the primal *qi* to get excreted.) Thus, the discourse further explains that when you simply breathe in the ordinary manner with your *qi* unattended, all you can do is "penetrate and govern the vital organs so as to digest grains and foods" 通治藏府 消化穀食; you are unable to "revert the *yin* and return to *yang* in order to replenish and supplement your blood and brain" 還陰返陽 填補血腦 (4b). In other words, by focusing the mind on the subtle inner *qi* while breathing, you can purify, nourish, and heal the body in a far profounder way than through the mere digestion of foods; indeed, if the digestion of food causes the depletion of vital *qi*, it perhaps cannot even be said to be beneficial at all. The implication is perhaps that one ought to eschew the eating and digestion of foods entirely, in favor of the inner circulation of the *qi*; as we saw, the *Embryonic Breathing* commentary does specifically mention the satiation of all hunger as one of the benefits of embryonic breathing.

This, then, we are told, is how "the breathing of ordinary people differs from that of the sages" 凡人呼吸與聖人之呼吸殊; the *qi* of sages is thus said to have "deep roots" 深根, and this is what the phrase "deepen the roots and solidify the stem" 深根固蔕 (from the fifty-ninth chapter of the *Laozi*) means[34] (*The Embryonic Subtleties* 4b). The interlinear commentary attached to this portion of the discourse in *The Embryonic Subtleties*, further citing ancient Daoist philosophy states:

是故南華經云 凡人之息以喉 真人之息以踵 踵猶根也

Therefore the *Nanhua jing* (the *Zhuangzi*) says, "Ordinary people breathe with their throats; Genuine Persons breathe with their heels." The heels are like the root. (*The Embryonic Subtleties*, 4b)

The passage alluded to is found in the sixth chapter of the *Zhuangzi*, which also tells us, regarding Genuine Persons, that their breathing is deep, that they do not dream when sleeping, that they never worry when awake, and that they do not take pleasure in their food (2/1b). Although it is hard to say whether Zhuang Zhou back in the fourth century BCE would have specifically endorsed any of the embryonic breathing methods of medieval Daoism, this statement would indicate that he recommended maintaining a placid mental state that is characterized by few desires and concerns, and which physiologically is accompanied by breathing that is deep. He and most Tang authors on embryonic breathing would agree that most people, in most situations, ought to first of all "calm down and take a deep breath."

At the end, the "Marvelous Functions Lesson" in *The Embryonic Subtleties* concludes:

若胎息道成 精氣有主 故使男子莖中無聚精 夫人臍中不結嬰 雖有情欲 終不能與神爭 是謂胎息之真 反精爲神

If the Way of embryonic breathing is accomplished, your essence and *qi* will have a master. Therefore, it will cause a male to not gather essence in his stalk, and a female to not form an infant inside her navel. Even if they have emotions and desires, they will in the end not be able to compete against the spirit. This is what is called the authenticity of the embryonic breathing. You reverse the essence and make it into spirit. (*The Embryonic Subtleties* 5b)

In other words, the practice of Embryonic Breathing in which you concentrate the mind on the *qi* and circulate it throughout the body not only purifies, nourishes and heals the body, but also endows you with complete control over your sexual impulses. Thus, if you are a man you will not ejaculate (and perhaps not have erections either—depending on how one interprets "not gather essence in the stalk"), and if you are a woman you will not become pregnant; presumably this is regarded as beneficial because seminal ejaculation and childbirth are also physiological functions that incur substantial loss of vital *qi*. The fact that this benefit of embryonic breathing gets touted in the "Marvelous Functions Lesson" (and it is touted in all four versions)[35] might seem to suggest that this particular embryonic breathing method was something propagated among practitioners of the sort who were committed to celibacy, and thus struggled to suppress their sexual impulses and functions.

Celibate Neidan traditions—perhaps most notably the Quanzhen tradition—would indeed develop theories and methods that in many ways resemble what is taught in the *Embryonic Breathing* scripture and commentary, and in the "Marvelous Function Lesson," and saw the elimination of sexual impulses and functions as an essential step in one's progress toward immortality.[36] They also perceived their regimens as functioning to ultimately transform essence into spirit. However, it is also possible to read and interpret the claims of the "Marvelous Functions Lesson" in a manner compatible to the agenda of practitioners of sexual yogic techniques. Its embryonic breathing method could plausibly be construed as a means of enabling you to resist ejaculation and the excess of lust leading thereto, even while in the middle of coitus. In fact, one might surmise that such perhaps is at least what the editor of *The Embryonic Subtleties* had in mind. In that text the "Marvelous Functions Lesson" is directly followed by another section that is entitled *Taixi shenhui neidan qifan jue* 胎息神會內丹七返訣 (The Embryonic Breathing Spirit-Meeting Internal Elixir Seven Returnings Lesson; 5b–7b). This is a short text that enjoins you to nurture your spirit, *qi*, brain, and essence, and to swallow saliva in a manner by which it transmutes successively into phlegm, blood, and then essence, after which it goes up into the brain; these transmuting fluids are what are here said to be the "inner elixir." The section concludes by saying:

房中之術百數 妙在還精補腦 初修道之人 元炁未通 難見妙旨

> As for the hundred different techniques of the bedroom, their marvel lies in the recycling of essence that supplements the brain. For people just beginning to cultivate the Way the marvelous principles are hard to see because the primal *qi* has not yet penetrated. (*The Embryonic Subtleties*, 7b)

Thus, in this discourse the value of sexual yogic techniques is affirmed, and its so-called method of embryonic breathing or Internal Alchemy is clearly intended to facilitate such techniques. The editor of *The Embryonic Subtleties* perhaps assumed the same thing about the embryonic breathing method of the "Marvelous Functions Lesson."

We embarked on our discussion of *Embryonic Breathing* with the notion that this scripture, in explicitly enjoining little more than clearing, calming, and focusing the mind inward, closely resembles *The Inscription* and offers a passive approach to embryonic breathing that differs from other more proactive approaches. It should now be pointed out first of all that even a straightforward reading of the *Embryonic Breathing* scripture brings to light an important distinction between it and *The Inscription* in terms of what it claims can come about from its method. *Embryonic Breathing* promises not only that *qi* will be retained and will keep you alive, but also that this *qi* will somehow come to breathe on its own. The full meaning and implication of this remains mysterious, but it seems as though some sort of new and marvelous entity is created within your being.

When one reads the *Embryonic Breathing* commentary and tries to further supplement the gaps in its information with information from *The Embryonic Origins*, *The Embryonic Subtleties*, *Holy Embryo*, and *Bodhidharma's Lesson*, one finds that the method for "subduing" the *qi* and creating the womb entailed—at least in the minds of some Tang period interpreters—a technique of mentally directing the primal *qi* toward the Elixir Field while inhaling and exhaling normally and internally visualizing a Mysterious Pearl. Once the womb had been formed and the internal "breathing" had commenced (bringing simultaneously a suspension of the ordinary sort of breathing), you were supposed to mentally guide the inwardly merged spirit and primal *qi* on an internal circuit up and down the body, while visualizing the internal, breathing Genuine Spirit. At this point one has to say that the method being carried out is not a passive one, but a proactive one. Whether it is a faithful interpretation of what the author of the *Embryonic Breathing* scripture had in mind is very hard to say.

The *Embryonic Breathing* commentary refers to its method also as Neidan or Internal Alchemy. It is not the only Tang period text that equates embryonic breathing to Neidan (as we have just seen), and it is certainly not the earliest instance of usage of the term *neidan* to be found in medieval religious literature (curiously, that honor perhaps goes to the Sui period Tiantai Buddhist master Huisi 慧思 [515–577]).[37] If one is to try to trace or identify the roots of Neidan theory and practice, one might look to the rather frequent instances of the usage of alchemical terms and metaphors in early medieval Daoist meditation texts; these occur already in the Shangqing scriptures, and in even earlier texts such as *Taishang laojun zhongjing* and *Taishang huangting waijing yujing*. Or, one might try to investigate the role that meditation played in the practice of laboratory alchemists, or ascertain the point at which commentators started to interpret alchemical texts such as the *Zhouyi cantong qi* 周易參同契 in "internal" terms.

In any case, there is no doubt that theories and methods of embryonic breathing—particularly those discussed in this chapter—represent an important precursor to Neidan methods that developed and flourished in subsequent periods. Neidan authors would heavily borrow and adapt embryonic breathing theories to their own methods, which also placed a primary emphasis on inner serenity. Effects such as the overcoming of hunger and the cessation of arousal and ejaculation would come to be considered essential physical phenomena that needed to be brought about through the serenity of Neidan, as would the suspension of breathing itself (which in the view of Ge Hong was what the term "embryonic breathing" meant).

# EIGHT

# Conclusion

Daoists during the Latter Han through Tang periods applied the ancient Daoist principles of serenity and nonaction to meditation in various ways, with various results. The effects brought about (or hoped for) thereby to some degree resembled what was promised in the *Laozi*, *Zhuangzi*, and *Neiye*, but in many ways went far beyond anything mentioned in them. It is now time to sum up what the texts highlighted in chapters 2 through 7 have to say in regard to meditation, the cultivation of serenity, and the effects that this will bring about. Though the texts were selected for being representative of passive approaches to meditation as opposed to proactive ones, it turns out that these approaches are not uniform, and for some of them it can be debated as to how well they actually fit the description of "passive"; there is often some degree of volition involved in fostering serenity or in creating the conditions from which various wondrous (or in some cases disturbing or hazardous) phenomena can subsequently spontaneously unfold. Also, although some of the texts hold the position that techniques involving the visualization of specific, concrete forms either constitute an inferior level of practice or should be eschewed all together, others betray no such view or attitude.

In the Taiping Group texts (*The Great Peace, GP Synopsis, GP Instructions*, and quotes from the *Taiping jing* found in other sources) we find evidence of various techniques of meditation. It bears keeping in mind that this variety could in part be due to the fact that the original second century *Taiping jing* was itself a very large text that developed by accumulating material from different hands over the course of many years, and that even more material got added during the Six Dynasties and Tang when our extant Taiping Group texts took shape. In any case, the meditation methods of the Taiping Group texts—at least some of which were carried out in a reclining position, rather than a seated one—certainly include some highly proactive ones, such as the visualization of the deities of the five viscera in specific sizes and countenances, clad in specific sorts of colored clothing, that is aided by looking at pictures of them that are displayed in your room. However, we can also find stated or implied in some passages a priority or higher esteem that is placed on approaches that are much simpler and/or which involve little or no concrete imaginary sensory content. The term used most frequently to denote meditation is Guarding the One, and in *GP Synopsis* it is stated that it is better to guard the One than it is to guard the Two or the Three. It thus seems to be saying that it is better to focus the mind on one thing than it is to busily engage it in many things. As far as what this one thing should be, it is perhaps preferable that it be devoid of any concrete form. This, at least, is the impression conveyed in a ranking scheme of practices that is found in all three of our principal Taiping Group texts. In this scheme, the highest method that confers the highest level of immortality (the Non-action of the Primal *Qi*) is one that entails just thinking of your body as blank and formless, and the second one (the Naturalness of Empty Nothingness) entails imagining it as hollow and filled with bright radiance. Methods for visualizing the deities of the five viscera or other spirit beings rank lower; in fact, they are said to not actually confer immortality but rather to be useful for prognostication or for the subduing of demons. It is true that even the visualization of something formless is a sort of visualization, and is not pure passive observation. But in any case, whatever the specific meditation technique is that is being described, "clarity and calmness" (*qingjing* 清靜) seems to be the most essential underlying condition for enabling any sort of good result. It is the degree of your inner serenity that determines your ability to perceive marvelous things, whether they be things that you visualize or things that spontaneously emerge from within or arrive from without. In fact, the fostering of serenity in secluded contemplation seems to be recommended even for those of lower spiritual caliber with little prospect of higher attainments, simply because such cultivation might temper the mood swings by which they tend to too often bring injury to society.

*Laozi-Xiang'er*, in stark contrast to the Taiping Group texts, seems to have little to say about meditation, and is explicitly, harshly critical of the visualization of bodily deities. However, *Laozi-Xiang'er* lays great emphasis on the fostering of inner purity and calmness. It particularly emphasizes purity of mind in the sense of keeping the mind free of evil thoughts so as to enable you to obey the moral precepts of the religion. However, there are also passages where the term "clarity and calmness" (*qingjing* 清靜) is perhaps meant to refer to a particular meditation technique that could enable you to "observe the various subtleties" and which was to be practiced "at sunrise and sunset."

The "Plain Way" section of *The Manifest Dao* describes a meditation technique that is carried out in a reclining position, naked, in your meditation chamber during the daytime. The mental technique employed primarily seems to be that of simply directing and holding your attention on the Elixir Field in the lower abdomen to await and observe the spontaneous emergence of the Dao-*qi* from there. Though it appears to be desirable that your breaths become long and slow, the text states that this should be allowed to come about naturally and must not be forced. The invocation (and visualization?) of the deities of the five viscera does figure into the technique, but apparently only at the beginning of the meditation session, when you are to call out their names and invite them to all gather inside the Elixir Field; the purpose of this is to aid the process by which the *qi* of the entire body will concentrate toward the Elixir Field and ultimately lead to the emergence of the Dao-*qi*. The undertaking of the Plain Way is preceded by the observance of a retreat during which you cleanse your body and expiate your transgressions, but the Plain Way itself calls for a state of mind that is peaceful and relaxed. During the course of the regimen, sexual activity is refrained from, and dietary intake is limited.

The meditation technique of *Contemplating the Baby* also entails primarily focusing attention on a particular part of the body and observing what occurs; however, this location progressively shifts from the region of the kidneys (roughly corresponding to the Lower Elixir Field), to the heart, and finally to the head. The text does make frequent references to entities or inner personages such as the red-color *yuan*, the Female and the Male, the Masculine and the Feminine, the Baby and the Genuine Person, which you perhaps can or should visualize—though this is unclear. What does seem clear, however, is that you are supposed to await and observe the subtle, mysterious Dao and the various (sometimes alarming) manifestations and revelations that spontaneously come about at the naturally proper time—you cannot make them come about through your own effort at just any time you desire. Thus the text prescribes specific hours on specific days for practice that must not be missed or altered.

*The True Record* describes or alludes to a large and diverse variety of practices, among which only one—the method described in LLS#2—fits the description of "passive meditation." That method consists simply of making your mind clear and calm, and then once you have become calm, you are to turn your hearing and observing capacities inward upon your own body. When reading *The True Record* alone it is difficult to discern how LLS#2 and its method relate to other passages in the text. However, in *The Way of Transcendence* and *The Holy Chronicle*, as well as in a Neidan anthology of circa 1300 (*Zhuzhen neidan jiyao*), this method is clearly identified as the means of bringing forth the Red Snake-Queen Mother vision sequence (which *The True Record* describes vividly at length in LLS#4, but does not seem to clearly link to the method of LLS#2).

*The Western Ascension* recommends progressing through different levels and approaches to meditation. At first you can and should visualize various spirits, radiances, or vital forces within the body, and perhaps engage in the guiding of internal *qi* (according to the interpretation of the commentator Li Rong). However—at least according to the interpretation of the text's earliest known commentator Wei Jie—you must eventually move beyond harboring any thoughts or images.

*The Original Arising* presents a graded scheme of meditation practices, somewhat reminiscent in content and terminology, and perhaps even related in its provenance, to that proposed in the Taiping Group texts. The supreme practice in this graded scheme, referred to as the method of the Great Naturalness of Empty Nothingness, consists simply of emptying the mind of all thoughts and focusing its attention inwardly toward the region of the heart. The Intermediate and Small methods of the Naturalness of Empty Nothingness both entail the visualization of deities and spirits, and are said to lead to levels of attainment that are inferior to that which results from the Great method. They also fail to bring forth a direct apprehension of a crucial fundamental fact, namely that your spirit issues from the Dao and is originally clear and pure. In fact, all of your attempts at meditation, if they are to meet with any success at all, must be grounded on the theoretical understanding of this fact. Otherwise, you become like the adherents of "the school(s) of the outside way(s)" (meaning Buddhists?) who in vain "try to force themselves to close their ears and eyes and cut off their emotions and desires." In other words, the idea seems to be that when you are not mindful of the fact that your spirit is originally, in its basic essence, pure, you start to try too hard to make it pure, which actually hinders it from reverting to its natural, pure state. However, knowing in theory that the spirit is originally pure is not the same thing as directly witnessing your spirit's original purity and unity with the Dao, and this direct witnessing can only come about through the practice of the method of the Great Naturalness of Empty Nothingness.

*The Original Juncture*, one could argue, does not really describe any passive meditation technique. However, it does describe a method of contemplating the Dharma Body—also known as the True Dao, the Dao Body, or the Dao Nature—which is utterly formless, clear, and pure. This, being that it is a method of visualizing something that is formless, could be said to be similar to the method of the Non-action of Primal *Qi* endorsed in the Taiping Group texts. However, in *The Original Juncture* there is no claim that this is the superior meditation technique. The text equally endorses the method of visualizing in detail the 72 marks and 81 signs of the body of the Primordial Heavenly Worthy. It also states that merit equal to that gained by such contemplative practices can also be gained by worshipping an image of the Primordial Heavenly Worthy. In *The Original Juncture* the main teaching actually pertains not so much to contemplative techniques, but rather to metaphysical insights that can properly orient your practice when theoretically understood, and that constitute your very salvation when directly apprehended. One of these basic insights pertains to what is also emphasized in *The Original Arising*—the idea that the spirit is originally and fundamentally pure. It is equivalent to the Dao, which according to what can be deduced from *The Original Juncture*, also makes it equivalent to the Dharma Body—the True Body of the Primordial Heavenly Worthy. But beyond this insight that reassures you of your pure origins and your prospects for salvation, are insights of the Twofold Mystery doctrine that conduce to detachment from the things and notions (including detachment itself) that bind you to ignorance and *saṃsāra*. These insights pertain to Emptiness (lack of inherent existence), and the Emptiness of Emptiness.

*The Five Kitchens* (consisting merely of five sets of four lines of five-character verse) primarily describes a sort of mental attitude and approach that would be ordained by the insights of the Twofold Mystery doctrine (though terms such as "Twofold Mystery" or "Emptiness" do not actually appear in it). That attitude and approach is one in which you, while abiding in harmony and not engaging in any thinking, do not regard yourself as being in harmony, and do not make any intentional effort to cease or abstain from thinking. Although the text thus pertains primarily to mental states, references to *qi* and perhaps to more physical practices or concerns do occur briefly at the very beginning and end of the text. The text's very first line of verse refers to a peaceful harmony that occurs when the "*qi* of the One" is harmonious. Though one might begin to infer or conjecture that there is some particular technique that brings about this "harmony of the *qi* of the One," no clarification on this is to be found in the text itself, although Yin Yin's commentary does advertise the benefits that this harmony brings to the five viscera and their resident spirits. The text's final set of verses speaks of the *qi* that is introduced into the body through the taking of foods, and of how this cannot be permanently retained; the point being made seems to pertain to the impermanence of the body and of what sustains it, and the consequent futility of clinging to physical existence. As it turns out, the most important sort of practice that came to be connected to *The Five Kitchens* is one that the text does not even mention. That practice is the recitation of the text itself, which within both Daoist and Buddhist circles was thought to have the effect of subduing hunger.

*The Clarity and Calmness* has similarly enjoyed great popularity (to this very day in fact) as a text for recitation. The text itself in content is much more about encouraging and guiding insights than it is about meditation techniques. All that it tells you to do is to get rid of your desires, and reassures you that you can do this and remain free of desires because the spirit is basically fond of clarity and the mind is basically fond of calmness. It also provides insights by which you can become and remain detached from things that might otherwise elicit your desire; these insights pertain to Emptiness and to the Emptiness of Emptiness itself. Guided by these insights it is maintained that you can always maintain your inner clarity and calmness, even while responding to things that you encounter. The ultimate paradox, however, is that in gaining this blessed state of constant serenity you really gain nothing, for it is actually something that we all latently possess all along. This understanding precludes pretensions of being "virtuous" or of competing for recognition for this. Beyond what the text itself states, Daoist tradition also came to maintain that the exercise of reciting *The Clarity and Calmness* itself conduces greatly to the cultivation of serenity, and can also bring forth other blessings.

*Sitting and Forgetting* explains its own title (which is of course inspired by alleged statements by Yan Hui recorded in the sixth chapter of the *Zhuangzi*) as signifying a condition where you become oblivious both of yourself and of the world around you, and thereby achieve union with the Dao. As for how you are to go about attaining this condition, you should ground yourself on the insight that "there is nothing to be regarded as existing" (*wu suoyou* 無所有); this amounts again to saying that everything is Empty, and thus not worth becoming attached to. However, *Sitting and Forgetting* also warns that the concept of Emptiness itself can become an object of attachment, and that when there are any objects of attachment, this exhausts the mind and can also lead to disease. Also, while you should eliminate harmful thoughts and desires, this does not mean that you should eliminate all mental activity; at the very least you need to remain conscious and attentive, presumably so that you can guard against falling into delusions, and so that the ultimate union with the Dao can be experienced when it does come about. As for this union, however, you must not anxiously anticipate it or purposely seek it. The text thus states, "If people are able to empty their minds and practice non-action, even if they have no desire for the Dao, the Dao will come to them on its own."

*Stability and Observation* enjoins the method of "sitting peacefully" and "inwardly observing the arising of the mind." This you are to do so that as soon as you notice the emergence of any thought, you can eliminate it. All thoughts, even seemingly trivial and random ones, should be eliminated because they can lead to the formation of desires. Although the mind must be always kept free of thoughts, it must not become unconscious or inattentive, because you need to pay attention in order to detect the emergence of a thought and remove it. Yet, although constant attention is necessary, you must not strain your mind too hard. If the mind does not happen to be generating thoughts, you can relax; you need not be making any effort to make it or keep it calm. Straining the mind and trying too hard can actually lead to illness or to insanity. Thus, proper moderation in your degree of vigilance and relaxation is of the essence. Ultimately, out of a properly moderated state of mind there should emerge "wisdom" (*hui* 慧), but this wisdom must not be eagerly anticipated or sought. A person eager for wisdom is liable to fall into delusion or grandiosity.

*The Inscription* prescribes a method of simply calming the mind and focusing it on the Sea of *Qi* (also known as the Elixir Field). The relationship between the *qi* and the spirit is compared to that between a mother and child, and the method is in one place referred to as "the meditative stability observation that enters the womb," and in another as "the meditative stability observation of embryonic breathing." *The Inscription* also states that its method requires neither the imbibing of *qi* nor the swallowing of saliva, and does not entail "hard suffering" (even though it does require "the elimination of kernels"). The main stated purpose is to retain spirit and primal *qi* together in the body so as to keep the body alive. However, the text also speaks of higher insights and states of union with the Dao or with your True Nature, and takes apparent recourse to Buddhist terms such as "life of wisdom" and "spiritual penetration" (though interpretation of this portion of the text is made difficult by variations in wording in its two versions). It appears to have an author who is conversant in the Buddho-Daoist metaphysical discourse of the Tang period, but combines this metaphysics with his more quintessentially Daoist theory on spirit, *qi*, and physical vitality.

*Embryonic Breathing* is similar to *The Inscription* because it describes its meditation method as one of embryonic breathing, and this method is one that seems to involve little or no more than just turning the mind's attention inward (toward the Lower Elixir Field, according to the commentary) so as to retain the primal *qi* and ensure the body's vitality. This represents a contrast against embryonic breathing methods described in other texts that involve more deliberate, proactive measures such the holding of breath, the swallowing of saliva, or visualizations. However, there are also a few notable differences between *Embryonic Breathing* and *The Inscription*. For one thing, in *Embryonic Breathing* there is no Buddhistic terminology or metaphysics, nor any mention of states of wisdom or mystical union. Also, *Embryonic Breathing* speaks of how by subduing the *qi* within you (this is perhaps done by mentally directing the *qi* toward the Elixir Field while breathing normally through the nose), you form a "womb," and of how eventually "breathing" (carried out by the "spirit-child," according to the commentary) starts to occur within this womb. What exactly this means and what it is that you are likely to witness or experience as indications that this has occurred is unclear—though certain possibilities come to mind (a matter that we return to later). It would also appear, at least according to our conjectures made on the basis of information in *The Embryonic Origins*, *The Embryonic Subtleties*, *Holy Embryo*, and *Bodhidharma's Lesson*, that the formation of the womb forms a point from where the meditation practice transitions into a more proactive phase in which you mentally guide the spirit and primal *qi* on an inner circuit that extends throughout the body and head. In any case, this formation of the womb seems to constitute a monumental turning point in your experiences, capacities, and mental activities. The *Embryonic Breathing* commentary declares that its method is what is known as "Internal Alchemy, the Way of Immortality"; it seems perhaps that the inner "elixir" is the inner womb of spirit and *qi* that can be employed to thoroughly sustain, nurture, and heal the entire body.

Although the meditation techniques described in our texts are thus extremely varied, what they do have in common is that they require you to be undistracted, calm, and focused so as to observe or experience something—be it sensory, physical, psychological, noetic, or supernatural—that is ultimately going to arise spontaneously on its own, not by your compelling or forcing it. Visualization and other proactive measures can aid you in gaining the desired level of concentration, but they can also impede the emergence of the spontaneous phenomena. So then, what are these various phenomena to be observed or experienced?

Visions feature very prominently in a number of our texts. In the Taiping Group texts a particularly intimate connection was drawn out between mental serenity and the ability to see various marvelous things that are invisible otherwise. *GP Synopsis* outlines how as you begin to be more relaxed, patient, and focused in your confined contemplation practice, you begin to see images (though it is unclear whether these are things you are visualizing) clearly as though you are seeing them reflected in a mirror or on clear water. *GP Instructions* explains that as you become better at being pure and calm, you begin to see a divine radiance that will get increasingly brighter. With this bright radiance you become able to see distant things in all directions, and see the forms of spirits. You see spirits not only because of the increased acuity of vision wrought by your serenity, but also because—as *GP Synopsis* explains—the calm, joyful radiance that you exude attracts divine spirits to your midst.

*The Manifest Dao* also conveys the sense that good forces and spirits come to the company and protection of the serene practitioner who thinks only good thoughts. It also describes visions of light that shine forth from the Elixir Field. However, what really grabs one's attention in this text as far as visions are concerned is the strange and hazardous vision of "specters" in the form of an elderly woman attended by a girl, which is furthermore accompanied by symptoms of shaking and babbling on the part of the practitioner. In the text Laozi explains that this happens because your mind is lacking in concentration. You certainly must not become prideful or self-satisfied over seeing such a vision, and you must take greatest care not to converse with the old woman. Doing so will cause you to be "taken away" by her. In concrete terms it is difficult to determine what this is supposed to imply, but one might surmise that this could mean that being drawn into conversation with the old woman could lead you to lose your mind or even your life (?). The way to survive this hazard is to just maintain your composure and continue to contemplate the Elixir Field and circulate the primal *qi* (in a manner spontaneously synchronized with your ordinary respiration) as before. Although the old woman seems to be a malignant force that arrives from without, with the intention of exploiting your lack of concentration, Laozi also later in the text explains that specters are "intermediaries" of Genuine Persons, and that you therefore must not insult the specters, nor should you let other people know that you have encountered them. The idea here is perhaps that the specters are dispatched by holy, benevolent beings to test you, or that their appearance forms a prelude to subsequent auspicious epiphanies of holy beings (though this idea is not conveyed clearly the way it is in *Contemplating the Baby* or *The True Record*). We might also conjecture as to the possibility that the specters arrive from within your physical or psychic being. The text explains that the shaking and babbling that accompany the vision of the old woman and the girl are the effects of the activity of the primal *qi* that emerges from the Elixir Field. We might further conjecture that the vision could also be a hallucination linked to the somatic phenomenon regarded as the emergence of primal *qi*. It also seems highly plausible to regard the visual images as memories or archetypes that have emerged from the subconscious. The text states that the vision of the old woman and the girl occurs at least twenty or thirty days after you have commenced your practice, and thus one might surmise that the rigors of the lengthy desolation are beginning to have an effect.

The old woman and her girl attendant seem to reappear—albeit with somewhat altered attributes—in the Red Snake-Queen Mother vision sequence of *Contemplating the Baby*, *The True Record*, and other texts. This seeming reappearance is perhaps evidence in favor of the hypothesis that these visions are manifestations of archetypes from the subconscious. It bears questioning whether the descriptions in these different texts really do result from occurrences of similar experiences in different people, or are merely textual imagery that is borrowed to describe what is anticipated, rather than actually experienced. In any case, in the Red Snake-Queen Mother vision sequence it seems as though the old woman has become the more divine—albeit also crankier—figure of the Queen Mother of the West. In *The True Record* she also later on appears again as just an old woman, and at the 25-day juncture her girl attendant seems to make an appearance, albeit in the form of "two women." Both *Contemplating the*

*Baby* and *The True Record* speak of additional tempting, deluding visions that come in variously divine, anthropomorphic, and zoomorphic form, and explain that these are merely the mischievous crafting of the spirits that inhabit your body. Unique to *The True Record* is the intriguing description of the final trial occurring at the 150-day juncture, where you encounter "evil spirits claiming to be your father, mother, wife, and children." These sound a great deal like effects manifested by the complex, ambivalent, deep-seated feelings that we tend to harbor in regard to the people closest to us.

However, not all of the visions that you encounter are of the deluding, malicious variety. In *Contemplating the Baby* it is said that at certain points the Great Dao itself does appear before you (though it is difficult to discern as to exactly what things mentioned in the text constitute the epiphany as opposed to illusion), and at the very end Laozi declares that he will show you and tell you everything that you need to see and know about his Great Dao. Both *Contemplating the Baby* and *The True Record* also mention certain holy beings (elderly gentleman/white-haired elder riding a deer, Genuine Person[s], Heavenly Master[s]) who are genuinely holy and to whom you should speak truthfully and respectfully. Then there is the fiery red snake, which, shocking though it is, is not a malicious or deluding entity—though allowing yourself to be shocked by it does undermine all your efforts. From what is described in *Contemplating the Baby*, where the red snake is said to be both the Baby and the essence of the sun, we can conjecture that it represents your new core of awareness that has freshly emerged from the depths of your organic being, yet is at the same time perhaps an infusion of cosmic energy or awareness that comes from without. This vision could perhaps be said to embody the notion that the force that engenders and sustains your consciousness and vitality is the same as that which creates, animates, and bestows consciousness to the entire world. It also seems to pertain to a state of consciousness where the distinction between inside and outside, or subject and object, has been blurred or transcended.[1]

It should also be noted in regard to *The True Record* that in LLS#2, where it describes that simple method of becoming calm and then turning your senses inward (the method that *The Way of Transcendence*, *The Holy Chronicle*, and *Zhuzhen neidan jiyao* explicitly link to the Red

Snake-Queen Mother vision sequence), it states that you will see colorless colors, hear soundless sounds, taste flavorless flavors, and revere wordless utterances. Thus it promises a whole different way of sensing and apprehending things that eludes the categories of our normal experiences and understanding. In addition it mentions that your serenity also brings about a sympathetic inter-feeling with divine beings that causes them to come to your midst. It would seem, then, that the oddly nonsensory visions (and sounds and flavors) would perhaps also be accompanied by sensory visions of these deities. And there is again the question of whether the Red Snake-Queen Mother vision sequence is supposed to proceed from this.

*The Original Arising* describes how, when you practice its supreme meditation method of emptying the mind of all thoughts and focusing on your heart, you enter a condition where you can no longer tell whether you are breathing, or whether you still possess a body; you then experience your spirit hovering up amidst the empty nothingness above the heavens, and see all around you a blank whiteness similar to that which appears when a fresh snow has just covered all the mountains and trees. As for why you experience this, the text explains that your spirit really has risen above the skies and is on the verge of returning permanently into the empty nothingness of the Dao. Because you are to be compassionate and must tend to the needs of the suffering sentient beings in *saṃsāra*, you should at this point think of them and return to your body. This, it would appear, also has the effect of preventing the death that your body is on the verge of undergoing as it sits there with its breathing severely retarded or suspended. By witnessing what you did above the heavens you directly see for yourself that the spirit has the empty nothingness of the Dao as its original source and essence, and this somehow endows you with the ability to "show deaths and births" at will to act as a savior in the realm of *saṃsāra*. However, aside from this supreme visionary experience, *The Original Arising* also acknowledges that during your practice it is also likely that you will see wicked spirits, and—similarly to *The Manifest Dao*, *Contemplating the Baby*, and *The True Record*—warns that you must not converse with them. It also states that you should not bother yourself with the endeavor of trying to see spirits, for this is an inferior goal that detracts from the higher endeavor of directly encountering the empty nothingness of the Dao itself, and attaining the omniscience that this confers.

In *The Original Juncture*, the Primordial Heavenly Worthy, while announcing his departure from the world, declares to his bereaved, adoring audience that by practicing correct insight they will be able to see his body clearly. "Correct insight," as is stated clearly elsewhere in the text, refers to that of the Twofold Mystery. The sort of vision promised here is of the same sort promised by the Śākyamuni Buddha in the sixteenth chapter of the *Lotus Sūtra*, although there the vision is promised to all "who practice meritorious ways, who are gentle, peaceful, honest and upright."

In *Stability and Observation* it is warned that if you give rise to thoughts while in meditation, this is likely to cause you to see visions of all sorts of spirits. The explanation given for this is that your unnecessary and unwholesome thoughts evoke responses from these spirits; they seem to be drawn to you, motivated by the will to capitalize on your vulnerability. Among the visions that you are likely to see are also those of Heavenly Worthies, Genuine Persons, and Transcendents; ambiguities in the text make it difficult for us to ascertain whether these are to be regarded as deceitful apparitions crafted by malevolent spirits, or actual auspicious epiphanies.

Thus many—but not all—of our texts speak of visions that are likely to occur when you undertake the meditation methods that they propose. These visions can be variously hazardous or auspicious, and their source may be your own mind and body, or some place outside of you.

Another phenomenon that is noted in many of our texts is the decrease of hunger, and the gaining of the ability to survive without taking food. In *The Great Peace* it is maintained that at the time of their initial creation, human beings neither ate nor drank. Because they "embraced the primal *qi* naturally," their breathing alone was sufficient for nourishing them. The text further states these primitive people "exhaled and inhaled faintly" and could therefore contain the primal *qi* and survive without eating and drinking. *GP Synopsis* describes the condition of fetuses as one where they do not eat and do not even breathe, and yet they grow and flourish because they have the "*qi* of naturalness" within their bellies. Thus it is recommended that you should "revert to the *qi* of naturalness" and make your mind "like that of an infant." The Taiping Group texts thus seem to be saying that it is possible and desirable to attain a condition where you no longer eat or drink, and that this condition entails having simplicity of mind akin to primitives and infants, and a manner of respiration that is either very faint or completely dormant. From this one might further conjecture that it might be possible for a hunger-free state to come about naturally in the course of calm meditation, and we did indeed find one passage in *The Great Peace* that states, "Enter the room and contemplate the Dao. Naturally you will not eat and you will be bound together with *qi*." However, the authors of the Taiping Group texts also appear to have recognized that this did not come about quite so simply and easily in actual practice. Thus much more deliberate approaches such as "eating *qi*" (meaning most likely to swallow air), gradually reducing your daily food intake, or ingesting hunger-suppressing medicines are frequently mentioned and endorsed.

In *Laozi Xiang'er* the ability to survive without eating "grains" is mentioned as one of the definitive traits of the immortal Transcendents (*xianren* 仙人), though there is nothing wrong with eating grains per se, if they are available. Transcendents are able to do without ordinary food because they can eat *qi*. Although it is possible that the swallowing of air is what is meant here—as is what seems to be the case in the Taiping Group texts—it is also possible that *Laozi-Xiang'er* means something different by this term. Right after stating that Transcendents can eat *qi*, the text speaks of how *qi* can fill the belly, and in regard to how the *qi* fills the belly, the text tells the reader that it has already explained this in a previous chapter. As has been conjectured by Bokenkamp,[2] the chapter thus alluded to seems be the one near the very beginning of the extant text that explains how the Dao or its *qi* fills the bellies of those people whose minds are free of evil thoughts. It is perhaps thus considered possible that total purity of mind can lead to complete absence of hunger.

In early Daoist religion there thus existed theories according to which the elimination of hunger seemingly ought to occur naturally as a result of a pure mind and a calm mind and body (especially one that breathes very softly or slowly). However, as a practical matter various more deliberate and proactive techniques were employed for realizing this most difficult and arduous objective of conquering hunger. This state of affairs is fully embodied in *The Manifest Dao*. The third section of this text is a manual on fasting in which the method primarily entails the swallowing of air and saliva, and in which vivid descriptions are provided of the miserable and later glorious effects that the mind and body experience as they undergo a radical transformation. The text's second section ("Sudao jie") that describes the largely passive meditation method of the Plain Way allows for certain types of foods to be eaten in limited amounts while carrying out the regimen. However, it also maintains that the complete "elimination of grains" is necessary if you are to "transcend the world" (*dushi* 度世) as an immortal being, and that through the sustained practice of the method and beneficial effects of the Dao-*qi*, you certainly can get to where you never become thirsty or hungry. This Dao-*qi* is naturally activated from the Elixir Field in the belly by simply calmly focusing your attention there. The text also seems to say that as you continue to focus there and breathe normally, the Dao-*qi* will circulate your five viscera in a manner synchronized with your respirations, and then converge upon the stomach—which one might conjecture would have the effect of satiating hunger. Although the text states that you should just breathe naturally and not deliberately try to make your breaths "long," it does imply that your breathing will naturally become slower and deeper without any conscious effort to that end. One can surmise here that there could be an underlying connection between the slowing of breathing and the lessening of hunger. Though the text's second section thus does seem to proclaim the possibility of the elimination of hunger occurring naturally as an effect of its largely passive meditation regimen, one wonders whether the editor of *The Manifest Dao* added the third section so that its proactive fasting method could be employed as a supplement to the Plain Way, the regimen of which could prove too arduous otherwise.

Prescriptions for the limiting of eating, or the notion that the subduing of hunger constitutes an integral aspect of one's progress in cultivation can be found in some of our other texts. *Contemplating the Baby* and *The Original Arising* both prescribe "eating little food," but do not discuss in any more specific terms what this entails. *The Western Ascension* states that "the gentleman to the end of the day does not look, does not listen, does not speak and *does not eat*" (emphasis added), though the commentator Li Rong interprets this as merely meaning that you should limit your food intake and avoid particularly tasty foods. In *The True Record*, in LLS#4, after the description of the meditations of the Nine Rooms (which is preceded by the description of the Red Snake-Queen Mother vision sequence), it is stated that the practitioner's attendant should not become alarmed or dismayed if the practitioner stops taking the food that is left for him or her by the entrance of the meditation chamber, for this is a sign that the proper transformation is taking place. It should be noted here, however, that the Nine Rooms meditations that are apparently supposed to cause this transformation seem to be proactive techniques that involve much visualization, though they may also involve observation of spontaneous visions (this is extremely hard to tell from the text). In the case of *The Five Kitchens* we have a text that in content (despite its title) seems to say little or nothing about fasting, yet which came to be recited by both Daoists and Buddhists for its acclaimed efficacy for subduing hunger.

In *The Inscription*, the *Embryonic Breathing* commentary and the "Marvelous Functions Lesson" we find the claim clearly made that through the natural effects of internal *qi*, brought about by and large by just calmly turning the mind inward, you can eliminate hunger. In *The Inscription* it is maintained that if the Sea of *Qi*—that is, the Lower Elixir Field—contains in it a plenitude of primal *qi* wherein your spirit is snugly nestled, you will "naturally be satiated." In the *Embryonic Breathing* commentary it is explained that when the spirit stays within your body, this prevents the *qi* from scattering; the result is an inner plenitude where there is no more hunger or thirst. The commentary—citing Wu Yun's *Xuangang lun*—further explains that primal *qi* is *yang* whereas the *qi* acquired from foods is *yin*, and that therefore you need to reduce your food intake and your desires, and make the primal *qi* circulate within you; this fills you with *yang*, purges you of *yin*, and eliminates all ailments and defects from the body.

In thus speaking of the circulation of primal *qi* (and the reduction of desires—especially if this means sexual desires), the *Embryonic Breathing* commentary seems to address a subject that is not actually mentioned in the *Embryonic Breathing* scripture, but is discussed in the various versions of the "Marvelous Functions Lesson" found in *The Embryonic Origins*, *The Embryonic Subtleties*, *Holy Embryo*, and *Bodhidharma's Lesson*. This subject is the more proactive method of mentally guiding the embryo (composed of spirit and *qi*) on a circuit throughout the body that can ensue once the embryo has formed and has started to "breathe." The "Marvelous Functions Lesson" indicates (in wording that unfortunately varies in its different versions) that when you engage in this inner circulation your ordinary breathing through the nose becomes suspended—or perhaps that you just cease to exhale air (and the air you inhale perhaps departs through your pores); *Bodhidharma's Lesson* refers to this condition as "true embryonic breathing." If the condition is in fact one of suspended breathing, this indeed is what Ge Hong back in the early fourth century had considered to constitute embryonic breathing. In fact, the *Embryonic Breathing* scripture, while it does not speak of the internal circuit, does contain sentences (e.g., "If your mind does not give rise to thoughts, it will not come and go. Not leaving and entering, it naturally constantly stays.") that could be interpreted as meaning that your breathing becomes suspended. (Note also here that Ge Hong was familiar with a text entitled *Taixi jing*, though we do not know whether this was the same text as the *Embryonic Breathing* scripture.)

Additionally, in regard to the matter of breathing, note that *The Original Arising* maintains that when you practice its method of the Great Naturalness of Empty Nothingness, your breathing will become faint, and you will come to the point where you are not "aware of any breathing." This is its claim, even though it does not purport to be a text on "embryonic breathing," and its method is not described as one in which primal *qi* concentrates on or emerges from the navel, or starts to undertake any inner "breathing."

On the other hand, the Plain Way of *The Manifest Dao* does closely resemble our embryonic breathing texts, because its main emphasis is on the emergence of primal *qi* from the Elixir Field, and it also describes an inner circulation of this primal *qi*, albeit along a shorter route than that described in the "Marvelous Functions Lesson." This circulation, however, seems to occur simultaneously with normal respiration, in a manner synchronized with it. Though the text does imply that your breathing will naturally become longer and slower, it does not mention the suspension of breathing.

In addition to the phenomenon of suspended breathing (or at least suspended exhalation), the "Marvelous Functions Lesson" asserts that when you completely master the method of embryonic breathing, you will gain control over your sexual desires, and will prevent all body functions that can lead to ejaculation or to pregnancy ("it will cause a male to not gather essence in his stalk, and a female to not form an infant inside her navel"). Though it is quite possible that the author of the "Marvelous Functions Lesson" (or at least the editor of *The Embryonic Subtleties*) actually saw this sexual self-control as an attribute that might prove beneficial in the practice of sexual yogic techniques, we can note that adherents of subsequent celibate varieties of Neidan such as that of the Quanzhen tradition would place a great emphasis on the endeavor of harnessing and transforming the "essence," and considered the total elimination of sexual desire and shutting down of the body's sexual functions (especially, seminal emission and menstruation) to be natural effects that are supposed to come about through the inner serenity cultivated through their regimen.[3] This particular claim is not to be found in any of the materials examined in our current study (with the possible exception of the "Marvelous Functions Lesson"). However, the notion that the depletion of essence through sexual activity is injurious to the body certainly occurred quite early, and thus *Laozi Xiang'er* recommends restraint in sexual activity, and considers the ability to abstain as one of the definitive traits of immortal beings. In *The Manifest Dao* it is clear that the practice of the Plain Way requires abstinence from sexual activity, and it is stated unequivocally that celibacy must be maintained permanently if one is to hope to "transcend the world as a Flying Transcendent." The dual notions that sexual intercourse endangers health and that celibacy enhances the effectiveness of a longevity regimen are also readily found in the scriptures of the influential Shangqing movement of the late fourth century, as I have discussed in a previous study.[4] However, in all of these instances it seems to be by means of superior effort and discipline that sexual urges and impulses are to be resisted and subdued. The notion that one's sexual impulses and functions can shut down naturally as an effect of meditation or inner serenity is difficult to find in material prior to the late Tang.

In *The Original Arising* we find a description of yet another phenomenon that would become very prominent in Neidan literature from the late Tang onward,[5] but is not found elsewhere among the texts highlighted in our current study. That phenomenon is the experience of rising up beyond the heavens, which as the text explains, comes about because your spirit really has left your body (while the body in the mean time is barely breathing, if at all). *The Original Arising* tells you to make sure to come back down into your body because you will otherwise merge eternally into the empty nothingness of the Dao and will be unable to remain on earth and help your fellow sentient beings. Neidan texts similarly warn you to return quickly to your body; however, this is not because you do not want to ascend to transcendent bliss, but rather because it is feared that your spirit is still immature, and is likely to end up as a wandering ghost that will need to find a residence in another body or womb.[6] But in both the cases of *The Original Arising* and of Neidan texts, the tacit fear seems to be that actual physical death can occur in the midst of meditation if the spirit wanders for too long, particularly—one would think—if breathing is indeed suspended.

It merits noting here that the phenomenon of suspended breathing is also attested to within Buddhist literature. Various Buddhist texts—including very early Indian ones found in the Pali Canon—speak of a progression of four "Meditations" (*dhyāna* in Sanskrit; *jhāna* in Pali; *chan* 禪 in Chinese). These are meditative trance states that Śākyamuni Buddha himself is said to have progressed through and beyond. Although sometimes the distinctive traits of the Four Meditations are described as pertaining entirely to one's state of mind,[7] in some texts the suspension of breathing is said to occur when one progresses to the Fourth Meditation.[8] One's condition while in the Four Meditations is said to correspond to (and confer rebirth into) the condition of beings that dwell beyond the Realm of Desire 欲界, in the four highest heavens (the Four Meditations Heavens 四禪天) within the Realm of Form 色界. Beyond these Four Meditations are said to be the Four Formless Trances (四無色定) that constitute even subtler mental states and which correspond to the heavens of the Realm of No Form 無色界. The Trance of Complete Extinction (*miejin ding* 滅盡定; *nirodha-samāpatti* in Sanskrit) is the meditative trance stage that surpasses even the Four Formless Trances. It is a trance state that can be entered by a so-called nonreturner (*buhuan* 不還; *anāgāmin* in Sanskrit)—one who has overcome ignorance and confusion to the point where there will be no more rebirths in the human realm (and thus *nirvāṇa* is to be attained in the future while dwelling in one of the heavens). This trance state is characterized by a complete cessation of thoughts.⁹ In some early texts one finds evidence that the Trance of Complete Extinction may well have entailed a suspension or dramatic slowing of both breathing and pulse, because apparently on more than one occasion a learned monastic disciple (a nun, in one documented case) of the Buddha had to respond to the question of whether there is any difference between the condition of a dead person and that of one who has entered into the Trance of Complete Extinction. The difference, it is explained, lies in the fact that the person in the Trance of Complete Extinction remains alive, retains bodily warmth, and does not physically decompose.¹⁰ Also, in the *Huayan jing* 華嚴經 (*Avataṃsaka Sūtra*), one of the most influential Mahāyāna scriptures in China, we can find a passage where the Trance of Complete Extinction is described in terms suggesting that it is a condition difficult to distinguish from death.¹¹

As discussed in chapter 2, it is suggested in *GP Synopsis* (4/1a; 8/19b–20a) that breathing in the ordinary manner is what causes mortality, and that one ought to revert to the condition of the fetus that does not inhale and exhale from the mouth and nose. This sort of logic seems to lie behind the various *Embryonic Breathing* methods and theories that developed wherein the suspension of breathing (or at least of exhalation) was in some cases said to occur. It does not seem necessary to assume Buddhist influence in our texts where they mention or suggest the suspension of breathing. However, it should be noted that Buddhist theories and terms (such as the Four Meditations and the Trance of Complete Extinction) would be explicitly drawn upon at later periods by Daoist Neidan authors in regard to the suspension of breathing and pulse.¹²

On the topic of how the theories and phenomena described in our texts constitute parallels or precedents to what we find in later Neidan materials, one must also take note of how *Contemplating the Baby* describes a progression in your method of practice in which you first calmly focus your attention on the region of your kidneys, but later transfer your focus to your heart, and finally to your head. What you observe or feel (?) rising from your kidneys (an organ that in China was traditionally attributed with a chiefly reproductive function) is the apparently organic, impersonal *yuan* half of the *yuanqi* (primal *qi*). But when this rises from your heart to your head, this impersonal vital force manifests itself as a fiery red snake and then as the Baby, and this Baby seems to personify and subsequently function as the new core of your awareness. All of this is very similar to how in Neidan theories such as those developed by major figures in the Quanzhen tradition such as Li Daochun 李道純 (fl. 1288–1306) and Wu Shouyang 伍守陽 (1573–1640), you progressively refine essence (the impersonal, reproductive force from your kidneys) into *qi*, then *qi* into spirit (your Single Numinous Genuine Nature [*yiling zhenxing* 一靈真性]), and then finally refine spirit and make it return to the void. In the writings of Wu Shouyang it is clearly stated that the focus of attention shifts accordingly from the Lower Elixir Field, to the Middle Elixir Field and to the Upper Elixir Field.[13]

One of the intriguing questions that we are left with in *Contemplating the Baby* is what it is exactly that you are supposed to witness or feel when the *yuan* rises from the kidneys to the heart, and why this is likely to agitate you. Similarly, our texts on embryonic breathing left us wondering what it is that occurs that allows you to know that the "embryo" has formed inside you and has begun to breathe. One wonders here whether some answers to these questions might actually be found in *The Manifest Dao*, which describes rumbling in the intestines, quickening pulse, a drop in body temperature, aching in the hands and feet, visions, shaking in the limbs and babbling speech that occur when the primal *qi* is activated from the Elixir Field (an occurrence that should take place in two or three days for men, or four or five days for women). These sorts of things it describes as "signs of proof" (*zhengyan* 證驗). Perhaps practitioners of the methods of *Contemplating the Baby*, *Embryonic Breathing*, or the "Marvelous Functions Lesson" experienced some of these same things and thereby found in them verification that the *yuan* had risen to the heart, or that the embryo had formed and had started to breathe. In this regard it seems particularly relevant to mention that in *The Manifest Dao*, the moment when "the *qi* first arrives" is also known as the moment when "the breathing is obtained."

*The Manifest Dao* can be said to be unique among our texts in the degree to which it provides concrete descriptions of tactile sensations and physical symptoms that occur from deep states of serenity. On the other hand it can be noted that some of the texts that we have highlighted in our study have little or nothing to say about physical effects or benefits.

By probably no coincidence, these texts are ones that are heavily influenced by Buddhism.

*The Original Juncture* seems to represent among our materials the most extreme example of this. Its core teachings pertain to the metaphysics of the Twofold Mystery, and have to do with the gaining of enlightenment, rather than physical longevity or transformation. Even the contemplative and devotional practices that it describes (such as the visualization of the Primordial Heavenly Worthy's "marks" and "signs," and the veneration of a statue of him) seem to be based on Buddhist models. Aside from the fact that it gives Daoist names to its protagonists and employs certain terms and concepts from the *Laozi* in its metaphysical exposition, it is difficult to find much in *The Original Juncture* that distinguishes it from a Buddhist text.

*The Five Kitchens* and *The Clarity and Calmness* in content also seem to pertain almost entirely to mental cultivation and enlightenment. *The Five Kitchens* does, however, in its first line at least make mention of the "harmony of the *qi* of the One," which seems to describe some sort of optimal physical condition. *The Clarity and Calmness* does contain the ambiguous and all too vague phrase stating that "heaven and earth will all return," which would eventually be given a physiological interpretation by the twelfth-century Quanzhen master Ma Yu.

*The Original Arising* mentions the various sorts of Daoist methods designed to transform the body and bring about immortality, the power of flight, heavenly ascension, and the like, and does acknowledge their efficacy. However, the supreme method that it endorses is one that is geared toward gaining a supreme insight, and its practitioner is to shun any selfish goal such as physical immortality or heavenly ascension (or *nirvāṇa*, for that matter). The insight you attain confers you with the power to direct your own destiny and transform at will, but you must compassionately use that power to remain eternally in *saṃsāra*, continually "showing deaths and births."

*The Western Ascension*, on the surface at least, seems at times to reject the goal of physical immortality in the most radical of terms. It states that "the false way is to nurture the body and the True Way is to nurture the spirit." It rhetorically asks, "If you can disappear into empty space and become nothing, what need is there to fly away as a Transcendent?" It even depicts Laozi/Lord Lao himself declaring, "Even I have white hair, and have become decrepit and ripe in years."

By the eighth century or so the apparent tendency among some Daoists to de-emphasize the body and its immortal transformation had perhaps reached a point where a backlash was inevitable. The possibility and necessity of making the body immortal had to be reasserted, and this task is consciously taken on in *Sitting and Forgetting*, and in the discourse on the Seven Phases of physical transformation found in *Zuowang shuyi* (the appendix to *Sitting and Forgetting* version A), *Stability and Observation* and *The Inscription*.

*Sitting and Forgetting* argues that when the mind is empty, this naturally (with no such deliberate intention on your part) allows the Dao to enter into it, and when the Dao enters into you, it has the power to transform both your spirit and your body. If it so ends up that only your spirit is transformed—meaning that your mind attains wisdom but you end up undergoing physical death anyway—your level of attainment is still shallow. Through the power of the Dao the body should get refined to the point where you become a Divine Person whose body and spirit are eternally united as one, and can at will merge with the Dao or transform in any manner. This basic argument is in essence not too different from that put forth in *Laozi-Xiang'er*, where it states that if your mind is free of evil thoughts, the Dao—or its ubiquitous, life-giving *qi*—will fill your belly and keep you alive.

The Seven Phases of physical transformation are said to occur once the mind has attained a state of complete, constant calmness, which constitutes the last of the mind's Five Stages, as outlined in *Zuowang shuyi* and *The Inscription*. Thus, in these two texts, and in *Stability and Observation*, a severe rebuke is issued toward practitioners who think that they have attained great things even though no improvement or transformation has occurred in their physical condition.

*The Western Ascension* at closer examination also has a great deal positive to say about the body, and is in fact quoted as an authority in *Sitting and Forgetting* (as well as in the *Embryonic Breathing* commentary). It is indeed the thirty-sixth chapter of *The Western Ascension* that is being quoted by *Sitting and Forgetting* when it states, "If people are able to empty their minds and practice non-action, even if they have no desire for the Dao, the Dao will come to them on its own." It is in a similar paradoxical sense—that which holds that something good or desirable is actually more likely to occur if you do not purposely seek or desire it—that the reader needs to understand the comments in *The Western Ascension* that seemingly disparage the body and the possibility of immortality. *The Western Ascension* wants you to disregard and forget about the body—to revert to your original, pristine, worry-free condition that you possessed prior to becoming born and possessing a body. This, ironically, is what will best enable you to stay alive. There is also a passage in the text's twentieth chapter that in version B reads, "If you can always maintain [a condition of] clarity, calmness and non-action, *qi* will return." The text's earliest known commentator Wei Jie glosses this passage by stating, "When Dao-*qi* returns again to the body, you forget your body." In other words, the optimal state of consciousness coincides with or is brought about by an infusion of *qi*—apparently the very same *qi* of the Dao that is said to enter the bellies of the pure-hearted in *Laozi-Xiang'er*, and is said to emerge from the Elixir Field in *The Manifest Dao*.

In *The Western Ascension* the relationship between the body and the spirit is compared to that between a chariot and its rider, a house and its resident, or a host and his guest. As it turns out, the two counterparts need each other and must be kept together for their mutual benefit. Essentially, to keep the spirit in the body you must keep calm. Only if the spirit stays in the body can the body stay alive. The spirit, however, also needs the body, because it is only through dwelling in a body that the spirit can be "completed" (*cheng* 成). For the spirit to be completed means for it to attain the supreme level of consciousness, and the progression toward this attainment—given the deepness of our attachments and ignorance—requires the experience of embodied existence (actually, numerous embodied existences). The completed spirit appears to be equivalent to what is referred to as the "Genuine Spirit" in the text's seventh chapter, and is there described as something that "corresponds with the Dao" and that "can perish and can survive [as it pleases]" and can also "make the body fly" and "move mountains."

In *The Inscription* and *Embryonic Breathing* the main idea expounded in common is that through calm inner concentration you must keep your spirit inside your body; indeed the *Embryonic Breathing* commentary cites *The Western Ascension*'s house and host metaphors to help illustrate this point. Both *The Inscription* and *Embryonic Breathing* explain that as long as the spirit stays within the body, so will the primal *qi*, and thus the body will stay alive. But *The Inscription* also says that when the spirit (the "child") lies snugly within the primal *qi* (the "mother") in the Sea of *Qi*, your mind enters a state of meditative trance or "stability" (or *samādhi* in Sanskrit), which enables you to "dwell at the source of the Dao" and be a sage endowed with wisdom. According to the wording of version A, the text also seems to say that your enlightened spirit partakes of the "life of wisdom" (*huiming* 慧命), a term that in Buddhist literature denotes the eternal life of the Buddha's Dharma Body that you can partake in as long as you possess the wisdom of enlightenment. In any case, *The Inscription*, somewhat like Wei Jie's commentary to *The Western Ascension*, attributes to the vitality-sustaining *qi* the additional property of engendering a higher state of consciousness and wisdom that reconnects you to your original source and Genuine Nature (the Dao; the Dharma Body).

While the influx of Buddhist doctrines into medieval Daoism apparently provoked a protest against the seeming neglect of bodily cultivation that it engendered, Buddhism's impact on the Daoist religion was permanent. Even protesting texts such as *Sitting and Forgetting*, *Stability and Observation*, and *The Inscription* take recourse to Buddhist terminology and metaphysics. Buddhist insight-based strategies toward fostering detachment provided Daoists with indispensable tools for fostering serenity. Mahāyāna Buddhist teachings pertaining to the Buddha's eternal Dharma Body and the universal Buddha Nature of sentient beings tended to confirm and add an extra compassionate dimension to Daoist notions of an eternal Dao that imbues all of us, and which we can best encounter when we forget about ourselves. However, to merely say something to the effect that enlightenment somehow endows the spirit with the power to transform the body, or brings about an infusion of the Dao and its life-sustaining and transforming power, may seem far too simple and shallow as descriptions and explanations of what happens in an organism so complex as the human being. Daoists of subsequent periods were left with the continued task of properly understanding and explaining the intricacies of mind and body while integrating that understanding with practical approaches that were sufficiently simple and passive so as to not undermine the salubrious natural processes of the mind and body.

This task would be carried out in a thorough and influential manner by proponents of what one might call the "passive-reactive" approach to Neidan meditation, which would eventually be given its most concrete and thorough expositions by Wu Shouyang 伍守陽 (1574–1644) and Liu Huayang 柳華陽 (fl. 1794; a self-professed Buddhist, curiously enough). Some Neidan regimens—such as that promoted in *Bichuan Zhengyang zhenren lingbao bifa* 祕傳正陽真人靈寶畢法[14] and *Zhong-Lü chuan-dao ji* 鍾呂傳道集[15] of the Northern Song 北宋 (960–1127) period—entailed many complicated, proactive methods of controlled respiration, saliva-swallowing, visualizations, postures, stretches, tensing of muscles, and the like. Some forms of Neidan would entail sexual intercourse (or paired practice by a man and woman that entailed no actual contact). Proponents of passive-reactive Neidan were critical or dismissive of all such methods of mental and physiological self-manipulation, and asserted that such things needed to be pursued only at the rudimentary stages of self-cultivation, or be eschewed altogether. They advocated passively observing the spontaneous stirrings of fresh psychic or physiological activity that emerge from the depths of stillness, and then reacting to these with certain acts of mental volition, such as the guiding of the *qi* up the spine, or the projection of the spirit out of the top of the skull. I hope to discuss all of this in a sequel to the current book.

# Notes

CHAPTER 1. INTRODUCTION

1. "Mystical" here means an experience or insight that is beyond ordinary sense perception or rational knowledge.
2. The character 氣 for *qi* is thought to derive from a pictograph of steam rising up from the character 米 (*mi*; "kernel[s] of grain"), and thus in its most fundamental, archaic sense seems to denote steam, air, or things of a gaseous nature. However, it is sometimes used in a much broader, metaphysical sense to denote something like the fundamental energy or substratum of the universe that in itself is neither spirit nor matter, but which can condense into solid and liquid forms, or rarify into gaseous forms, or into spirit. Perhaps most notable, then, is that in this metaphysics, spirit and matter are not distinctly different entities; both are *qi*, albeit in very different degrees of condensation or rarefaction.

In discussions pertaining to the human mind and body, *qi* is frequently presented as part of a triad with essence (*jing* 精) and spirit (*shen* 神). In such cases, *qi* refers to that which animates us, and which circulates though the body as breath or as currents of energy. Essence is that which nourishes the body if kept within and which procreates when interacting outwardly; it is primarily associated with bodily fluids, and with sexual fluids in particular. Spirit is formless and is what makes you conscious and intelligent.

3. See Isabelle Robinet, *Taoist Meditation: The Mao-Shan Tradition of Great Purity*, translated by Norman Girardot and Julian Pas. Originally published in French as *Meditation taoïste*; and *La revelation du Shangqing dans l'histoire du taoïsme*.

4. There does not yet seem to be a clear consensus among scholars regarding the definition of Neidan and the historical period at which it originates. However, I would tentatively define it as a theory and method of meditation that takes recourse to the terminology, metaphysics, and practical model (of progressive praxis and transformation) of alchemy—particularly that of the sort expounded in the *Zhouyi cantong qi* 周易參同契 (DZ999/TT621). Thus, by "Neidan" I refer to a phenomenon that seems to have its origins in the mid- to latter part of Tang period, and which gained prominence from the Song period onward. The usage of the term *Neidan* is also something that we see emerging among Daoists during the Tang, and becoming frequent and pervasive from the Song onward. However, there are many passages in the Shangqing scriptures and in even earlier texts—such as the *Taishang Laojun zhongjing* 太上老君中經 (DZ1168/TT839; also in *Yunji qiqian* 18 and 19; second century?) and *Taishang huangting waijing yujing* 太上黃庭外景玉經 (DZ332/TT167; pre-255)—that amply employ terminology from laboratory alchemy and feature concepts such as that of an inner "baby" (representing one's true inner self) or "embryo" of immortality that would feature prominently in later Neidan. For an excellent study and translation of the *Zhouyi cantong qi*, see Fabrizio Pregadio, *The Seal and Unity of the Three: A Study and Translation of the* Cantong qi, *the Source of the Taoist Way of the Golden Elixir*. On the precedents to Neidan terminology and concepts in *Taishang laojun zhong jing* and *Taishang huangting neijing yujing*, see Pregadio 2011, 58–63.

In citations of texts from the *Daoist Canon* (meaning the extant Ming dynasty canon consisting of the *Zhengtong daozang* 正統道藏 of 1445 and *Xu daozang* 續道藏 of 1607), the DZ number denotes the "work number" assigned to the text in Kristofer Schipper and Franciscus Verellen, eds., *The Taoist Canon: A Historical Companion to the* Daozang. The TT number denotes the number of the fascicle(s) containing the text in the 1926 Shanghai Hanfenlou 涵芬樓 facsimile reprint edition of the *Daoist Canon*.

5. See Harold D. Roth, *Original Tao: Inward Training and the Foundation of Taoist Mysticism*.
6. Page citations for the *Laozi* refer to the version in the *Daozang* that bears the commentary of Heshanggong 河上公 (*Daode zhenjing zhu* 道德真經註 [True Classic of the Tao and the Virtue, with Commentary]; DZ682/TT363).
7. See James Legge, *The Texts of Taoism*, 95.
8. Page citations for the *Zhuangzi* refer to the nonannotated version in the *Daozang* (*Nanhua zhenjing* 南華真經 [True Classic of the Southern Florescence]; DZ670/TT349–351).
9. See Legge 1959, 305.
10. See Livia Kohn, *Seven Steps to the Tao: Sima Chengzhen's* Zuowang lun, and *Sitting in Oblivion: The Heart of Daoist Meditation*.
11. For a full study and translation of the *Guanzi*, see W. Allyn Rickett, Guanzi*: Political, Economic and Philosophical Essays from Early China*. The book is attributed to Guan Zhong 管仲 (725–645), but was probably compiled during the Warring States (403–221 BCE) period.
12. This critical edition with full English translation is found in Roth 1999, 45–97.
13. The end of the first chapter of the *Xunzi* 荀子 (by Xun Kuang 荀況; ca. 313–238 BCE) has the following statement: "Once your conduct is virtuous you can be stable. Once you are able to be stable, you can respond [to things]. If you are able to be stable and able to respond, you are what is called an accomplished person" 德操然後能定　能定然後能應　能定能應　夫是之謂成人 (*Xunzi*, 9). This is an instance in a text close in date to the *Neiye* where rectitude in moral virtue and conduct is put forth as a prerequisite for *ding*, which constitutes a sort of mental stability that conduces to good judgement and proper action. John Knoblock translates *ding* as "firm of purpose." See John Knoblock trans., *Xunzi: A Translation and Study of the Complete Works*, vol. 1, 142.
14. Mencius is recorded as stating, "I am good at cultivating my flood-like *ch'i* (*qi*)." (D.C. Lau trans., *Mencius*, 77.) See *Mengzi* 孟子 (*Sibu congkan chubian* 四部叢刊初編 4) 3/6b.
15. This phrase is emended and translated by Roth as "it abides within the excellent mind" 善心焉處. See Roth 1999, 54–55.
16. Here the texts are referred to by our ad hoc appellations, with their

full Chinese titles in parentheses. More complete title and bibliographical information for our principal texts is provided in the respective chapters where they are discussed.

17. *Benqi* 本起 or "original arising" seems to refer to the cosmic processes that brought about the world as we know it, because the first portion of *The Original Arising* consists of a description of cosmogonic processes. The word *benqi* happens to figure in the titles in a number of Buddhist scriptures pertaining to the life of the Buddha. It is possible that the author of *The Original Arising* got the idea to use the word from seeing it in the titles of such Buddhist works. However, the meaning of the term within the title of our Daoist text seems to be a cosmogonic one, because in *The Original Arising* there is no discussion pertaining to the biography of the Buddha or anybody else.

18. The Quanzhen School was founded by Wang Zhe 王嚞 (1113–1170) and developed into a prominent monastic order under the Yuan 元 dynasty. It currently remains the predominant school of monastic Daoism in China. In recent years several Western language monographs on the early phases of this movement have been published. See Eskildsen, *The Teachings and Practices of the Early Quanzhen Taoist Masters*; Louis Komjathy, *Cultivating Perfection: Mysticism and Self-transformation in Early Quanzhen Daoism* and *The Way of Complete Perfection: A Quanzhen Daoist Anthology*; and Pierre Marsone, *Wang Chongyang (1113–1170) et la foundation du Quanzhen: ascètes taoïstes et alchimie intérieure*.

CHAPTER 2.
THE EARLIEST-KNOWN DAOIST RELIGIOUS MOVEMENTS

1. Pei Songzhi notes that this person's name was actually Zhang Heng 張衡. Zhang Heng was the son of the 1st Heavenly Master (*tianshi* 天師) Zhang Daoling 張道陵 and the father of the 3rd Heavenly Master Zhang Lu 張魯.
2. Citation is from *Sanguo zhi*.
3. See Anna Seidel, *La divinasation de Lao Tseu dans le taoïsme des Han*.
4. Citation is from *Houhan shu*.

5. See Seidel 1969, 48–50.
6. The 75th *juan* of the *Han shu* 漢書 records that during the reign of Han Emperor Cheng 成帝 (r. 33–7 BCE) a certain man of the region of Qi 齊 (Shandong) named Gan Zhongke 甘忠可 fabricated a book in 12 *juan* entitled *Tianguan li baoyuan taiping jing* 天官曆包元太平經. He claimed that this book constituted the teachings that he had received from the Genuine Man Chijingzi 真人赤精子, who had been dispatched as an envoy by the Emperor of Heaven (Tiandi 天帝) to proclaim that the Han royal house was on the verge of being confronted with the end of the world, and needed to receive the Mandate of Heaven anew. The book was later presented to the court of Emperor Ai 哀帝 (r. 7–1 BCE). It can be said the title of Genuine Man borne by Chijingzi, the notion that he was an envoy of a supreme divine being of heaven, as well as the theme of restoring the virtue of the regime so as to avert cosmic disaster, bear strong resonances with the *Taiping jing* or what survives of it. See Ban Gu 班固 (32–92), *Han shu*.
7. These texts include the *Zhengyi fawen tianshi jiaojie kejing* 正一法文天師教戒科經 (DZ789/TT563), the *Taishang Laojun jinglü* 太上老君經律 (DZ786/562), and the *Santian neijie jing* 三天內解經 (DZ1205/TT876). See Kristofer Schipper, "*Zhengyi fawen tianshi jiaojie kejing*," and "*Taiping jing*," in Schipper and Verellen, 120–122, 277–280. According to the view put forth in these texts, Gan Ji received his revelation from Lord Lao, which took place during the Zhou dynasty (ca. 1020–256 BC). In the *Zhengyi fawen tianshi jiaojie kejing*, in a section entitled *Daodao jialing jie* 大道家令戒 (Commands and Admonitions for the Families of the Great Dao), Zhang Jue is denounced for causing tens of millions of deaths, and his movement is referred to as a "deviant Dao." See Stephen Bokenkamp, *Early Daoist Scriptures*, 172.
8. DZ1101.a/TT746–755.
9. The *juan* that survive in it are *juan* numbers 35–37, 39–51, 53–55, 65–72, 86, 88–93, 96–114, 116–119.
10. DZ1101.b/TT746–747.
11. DZ1102/TT755. A partial translation of this text (1a–3b) is found in Livia Kohn, *The Taoist Experience: An Anthology*, 193–197.

12. Some scholars, beginning with Tang Yongtong 湯用彤 and including Wang Ming 王明, have subscribed to the view that *GP Synopsis* was edited and compiled by Lüqiu Fangyuan 閭丘方遠 (d. 902), who has been described as having been a practitioner of the meditation of Guarding the One (a prominent theme in the *Taiping jing*) and is known to have produced a book of "selections" (*quan* 銓 or *quan* 詮) from the *Taiping jing*. However, others such as Kristofer Schipper maintain that such cannot be the case, because Jia Shanxiang's 賈善翔 (ca. 1086–1100) *Youlong zhuan* 猶龍傳 (DZ774/TT555; 4/18a) states that there is a "synopsis" of the *Taiping jing* in 10 *juan* (apparently meaning *GP Synopsis*), the author of which is unknown, while also mentioning Lüqiu Fangyuan's *Taiping jing* selections, which amounted to 30 *juan* in length. This would seem to indicate that Lüqiu Fangyuan's compilation was not *GP Synopsis*. See Tang Yongtong, "Du *Taiping jing* shu suojian" 讀《太平經》書所見, *Guoxue jikan* 國學集刊, 7–38; Wang Ming 王明, *Taiping jing hejiao* 太平經合校, "Introduction," 15 ff; Schipper, "*Taiping jing chao*," in Schipper and Verellen, 493–494; *Xu xian zhuan* 續仙傳 (DZ295/138; by Shen Fen 沈汾) 3/4a–6a.

13. See Wang 1960, "Introduction," 15 ff. Wang Ming further speculates that *GP Instructions* was also put together by Lüqiu Fangyuan, whom he regards as the editor/compiler of *GP Synopsis*. Yoshioka Yoshitoyo 吉岡義豊 also views *GP Instructions* as being of provenance closely related to *GP Synopsis*. Grégoire Espesset regards *GP Instructions* as largely preserving what would have been found in the now-lost 38th *juan* of *The Great Peace*. This is because an important manuscript from the caves of Dunhuang (Stein manuscript, no. 4226)—that which preserves a table of contents with section titles for the entire original 170-*juan* text of *The Great Peace*—indicates that the 38th *juan* bore the title of "Shouyi fa" 守一法 (Method for Guarding the One) and consisted of a "section 49" that bore the same title. Barbara Hendrischke, however, takes a more reserved attitude toward *GP Instructions*, observing that its style of writing, which employs eloquent four character phrases, rhymes, and rhetorical devices, is highly dissimilar to the portions of *The Great Peace* that she regards as most likely of second-century provenance (what she calls "layer A

material") and is more reminiscent of its portions that she regards most likely to be added later by sixth-century editors ("layer C material"). See Yoshioka Yoshitoyo, "Taihei-kyō no shuitsu shisō" 太平経の守一思想, in Yamazaki sensei taikan kinenkai 山崎先生退官記念会 ed., *Tōyō shigaku ronshū* 東洋史学論集, 491–500; Grégoire Espesset, "Cosmologie et trifonctionnalité dans l'idéologie du Livre de la Grande paix"; Barbara Hendrischke, *The Scripture on Great Peace: The Taiping jing and the Beginnings of Daoism*, 161, nn. 1.

14. DZ1130/TT764.
15. DZ1139/TT780–782. As has been pointed out by Florian Reiter, about two-thirds of this encyclopedia has been lost. Its compiler, Wang Xuanhe 王懸河, was a court Daoist active around 680. See Reiter, "*Sandong zhunang*," in Schipper and Verellen, 440–441.
16. See Fukui Kōjun, "*Taihei kyō* no ichi kōsatsu" 太平経の一考察, *Tōyō shi kai kiyō* 東洋史会紀要, 1–2 (1936–1937): 141–178. Yoshioka Yoshitoyo, *Dōkyō to Bukkyō* 道教と仏教, vol. 2, 103–104, 130–131.
17. See Schipper, "*Taiping jing*," in Schipper and Verellen, 277–280.
18. See Schipper, "*Taiping jing chao*," and "*Taiping jing shengjun bizhi*," in Schipper and Verellen, 493–495.
19. See Hendrischke 2006, 67–342.
20. Ibid., 38–47.
21. Roth here emends the character *gan* 敢 with *fang* 放.
22. See Kubo Noritada 窪徳忠, *Kōshin shinkō no kenkyū* 庚申信仰の研究; and Eskildsen, *Asceticism in Early Taoist Religion*, 46, 61.
23. The terms loosely translated here as "feet" and "inches" are *chi* 尺 and *cun* 寸. During the second century, one *chi* equaled 23.04 centimeters, and one *cun* was 2.304 centimeters.
24. The difficulty in translation here lies in the problem of understanding the character *de* 德, which perhaps here, like its homophone *de* 得, means to "acquire." Or, perhaps it is best rendered in its most usual sense as "virtue."
25. For cognate passages see *GP Synopsis* 5/5a–b; and *GP Instructions* 2b–3b.
26. See *The Great Peace* 42/1a–b.
27. See Edward Conze ed., *Buddhist Texts through the Ages*, 56–59 (esp., 57; translation from Pali by I.B. Horner); Bhikkhu Ñāṇamoli and

Bhikkhu Bodhi trans., *The Middle Length Discourses of the Buddha: A New Translation of the* Majjhima Nikāya, 949–958 (esp., 951; *Kāyagatāsati Sutta* [Sutta #119]).

28. See Tilmann Vetter, *A Lexicographical Study of An Shigao's and his Circle's Chinese Translations of Buddhist Texts*, 82–83. An example of an early translation that deals with this and other meditative concentration techniques related to breathing is the *Foshuo anban shouyi jing* 佛說安般守意經 (*Taishō Canon*, no. 602, vol. 15), translated by the Parthian An Shigao 安世高 (fl. 148–170).

29. Here I comply with Wang Ming's emendation of the text in *Taiping jing hejiao*, which certainly makes better sense in this context.

30. In the *Agañña Sutta* (Sutta #27 of the *Digha Nikaya*) we find a description of how when the world newly evolves, the beings that inhabit it are made of mind (not body), feed on rapture (not food), and radiate their own light. Eventually, their greed incites them to eat various things that appear in the world (first an "earth essence," then a "fragrant earth," then "a creeper," and then rice), and this causes them to lose their radiance, form physical bodies, engage in sexual intercourse and give rise to human culture with all of its other vices. (See T.W. Rhys Davids and C.A.F. Rhys Davids trans., *Dialogues of the Buddha*, 77–94; also Steven Collins, *Nirvana and Other Buddhist Felicities: Utopias of the Pali Imaginaire*, 627–634.) Thus, in both this Buddhist account and *The Great Peace*, our predecessors long ago are said to have not eaten food, and their loss or lack of purity or innocence causes them to eat. However, in *The Great Peace* our forebears are already embodied as humans at the time of primal innocence, the primal *qi* is what sustains them, and heaven and earth generate solid and liquid nourishment out of pity for their hunger and mortality—none of which are the case in the Buddhist account. In sum, although it is possible that the author(s) of *The Great Peace* were somehow, to some degree influenced by the Buddhist myth, there does not seem to be adequate reason to make such a conclusion.

31. The remaining eight types of persons, in descending rank, with their respective tasks, are as follows: (1) Great Divine Persons (*da shenren* 大神人), regulate heaven; (2) Genuine Persons (*zhenren* 真人) regulate earth; (3) Transcendents (*xianren* 仙人), regulate the four

seasons; (4) Great Persons of the Dao (*da daoren* 大道人), regulate the five agents; (5) Sages (*shengren* 聖人), regulate the *yin* and *yang*; (6) Worthies (*xianren* 賢人), regulate the documents and books; (7) commoners (*fanren* 凡人), regulate the grasses, trees and five varieties of grain; and (8) servants and slaves (*nubi* 奴婢), regulate property and money.

32. See Rao Zongyi 饒宗頤, *Laozi Xiang'er zhu jiaozheng* 老子想爾注校證.

33. These sources include *Chuanshou jingjie yi zhujue* 傳授經戒儀注訣 (DZ1238/TT989); Lu Deming's 陸德明 (556–627) *Jingdian shiwen* 經典釋文 (In *Sibu congkan* 四部叢刊, vols. 52–63); *Sandong fengdao kejie yifan* 三洞奉道科誡儀範 (Dunhuang Pelliot Manuscript, no. 2337); Zhang Wanfu's 張萬福 (early eighth c.) *Chuanshou sandong jingjie falu lüeshuo* 傳授三洞經戒法籙略說 (DZ1241/TT990); and Du Guangting's 杜光庭 (850–933) *Daode zhenjing guangsheng yi* 道德真經廣聖義 (DZ725/TT440–448). See Ōfuchi Ninji, *Shoki no dōkyō* 初期の道教, 248.

34. The precepts referred to here are not expressly enumerated anywhere in what survives of *Laozi-Xiang'er*. However, as various scholars have pointed out, they are most likely a set of 36 precepts (9 prescriptive and 27 proscriptive) that were transmitted within early Heavenly Masters circles and have been preserved in several extant sources. The earliest of these (dating perhaps as early as the third century) is the *Taishang Laojun jinglü* 太上老君經律 (Canonical Rules of the Most High Lord Lao; DZ786/TT562), where the precepts are enumerated under the heading "Daode zunjing Xiang'er jie" 道德尊經想爾戒 (Xiang'er Precepts of the Venerable Scripture of the Dao and the Virtue). The prescriptive precepts are drawn from the *Laozi* main text, and include things such as "practice nonaction" 行無爲, "practice clarity and calmness" 行清靜, and "practice nondesire" 行無欲. The proscriptive items are drawn from the *Laozi-Xiang'er* commentary, and admonish against a wide range of things including meat-eating, killing, coveting, seeking fame, and wastefully expending essence and *qi*. The other texts that enumerate the *Xiang'er* precepts are the *Taishang jingjie* 太上經戒 (DZ787/TT562), the *Yaoxiu keyi jielü chao* 要修科儀戒律鈔 (DZ463/TT204–207), and the "Shuo jie"

說戒 (Proclaiming the Precepts) section of the *Yunji qiqian* 雲笈七籤 (DZ1032/TT677–702), where they are referred to as "Lord Lao's 27 Precepts" 老君二十七戒 (38/18a–19a). See Schipper, "*Taishang Laojun jinglü*," in Schipper and Verellen, 131–132; and Bokenkamp 1997, 48–51. For a full translation of the lists of prescriptive and proscriptive *Xiang'er* Precepts, see Bokenkamp 1997, 49–50.

35. These sources are *Chuanshou jingjie yi zhujue* (3b) and *Jingdian shiwen*. While the former source is unequivocal in ascribing authorship to Zhang Lu, the latter states that it is variously maintained that the author is Zhang Lu, or Liu Biao 劉表 (d. 218; a famous military commander). See Schipper, "*Laozi Xiang'er zhu*," in Schipper and Verellen, 74–77.
36. These sources are *Tang Xuanzong yuzhi Daode zhenjing shu* 唐玄宗御製道德真經疏 (DZ679/TT358; Waizhuan, 1b) and *Daode zhenjing guangshengyi* (preface, 2b). See Schipper, "*Laozi Xiang'er zhu*," in Schipper and Verellen, 74–77.
37. See Schipper, "*Laozi Xiang'er zhu*," in Schipper and Verellen, 74–77.
38. See, for example, the discussions on this issue in Kusuyama Haruki 楠山春樹, *Rōshi densetsu no kenkyū* 老子傳說の研究; and Kobayashi Masayoshi 小林正美, *Rikuchō dōkyōshi kenkyū* 六朝道教史研究 (Tokyo: Sōbunsha 創文社, 1990).
39. See Chen Shixiang 陳世驤, "Xiang'er Laozi daojing Dunhuan canjuan lunzheng" 想爾老子道經敦煌殘卷論證, *Ts'ing Hua Journal of Chinese Studies* 清華學報, 41–62.
40. See Ōfuchi 1991, 247–308.
41. See Bokenkamp 1997, 29–77.
42. This text is contained in *Zhengyi fawen tianshi jiaojie kejing*, 12a–19b.
43. It is however unclear whether the word in this case refers to *Laozi-Xiang'er*, or to the *Xiang'er* precepts, or rather should be rendered "[the Dao] thinks of you," as Bokenkamp does. See Bokenkamp 1997, 172, 184 (nn. 4).
44. *Chuanshou jingjie yi zhujue* (3b) explains that Zhang Lu wrote his *Xiang'er* commentary in order to guide the simple and shallow-minded people of the Shu 蜀 (Sichuan) region, and to do so claimed to have met and received his teachings from Xiang'er (or Xiang Er, if

the understanding is to be that Xiang was his surname). See Schipper, *Laozi Xiang'er zhu*, in Schipper and Verellen, 74–77.
45. See Bokenkamp 1997, 61–62; Ōfuchi 1991, 297–298. In this view, then, the author of *Chuanshou jingjie yi zhujue* and his contemporaries had taken what was originally something of a watch word or slogan of the early Heavenly Masters movement and construed it as the name of a holy personage.
46. See Bokenkamp 1997, 29–148.
47. See Gu Baotian 顧寶田, Zhang Zhongli 張忠利 and Fu Wuguang 傅武光 eds., *Xinyi Laozi Xiang'er zhu* 新譯老子想爾注 (full original text of the *Laozi Xiang'er zhu* with introduction, modern Chinese translation and notes).
48. For quotations from *Laozi-Xiang'er* we refer to the number of the page(s) at which the original Classical Chinese text for the passage is provided in Gu, Zhang, and Fu 1997. Also see Bokenkamp's translation of the same passage.
49. The manuscript has the character *ling* 靈 here, where the received *Laozi* has the character *xu* 虛.
50. See Bokenkamp 1997, 41–42. Bokenkamp also further interprets the passage as meaning that you should make the "pneumas" (*qi*) of morning and evening descend into your body so that you can mix them with yours, and distribute them through the body. My impression is that the text is simply drawing a parallel between the body's natural *qi* circulation and that of the cosmos.
51. It is clear (from critical passages contained in the important Shangqing school compilation the *Zhen'gao* 真誥 [DZ1016/TT637–640]) that by at least the fourth century the rite was flourishing among Heavenly Masters adherents in the south, and that its origins were being ascribed to the first Heavenly Master Zhang Daoling (see Eskildsen 1998, 77–79). Strong evidence that the rite was occurring within the movement by at least some point in the third century is found in an internal source, the *Nüqing guilü* 女青鬼律 (DZ790/TT563). (See Adrianus Dudink, "*Nüqing guilü*," in Schipper and Verellen, 127–129.) However, one does wonder why the rite is not mentioned in the passages in the dynastic histories describing the

practices of the Heavenly Masters and other "sinister bandits," because such activity might normally tend to get noticed and sensationalized by an unsympathetic reporter. Ōfuchi draws from *Laozi-Xiang'er* the conclusion that the Heavenly Masters movement in its earliest days did not engage in the Merging of *Qi*, or any other sexual ritual or technique. See Ōfuchi 1991, 330–334.

52. See Bokenkamp 1997, 43–44. The principal primary sources available for attempting to understand the rite of "merging the *qi*" are the *Dongzhen huangshu* 洞真黃書 (DZ1343/TT1031) and the *Shangqing huangshu guodu yi* 上清黃書過渡儀 (DZ1294/TT1009).

53. These are issues that I intend to discuss in the sequel to the current study. In what can be called the "passive-reactive" approach to Neidan subscribed to by Wu Shouyang, Liu Huayang and others, the key undertaking in the early stages of the regimen is the calm observation and detection of the moment at which a new movement of vital force emerges from the depths of stillness. In terms of concrete symptoms, this can cause a movement of essence toward the tip of the penis that can (but must not be allowed to) lead to ejaculation, and/or to erection. The fresh movement of vital force is awaited for in meditation, but must also be anticipated to occur during sleep. See Wu Shouyang, *Tianxian zhengli zhilun zengzhu* 天仙正理直論增註, in *Zangwai daoshu* 藏外道書 5:836b–837b; *Xianfo hezong yulu* 仙佛合宗語錄, in *Zangwai daoshu* 5:661a; Liu Huayang, *Huiming jing* 慧命經, in *Zangwai daoshu* 5:892b.

54. It strikes one as somewhat odd or atypical of a Daoist scripture for the discussion to pertain to the immortality of the spirit, rather than of the whole person that involves a physical component. This occurs here perhaps simply because the *Laozi* passage being glossed speaks specifically of spirit. Another possibility is that the author has in mind the process of postmortem immortality that is mentioned in the gloss to the final phrase of what corresponds to *Laozi*, chapter 16 that reads, "you will die, but will still not be in danger" 没身不殆. There it explains that there is a "palace for refining the body" 練形之宮 called the Great Yin 太陰 where Worthies 賢者 go "feigning death" 託死, after which they emerge alive—thus they are in no danger. People who have not accumulated good deeds, however, undergo

"true death" 真死 and pass into custody of the Earth Officials 地官 (see *Laozi-Xiang'er*, 72; see also Bokenkamp 1997, 102). The idea is perhaps that the creation of an undying spirit through the binding-up and retention of essence helps ensure the attainment of this postmortem immortality.

55. Bokenkamp, being quite confident that *Laozi-Xiang'er* belongs to the early Heaven Masters movement, and that the Merging of *Qi* was an integral component of the movement already at this early phase, points out that this passage can be understood as recommending termination of sexual intercourse leading to procreation, but not of sexual intercourse per se—thus leaving open the possibility that the author endorsed the Merging of *Qi*. See Bokenkamp 1997, 45.
56. I comply here with Bokenkamp's emendation and interpretation of the text. The text here actually reads "Transcendents wives" 仙人妻, but this is probably due to a scribal error that omitted the character *wu* 無 ("not have") that is found in the four clauses that surround it.
57. This is also intended as a major point of discussion in the sequel to the current study. I have previously discussed this in my article "Wu Shouyang, Wu Zhenyang he Liu Huayang de fojing jieshi yu fojiao piping" 伍守陽，伍真陽和柳華陽的佛經解釋與佛教批評 in Zhao Weidong 趙衛東 ed., *Quanzhen dao yanjiu* 全真道研究, 120–143.
58. See Bokenkamp 1997, 42–43, 112 n.

CHAPTER 3. DRAMATIC PHYSICAL AND SENSORY EFFECTS

1. DZ1168/TT839; also in *Yunji qiqian*, 18 and 19. The version in the *Yunji qiqian* is entitled *Laozi zhongjing* 老子中經, and also bears a note stating that its alternate title is *Zhugong yuli* 珠宮玉曆. The end of the text contains a pronouncement by Laozi to the effect that he shall make an appearance during the Han dynasty. See Schipper, "*Taishang Laojun zhongjing*," in Schipper and Verellen, 92–94.
2. DZ332/TT167. The *Zhengyi fawen tianshi jiaojie kejing* 正一法文天師教戒科經 (dating to 255) mentions this as an important text. See Schipper, "*Zhengyi fawen tianshi jiaojie kejing*," in Schipper and Verellen, 96–97.

3. Some of the translated passages and discussion in this section on *The Manifest Dao* have previously appeared in Eskildsen, "Some Troubles and Perils of Taoist Meditation," 259–291.
4. DZ862/TT578.
5. DZ132/TT59. Schipper dates this text to the third or fourth century. See "*Taiqing zhenren luoming jue*," in Schipper and Verellen, 94–95.
6. See Schipper and Verellen, 95; Sun Qi 孫齊 2013.4; and *Baopuzi neipian* 抱朴子內篇 (DZ1185/TT868–870) 4/1b, 19/5b.
7. In this manner of translating the words *hun* and *po*, I follow the example of Bokenkamp 1997. Theories maintaining the existence of multiple spirits or souls in a person were developed in great abundance and variety within Daoist religious texts, where there are often said to be three *hun* and seven *po*. However, the notion of the *hun* and *po* had existed within the larger Chinese culture much earlier, as is attested to in pre-Common Era texts such as the *Zuo zhuan* 左傳 or the *Li ji* 禮記. However, recently scholars have cautioned that explanations given in such literati works, wherein *hun* and *po* get described as separating at death to return respectively to the heavens and to the earth, or are associated respectively with the principles of *yang* and *yin*, do not necessarily—or even very often—reflect the beliefs of real practitioners of Chinese religion during ancient or modern times. See Mu-chou Poo, *In Search of Personal Welfare: A View of Ancient Chinese Religion*, 62–66, 163–164; K.E. Brashier, *Ancestral Memory in Early China*, 91–92.
8. Passages corresponding to these passages in *The Manifest Dao* 2a–b can be found in *The Embryonic Subtleties* (*Taixi jingwei lun* 胎息精微論 [DZ829/TT571]; 1b–2a), a Tang period collection on embryonic breathing methods that figures into the discussion in chapter 7.
9. For a thorough overview and discussion of the lore of Laozi/Lord Lao, and the Daoist canonical literature ascribed to this sage-deity, see Livia Kohn, *God of the Dao: Lord Lao in History and Myth*.
10. An extensive discussion on "cutting off grains" is found in the 15th chapter ("Zaying" 雜應 [Miscellanea]; 1a–5b) of Ge Hong's 葛洪 (283–343) *Baopuzi neipian* 抱朴子內篇 (DZ1185/TT868–870). There Ge Hong presents his views on the benefits of not eating and on the various methods by which this is attempted. He also calls out

specifically for criticism those "shallow and superficial Daoist adepts" (*qianbo daoshi* 淺薄道士) who merely refrain from eating rice gruel while all along indulging in wine, dried meats, puddings, jujubes, chestnuts, eggs, and meats. He points out that they are no better than ordinary wine drinkers (*jiuke* 酒客) who, while holding no pretentions of being "Daoist adepts" or of "cutting off grains," do not consume grains, because they only eat dried meats to go with their wine (*Baopuzi neipian*, 15/4b–5a; *Alchemy, Medicine, Religion in the China of A.D. 320: The Nei P'ien of Ko Hung (Pao-p'u tzu)*, translated by James R. Ware, 248). From this it appears that in the early fourth century there were some people who understood "cutting off grains" as merely meaning avoiding starches; however, this was viewed as an incorrect or aberrant understanding by Ge Hong, the great expert on immortality methods of his time.

As I have discussed previously, Wang Chong 王充 (23–100 CE) appears to have equated the practice of "avoiding grains" to that of "not eating" (*bushi* 不食), and refuted the practice on the grounds that we are equipped with mouths, teeth, and anuses for a reason, and that to not eat is simply unnatural. He has nothing to say in his arguments regarding the virtues or detriments of grains specifically. See Eskildsen 1998, 43–68.

11. If one is to understand the "elimination of grains" as pertaining primarily to a taboo specifically against starches, rather than a reduction of overall dietary intake, one would be inclined to place "rice porridge" in the preceding sentence and interpret the text here as saying that rice porridge is among the grains that must be abstained from after the 100 days. Doing so, however, then leaves one with a problem with what to do with "as well as eat pure things" (*ji er qingwu* 及餌清物), because *ji* 及 interpreted as "as well as" or "and" always implies that both the noun before it (in this case "rice porridge") and after it are associated together with some common action or attribute.
12. As Kristofer Schipper has pointed out, similar names for these spirits are given in the *Taishang Laojun zhongjing* (1/21a–b) and the *Taiqing zhenren luoming jue* (3b–4a).
13. In *Contemplating the Baby* (*Rushi si chizi fa* 入室思赤子法) it states,

"The *maoyou* is the Hall of Light, which is also one *cun* square. It is right between the two eyebrows" 卯酉者明堂也 亦方圓一寸 正在兩眉間 (*Yunji qiqian* 雲笈七籤 55/13b–14a).

The Wuchengzi 務成子 commentary to the *Huangting waijing jing* 黃庭外景經 states, "The palace of the Hall of Light is three *cun* square and is the dwelling of gods. It is right between the eyes" 明堂之宮 方圓三寸神所居 正在目中央 (*Yunji qiqian* 12/31a).

14. A similar set of instructions concerning daytime and nighttime contemplation is to be found in the important thirteenth century Quanzhen Neidan manual, *Dadan zhizhi* 大丹直指 (DZ244/TT115; 2/11b–12a), attributed to Qiu Chuji 丘處機 (1143–1227). That text prescribes "practicing the Stem of Life during the day" (*ri xing mingdi* 日行命蒂) and "practicing the Root of One's Nature during the night" (*ye xing xinggen* 夜行性根). To practice the former, one first warms one's hands by rubbing them together and then presses them against the navel. One then concentrates single-mindedly on the navel; when in the depth of serenity thus brought about, one will spontaneously come to feel spurts of True Water (*zhenshui* 真水) rising from the Elixir Field (under the navel) and spurting up to the crown of the head repeatedly. After a long while this will cause the Elixir Field to have the sensation of containing the "essence of fire" and bring on an indescribable rapture. To "practice the Root of one's Nature at night," one presses one's tongue up against one's upper soft palate and single-mindedly concentrates on the crown of the head. This, at the depth of serenity, causes True Fire (*zhenhuo* 真火) to rise up from below, right up to the crown of the head. If practiced at length, this will enable one to hear the "music of Immortals" (*xianyue* 仙樂) and smell indescribably exquisite aromas through the nose.

15. Or, this is perhaps better punctuated and translated, "[In practicing] the Dao, when the *qi* emerges and enters . . ." 道 氣出入.

16. *Taishang Laojun zhongjing* (sec. 17; 1/12b–13a) reads as follows:

> 丹田者人之根也 精神之所藏也 五炁之元也 赤子之府 男子以藏精 女子以藏月水 主生子合陰陽之門戶也 在臍下三寸附著脊膂 兩腎根也.

> The Elixir Field is the root of a person. It is where the essence and spirit are stored. It is the origin of the five *qi*. It is the residence

of the Baby. With it boys store their essence. With it girls store their monthly waters. It is the gateway for producing children and combining the *yin* and *yang*. It is located 3 *cun* below the navel, and is attached to the backbone. It is the root of the two kidneys.

The passage goes on to state that the resident spirit of the Elixir Field has the surname Kong 孔, the personal name Qiu 丘, and the style name Zhongni 仲尼. It then describes an inner visualization.

17. The Three Burners (*sanjiao* 三焦) is a somewhat obscure physiological term that refers to certain portions of the digestive system. According to the ancient medical text *Huangdi bashiyinan jing* 黃帝八十一難經 (aka *Nan jing* 難經; attributed to the Warring States period physician Qin Yueren 秦越人 [aka Bian Que 扁鵲]), the Three Burners are "roads for water and grains." The Upper Burner is located under the heart and at the entrance to the stomach, the Middle Burner is located inside the stomach, and the Lower Burner is located beneath the navel, above the entrance to the bladder. See Wang Jiusi 王九思 (1468–1551) et al., *Nan jing jizhu* 難經集注 (*Sibu congkan chubian* 四部叢刊初編 38) 3/28b–31a.

18. According to Jungian theory the old woman and/or the girl could perhaps be understood as the *anima*—the archetype representing the subconscious, feminine, affective character in men, which can manifest as female figures in dreams and visions, and is the deposit of all experiences that men have with women. See C.G. Jung, *Alchemical Studies*, 39–41.

19. As we have seen, in the *Taiping jing* a Genuine Person appears frequently in the role of the interlocutor who receives sublime teachings from a Heavenly Master. It would appear that the Genuine Person there is a Daoist whose attainments are still not at the highest level, who still requires the guidance of a teacher. In *The Manifest Dao*, a Genuine Person is a full-fledged immortal or transcendent being whose company constitutes a most lofty privilege for any ordinary mortal.

20. DZ1185/TT868–870.

21. In the Shangqing scriptures most of these names are altered by adding an extra character, but are still easily recognizable. Yuanxian becomes Sanyuanxian 三元先, Zidan become Zinandan 子南丹,

Guangjian becomes Zhongguangjian 中光堅, Yuanyang becomes Yuanyangchang 元陽昌, and Guxuan becomes Guxiaxuan 谷下玄. See *Huangtian shangqing jinque dijun lingshu ziwen shangjing* 皇天上清金闕帝君靈書紫文上經 (DZ639/TT342) 11b.

22. See Eskildsen, "Some Troubles and Perils of Daoist Meditation," *Monumenta Serica*, 259–291.

23. Some of the translated passages and discussion on *Contemplating the Baby* in this section has previously appeared in Eskildsen, "Red Snakes and Angry Queen Mothers: Hallucinations and Epiphanies in Medieval Daoist Meditation," 149–184.

24. The other five are *The True Record* (*Taishang hunyuan zhenlu* 太上混元真錄; DZ954/TT604); *The Way of Transcendence* (*Xiantian Xuanmiao Yunü Taishang Shengmu zichuan xiandao* 先天玄妙玉女太上聖母資傳仙道; DZ868/TT579); *The Holy Chronicle* (*Hunyuan shengji* 混元聖紀; DZ770/TT551–553); *Zhuzhen neidan jiyao* 諸真内丹集要 (Collected Neidan Essentials from the Genuine Ones; DZ1258/TT999); and *Dacheng jieyao* 大成捷要 (Expedient Essentials for the Great Accomplishment; the two most complete editions of this text in circulation are those published by Shanxi Renmin Chubanshe 山西人民出版社 of Taiyuan 太原 [1988; prefaces dated 1929 and 1933] and Zhenshanmei Chubanshe 真善美出版社 of Taipei 臺北 [1966]. The latter Taipei edition bears the title, *Tianji biwen* 天機秘文 [Secret Writ on the Functioning of Heaven]).

*The True Record*, *The Way of Transcendence*, and *The Holy Chronicle* are discussed in the next section of chapter 3. *Dacheng jieyao* is a lengthy Neidan manual written most likely in the early twentieth century. Its author professes affiliation to the Quanzhen Longmen lineage and is strongly influenced by the writings of the Qing period (ca. 1700) Neidan master-Buddhist monk Liu Huayang; the author may also have been connected with one of the "redemptive societies" (such as Tongshan She 同善社, Xiantian Dao 先天道) that rose to prominence in the late imperial and Republican (1911–1948) periods.

25. DZ1032/TT677–702. See Schipper, "*Yunji qiqian*," in Schipper and Verellen, 2:943–945.

26. By "mile" here is meant the Chinese mile or *li* 里, which today

is about 500 meters, but which in medieval times varied between roughly 450 to 550 meters, depending on the dynasty.
27. It is difficult to determine here whether this means that there is no tangible sensory data to be witnessed, or rather that you no longer regard things and concepts as possessing inherent existence (and can therefore detach from them). The latter meaning is what the term *wu suoyou*—or its synonym *wu suode* 無所得—has within the context of Buddhist literature. (See entry on "mu sho u" 無所得 in Nakamura Hajime 中村元 et al., *Iwanami Bukkyō jiten* 岩波仏教辞典, 990.) The occurrence of the term *wu suoyou* here could thus be regarded as evidence of Buddhist influence on the author of *Contemplating the Baby*. However, judging from the fact that this sort of ontological discourse is otherwise absent in the text, it seems somewhat more likely that Buddhist meaning is not intended here.
28. In the traditional Chinese method, days and years are designated and enumerated according to a sequence of ten characters known as the "ten heavenly stems (*gan* 干*)*." *Jia* and *gui* are, respectively, days 1 and 10 in this sequence.
29. Chinese days or years can also be enumerated in a sequence of 60 days, designated by sequential combinations of the ten heavenly stems with the twelve earthly branches (*zhi* 支).
30. The supreme female Immortal who dwells on Mt. Kunlun 崑崙山; her cult/lore existed already by the Warring States Period. Around 3 BC a popular cult flourished that worshipped the Queen Mother in the hope that she would bestow immortality. For an in-depth study see Suzanne Cahill, *Transcendence and Divine Passion: The Queen Mother of the West in Medieval China*.
31. See chapter 3, nn. 16 above.
32. See *Huangting waijing yujing zhu* 黃庭外景玉經註 in *Xiuzhen shishu* 修真十書 (DZ263.58/TT131), 58/1b.
33. Some of the translated passages and discussion on *The True Record* in this section has previously appeared in Eskildsen, "Red Snakes and Angry Queen Mothers: Hallucinations and Epiphanies in Medieval Daoist Meditation," in *Hindu, Buddhist and Daoist Meditation: Cultural Histories*, ed. Halvor Eifring, 149–184.
34. DZ954/TT604.

35. As Franciscus Verellen and Kusuyama Haruki both point out, the Tang authorship of this text appears clear from how it avoids using the character *shi* 世 that was made taboo during that period in deference to Li Shimin 李世民 (Emperor Taizong 太宗 [r. 626–649]). In Verellen's view, this text "stands as an early representative of a new phase of the development of Laozi's annals" that "took shape against the background of the sage's adoption as the Tang imperial family's ancestor." As further reasons for regarding *The True Record* as a Tang work, Kusuyama also notes how the text's author seems compelled to argue against possible objections that Lord Lao embarked on his westward journey during the reign of King Zhao 昭王 (not King You 幽王), and that he met Yin Xi at the Hangu Pass (not the Sanguan 散關 or the Longguan 壟關 passes)—points that would be taken for granted at later periods. See Verellen, "*Taishang hunyuan zhenlu*," in Schipper and Verellen, 414–415; and Kusuyama 1979, 393–422.

36. In Kusuyama's view, Yin Wencao was the person primarily responsible for establishing the reign of King Zhao as the time of Laozi's westward departure—a point that is vigorously asserted in *The True Record*. Speculating further that Yin Wencao perhaps claimed himself to be a descendant of Yin Xi, Kusuyama notes that *The True Record* specifically mentions that Yin Xi's father had established the family home in Tianshui 天水 (Gansu)—which also happened to be where Yin Wencao was from—and generally seems intent on glorifying Yin Xi. See Kusuyama 1979, 393–422. On Yin Wencao see Schipper and Verellen, 3:1286; *Zhongnan shan shuojingtai lidai zhenxian beiji* 終南山說經臺歷代真仙碑記 (DZ956/TT605), 16b–17a; and *Gu Louguan ziyun yanqing ji* 古樓觀紫雲衍慶集 (DZ957/TT605), 1/4b–9b.

Though the *Xuanyuan huangdi shengji* itself no longer survives, it appears to have served as a major source for later large collections of Laozi lore that have survived, such as Jia Shanxiang's 賈善翔 *Youlong zhuan* 猶龍傳 (DZ774/TT555) and Xie Shouhao's 謝守灝 *The Holy Chronicle* (*Hunyuan shengji* 混元聖紀; Holy Chronicle of the Chaotic Origin; DZ770/TT551–553).

37. See Kusuyama 1979, 418–420.
38. DZ868/TT579.

39. DZ770/TT551–553. See Verellen, "*Hunyuan shengji*," in Schipper and Verellen, 2:872–874.
40. See Schipper, "*Xiantian Xuanmiao yunü Taishang shengmu zichuan xiandao*," in Schipper and Verellen, 359–360. Schipper notes that the Jade Maiden of Obscure Mystery (Xuanmiao Yunü 玄妙玉女), Laozi's mother who is cast in the role of revealer (to her son) in the first half of the text, was given the honorary title of Xiantian Taihou 先天太后 (Great Empress of Prior Heaven) by Empress Wu Zetian 武則天 in 666; he thus conjectures that the first word *xiantian* in the scriptures title reflects this bestowal of title, and suggests that the text therefore likely dates to around that time.
41. *Shiji*, 2139–2143 (63rd *juan*).
42. There are a number of fine studies available on the development of the lore of Laozi/Lord Lao. These include Seidel 1969; Kusuyama 1979; and Kohn 1999.
43. There is a biography of Qian Chengshu in the 60th *juan* of the standard history of the Jin 晉 dynasty. See Fang Xuanling 房玄齡 (578–648) et al., *Jinshu* 晉書, 1635–1636.
44. There is a biography of Xue Daoheng in the 57th *juan* of the standard history of the Sui 隋 dynasty. See Wei Zheng 魏徵 et al. (completed in 636), *Suishu* 隋書, 1405–1414. His poem is also quoted in *The Holy Chronicle* (3/2b), where it is indicated that the poem had been inscribed on a stele called the *Citingbei* 祠庭碑 (Ancestral Hall Courtyard Stele).
45. "Daqin" 大秦 appears in the "Account of the Western Regions" of the *Houhan shu* (88th *juan*) as the name of a great empire west of the sea, which means in all likelihood the Roman Empire (see *Houhan shu*, 10:2919–2920). The idea that Laozi traveled to Daqin is conveyed in both the *Liexian zhuan* 列仙傳 (DZ294/TT138; 1/4b–5a) and the *Taiqing jinye shendan jing* 太清金液神丹經 (DZ880/TT582; 3/13b–14a). Although the authorship of the *Liexian zhuan* is ascribed to Liu Xiang 劉向 (77–6 BCE), scholars have come to the view that it could have been authored no earlier than the Latter Han period, and that the text as we have it has likely undergone both omissions and interpolations. The 3rd *juan* of the *Taiqing jinye shendan jing* (wherein Laozi's trip to Daqin is mentioned) is an essay describing

things in foreign lands, ascribed to Ge Hong (283–343), but which is thought to perhaps date to the early sixth century. See Fabrizio Pregadio, *Great Clarity: Daoism and Alchemy in Early Medieval China*, 57; Schipper, "*Taiqing jinye shendan jing,*" and "*Liexian zhuan,*" in Schipper and Verellen, 104–105, 114; T.H. Barrett, "Buddhism, Daoism and the Eighth Century Chinese Term for Christianity. A Response to the Recent Work of Antonino Forte and Others," in Jingjiao*: The Church of the East in China and Central Asia*, 45–56 (esp., 49).

In Tang times the name "Daqin" came to be connected with Nestorian Christianity. As is evidenced in the famous Nestorian Monument inscribed in 781, the religion referred to itself as "Daqin Jingjiao" 大秦景教 (Luminous Religion of Daqin), and the inscription uses the name Daqin very broadly, to refer both to the region where Jesus lived, and the place (Sasanian Persia) from which the first group of Nestorian missionaries, led by a certain Aluoben 阿羅本 (Abraham?) came (in 635). Nestorian Christian churches, in accordance with an edict issued in 745, bore the name of Daqinsi (Daqin Temple; prior to this they bore the name Bosisi 波斯寺, or "Persian Temple"). Interestingly, in the Nestorian monument there is a passage implying that the introduction of Christianity to Tang China constituted the return of the true Way that had previously departed from China during the Zhou period when Laozi had left. (The passage reads, "When the virtue of the clan of Zhou was lost, [Laozi] mounted a black [ox] and ascended to the west. When the Dao of the great Tang radiated, the luminous wind fanned toward the east" 宗周德喪 青駕西昇 巨唐道光 景風東扇.) Another Nestorian text (recovered from Dunhuang), the *Zhixuan anle jing* 志玄安樂經, has Jesus mentioning how he has various extraordinary physical features, including the mark of the figure ten 十; as Saeki Yoshirō 佐伯好郎 has pointed out, Laozi is described as possessing the mark of the figure ten on his hand in sources such as the *Shenxian zhuan* 神仙傳 and the *Mouzi lihuo lun* 牟子理惑論. It thus seems that Nestorian Christians in China may have been claiming that Jesus was a transformation or manifestation of Laozi/Lord Lao. See Saeki Yoshirō, *The Nestorian Documents and Relics in China*, Part IV, 78, 307 and *Keikyō no kenkyū* 景教の研究; Eskildsen, "Parallel Themes in Chinese Nestorianism and Medieval Daoist Religion," in Malek 2006, 73, and "Christology and Soteriology in the Chinese Nestorian Tests," in *The Chinese Face of Jesus Christ*, vol. 1, ed. Roman Malek, 181–218.

46. The alchemical texts mentioned here appear to be connected to the so-called Taiqing 太清 (Great Clarity) alchemical tradition that flourished in the region south of the lower Yangzi River during the third and fourth centuries and which is famously championed by Ge Hong in the *Baopuzi neipian*. There (4/2a–b; Ware 1966, 69–70) he states that the *Taiqing danjing* 太清丹經 (Great Clarity Elixir Scripture[s]) in 3 *juan*, the *Jiuding danjing* 九鼎丹經 (Nine Tripod Elixir Scripture) in 1 *juan* and the *Jinye danjing* 金液丹經 (Golden Liquid Elixir Scripture) in 1 *juan* were divinely revealed to Zuo Ci 左慈 at the end of the Han dynasty and subsequently passed on to Ge Xuan 葛玄 (Ge Hong's great uncle), Zheng Yin 鄭隱 (Ge Hong's teacher), and then to Ge Hong himself. He also specifically mentions the *Taiqing guantian jing* 太清觀天經 (see 4/8b; Ware 1966, 79). The brief alchemical discussion in *The True Record* enumerates "Nine Elixirs" (*jiudan* 九丹; see 7b–8a), and the names of these elixirs match those given in *Baopuzi neipian* (4/7a–8b; Ware 1966, 76–78). For a superb study of Taiqing laboratory alchemy based on extant remnants of this tradition preserved in the *Daoist Canon* see Pregadio 2006. According to Pregadio (p. 57), the *Taiqing jinye shendan jing* (see chapter 3, nn. 45, earlier), in content, despite its title, does not seem to have been part of the Taiqing corpus transmitted to Ge Hong. However, it certainly appears possible that the author of *The True Record* was familiar with it and its passages concerning Laozi's journey to Daqin.

47. The *Taishang Laojun zhongjing* has 55 chapters, and the version of it included in the *Yunji qiqian* bears the alternative title of *Zhugong yuli* 珠宮玉曆. Ge Hong lists a *Laojun yuli zhenjing* 老君玉曆真經 among the texts he saw in his teacher Zheng Yin's library (see *Baopuzi neipian* 19/4a).

48. This likely corresponds to the text by the same title listed by Ge Hong as one of the texts he saw in his teacher Zheng Yin's library (see *Baopuzi neipian* 19/4a).

49. This perhaps corresponds to the text entitled *Lizang yannian jing* 歷

藏延年經 that is listed by Ge Hong as one of the texts he saw in his teacher Zheng Yin's library (see *Baopuzi neipian* 19/5a). Interestingly, the text that directly precedes it on this list is a *Wenshi xiansheng jing* 文始先生經—Wenshi xiansheng was a title used to refer to Yin Xi.

50. The *Huangting jing* is listed by Ge Hong as one of the texts he saw in his teacher Zheng Yin's library (see *Baopuzi neipian* 19/5a). This probably refers to the *Huangting waijing jing* rather than the *Huanting neijing jing*, because the latter is thought to be a fourth-century work connected to Shangqing movement. See Schipper, "*Taishang huangting neijing yujing*," in Schipper and Verellen, 184–185.

51. See Kusuyama 1979, 199–238. Among Ge Hong's list of texts in Zheng Yin's library we also find a *Jiejie jing* 節解經 (see *Baopuzi neipian* 19/5a), which might perhaps correspond to the *Laozi jiejie*. Kusuyama, however, urges caution in drawing this conclusion because in his view Ge Hong should have placed the name "Laozi" at the head of the text's title if that text was indeed the *Laozi* commentary that we are concerned with. Another lost commentary to the *Laozi* that seems to have borne a close relationship to the *Laozi jiejie* and to have resembled it considerably in content was the *Neijie* 內解 (Inner Commentary), attributed to Yin Xi. Two short passages from this text are quoted in the *Yangxing yanming lu* 養性延命錄 (DZ838/ TT572 [1/6b, 2/5a]; attributed variously to Tao Hongjing 陶弘景 [456–536] or Sun Simiao 孫思邈 [581–682]), and the first of these is also found in the Japanese compendium *Ishinpō* 醫心方 (written in 984) of Tanba no Yasuyori 丹波康賴 (27th *juan*, section 4 ["Yong qi" 用氣]), who indicates that this passage of the "*Laozi Yinshi neijie*" 老子尹氏內解 (Mr. Yin's Inner Commentary to the *Laozi*) was found in the *Yangsheng yaoji* 養生要集 (by Zhang Zhan 張湛 of the fourth century, another important lost text). See T.H. Barrett, "Taoist and Buddhist Mysteries in the Interpretation of the *Tao-te-ching*," *Journal of the Royal Asiatic Society*, 35–43; T.H. Barrett and Livia, Kohn, "*Yangsheng yaoji*," in *The Encyclopedia of Taoism*, 1151–1152; Schipper, "*Yangxing yanming lu*," in Schipper and Verellen, 345–346.

52. These commentaries are *Daode zhenjing zhushu* 道德真經註疏 (DZ710/TT404–406; compiled after 1101, but attributed to Gu Huan 顧歡 [420–483]) and *Daode zhenjing xuande zuanshu* 道德真

經玄德纂疏 (DZ711/TT407–413; compiled by Qiang Siqi 強思齊 [ninth c.]).
53. *Taishō Canon*, no. 2110, 50:500.
54. One *cun* during the third century was equal to 2.4 centimeters. During the Tang dynasty it was equal to 3.1 centimeters. Roughly speaking, thus, a *cun* is equal to one inch or a bit more.
55. DZ1258/TT999 (2/9a–13a). Compiled by a certain Xuanquanzi 玄全子 (Master of the Completion of Mystery), perhaps around 1300. Xuanquanzi, an otherwise obscure figure, also compiled the *Zhenxian zhizhi yulu* 真仙直指語錄 (DZ1256/TT998; A Record of Sayings that are the Direct Instructions of Realized Immortals), an anthology of discourses by the famous Quanzhen masters Ma Yu 馬鈺 (1123–1184), Tan Chuduan 譚處端 (1123–1185), Liu Chuxuan 劉處玄 (1147–1203), Qiu Chuji 丘處機 (1143–1227), Hao Datong 郝大通 (1140–1212), and Yin Zhiping 尹志平 (1169–1251).
56. The passage is found within a section of *Zhuzhen neidan jiyao* that bears the heading, *Jindan huohou bijue shi'erju* 金丹火候祕訣十二句. This section is constituted by two segments of verse, each of which is followed by a segment of prose commentary. The first prose commentary segment commences with the words, "Genuine Man Chunyang (Lü Dongbin's sobriquet) said. . . ." 純陽真人云. The second prose commentary segment is where the discourse that concerns us is found. Though this second segment does not start with the words, "Genuine Man Chunyang said . . . ," such an attribution seems to be implied.
57. *Zhuzhen neidan jiyao* 2/8a–9a.
58. See *Taiping yulan* 太平御覽, 1663 (*juan* 361). The *Taiping yulan* was compiled by Li Fang 李昉 et al. by order of Song Emperor Taizong 太宗, and was completed in 984. The *Laixiang ji* was apparently authored prior to the Tang, because its testimony regarding Laozi, the white deer, and Mother Li's conception is also cited in the 95th *juan* of the *Yiwen leiju* 藝文類聚, compiled by Ouyang Xun 歐陽詢 (557–642) in 624. See *Yiwen leiju*, 1648–1649.
59. This episode also occurs in the *Youlong zhuan* 猶龍傳 (DZ774/TT555; by Jia Shanxiang 賈善翔, ca. 1086–1100), 3/3a.
60. This refers to a strain of Neidan theory and practice developed in the

writings of a lineage of masters of the Song period. The so-called Five Patriarchs (*wuzu* 五祖) of the Southern School were Zhang Boduan 張伯端 (sobriquet, Ziyang 紫陽; 984?–1082), Shi Tai 石泰 (sobriquet, Xinglin 杏林; d. 1158), Xue Daoguang 薛道光 (sobriquet, Zixian 紫賢; 1078?–1191), Chen Nan 陳楠 (sobriquet, Niwan 泥丸; d. 1213), and Bai Yuchan 白玉蟾 (sobriquet, Haiqiong 海瓊; 1134?–1229). See Schipper and Verellen, 2:812–840.

61. The Nine Contemplations are enumerated as: (1) Contemplation of No Evil (*wuxie si* 無邪思); (2) Contemplation for Rectifying the Body (*zhengshen si* 正身思); (3) Contemplation for Bringing forth Governance (*zhizheng si* 致政思); (4) Contemplation of Great Rectitude (*dazheng si* 大正思); (5) Contemplation of Extreme Rectitude (*jizheng si* 極正思); (6) Contemplation of Bodily Rectitude (*shenzheng si* 身正思); (7) Contemplation of Correct Truth (*zhengzhen si* 正真思); (8) Contemplation of Cavern Mystery (*dongxuan si* 洞玄思); and (9) Contemplation of the Great Cavern (*dadong si* 大洞思). Neither text provides any description or summary of what each contemplation entails—unlike LLS#4.

62. Second Room: Contemplation for Rectifying the Body (*zhengshen si* 正身思), "Combine with the essence and *qi* to take control. Ghosts and specters shall all dwell outside. Gaze at what is right and what is not right. House the spirit(s) inside. See if they can be completed or not" 與精氣合為理 鬼物俱居外 瞻正與不正 宅神居內 視可成不也.

Third Room: Contemplation for Bringing forth Rectitude (*zhizheng si* 致正思), "Essence, *qi*, ghosts and specters all combine into one, as though they were living in a city (?). Spirit(s) dwells outside of them. Do not consider this strange" 精氣鬼物皆合為一 若居都市中 神居其外 勿怪之.

Fourth Room: Contemplation of Great Rectitude (*dazheng zi* 大正思), "A person's essence can have a small merging with the spirit(s)" 人精得與神小合也.

Fifth Room: Contemplation of Extreme Rectitude (*jizheng si* 極正思), "The genuine spirit(s) can enter inside it, and the essence and *qi* come after it. Ghosts and specters dwell outside of it. Thereby say, 'Go!'" 真神得入其內 精氣次之 鬼物居其外 方曰去也.

Sixth Room: Contemplation of Deep Rectitude (*shenzheng si* 深正思), "Spirit and essence are rectified, and the circulation of *qi* is rectified. Thus they find their place. Old *qi*, ghosts, specters, wickedness and evil are thereby eliminated" 神精正 行氣正 以得其所 故氣鬼物邪惡以除去也.

Seventh Room: Contemplation of Correct Truth (*zhengzhen si* 正真思), "The Great Genuine Spirit arrives. All the wicked ones recognize him as superior, and thus all are eliminated. Only the Genuine Spirit remains" 大真神至 衆邪長之 悉除去 獨有真神在也.

Eighth Room: Contemplation of the Mysterious Cavern (*xuandong si* 玄洞思), "Your body and the Genuine Spirit combine to form a person. From morning to evening never think of a single worldly affair on earth" 身與真神都合爲人也 旦夕未嘗念地上俗閒一事也.

Ninth Room: Contemplation of the Great Cavern (*dadong si* 大洞思), "You have already become a Genuine Person. Accord with the *qi* and lie down. The Dao of the Great Cavern is there intact" 已成真人也 隨氣而臥 大洞道備矣 (*The True Record* 26b–27a).

63. Very likely the textual source drawn upon here is the *Taishang Laojun zhongjing*. In its 21st section it states, "If you cannot ingest the Divine Cinnabar and Golden Liquid, you but belabor yourself with intensive contemplation, only to torment yourself in vain" 兆不能服神丹金液 勞精思念 當自苦耳 (1/16a).

CHAPTER 4. INTEGRATING BUDDHISM: EARLIER PHASE

1. DZ726/TT449.
2. DZ666/TT167.
3. See Livia Kohn, *Taoist Mystical Philosophy: The Scripture of the Western Ascension* (Albany: State University of New York Press, 1991); and *Sitting in Oblivion: The Heart of Daoist Meditation* (Dunedin, FL: Three Pines Press, 2010), 34–36.
4. Variations in the texts of the two versions of *The Western Ascension* will be indicated by an underscore and a slash-mark. On the left side of the slash-mark is the character that appears in version A, and on the

right side, the character appearing in version B. An x on either side of the slash-mark indicates a missing character.
5. See Eskildsen 1998, 72–75, 121–128.
6. See Tilmann Vetter, *A Lexicographical Study of An Shigao's and his Circle's Chinese Translations of Buddhist Texts*, 183; Nakamura Hajime 中村元 et al., *Iwanami Bukkyō Jiten* 岩波仏教辞典, 980–981.
7. Buddhistic usage of the word *kong* can be found within the fifth century Lingbao corpus of scriptures. For an example see *Taishang dongxuan lingbao zhihui dingzhi tongwei jing* 太上洞玄靈寶智慧定志通微經 (DZ325/TT167) 4b; and Eskildsen 1998, 124.
8. In the mainstream Buddhist understanding as has been established in India, there is no self (*atman*) or anything such as a spirit or soul that constitutes the permanent core of one's being, or which transmigrates from body to body. However, the fact that medieval Chinese Buddhists typically inferred from the doctrine of *saṃsāra* the presence of an immortal spirit is reflected in writings by eminent Buddhists such as Huiyuan 慧遠 (334–416), and in the reaction stirred up by Fan Zhen's 范縝 (ca. 450–515) anti-Buddhist treatise *Shenmie lun* 神滅論 (Treatise on the Mortality of the Spirit) among the Buddhist faithful, which included Liang Emperor Wu 梁武帝 (r. 502–549). See Nakamura et al. 2002, 583; and Kenneth Ch'en, *Buddhism in China: A Historical Survey*, 138–142.
9. Some of the translated passages and discussion on *The Original Arising* in this section has previously appeared in Eskildsen, "Mystical Ascent and Out-of-Body Experience in Medieval Daoism," 36–62.
10. DZ1032/TT677–702. Compiled by Zhang Junfang 張君房 (fl. 1008–1025).
11. DZ1438/TT1059.
12. See John Lagerwey, "*Taishang laojun xuwu ziran benqi jing*," in Schipper and Verellen, 531–532.
13. See *The Original Arising* 8b, 10b, and 11b.
14. See *Miaofa lianhua jing* 妙法蓮華經 (*Taishō Canon*, no. 262), 9:42b–44a; and Burton Watson trans., *The Lotus Sūtra*, 224–232. The *Lotus Sūtra* (comp. ca. 50–150) does not specifically employ the terms *nirmāṇakāya* and *dharmakāya*; the *trikāya* (three Buddha bodies) scheme that employed these terms was devised around the fifth

century by the Yogacara school (see Edward Conze, *Buddhism: Its Essence and Development*, 171–172).

15. As has been pointed out by Michel Strickmann, Stephen Bokenkamp, and others, the Shangqing scriptures of the late fourth century had forcefully asserted that the Genuine Persons (*zhenren*) were a category of exalted beings superior even to the Immortals (or Transcendents; *xianren*) extolled in earlier traditions. See Strickmann, "The Maoshan Revelations," *T'oung Pao* 63 (1977): 1–64; and Bokenkamp 1997, 266–267.

16. This Neidan material is intended as the focus of the sequel to the current study. For now it can be pointed out, for example, that the sending out of the pure *yang* spirit is perceived as the paramount attainment in the literature of the early Quanzhen tradition, and that the Neidan method of that tradition laid prime emphasis on the cultivation of serenity (see Eskildsen 2004, 21–38, 93–94, and 121–126). More detailed discussions addressing how deep serenity directly leads to the moment where the spirit can exit are to be found in the writings of the late Ming Quanzhen master Wu Shouyang 伍守陽. He describes how at the moment when all traces and stirrings of thought and emotion are eliminated from the mind, and breathing (and pulse) has come to full suspension, you see a spontaneous vision of "flowers" or snowflakes falling from the sky. At this moment you are to project your spirit out of the top of your head (see *Xianfo hezong yulu*, in *Zangwai daoshu* 5:689a–b).

17. See Robinet 1993, 171–226.

18. The passage being alluded to here reads, "[The sage] shines but does not dazzle" 光而不耀. The original gist of the passage seems to pertain to how the sagely ruler, though he may possess intelligence or some other brilliant quality, does not flaunt it. The author of the *Xuwu benqi jing* has given the passage a creative, meditation-related interpretation, by interpreting the word *yao* 曜/耀 (shine; dazzle) as meaning to generate "sparks" or visions of gods.

19. The term *shijie* or Liberation by the Corpse is used widely throughout medieval Daoist literature, but without complete consistency in meaning. It is variously used to denote situations where somebody has attained physical immortality while feigning death (by means such

as transforming a sword or bamboo staff into a semblance of one's dead body), become bodily resurrected or reconstituted after actually dying, or attained blessed immortality in the spirit that had cast off the body. For a fine study on this phenomenon, see Ursula-Angelika Cedzich, "Corpse Deliverance, Substitute Bodies, Name Change, and Feigned Death: Aspects of Metamorphosis and Immortality in Early Medieval China," *Journal of Chinese Religions* 29 (2001): 1–68.

## CHAPTER 5. INTEGRATING BUDDHISM: EMPTINESS AND THE TWOFOLD MYSTERY

1. DZ1111/TT758.
2. DZ59/TT31.
3. DZ1123/760. Compiled 712–723 by Shi Chong 史崇 et al.
4. Compiled by Xu Jian 徐堅 et al., 659–729.
5. See Hans-Hermann Schmidt, "*Taixuan zhenyi benji miaojing*," and "*Yuanshi dongzhen jueyi jing*," in Schipper and Verellen, 520–522.
6. DZ329/TT167.
7. See *Pen-tsi king: Livre de terme originel*.
8. See Frederike Assandri, 57.
9. See Wu 1960, Introduction, 11–14.
10. *Taishō Canon*, no. 2112, vol. 52.
11. See Assandri 2009, 152–172.
12. Ibid., 59.
13. Ibid., 59, 168–172.
14. "*The Original Juncture*\*" refers to the version of the 2nd *juan* of *The Original Juncture* that is found in the *Daoist Canon* under the title *Taixuan zhenyi benji miaojing*.
15. Translation borrowed from Watson 1993, 230–231. See *Miaofa lianhua jing*, 43b–44a.
16. This notion is lucidly articulated in the writings of the late Ming Neidan master Wu Shouyang 伍守陽 (1573–1640). See Eskildsen 2011.
17. One of the influential sūtras describing and promoting this practice is the *Foshuo guanfo sanmeihai jing* 佛說觀佛三昧海經 (*Taishō Canon*, no. 643, vol. 15) that is said to have been translated by Buddhabhadra

(Foduobatuo 佛馱跋陀; 359–429). The text and its method would come to be particularly strongly emphasized within Pure Land tradition. See Nakamura et al. 2002, 186.

18. In Chinese Buddhist (and medieval Daoist) literature, this refers to *abhijñā*, the supernormal powers that a holy person acquires through training—particularly meditation. Of these *abhijñā* there are said to be six (*liutong* 六通): 1) *abhijñā* of the Divine Foot—the ability to go anywhere instantaneously, (2) *Abhijñā* of the Heavenly Eye—the ability to see into the past and future, (3) *Abhijñā* of the Heavenly Ear—the ability to hear sounds that ordinary people cannot, (4) *Abhijñā* of the Minds of Others— the ability to read minds, (5) *Abhijñā* of Past Lives—the ability to know of one's past lives, (6) *Abhijñā* of No Outflowings—the ability to be without the craving for existence, the craving for sensual pleasures and ignorance. See Nakamura et al. 2002, 1070.

19. This important school of Buddhist philosophy originated from the treatises of Nagarjuna (Longshu 龍樹 ca. 150–250) in India. See Nakamura et al. 2002, 706–707; Chen 1964, 84–88; and Richard H. Robinson, *Early Mādhyamika in India and China*.

20. See Assandri 2009; also, Livia Kohn and Russell Kirkland, "Daoism in the Tang (618–907)," 339–383.

21. This version bears the title *Laozi shuo wuchu jing zhu* 老子說五廚經註 (The Scripture of the Five Kitchens Spoken by Laozi; DZ763/TT533).

22. This version bears the title *Wuchu jing qifa* 五厨經氣法 (The *Qi* Method of the Scripture of the Five Kitchens), and is found in the *Yunji qiqian* (61/5b–10b). Yin Yin's preface to this version gives the year 735 (Kaiyuan era, 23rd year 開元二十三年) as the date of its writing. For some reason, this date is missing from the preface to *Wuchu jing* version A.

23. See Livia Kohn, *Sitting in Oblivion: The Heart of Daoist Meditation*, 198–206.

24. See *Yunji qiqian*, 57/10a–11b. The other version of the *Fuqi jingyi lun* (DZ830/TT571) in the *Daoist Canon* for some reason does not contain the *Wuchu jing* verses and accompanying method.

25. The first set of verses, the "Eastern Direction Long Life Chapter," is

recited 90 times, followed by 30 recitations of the "Southern Direction Not-Hungry Chapter," 120 recitations of the "Central Direction Not-Hot Chapter," 70 recitations of the "Western Direction Not-Cold Chapter," and 50 recitations of the "Northern Direction Not-Thirsty Chapter." The recitations are to be done silently ("recite with the heart" 心誦) with the eyes and mouth closed, facing the direction to which the verses being recited are addressed. At the same time, you are to use your tongue to stimulate the flow of saliva from the salivary glands in the mouth and swallow it along with air, and make the *qi* thus absorbed enter into the organ corresponding to the direction of the verses being recited. All of this is concluded with the recitation of a "Hymn to the Great Dao." If you are suffering specifically from disharmony of energy, hunger, heat, cold, or thirst, you can recite individually the verses designated for those conditions. Interestingly, the text also states that this method should be supplemented with the ingestion of talisman water and drugs, because it can lead to "empty melancholy" (*xuchuo* 虛惙) otherwise.

26. *Taishō Canon*, no. 2894, vol. 85. Aside from the version included in the *Taishō Canon*, there are three other recensions of the text among manuscripts that have been found at Dunhuang and at Mt. Kōya 高野山 in Japan. One of these recensions is entitled *Foshuo tingchu jing* 佛說停廚經, and another is entitled *Foshuo san tingchujing* 佛說三停廚經. See Christine Mollier, *Buddhism and Taoism Face to Face: Scripture, Ritual and Iconographic Exchange in Medieval China*, 26–27.

27. The procedures prescribed here involve most of what is described in the *Fuqi jingyi lun*, plus several other elements. This Buddhist text in one place calls for the adept to concentrate on the region of the navel while reciting each verse facing the appropriate direction. It also promises that eventually the adept will enjoy dreams and visions where he or she sees, smells, and tastes the delectable foods of the paradises. There is also provided a chant with which one can transform a bowl of water into a bowl of heavenly delicacies. The text also describes vividly the process in which the body first suffers weakening and emaciation, but by the seventh day regains its strength.

28. See *Daojiao lingyan ji* (DZ590/TT325–326), 12/2b–3b. See also *Yunji qiqian* 119/24a–25a.
29. See Mollier 2008, 23–54.
30. The clearest and most thorough description of a method for ingesting the Five Sprouts is found in the *Fuqi jingyi lun* 服氣精義論 (DZ830/TT573; 2b–5a). However, the method has its earlier precedents in the Lingbao and Shangqing traditions, and the earliest extant description of it is found in the *Taishang lingbao wufu xu* 太上靈寶五符序 (DZ388/TT183). The *Taiqing zhonghuang zhenjing* 太清中黃真經 (DZ817/TT586) describes yet another set of methods where one first engages in rigorous fasting sustained by the imbibing of air; this is said to make the colored *qi* ("sprouts") of the five viscera visible. Then through intensive visualization and breath-holding one is to mobilize the five visceral *qi* to transform the body and bring about immortal ascension. (See Eskildsen 1998, 44–51.)
31. Yin Yin's precise words here are, "Once the utmost harmony has come to pervade, not only is there no One, there is also no harmony" 至和既暢 非但無一 亦復無和 (A 2a, B 7b).
32. Text of version B. Character variations in version A are indicated in parentheses.
33. Version A here has the character *ling* 令 instead of *jin* 今 at the beginning of this passage. If one complies with version A, the passage would translate into "If you cause your mouth to take in flavors and thereby fill the five viscera, the body will assemble like a soap bubble, and with it carry its form." This would seem to be blaming the coming about of the flawed, corruptable body specifically on one's choice to eat foods. Read in this way, Yin Yin could be understood as enjoining his readers to fast. However, the text read in this way seems somewhat awkward grammatically and less coherent in meaning with the main text and with Yin Yin's statements that follow.
34. The translation here is based on the text of version B, which appears to be more coherent.
35. A possible Buddhist source of inspiration for this image is the *Diamond Sutra* (*Jin'gang bore boluomi jing* 金剛般若波羅蜜經; *Taishō Canon*, no. 235, vol. 8) where it is proclaimed that all phenomena

formed by causes are fleeting, like a dream, a mirage, a soap bubble, a shadow, dew, or lightning (see 752b).

36. This is the set of elements that typically figures in Buddhist discourse. The fact that Yin Yin prefers to speak in terms of this set rather than in terms of the indigenously conceived set of five agents (*wuxing* 五行; wood, fire, earth, metal, and fire) reflects the profound influence of Buddhism on his thinking, and can perhaps be taken as a hint that Yin Yin's intention here is to point out that the body is inherently impermanent and flawed, rather than to enjoin fasting.

37. Text of version B. Character variations in version A are indicated in parentheses.

38. Here the text of version A would translate into something like "As for the One . . .," and is very difficult to conjoin coherently with the phrases that follow.

39. The translation here is based on the text of version B, which appears to be more coherent.

40. DZ620/TT341. Full title, *Taishang Laojun shuo chang qingjing miaojing* 太上老君說常清靜妙經 (The Marvelous Scripture on Constant Clarity and Calmness, Spoken by the Most High Lord Lao). A full English translation of this text is found in Legge 1959, 689–696.

41. See "*Taishang Laojun shuo chang qingjing miaojing*," in Schipper and Verellen , 562. Sima Chengzhen's commentary is mentioned in one of the extant commentaries to *The Clarity and Calmness* (*Taishang Laojun shuo chang qingjing jing zhu* 太上老君說常清靜妙經註 [DZ757/TT532], 23a). Li Simu's commentary is mentioned in *Nanyue zongsheng ji* 南嶽總勝集 (*Taishō Canon*, no. 2097; 51:7a [*juan* 3]). Huaisu's manuscript is listed in the *Bidian zhulin* 祕殿珠林 (compiled by Zhang Zhao 張照 [b. 1650], Liang Shizheng 梁詩正 [1697–1763] et al.).

42. Full title, *Bore boluomiduo xin jing* 般若波羅蜜多心經 (*Prajnaparamita hrdaya sūtra* in Sanskrit). There are seven different Chinese translations of this scripture in the eighth volume of the *Taishō Canon*, including those of (or attributed to) Kumarajiva 鳩摩羅什 (344–413; no. 245) and Xuanzang 玄奘 (602–664; no. 251). The date of the *sūtra* itself has become a hugely controversial issue. Edward Conze has dated it to around 350, whereas Nakamura Hajime has dated it to the

second century. Jan Nattier, however, has argued that it was probably composed in China in Chinese, and then translated into Sanskrit in the seventh century. See Nakamura, *Indian Buddhism: A Survey with Bibliographical Notes*, 160; Conze, *The Prajñāpāramitā Literature*, 9; Nattier, "The *Heart Sūtra*: A Chinese Apocryphal Text?," *The Journal of the International Association of Buddhist Studies*, 153–223; Donald Lopez, *Elaborations on Emptiness: Uses of the* Heart Sūtra, xi.

43. See *Zhongnanshan shenxian Chongyang zhenren Quanzhen jiaozu bei* 終南山神仙重陽真人全真教祖碑 in *Ganshui xianyuan lu* 甘水仙源錄 (DZ973/TT611–613) 1/8a; and Eskildsen 2004, 14. The *Classic of Filial Piety* is an important Confucian classic of ancient but uncertain date, traditionally attributed to Zeng Shen 曾參 (ca. 509–436), a disciple of Confucius.
44. DZ1169/TT839. This alternate version is also included in the *Yunji qiqian* (17/13b–15b), where it bears the title, *Laojun qingjing xin jing* 老君清淨心經 (Lord Lao's Heart Sūtra of Clarity and Purity).
45. DZ755/TT532.
46. As Schmidt has pointed out, there is a passage in this commentary (60a) that reads "in the past, in the first year of the Xining era (1068) of Song times" 昔宋時熙寧元年, which betrays the fact that the author is writing after the Song period.
47. DZ756/TT532.
48. Actually, there was no such reign era during the Tang; however, during the Northern Song dynasty there was a Qingli 慶曆 reign era that lasted from 1041 to 1048.
49. DZ1057/728. Compiled by Wang Yizhong 王頤中.
50. See Eskildsen 2004, 57–94.

CHAPTER 6. SERENITY AND THE
REAFFIRMATION OF PHYSICAL TRANSFORMATION

1. DZ1036/TT740.
2. *Yunji qiqian* 94/1a–16b.
3. The designation *jushi* 居士 is typically used in Buddhist contexts to refer to a lay devotee. Zhenjing perhaps was a Buddhist, though this

more likely seems to be a case where the designation of *jushi* has been applied to a Daoist devotee. The term *jushi* can also be used to refer to a person of some talent or learning who chooses not to seek or assume government employment. However, the name Zhenjing 真靜, which translates into "Genuine Calm" would seem to somewhat suggest a religious affiliation or purpose in this person's manner of being a *jushi*.

4. The author's preface to version B states that the text lays out the "method of pacifying the mind and of sitting and forgetting" 安心坐忘之法 in seven stages, to which is also appended a "Wings of the Pivot" (*shuyi* 樞翼). Apparently the appendix came to be lost or omitted from version B.

5. DZ1017/TT641–648.

6. DZ1026/TT672. What the colophon most likely means to say is that its discourse was uttered by Sima Chengzhen, who was summarizing what he had heard from the mysterious and otherwise unknown Tianyinzi. A full translation of the *Tianyinzi* is found in Kohn 2010, 188–197.

7. The text of this stele inscription is preserved in the *Jigu lumu* 集古錄目, compiled in 1069 by Ouyang Fei 歐陽棐.

8. The Five Peaks (*wuyue* 五嶽) traditionally revered in China are the eastern peak Taishan 泰山 (Shandong), southern peak Hengshan 衡山 (Hunan), western peak Huashan 華山 (Shaanxi), northern peak Hengshan 恆山 (Shanxi), and central peak Songshan 嵩山 (Henan).

9. See Kohn 2010, 53–56.

10. Ibid., 60–63.

11. Interestingly, among the collected sayings of the famous brother duo of Confucian philosophers Cheng Hao 程顥 (1032–1085) and Cheng Yi 程頤 (1033–1107) we find the statement, "In the past Sima Ziwei (Sima Chengzhen) wrote the *Zuowang lun*. It (what it teaches) is what is called 'sitting and hurrying'." 司馬子微嘗作坐忘論 是所謂坐馳也 (Zhu Xi 朱熹 [1130–1200] and Lü Zuqian 呂祖謙 [1137–1181] eds., *Jinsi lu* 近思錄, *juan* 4, 5; also *Yishu* 遺書 2A/24b in Zhu Xi ed., *Er Cheng quanshu* 二程全書 [*Sibu beiyao* 四部備要 edition]). Thus, here it is Sima Chengzhen himself who is accused of writing a "*Treatise on Sitting and Forgetting*" that actually conduces to "sitting and hurrying." Unfortunately it is impossible

to tell whether it is our *Sitting and Forgetting* in seven sections that Master Cheng is criticizing and ascribing to Sima Chengzhen. Also, as is pointed out by Wing-tsit Chan 陳榮捷, it is not clear as to which Cheng brother uttered the statement, though commentators have attributed it to Cheng Yi. See Wing-tsit Chan trans., *Reflections on Things at Hand: The Neo-Confucian Anthology Compiled by Chu Hsi and Lü Tsu-ch'ien*, 130, n. 32.

12. See Kohn 2010.
13. Kamitsuka Yoshiko 神塚淑子 has argued that *Sitting and Forgetting* is a Daoist treatise on seated meditation that came about as a result of stimulus provided by Buddhist treatises on seated meditation. In particular she speculates that an important model for emulation was provided by Tiantai Buddhist master Zhiyi's 智顗 (538–598) *Xiuxi zhiguan zuochan fayao* 修習止觀坐禪法要 (Dharma Essentials on Practicing and Learning the Seated Meditation of Concentration and Insight; *Taishō Canon*, no. 1915, vol. 46)—which is perhaps more widely known as the *Tiantai xiao zhiguan* 天台小止觀 (Small Tiantai [Discourse on] Concentration and Insight). *Xiuxi zhiguan zuochan fayao* bears a 10-part structure that in Kamitsuka's view likely provided a model for the seven-part structure of *Sitting and Forgetting*. She states that the subject matter of *Sitting and Forgetting* sections 2 and 4 corresponds roughly to sections 1 ("Being Equipped with Causes" 具緣), 2 ("Rebuking Desires" 訶欲), and 3 ("Abandoning the Covers" 棄蓋) of the *Xiuxi zhiguan zuochan fayao*; that sections 3 and 5 correspond to section 6 ("Proper Training" 正修行); section 6 corresponds to section 7 ("Roots of Goodness Emerge" 善根發); and section 7 corresponds to section 10 ("Attaining the Fruits" 證果). Kamitsuka also notes that the term *anxin* 安心 ("pacify the mind," or "peaceful mind") that figures in the author's preface (in version B but not A) and in section 3 of *Sitting and Forgetting* was a key term in the literature of both the Tiantai and Chan schools of Buddhism. For good measure she points out that Sima Chengzhen spent a good part of his career at Mt. Tiantai, and thus very likely was in contact with Tiantai Buddhists and was familiar with their literature. See Kamitsuka Yoshiko, "Shiba Shōtei, *Zabō ron* ni tsuite" 司馬承禎『坐忘論』について, 213–242.

There is certainly no doubt that *Sitting and Forgetting* (and many other medieval Daoist works) was written under Buddhist influence or stimulus. It is certainly also likely that the author of *Sitting and Forgetting* had read the *Xiuxi zhiguan zuochan fayao* and could have emulated its structure. Having said this, it must be said that the most central notions of *Sitting and Forgetting*—the notion that a clear and calm mind evokes an infusion of the Dao, and that this power transforms both mind and body—are not found in the *Xiuxi zhiguan zuochan fayao*. It is also to be noted that the *Xiuxi zhiguan zuochan fayao* gives far more detailed instructions on the actual mechanics of meditation such as how to sit, how to breathe or where to focus the mind's attention. Interestingly, one of the locations of the body that is recommended as a focus for concentration is the navel, which by concentrating on it you can calm a mind that is becoming agitated or distracted (see p. 466a; it also states that if your mind is becoming dull and drowsy, you should focus on the tip of your nose). It also states that by focusing on a place located one inch under the navel you can heal various diseases; it furthermore states that that location is known as the *youtuona* 憂陀那 (Sanskrit: *udāna* [?]; this is normally a term denoting a genre of Buddhist *sūtra* wherein the Buddha utters a discourse that is not elicited by an interlocutor), or as the Elixir Field (see p. 471c). Here the *Xiuxi zhiguan zuochan fayao* seems to betray influence from Daoism; ironically, neither the notion of the Elixir Field or of focusing on the navel occurs in *Sitting and Forgetting*. In the *Xiuxi zhiguan zuochan fayao* we also find some fairly vivid descriptions of certain bodily sensations that occur in meditation and which constitute positive signs of progress (described as "emergences of roots of goodness"; see p. 496b), as well as descriptions of various distracting visions that occur through the mischief of demonic beings. This latter theme does occur in the *Zuowang shuyi*, as well as in *Stability and Observation*.

14. Underscoring and slash marks will be used to indicate textual variants between versions A and B. The left side of the slash mark indicates what is found in version A, and the right side indicates what is found in version B. An "x" indicates the absence of a character.
15. See entry on *mu shotoku* 無所得 in Nakamura et al. 2002, 990.

Another possible rendering of *wu suoyou* might be "there is nothing to possess."

16. In the 36th chapter of *The Western Ascension* is a passage that reads, "If people can be in a state of empty, vacant non-action, even if they have no desire for the Dao, the Dao will come to them on its own" 人能虛空無爲 非欲於道 道自歸之 (A 6/9b; B 3/18b).
17. See chapter 4, nn. 19.
18. In most versions of the *Laozi*, the passage quoted here from chapter 23 contains an additional character (*le* 樂) and reads, "the Dao also rejoices in obtaining them." The wording here of *Sitting and Forgetting* conforms to that found in the version of the *Laozi* that bears the commentary of Tang Emperor Xuanzong (DZ677/TT355). The passage quoted from chapter 62, in some versions such as that bearing the commentary of Wang Bi 王弼 (226–249; DZ690/TT373), has the character *yue* 曰 instead of *ri* 日, and thus translates best into a rhetorical question something like "Is it not said that you will obtain it if you seek it, and if you bear any guilt it will be absolved because of it?" The wording of *Sitting and Forgetting* here follows that of the version of the *Laozi* that bears the commentary attributed to the mysterious Han period figure Heshanggong 河上公 (DZ682/TT363).
19. Interestingly, it can be noted here that one of the (actual or purported) Nestorian Christian Chinese manuscripts recovered (at least allegedly) from the caves of Dunhuang quotes this very same passage, and in doing so seems to be speaking of how the Christian God has the power to immediately redeem sinners of all their sins. This manuscript, entitled *Daqin jingjiao xuanyuan zhiben jing* 大秦景教宣元至本經 (The Scripture that Proclaims the Origins and Reaches the Basis, of the Luminous Religion of the Land of Daqing) bears a colophon indicating that it was written down in the year 718 by a certain Zhang Ju 張駒. However, Lin Wushu 林悟殊 has argued that it is a modern forgery. See Eskildsen, "Parallel Themes in Chinese Nestorianism and Medieval Daoist Religion," in Malek 2006, 57–91; Lin Wushu, *Tangdai jingjiao zaiyanjiu* 唐代景教再研究, 156–174.
20. See James Benn, *Burning for the Buddha: Self-Immolation in Chinese Buddhism*.
21. DZ1312/TT1024. On the date of this text's authorship, see Eskildsen,

"Severe Asceticism in Early Daoist Religion" (PhD Thesis, University of British Columbia, 1994), 534–538.
22. See Eskildsen 1998, 129–152.
23. DZ400/TT189.
24. *Yunji qiqian* 17/6b–13a.
25. See Kohn 2010, 163–173.
26. If one is to draw parallels here to roughly contemporaneous Chan Buddhist theories of meditation, one can say that the approach thus advocated in *Stability and Observation* differs from that advocated in the *Platform Sūtra* 壇經 of the Sixth Patriarch Huineng 慧能 (638–713). There one is advised to observe the mind as it flows freely, without suppressing the emerging thoughts and feelings, but rather acknowledging them for what they are without attaching to them. More similar to the method of *Stability and Observation* is the method described in the enlightenment verse of Huineng's rival Shenxiu 神秀 (deemed as inferior the prologue of the *Platform Sūtra*), in which the "mirror" of the mind must be constantly wiped free of the dust of deluding thoughts. See Philip Yampolski trans., *The Platform Sūtra of the Sixth Patriarch*; and *Liuzu dashi fabao tan jing* 六祖大師法寶壇經 (*Taishō Canon*, no. 2008, vol. 48).
27. See Eskildsen 2004, 70–71; and Eskildsen 2011, 124–127.

## CHAPTER 7. SERENITY, PRIMAL *QI*, AND EMBRYONIC BREATHING

1. DZ834/TT571.
2. For a concise summary of the life and contributions of Sun Simiao, see Kohn 2010, 47–51.
3. *Yunji qiqian* 33/12a–14b.
4. From the layout of the text of the *Yunji qiqian* it is not entirely clear whether the editor regarded the *Taiqing cunshen lianqi wushi qihou jue* as a part of the *Sheyang zhenzhong fang*, or regarded them as separate treatises. The 33rd scroll of the *Yunji qiqian* constitutes part of a larger section that comprises scrolls 32 through 36 and bears the heading *Zaxiu she* 雜修攝 (Selections on Miscellaneous Cultivation Methods); the section includes miscellaneous writings from the hands

of various authors, named and anonymous. This being the case, one cannot conclude whether the editor even regarded the *Taiqing cunshen lianqi wushi qihou jue* as the work of Sun Simiao.

5. See Jean Lévi, "*Cunshen lianqi ming*," in Schipper and Verellen, 375–376.
6. See Kohn 2010, 174–178.
7. Citations of *The Inscription* refer to version A.
8. To give an early, authoritative example, Tiantai School founder Zhiyi 智顗 (538–598), in his *Miaofa lianhua jing wenju* 妙法蓮華經文句 (*Taishō Canon*, no. 1748, vol. 34), laments, "Take for example the infidels who hold to the [one-sided] view of emptiness. They willingly do evil things, and cause others to give rise to wickedness and cut off their roots of goodness. Once they have lost the Dharma Body, their life of wisdom also dies" 譬空見外道 恣意行惡教人起邪斷善根 法身既亡慧命亦死 (134a).
9. See chapter 5.
10. Here version B (*Yunji qiqian* 33/12b) has the character *zhu* 注 (focus; concentrate; pour) instead of *zhu* 住 (stay; stop; reside).
11. The underscored indicates a discrepancy between versions A and B. Left of the slash mark is the text as found in version A, and to the right of it is the text as found in version B.
12. See chapter 3, n. 10.
13. See, for example, Li Daochun 李道純 (fl. 1288–1306), *Zhonghe ji* 中和集 (DZ749/TT118) 2/4a–7b; and Wu Shouyang 伍守陽 (1573–1640), *Tianxian zhengli zhilun zengzhu* 天仙正理直論增註 (in *Zangwai daoshu*, 5:777a–855a), 836a–b.
14. DZ1185/TT868–870.
15. See Ware 1966, 139.
16. See Henri Maspero, *Taoism and Chinese Religion*, translated by Frank A. Kierman Jr., 459–460.
17. See Joseph Needham, *Science and Civilization in China*, vol. 5, no. 5, 145–146.
18. *Yunji qiqian* 58/13b–16b.
19. Needham understands this as referring to the meconium (a baby's first stools) that occlude the intestinal tract. See Needham 1983, 145–146.

20. DZ817/TT586; also in *Yunji qiqian* 13. This text consists of a main scripture text and a commentary. The commentary appears to date to around 700, but the main text could date to circa 300 or earlier, because *Zhonghuang jing* is among the titles mentioned by Ge Hong as having been among the books owned by his teacher Zheng Yin 鄭隱 (*Baopuzi neipian* 19/4b, 5a).
21. See Eskildsen 1998, 44–51.
22. The version that does not include the commentary is entitled *Gaoshang Yuhuang taixi jing* 高上玉皇胎息經 (The High and Supreme Jade Emperor's Scripture on Embryonic Breathing; DZ14/TT24). The two versions with the commentary—versions A and B—are entitled respectively *Taixi jing zhu* 胎息經註 (DZ130/TT59) and *Taixi jing* 胎息經 (*Yunji qiqi*an 60/27a–28b).
23. See *Baopuzi neipian* 19/4b.
24. It has been plausibly speculated—based on the minute, single-stroke difference in the first characters in the respective names—that this Mr. Huanzhen is one and the same as the Mr. Youzhen (Youzhen xiansheng 幼真先生) whose name graces the title of the treatise *Youzhen xiansheng fu nei yuanqi jue* 幼真先生服內元氣訣 (Mr. Youzhen's Lesson on Ingesting the Internal Primal *Qi*; DZ828/TT570 and *Yunji qiqian* 60/14a–17a). If so, it would appear that he lived during the eighth century, because one of the two versions of the *Youzhen xiansheng fu nei yuanqi jue*, bears a preface where the author describes how during the Tianbao 天寶 reign era (742–756) he had encountered and received instructions from a certain "Sir Wang, the Genuine Man of Luofu (a famous mountain in present day Guangdong 廣東 Province)" 羅浮真人王公 who had just returned from the Northern Peak 北嶽 (presumably Mt. Heng 恆山, in present day Shanxi 山西 Province). Oddly, in the *Daoist Canon* there also exists a text entitled *Songshan Taiwu xiansheng qijing* 嵩山太无先生氣經 (The Scripture on *qi* by Mister Taiwu of Mt. Song; DZ824/TT569) that in its contents is largely identical to the *Youzhen xiansheng fu nei yuanqi jue*; at the beginning of this text we find virtually the same story about an encounter with Sir Wang, which, however, is said to have occurred during the Dali 大曆 reign era (766–779), and presumably was experienced by Mister Taiwu—not Mr. Youzhen (unless

one person went by both names). As has been pointed out by Jean Lévi, one of the Song period bibliographies listing the title of the *Songshan Taiwu xiansheng qijing* states that its author is Li Fengshi 李奉時 (fl. 825), an attribution that also finds confirmation in the early twelfth century Daoist anthology, the *Daoshu* 道樞. See Jean Lévi, "*Songshan Taiwu xiansheng qijing*," in Schipper and Verellen, 370–371.

25. DZ1405/TT1050. This text must have been compiled sometime after 779, because it contains (on pp. 10a–b) a first-person testimony concerning an encounter with a certain "Sir Wang, the Genuine Man of Luofu" that occurred during the Dali 大歷 (sic, 大曆) era (766–779). As was mentioned in the previous note, this same testimony is found at the beginning of *Songshan Taiwu xiansheng qijing*. It seems unlikely that the narrator of the encounter incident is the compiler of the text, judging from its placement within the text. *The Embryonic Origins* as a whole is a quite eclectic, even haphazard-looking collection of discourses on various *qi*-related longevity techniques. The colophon states only that its commentary is by a certain Lang Zhao 郎肇. However, it is only on the first four folios (out of a total of nineteen folios) that there is any commentary to be found. It is on these same four folios that we find the discussion on embryonic breathing that concerns us, and which corresponds to *Bodhidharma's Lesson* and to certain portions of *The Embryonic Subtleties* (3a–5b; *Neizhen miaoyong jue* 內真妙用訣) and *Holy Embryo* (1a–2b).

26. DZ829/TT571. This is a short collection comprised of three sections; (1) the *Taixi jingwei lun* proper (1a–3a), (2) *Neizhen miaoyong jue* 內真妙用訣 (3a–5b), and (3) *Taixi shenhui neidan qifan jue* 胎息神會內丹七返訣 (5b–7b). The first section contains what looks like a quote from the *Embryonic Breathing* scripture. The second section corresponds to *Bodhidharma's Lesson* and to portions of *The Embryonic Origins* (1a–4b) and *Holy Embryo* (1a–2b). Interestingly, most of page 1b and part of the first line of page 2a match with *The Manifest Dao* 2a–b.

27. DZ826/570. This is a collection of various short discourses on embryonic breathing attributed to various authorities, many of which are prominent Daoist figures of the Northern Song Period, such as

"Genuine Man Haichan" (Liu Haichan 劉海蟾), "Divine Elder Xu" 徐神翁 (Xu Shouxin 徐守信), Chen Xiyi 陳希夷 (Chen Tuan 陳摶), Langranzi 朗然子 (Liu Xiyue 劉希嶽), and Transcendent Girl Cao 曹仙姑 (Cao Wenyi 曹文逸). Thus, the compilation dates to perhaps the twelfth century or later. However, it also appears to contain earlier material. On pages 1a–2b is found material that corresponds to *Embryonic Breathing*, *The Embryonic Origins*, *The Embryonic Subtleties* and *Bodhidharma's Lesson*.

28. This discourse is found in the *Yunji qiqian* (59/14b–18a), within a section bearing the heading "*Qi* Methods of Various Schools" (Zhuji qifa 諸家氣法). Interestingly, the discourse preceding it in this section (*Tanluan fashi fuqi fa* 曇鸞法師服氣法) is also attributed to a famous Buddhist figure, the Pure Land master Tanluan 曇鸞 (476–542).

29. See *Daode zhenjing zhu* 道德真經註 (DZ682/TT363), 1/5a–b; *The Embryonic Subtleties*, 3a. The Heshanggong commentary is attributed to a mysterious figure who is said to have been active at the end of the Warring States Period, or during the reign of Han emperor Wendi 文帝 (r. 179–157 BCE). Its actual date of authorship has been long debated, with estimates ranging between the Latter Han and the fifth century. The Daoist religion, beginning perhaps with the Lingbao movement in the fifth century, embraced it as a Laozi commentary most worthy of heeding, and for formal transmission to Daoist initiates. See Jan de Meyer, "*Daode zhenjing zhu*," in Schipper and Verellen, 72–74; and Eskildsen 1998, 123–124.

30. "B 1a" here corresponds to *Yunji qiqian* 60/27a.

31. For some reason, the form of the character *qi* written 炁—rather than 氣—is used here in the commentary in version A, but not in version B. 氣 is used throughout the main text in both versions. This may be the commentator's—or version A editor's—own way of conveying the concept of vital, primal *qi*, as opposed to air or ordinary breath.

32. The underscore indicates a discrepancy between versions A and B. On the left side of the slash mark is the text as shown in version A; on the right side is what is shown in version B.

33. The passage quoted is found in *Zongyuan xiansheng xuangang lun* 宗玄先生玄綱論 (DZ1052/TT727) 11b. For an extensive, detailed

study on Wu Yun and his writings, see Jan de Meyer, *Wu Yun's Way: Life and Works of an Eighth-century Daoist Master*.

34. This particular chapter of the *Laozi*, at least on the surface, seems to pertain more to wise statecraft than to personal macrobiotic cultivation. If so, "to deepen the roots and solidify the stem" would seem to mean to exercise the sort of frugality and moderation that keeps the state stable.
35. See *The Embryonic Origins*, 4b; *Holy Embryo*, 2b; and *Bodhidharma's Lesson*, Yunji qiqian 59/18a.
36. See chapter 2, nn. 57.
37. In his "Writ for Establishing My Vow," Huisi proclaims his intention to "take recourse to the power of the external elixir so as to cultivate the internal elixir." 藉外丹力修內丹 (*Nanyue Si dachanshi lishiyuan wen* 南嶽思大禪師立誓願文 [*Taishō Canon*, no. 1933, vol. 46], 791c). What he apparently means to say, however, is that he intends to take recourse to the various available herbal and medicinal remedies ("external elixir") in order to extend his lifespan and thus prolong as much as possible the amount of time he has to practice meditation (the "internal elixir"); he needs the extra time because he desires to attain nothing less than the fullest enlightenment. It appears thus that by internal elixir he is referring to Buddhist meditation, rather than anything that represents a precursor to Neidan methods of the sort that would later develop. See James Robson, "Buddhism and the Chinese Marchmount System: A Case Study of the Southern Marchmount," in *Religion and Chinese Society*, vol. 1 (Ancient and Medieval China), ed. John Lagerwey, 341–384 (esp., p. 360); James Robson, *Power of Place: The Religious Landscape of the Southern Peak (Nanyue) in Medieval China*, 218–219; Qing Xitai 卿希泰 ed., *Zhongguo daojiao shi* 中國道教史, 2:506–507 (by Zhao Zongcheng 趙宗誠).

## CHAPTER 8. CONCLUSION

1. In the terms of Jungian depth-psychology, one might also understand these images as projections of subconscious forces at work in a psychotherapeutic progress toward human wholeness (i.e., individuation).

The Baby and the Red Snake might perhaps be understood as embodying the archetype of the "self" (the essence of human wholeness wherein conscious and subconscious are integrated), or perhaps as the world-creating spirit (Mercurius, *prima materia*) imprisoned or concealed in matter, which acts as an agent of healing and renewal of one's personality. See C.G. Jung, *Psychology and Alchemy*, translated by R.F.C. Hull, 3–37, 144, 292–293.
2. See Bokenkamp 1997, 42–43, 112 n.
3. See Eskildsen 2004, 69–74; Eskildsen 2011, 124–128. For good discussions on female Neidan and the stopping of menstruation (decapitating the Red Dragon), see Catherine Despeux and Livia Kohn, *Women in Daoism*, 177–243.
4. See Eskildsen 1998, 75–79.
5. Notable among Tang Neidan materials that describe this sort of phenomenon are the *Zhen longhu jiuxian jing* 真龍虎九仙經 (DZ227/TT112; with commentaries attributed to Ye Fashan 葉法善 [ca. 616–720] and Luo Gongyuan 羅公遠 [ca. 655–758]) and *Taibai huandan pian* 太白還丹篇 (In *Daoshu* 27/4a–13a; attributed to Wang Yuanzheng 王元正 [fl. 785–805]).
6. On this problem, and on methods proposed to cope with premature death, see Eskildsen, "Emergency Death Meditations for Internal Alchemists," *T'oung Pao* 92:4–5 (2006): 373–409.
7. The Four *Dhyānas* are typically described as follows: (1) applied and sustained thought, with rapture and pleasure born from seclusion; (2) rapture and pleasure born from seclusion, without any more applied and sustained thought; (3) pleasure and equanimity, with neither rapture nor applied and sustained thought; and (4) no pleasure nor pain. See Ñāṇamoli and Bodhi 1995, 367–369 (translation of Sutta #39). See also Nakamura et al. 2002, 432.
8. In Sutta #33 (*Sangiti Suttanta*) of the *Digha Nikaya* we find the following statement: "by the attainment of the First Jhāna, sensuous perceptions cease, Second Jhāna, applied and sustained thought ceases, Third Jhāna, zest ceases, fourth Jhāna, respiration ceases." (T.W. Rhys Davids and C.A.F. Rhys Davids trans., *Dialogues of the Buddha*, part 3, 245). See also Bart Dessein, "Contemplation of the Repulsive: Bones and Skulls as Objects of Meditation," in Eifring 2014, 117–148 (esp., 145–146).

9. See Nakamura et al. 2002, 401, 999.
10. In Sūtra #210 (*Fala biqiuni jing* 法樂比丘尼經) of the *Zhong ahan jing* 中阿含經 (58th *juan*; *Taishō Canon*, no. 26, vol. 1) a female lay devotee named Bishequ 毘舍佉 asks, "Worthy Sage! What difference is there between dying and going into the Trance of Complete Extinction?" 賢聖 若死及入滅盡定者 有何差別. To this, the nun Fale 法樂 (Dharma Joy) replies, "As for dead people, their life has been extinguished. The warmth [of the body] leaves them, and their various sense faculties decay. When a monk enters the Trance of Complete Extinction, his life is not extinguished, warmth does not leave him, and his various sense organs do not decay. Thus it can be said that there is a difference between those who die and those who enter the Trance of Complete Extinction" 死者壽命滅訖 溫暖已去 諸根敗壞 比丘入滅盡定者 壽不滅訖 暖亦不去 諸根不敗壞 若死及入滅盡定者 是謂差別 (p. 789a).

    Similar conversations (between male interlocutors and monks) can be found in Sūtra #211 (*Dajuchiluo jing* 大拘絺羅經) of the *Zhong ahan jing* (58th *juan*; p. 791c), and in Sūtra #568 of the *Za ahan jing* 雜阿含經 (21st *juan*; *Taishō Canon*, no. 99, vol. 2, 150a). See Shi Yinrong 釋印融, "Lüetan miejin ding" 略滅盡定, in *Fuyan foxueyuan dibajie gaojibu xuesheng lunwenji* 福嚴佛學院第八屆高級部學生論文集, 69–83 (esp., 73).
11. The passage in question reads, "It is comparable to the case of a monk who has self-control of mind and has entered the Trance of Complete Extinction. All functioning of the six roots (thought, sight, hearing, smell, taste and touch) cease, and he is unaware of all speech. Because the power of trance sustains him, he does not enter final *nirvāṇa*" 譬如比丘得心自在 入滅盡定 六根作業皆悉不行 一切語言不知不覺 定力持故 不般涅槃. (*Dafang guangfo huayan jing* 大方廣佛華嚴經 [*Taishō Canon*, no. 279, vol. 10], 324a [60th *juan*].)
12. Qiu Chuji 丘處機 (1143–1227), the famous Quanzhen school Patriarch is recorded as having stated, "A man of old said, 'First thoughts stop, secondly breathing stops, thirdly pulse stops, and fourthly there is complete extinction and you enter into Great Stability'" 古人曰 初念住 二息住 三脈住 四滅盡 入乎大定 (*Zhenxian zhizhi yulu* 真仙直指語錄 [DZ1256/TT998] 1/13b–14a). Qiu Chuji thus used the specific term "complete extinction" to refer to the death-resembling

condition of breath-pulse suspension, and describes a fourfold progression of trance states that parallels—but does not quite match—the Buddhist one. A further four centuries later, Wu Shouyang and Wu Shouxu 伍守虛 (his disciple, cousin, and commentator) would similarly employ the term Trance of Complete Extinction to describe the condition of breath-pulse suspension, and would use the specific Buddhist term Four Meditations (*sichan* 四禪) to refer to the progression described by Qiu Chuji. In doing so, Wu Shouxu specifically quotes the *Avataṃsaka Sūtra*, although the passage he ostensibly quotes is curiously not to be found in either version of the *sūtra* in the *Taishō Canon* (see *Xianfo hezong yulu*, in *Zangwai daoshu* 5:675a; and Eskildsen 2011, 128–132), In the view of the two Wus, the suspension of breathing and pulse must come about, and you must witness of vision of "flowers" or snowflakes falling from the sky, before you send the spirit out of the body through the top of your head. The optimal trance condition is also referred to as *zhenkong* 真空 or "True Emptiness" (see *Xianfo hezong yulu*, in *Zangwai daoshu*, 5:689a–b).
13. See, for example, Li Daochun 李道純 (fl. 1288–1306), *Zhonghe ji* 中和集 (DZ749/TT118) 2/4a–7b; and Wu Shouyang伍守陽 (1573–1640), *Tianxian zhengli zhilun zengzhu* 天仙正理直論增註 (in *Zangwai daoshu*, 5:777a–855a), 836a–b.
14. DZ1191/TT874.
15. In *Xiuzhen shishu* 修真十書 (DZ263/TT131) 14–16.

# Bibliography

SOURCES IN ENGLISH AND FRENCH

Assandri, Frederike. *Beyond the Daode jing: Twofold Mystery in Tang Daoism*. Magdalena, NM: Three Pines Press, 2009.
Barrett, T.H. "Taoist and Buddhist Mysteries in the Interpretation of the *Tao-te-ching*." *Journal of the Royal Asiatic Society*, vol. 114, no. 1 (January 1982), 35–43.
———. "Buddhism, Daoism and the Eighth Century Chinese Term for Christianity. A Response to the Recent Work of Antonino Forte and Others." In Jingjiao: *The Church of the East in China and Central Asia*, edited by Roman Malek, 45–56. Sankt Augustin, Germany: Monumenta Serica Institute, 2006.
———, and Livia Kohn. "*Yangsheng yaoji*." In *The Encyclopedia of Taoism*, edited by Fabrizio Pregadio, 2:1151–1152. London and New York: Routledge, 2008.
Benn, James. *Burning for the Buddha: Self-Immolation in Chinese Buddhism*. Honolulu: University of Hawaii Press, 2007.
Bokenkamp, Stephen R. *Early Daoist Scriptures*. With a contribution by Peter Nickerson. Berkeley: University of California Press, 1997.
Brashier, K.E. *Ancestral Memory in Early China*. Cambridge: Harvard University Asia Center, 2011.

Cahill, Suzanne. *Transcendence and Divine Passion: The Queen Mother of the West in Medieval China*. Stanford: Stanford University Press, 1995.

Cedzich, Ursula-Angelika. "Corpse Deliverance, Substitute Bodies, Name Change, and Feigned Death: Aspects of Metamorphosis and Immortality in Early Medieval China." *Journal of Chinese Religions* 29 (2001): 1–68.

Chan, Wing-tsit, trans. *Reflections on Things at Hand: The Neo-Confucian Anthology Compiled by Chu Hsi and Lü Tsu-ch'ien*. New York: Columbia University Press, 1967.

Ch'en, Kenneth. *Buddhism in China: A Historical Survey*. Princeton: Princeton University Press, 1964.

Collins, Steven. *Nirvana and Other Buddhist Felicities: Utopias of the Pali Imaginaire*. Cambridge: Cambridge University Press, 1998.

Conze, Edward. *Buddhism: Its Essence and Development*. Oxford: Bruno Casirer, 1951.

———. *The Prajñāpāramitā Literature*. The Hague: Mouton, 1960.

———, ed., *Buddhist Texts through the Ages*. Oxford: Bruno Casirer, 1954.

Csikszentmihalyi, Mark, and Philip J. Ivanhoe, eds. *Religious and Philosophical Aspects of the* Laozi. Albany: State University of New York Press, 1999.

De Meyer, Jan. "*Daode zhenjing zhu*." In *The Taoist Canon: A Historical Companion to the* Daozang, edited by Kristofer Schipper and Franciscus Verellen, 1:72–74. Chicago: University of Chicago Press, 2004.

———. *Wu Yun's Way: Life and Works of an Eighth-century Daoist Master*. Leiden: Brill, 2006.

Despeux, Catherine, and Livia Kohn. *Women in Daoism*. Boston: Three Pines Press, 2005.

Dessein, Bart. "Contemplation of the Repulsive: Bones and Skulls as Objects of Meditation." In *Hindu, Buddhist and Daoist Meditation: Cultural Histories*, edited by Halvor Eifring, 117–148. Oslo: Hermes, 2014.

Dudink, Adrianus. "*Nüqing guilü*." In *The Taoist Canon: A Historical Companion to the* Daozang, edited by Kristofer Schipper and Franciscus Verellen, 1:127–129. Chicago: University of Chicago Press, 2004.

Eifring, Halvor, ed. *Hindu, Buddhist and Daoist Meditation: Cultural Histories*. Oslo: Hermes, 2014.

Eskildsen, Stephen. *Asceticism in Early Taoist Religion*. Albany: State University of New York Press, 1998.

———. "Christology and Soteriology in the Chinese Nestorian Tests." In *The Chinese Face of Jesus Christ*, edited by Roman Malek, vol. 1:181–218. Sankt Augustin, Germany: Monumenta Serica Institute, 2002.

———. *The Teachings and Practices of the Early Quanzhen Taoist Masters*. Albany: State University of New York Press, 2004.

———. "Emergency Death Meditations for Internal Alchemists." *T'oung Pao*, vol. 92, nos. 4–5 (2006): 373–409.

———. "Parallel Themes in Chinese Nestorianism and Medieval Daoist Religion." In *Jingjiao: The Church of the East in China and Central Asia*, edited by Roman Malek, 57–92. Sankt Augustin, Germany: Monumenta Serica Institute, 2006.

———. "Mystical Ascent and Out-of-Body Experience in Medieval Daoism." *Journal of Chinese Religions* 35 (2007): 36–62.

———. "Some Troubles and Perils of Taoist Meditation." *Monumenta Serica* 56 (2008): 259–291.

———. "Red Snakes and Angry Queen Mothers: Hallucinations and Epiphanies in Daoist Meditation." In *Hindu, Buddhist and Daoist Meditation: Cultural Histories*, edited by Halvor Eifring, 149–183. Oslo: Hermes, 2014.

Espesset, Grégoire. "Cosmologie et trifonctionnalité dans l'idéologie du Livre de la Grande paix." PhD Dissertation, Université Paris, 7. Paris, 2002.

Hendrischke, Barbara. *The Scripture on Great Peace: The Taiping jing and the Beginnings of Daoism*. Berkeley: University of California Press, 2006.

Jung, Carl G. *Alchemical Studies*. Translated by R.F.C. Hull. Princeton: Princeton University Press, 1967.

———. *Psychology and Alchemy*. Translated by R.F.C. Hull. Princeton: Princeton University Press, 1968.

Kaltenmark, Max. "The Ideology of the T'ai-p'ing-ching." In *Facets of Taoism*, edited by Holmes Welch and Anna Seidel, 19–52. New Haven: Yale University Press, 1979.

Kirkland, Russell, and Livia Kohn. "Daoism in the Tang (618–907)." In *Daoism Handbook*, edited by Livia Kohn, 339–383. Leiden: E.J. Brill, 2000.

Knoblock, John, trans. *Xunzi: A Translation and Study of the Complete Works*, vol. 1. Stanford: Stanford University Press, 1988.

Kohn, Livia. *Seven Steps to the Tao: Sima Chengzhen's Zuowang lun*. Sankt Augustin: Monumenta Serica Monograph XX, 1987.

———. *Taoist Mystical Philosophy: The Scripture of the Western Ascension*. Albany: State University of New York Press, 1991.

———. *The Taoist Experience: An Anthology*. Albany: State University of New York Press, 1993.

———. *God of the Dao: Lord Lao in History and Myth*. Ann Arbor: Center for Chinese Studies, University of Michigan, 1999.

———. *Sitting in Oblivion: The Heart of Daoist Meditation*. Dunedin, FL: Three Pines Press, 2010.

———, ed. *Daoism Handbook*. 2 vols. Leiden: Brill, 2000.

———, and Michael LaFargue, eds. *Lao-tzu and the Tao-te-ching*. Albany: State University of New York Press, 1998.

Komjathy, Louis. *Cultivating Perfection: Mysticism and Self-transformation in Early Quanzhen Daoism*. Leiden: Brill, 2007.

———. *The Way of Complete Perfection: A Quanzhen Daoist Anthology*. Albany: State University of New York Press, 2013.

Lagerwey, John. "*Taishang laojun xuwu ziran benqi jing*." In *The Taoist Canon: A Historical Companion to the* Daozang, edited by Kristofer Schipper and Franciscus Verellen, 1:531–532. Chicago: University of Chicago Press, 2004.

———, ed. *Religion and Chinese Society*, vol. 1 (Ancient and Medieval China). Hong Kong: Chinese University Press, 2004.

Lau, D.C., trans. *Mencius*. London: Penguin, 1970.

Legge, James (1815–1897). *The Texts of Taoism*. New York: Julian Press, 1959.

Lévi, Jean. "*Cunshen lianqi ming*." In *The Taoist Canon: A Historical Companion to the* Daozang, edited by Kristofer Schipper and Franciscus Verellen, 1:375–376. Chicago: University of Chicago Press, 2004.

———. "*Songshan Taiwu xiansheng qijing*." In *The Taoist Canon: A Historical Companion to the* Daozang, edited by Kristofer Schipper and Franciscus Verellen, 1:370–371. Chicago: University of Chicago Press, 2004.

Lopez, Donald. *Elaborations on Emptiness: Uses of the Heart Sūtra*. Princeton: Princeton University Press, 1996.

Malek, Roman, ed. *The Chinese Face of Jesus Christ.* Vol. 1. Sankt Augustin, Germany: Monumenta Serica Institute, 2002.

———, ed. *Jingjiao: The Church of the East in China and Central Asia.* Sankt Augustin, Germany: Monumenta Serica Institute, 2006.

Marsone, Pierre. *Wang Chongyang (1113–1170) et la foundation du Quanzhen: ascètes taoïstes et alchimie intérieure.* Paris: Institut des Hautes Études Chinoises (Collège du France), 2010.

Maspero, Henri. *Taoism and Chinese Religion.* Translated by Frank A. Kierman Jr. Amherst: University of Massachusetts Press, 1981.

Mollier, Christine. *Buddhism and Taoism Face to Face: Scripture, Ritual and Iconographic Exchange in Medieval China.* Honolulu: University of Hawai'i Press, 2008.

Nakamura Hajime. *Indian Buddhism: A Survey with Bibliographical Notes.* Delhi: Motilal Banarsidass, 1987.

Ñāṇamoli, Bhikku, and Bhikkhu Bodhi, trans. *The Middle Length Discourses of the Buddha: A New Translation of the* Majjhima Nikāya. Boston: Wisdom, 1995.

Nattier, Jan. "The *Heart Sūtra*: A Chinese Apocryphal Text?" *Journal of the International Association of Buddhist Studies* 15, no. 2 (1992), 153–223.

Needham, Joseph. *Science and Civilization in China.* Vol. 5, no. 5. Cambridge: Cambridge University Press, 1983.

Poo, Mu-chou. *In Search of Personal Welfare: A View of Ancient Chinese Religion.* Albany: State University of New York Press, 1998.

Pregadio, Fabrizio. *Great Clarity: Daoism and Alchemy in Early Medieval China.* Stanford: Stanford University Press, 2006.

———. *The Encyclopedia of Taoism.* 2 vols. London and New York: Routledge, 2008.

———. *The Seal and Unity of the Three: A Study and Translation of the* Cantong qi, *the Source of the Taoist Way of the Golden Elixir.* Mountain View, CA: Golden Elixir Press, 2011.

Reiter, Florian. "*Sandong zhunang.*" In *The Taoist Canon: A Historical Companion to the* Daozang, edited by Kristofer Schipper and Franciscus Verellen, 1:440–441. Chicago: University of Chicago Press, 2004.

Rhys Davids, T.W., and C.A.F. Rhys Davids, trans. *Dialogues of the Buddha*, part 3. London: Oxford University Press, 1921.

Rickett, W. Allyn. *Guanzi: Political, Economic and Philosophical Essays from Early China.* Princeton: Princeton University Press, 1985.

Robinet, Isabelle. *La meditation taoïste.* Paris: Albin Michel, 1979.

———. *La revelation du Shangqing dans l'histoire du taoïsme.* Paris: Ecole Française d'Extrême-Orient, 1984.

———. *Taoist Meditation: the Mao-Shan Tradition of Great Purity* (*La meditation taoïste*). Translated by Julian Pas and Norman Girardot. Albany: State University of New York Press, 1993.

Robinson, Richard H. *Early Mādhyamika in India and China.* Madison: University of Wisconsin Press, 1967.

Robson, James. "Buddhism and the Chinese Marchmount System: A Case Study of the Southern Marchmount." In *Religion and Chinese Society*, edited by John Lagerwey, 1:341–384. Hong Kong: Chinese University Press, 2004.

———. *Power of Place: The Religious Landscape of the Southern Peak (Nanyue) in Medieval China.* Cambridge, MA: Harvard University Asia Center, 2009.

Roth, Harold D. *Original Tao: Inward Training and the Foundation of Taoist Mysticism.* New York: Columbia University Press, 1999.

Saeki Yoshirō 佐伯好郎. *The Nestorian Documents and Relics in China.* Tokyo: Tōhō Bunka Gakuin, 1937 (1951).

Schipper, Kristofer. "*Liexian zhuan.*" In *The Taoist Canon: A Historical Companion to the* Daozang, edited by Kristofer Schipper and Franciscus Verellen, 1:114. Chicago: University of Chicago Press, 2004.

———. "*Taiping jing.*" In *The Taoist Canon: A Historical Companion to the* Daozang, edited by Kristofer Schipper and Franciscus Verellen, 1:277–280. Chicago: University of Chicago Press, 2004.

———. "*Taiping jing chao.*" In *The Taoist Canon: A Historical Companion to the* Daozang, edited by Kristofer Schipper and Franciscus Verellen, 1:493–494. Chicago: University of Chicago Press, 2004.

———. "*Taiping jing shengjun bizhi.*" In *The Taoist Canon: A Historical Companion to the* Daozang, edited by Kristofer Schipper and Franciscus Verellen, 1:494–495. Chicago: University of Chicago Press, 2004.

———. "*Taiqing jinye shendan jing.*" In *The Taoist Canon: A Historical Companion to the* Daozang, edited by Kristofer Schipper and Franciscus Verellen, 1:104–105. Chicago: University of Chicago Press, 2004.

———. "*Taiqing zhenren luoming jue.*" In *The Taoist Canon: A Historical Companion to the* Daozang, edited by Kristofer Schipper and Franciscus Verellen, 1:94–95. Chicago: University of Chicago Press, 2004.

———. "*Taishang huangting neijing yujing.*" In *The Taoist Canon: A Historical Companion to the* Daozang, edited by Kristofer Schipper and Franciscus Verellen, 1:184–185. Chicago: University of Chicago Press, 2004.

———. "*Taishang hunyuan zhenlu.*" In *The Taoist Canon: A Historical Companion to the* Daozang, edited by Kristofer Schipper and Franciscus Verellen, 1:414–415. Chicago: University of Chicago Press, 2004.

———. "*Taishang Laojun jinglü.*" In *The Taoist Canon: A Historical Companion to the* Daozang, edited by Kristofer Schipper and Franciscus Verellen, 1:131–132. Chicago: University of Chicago Press, 2004.

———. "*Taishang Laojun zhongjing.*" In *The Taoist Canon: A Historical Companion to the* Daozang, edited by Kristofer Schipper and Franciscus Verellen, 1:92–94. Chicago: University of Chicago Press, 2004.

———. "*Xiandao jing.*" In *The Taoist Canon: A Historical Companion to the* Daozang, edited by Kristofer Schipper and Franciscus Verellen, 1:95. Chicago: University of Chicago Press, 2004.

———. "*Xiantian Xuanmiao yunü Taishang shengmu zichuan xiandao.*" In *The Taoist Canon: A Historical Companion to the* Daozang, edited by Kristofer Schipper and Franciscus Verellen, 1:359–360. Chicago: University of Chicago Press, 2004.

———. "*Yangxing yanming lu.*" In *The Taoist Canon: A Historical Companion to the* Daozang, edited by Kristofer Schipper and Franciscus Verellen, 1:345–346. Chicago: University of Chicago Press, 2004.

———. "*Yunji qiqian.*" In *The Taoist Canon: A Historical Companion to the* Daozang, edited by Kristofer Schipper and Franciscus Verellen, 2:943–945. Chicago: University of Chicago Press, 2004.

———. "*Zhengyi fawen tianshi jiaojie kejing.*" In *The Taoist Canon: A Historical Companion to the* Daozang, edited by Kristofer Schipper and Franciscus Verellen, 1:96–97. Chicago: University of Chicago Press, 2004.

———, and Franciscus Verellen, eds. *The Taoist Canon: A Historical Companion to the* Daozang. 3 vols. Chicago: University of Chicago Press, 2004.

Schmidt, Hans-Hermann. "*Taishang Laojun shuo chang qingjing miaojing.*" In *The Taoist Canon: A Historical Companion to the* Daozang, edited by Kristofer Schipper and Franciscus Verellen, 1:562. Chicago: University of Chicago Press, 2004.

———. "*Taixuan zhenyi benji miaojing.*" In *The Taoist Canon: A Historical Companion to the* Daozang, edited by Kristofer Schipper and Franciscus Verellen, 1:520–521. Chicago: University of Chicago Press, 2004.

———. "*Yuanshi dongzhen jueyi jing.*" In *The Taoist Canon: A Historical Companion to the* Daozang, edited by Kristofer Schipper and Franciscus Verellen, 1:522. Chicago: University of Chicago Press, 2004.

Seidel, Anna. *La divinasation de Lao Tseu dans le taoïsme des Han.* Paris: Ecole Française d'Extreme-Orient, 1969.

Verellen, Franciscus. "*Hunyuan shengji.*" In *The Taoist Canon: A Historical Companion to the* Daozang, edited by Kristofer Schipper and Franciscus Verellen, 2:872–874. Chicago: University of Chicago Press, 2004.

Vetter, Tilmann. *A Lexicographical Study of An Shigao's and His Circle's Chinese Translations of Buddhist Texts.* Tokyo: International Institute for Buddhist Studies, 2012.

Ware, James R., trans. *Alchemy, Medicine, Religion in the China of A.D. 320: The Nei P'ien of Ko Hung (Pao-p'u tzu).* Cambridge: MIT Press, 1966.

Watson, Burton, trans. *The Lotus Sūtra.* New York: Columbia University Press, 1993.

Welch, Holmes, and Anna Seidel, eds. *Facets of Taoism: Essays in Chinese Religion.* New Haven: Yale University Press, 1979.

Wu Chi-yu 吳其昱. *Pen-tsi king: Livre de terme originel.* Paris: Centre National de la Recherche Scientifique, 1960.

Yampolski, Philip, trans. *The Platform Sūtra of the Sixth Patriarch.* New York: Columbia University Press, 1967.


SECONDARY SOURCES IN CHINESE AND JAPANESE

Chen Shixiang 陳世驤. "Xiang'er Laozi daojing Dunhuang canjuan lunzheng" 想爾老子道經敦煌殘卷論證. *Ts'ing Hua Journal of Chinese Studies* 清華學報, no. 1.2 (1957): 41–62.

Eskildsen, Stephen (Su Depu 蘇德樸). "Wu Shouyang, Wu Zhenyang

he Liu Huayang de fojing jieshi yu fojiao piping" 伍守陽，伍真陽和柳華陽的佛經解釋與佛教批評. In *Quanzhen dao yanjiu* 全真道研究, vol. 2, edited by Zhao Weidong 趙衛東: 120–143. Jinan: Qi-Lu Shushe 齊魯書社, 2011.

Fukui Kōjun 福井康順. "*Taihei kyō* no ichi kōsatsu" 太平経の一考察. *Tōyō shi kai kiyō* 東洋史会紀要, vol. 1–2 (1936–1937): 141–178.

Gu Baotian 顧寶田, Zhang Zhongli 張忠利 and Fu Wuguang 傅武光 eds. *Xinyi Laozi Xiang'er zhu* 新譯老子想爾注. Taipei: Sanmin Shuju 三民書局, 1997.

Kamitsuka Yoshiko 神塚淑子. "Shiba Shōtei, *Zabō ron* ni tsuite" 司馬承禎『坐忘論』について. *Tōyō Bunka* 東洋文化, no. 62 (March 1982), 213–242.

Kubo Noritada 窪德忠. *Kōshin shinkō no kenkyū* 庚申信仰の研究. Tokyo: Nihon Gakujutsu Shinkōkai 日本学術振興会, 1961.

Kusuyama Haruki 楠山春樹. *Rōshi densetsu no kenkyū* 老子傳説の研究. Tokyo: Sōbunsha 創文社, 1979.

Lin Wushu 林悟殊. *Tangdai jingjiao zaiyanjiu* 唐代景教再研究. Beijing: Zhongguo Shehui Kexueyuan Chubanshe 中國社會科學院出版社, 2003.

Nakamura Hajime 中村元 et al. *Iwanami Bukkyō jiten* 岩波仏教辞典. 2nd ed. Tokyo: Iwanami 岩波, 2002.

Ōfuchi Ninji 大淵忍爾. *Shoki no dōkyō* 初期の道教. Tokyo: Sōbunsha, 1991.

Qing Xitai 卿希泰 ed. *Zhongguo daojiao shi* 中國道教史. 4 vols. Chengdu: Sichuan Renmin Chubanshe 四川人民出版社, 1996.

Rao Zongyi 饒宗頤. *Laozi Xiang'er zhu jiaozheng* 老子想爾注校證. Shanghai: Shanghai Guji Chubanshe 上海古籍出版社, 1956.

Ren Jiyu 任繼愈, ed. *Zhongguo daojiao shi* 中國道教史. Shanghai: Shanghai Renmin Chubanshe 上海人民出版社, 1990.

Saeki Yoshirō 佐伯好郎. *Keikyō no kenkyū* 景教の研究. Tokyo: Tōhō Bunka Gakuin 東方文化学院, 1935.

Shi Yinrong 釋印融, "Lüetan miejin ding" 略談滅盡定. In *Fuyan foxueyuan dibajie gaojibu xuesheng lunwenji* 福嚴佛學院第八屆高級部學生論文集, pp. 69–83. Hsinchu, Taiwan: Fu Yan Buddhist Institute, 1999.

Sun Qi 孫齊. "Wang Tu, *Daoji jing* kao" 王圖《道機經》考. *Wenshi* 文史, no. 105 (2013.4), 5–22.

Tang Yongtong 湯用彤. "Du *Taiping jing* shu suojian" 讀《太平經》書所見. *Guoxue jikan* 國學集刊 5, no. 1 (1935): 7–38.

Wang Ming 王明. *Taiping jing hejiao* 太平經合校. Beijing: Zhonghua Shuju 中華書局, 1960.

Yoshioka Yoshitoyo. "Taihei-kyō no shuitsu shisō" 太平経の守一思想. In *Tōyō shigaku ronshū* 東洋史学論集, edited by Yamazaki sensei taikan kinenkai 山崎先生退官記念会: 491–500. Tokyo: Yamazaki sensei taikan kinenkai, 1967.

———. 吉岡義豊. *Dōkyō to bukkyō* 道教と仏教. Vol. 2. Tokyo: Toshima Shobō 豊島書房, 1970.

PRIMARY SOURCES IN THE *DAOIST CANON* (*ZHENGTONG DAOZANG* 正統道藏 [1445] AND *XU DAOZANG* 續道藏 [1607])

The DZ number denotes the "work number" assigned to the text in Kristofer Schipper and Franciscus Verellen, eds., *The Taoist Canon: A Historical Companion to the* Daozang (Chicago: University of Chicago Press, 2004). The TT number denotes the number of the fascicle(s) containing the text in the 1926 Shanghai Hanfenlou 涵芬樓 facsimile reprint edition of the *Taoist Canon*.

*Baopuzi neipian* 抱朴子內篇. DZ1185/TT868–870. By Ge Hong 葛洪 (283–343).

*Bichuan Zhengyang zhenren lingbao bifa* 祕傳正陽真人靈寶畢法. DZ1191/TT874. Ca. 11th c.

*Changsheng taiyuan shenyong jing* 長生胎元神用經 (*The Embryonic Origins*). DZ1405/TT1050. After 779.

*Chuanshou jingjie yi zhujue* 傳授經戒儀注訣. DZ1238/TT989. Late 6th or early 7th c.

*Chuanshou sandong jingjie falu lüeshuo* 傳授三洞經戒法籙略說. DZ1241/TT990. By Zhang Wanfu 張萬福. 713.

*Cunshen lianqi ming* 存神鍊氣銘 (*The Inscription*, version A). DZ834/TT571. Attributed to Sun Simiao 孫思邈 (581–682).

*Dadan zhizhi* 大丹直指. DZ244/TT115. Attributed to Qiu Chuji 丘處機 (1143–1227). 13th c.

*Damo dashi zhushi liuxing neizhen miaoyong jue* 達磨大師住世留形內真妙用訣 (Bodhidharma's Lesson). In *Yunji qiqian* (DZ1032/TT677–702) 59/14b–18a. 9th or 10th c.

*Danyang zhenren yulu* 丹陽真人語錄. DZ1057/728. Utterances of Ma Yu 馬鈺 (1123–1184). Compiled by Wang Yizhong 王頤中. 12th c.

*Daode zhenjing guangsheng yi* 道德真經廣聖義. DZ725/TT440–448. By Du Guangting 杜光庭. 901.

*Daode zhenjing xuande zuanshu* 道德真經玄德纂疏 (Laozi 老子 with commentaries). DZ711/TT407–413. Compiled by Qiang Siqi 強思齊. 9th c.

*Daode zhenjing zhu* 道德真經註 (Laozi with commentary). DZ682/TT363. Commentary attributed to Heshanggong 河上公 (1st or 2nd c. [?]).

*Daode zhenjing zhushu* 道德真經註疏 (Laozi with commentaries). DZ710/TT404–406. Compilation attributed to Gu Huan 顧歡 (420–483). Compiled after 1101.

*Daodian lun* 道典論. DZ1130/TT764. Ca. Tang dynasty (618–907).

*Daojiao lingyan ji* 道教靈驗記. DZ590/TT325–326. By Du Guangting 杜光庭 (850–930). After 905.

*Daoshu* 道樞. DZ1017/TT641–648. Compiled by Zeng Zao 曾慥. Ca. 1151.

*Dongxuan lingbao dingguan jing* 洞玄靈寶定觀經 (Stability and Observation, version B). In *Yunji qiqian* (DZ1032/TT677–702) 17/6b–13a. Ca. 8th c.

*Dongxuan lingbao dingguan jing zhu* 洞玄靈寶定觀經註 (Stability and Observation, version A). DZ400/TT189. Ca. 8th c.

*Dongzhen huangshu* 洞真黃書. DZ1343/TT1031. Ca. 3rd c.

*Fuqi jingyi lun* 服氣精義論. DZ830/TT571. By Sima Chengzhen 司馬承禎 (647–735).

*Fuqi jingyi lun* 服氣精義論. In *Yunji qiqian* (DZ1032/TT677–702) 57. By Sima Chengzhen 司馬承禎 (647–735).

*Ganshui xianyuan lu* 甘水仙源錄. DZ973/TT611–613. Compiled by Li Daoqian 李道謙. 1289.

*Gaoshang Yuhuang taixi jing* 高上玉皇胎息經 (*Embryonic Breathing*). DZ14/TT24. Six Dynasties (220–581), Sui (581–618) or Tang (618–907).

*Gu Louguan ziyun yanqing ji* 古樓觀紫雲衍慶集. DZ957/TT605. Compiled by Zhu Xiangxian 朱象先. Ca. 1308.

*Huangtian shangqing jinque dijun lingshu ziwen shangjing* 皇天上清金闕帝君靈書紫文上經. DZ639/TT342. Late 4th or early 5th c.

*Huangting waijing yujing zhu* 黃庭外景玉經註. In *Xiuzhen shishu* 修真十書 (DZ263/TT131) 58. Commentary by Bai Lüzhong 白履忠 (a.k.a., Liangqiuzi 梁丘子; fl. 722–729).

*Hunyuan shengji* 混元聖紀 (*The Holy Chronicle*). DZ770/TT551–553. By Xie Shouhao 謝守灝. Ca. 1191.

*Laojun qingjing xin jing* 老君清淨心經. In *Yunji qiqian* (DZ1032/TT677–702) 17/13b–15b. Ca. 8th c.

*Laozi shuo wuchu jing zhu* 老子說五廚經註 (*The Five Kitchens*, version A). DZ763/TT533. Commentary by Yin Yin written in 735.

*Laojun Taishang xuwu ziran benqi jing* 老君太上虛無自然本起經 (*The Original Arising*). In *Yunji qiqian* (DZ1032/TT677–702) 10. Between 5th and 7th c.

*Laozi zhongjing* 老子中經. In *Yunji qiqian* (DZ1032/TT677–702) 18 and 19. Ca. 2nd c.

*Liexian zhuan* 列仙傳. DZ294/TT138. Ascribed to Liu Xiang 劉向 (77–6 BCE). Ca. 2nd c.

*Nanhua zhenjing* 南華真經 (*Zhuangzi* 莊子). DZ670/TT349–351. 4th–2nd c. BCE.

*Nüqing guilü* 女青鬼律. DZ790/TT563. Ca. 3rd c.

*Rushi si chizi fa* 入室思赤子法 (*Contemplating the Baby*). In *Yunji qiqian* (DZ1032/TT677–702) 55/9b–14a. Six Dynasties (220–581).

*Sandong zhunang* 三洞珠囊. DZ1139/TT780–782. Compiled by Wang Xuanhe 王懸河. Ca. 680.

*Santian neijie jing* 三天內解經. DZ1205/TT876. By Xushi 徐氏. Ca. 421–478.

*Shangqing huangshu guodu yi* 上清黃書過渡儀. DZ1294/TT1009. Ca. 3rd c.

*Songshan Taiwu xiansheng qijing* 嵩山太无先生氣經. DZ824/TT569. Late 8th or early 9th c.

*Taibai huandan pian* 太白還丹篇. In *Daoshu* (DZ1017/TT641–648) 27/4a–13a. Attributed to Wang Yuanzheng 王元正 (fl. 785–805).

*Taiping jing* 太平經 (*The Great Peace*). DZ1101.a/TT746–755. Compiled ca. 6th c.

*Taiping jing chao* 太平經鈔 (*GP Synopsis*). DZ1101.b/TT746–747. Ca. Tang dynasty (618–907).

*Taiping jing shengjun bizhi* 太平經聖君祕旨 (*GP Instructions*). DZ1102/TT755. Ca. Tang dynasty (618–907).

*Taiqing cunshen lianqi wushi qihou jue* 太清存神鍊氣五時七候訣 (*The Inscription*, version B). In *Yunji qiqian* (DZ1032/TT677–702) 33/12a–14b. Attributed to Sun Simiao (581–682).

*Taiqing jinye shendan jing* 太清金液神丹經. DZ880/TT582. Attributed to Zhang Daoling 張道陵 (2nd c.), Yin Changsheng 陰長生 (1st-2nd c.) and Ge Hong 葛洪 (283–343). Ca. Six Dynasties (220–581).

*Taiqing zhenren luoming jue* 太清真人絡命訣. DZ132/TT59. Ca. 3rd or 4th c.

*Taiqing zhonghuang zhenjing* 太清中黃真經. DZ817/TT586. Commentary ca. 700 (Main text perhaps ca. 300).

*Taiqing zhonghuang zhenjing* 太清中黃真經. In *Yunji qiqian* (DZ1032/TT677–702) 13. Commentary ca. 700 (Main text perhaps ca. 300).

*Taishang dadao yuqing jing* 太上大道玉清經. DZ1312/TT1024. Before 753.

*Taishang dongxuan lingbao kaiyan bimi zang jing* 太上洞玄靈寶開演祕密藏經 (*The Original Juncture*, 9th *juan*). DZ329/TT167. Ca. 600.

*Taishang dongxuan lingbao zhihui dingzhi tongwei jing* 太上洞玄靈寶智慧定志通微經. DZ325/TT167. 5th c.

*Taishang huangting neijing yujing* 太上黃庭內景玉經. DZ331/TT167. 4th c.

*Taishang huangting waijing jing* 太上黃庭外景經. In *Yunji qiqian* (DZ1032/TT677–702) 12/28b–66b. With Commentary by Wuchengzi 務成子 (Ca. Tang dynasty [618–907]).

*Taishang huangting waijing yujing* 太上黃庭外景玉經. DZ332/TT167. Before 255.

*Taishang hunyuan zhenlu* 太上混元真錄 (*The True Record*). DZ954/TT604. Ca. 7th c.

*Taishang jingjie* 太上經戒. DZ787/TT562. Tang (618–907).

*Taishang Laojun jinglü* 太上老君經律. DZ786/562. Ca. 3rd c.

*Taishang Laojun qingjing xin jing* 太上老君清靜心經. DZ1169/TT839. Ca. 8th c.

*Taishang Laojun shuo chang qingjing jing zhu* 太上老君説常清靜經註 (*The Clarity and Calmness* with commentary). DZ755/TT532. Commentary by Li Daochun 李道純 (fl. 1288–1292).

*Taishang Laojun shuo chang qingjing jing zhu* 太上老君説常清靜經註 (*The Clarity and Calmness* with commentary). DZ756/TT532. Commentary by Wuming shi 無名氏 ("Mr. Anonymous"). Ca. Yuan dynasty (1279–1368).

*Taishang Laojun shuo chang qingjing jing zhu* 太上老君説常清靜經註. (*The Clarity and Calmness* with commentary). DZ757/TT532. Arranged and revised Bai Yuchan 白玉蟾 (1194–1229). Commentary by Wang Yuanhui 王元暉. 1312.

*Taishang Laojun shuo chang qingjing miaojing* 太上老君説常清靜妙經 (*The Clarity and Calmness*). DZ620/TT341. Ca. 8th c.

*Taishang Laojun xuwu ziran benqi jing* 太上老君虛無自然本起經 (*The Original Arising*). DZ1438/TT1059. Between 5th and 7th c.

*Taishang Laojun zhongjing* 太上老君中經. DZ1168/TT839. Ca. 2nd c.

*Taishang lingbao wufu xu* 太上靈寶五符序. DZ388/TT183. Compiled ca. 4th c.

*Taixi jing* 胎息經 (*Embryonic Breathing*, version B). In *Yunji qiqian* (DZ1032/TT677–702) 60/27a–28b. Commentary between late 8th c. and 1025.

*Taixi jing zhu* 胎息經註 (*Embryonic Breathing*, version A). DZ130/TT59. Commentary between late 8th c. and 1025.

*Taixi jingwei lun* 胎息精微論 (*The Embryonic Subtleties*). DZ829/TT571. Ca. 8th or 9th c.

*Taixi koujue* 胎息口訣. In *Yunji qiqian* (DZ1032/TT677–702) 58/13b–16b. Ca. Tang dynasty (618–907).

*Taixuan zhenyi benji miaojing* 太玄真一本際妙經 (*The Original Juncture**, 2nd *juan*). DZ1111/TT758. Ca. 600.

*Tang Xuanzong yuzhi Daode zhenjing shu* 唐玄宗御製道德真經疏. DZ679/TT358. Attributed to Tang Emperor Xuanzong (r. 712–756).

*Tianyinzi* 天隱子. DZ1026/TT672. 8th c.

*Wuchu jing qifa* 五厨經氣法 (*The Five Kitchens*, version B). In *Yunji qiqian* (DZ1032/TT677–702) 61/5b–10b. Commentary written by Yin Yin in 735.
*Wushang biyao* 無上祕要. DZ1138/TT768–779. Late 6th c.
*Xiandao jing* 顯道經 (*The Manifest Tao*). DZ862/TT578. Six Dynasties (220–581).
*Xiantian Xuanmiao Yunü Taishang Shengmu zichuan xiandao* 先天玄妙玉女太上聖母資傳仙道 (*The Way of Transcendence*). DZ868/TT579. Between 7th and 12th c.
*Xisheng jing* 西昇經 (*The Western Ascension*, version B). DZ666/TT167. Commentary by Emperor Huizong 徽宗 (r. 1100–1126).
*Xisheng jing jizhu* 西昇經集註 (*The Western Ascension*, version A). DZ726/TT449. Edited by Chen Jingyuan 陳景元 (1025–1094).
*Xiuzhen shishu* 修真十書. DZ263/TT131. Compiled ca. 1340.
*Xu xian zhuan* 續仙傳 (DZ295/138; by Shen Fen 沈汾 [fl. Ca. 937–975]).
*Yangxing yanming lu* 養性延命錄. DZ838/TT572. Attributed variously to Tao Hongjing 陶弘景 (456–536) or Sun Simiao 孫思邈 (581–682).
*Yaoxiu keyi jielü chao* 要修科儀戒律鈔. DZ463/TT204–207. By Zhu Junxu 朱君緒. Early 8th c.
*Yiqie daojing yinyi miaomen youqi* 一切道經音義妙門由起. Compiled by Shi Chong 史崇 et al. 712–713.
*Youlong zhuan* 猶龍傳. DZ774/TT555. By Jia Shanxiang 賈善翔. Ca. 1086–1100.
*Youzhen xiansheng fu nei yuanqi jue* 幼真先生服內元氣訣. DZ828/TT570. Latter half of 8th c.
*Youzhen xiansheng fu nei yuanqi jue* 幼真先生服內元氣訣. In *Yunji qiqian* (DZ1032/TT677–702) 60/14a–17a. Latter half of 8th c.
*Yuanshi dongzhen jueyi jing* 元始洞真決疑經 (*The Original Juncture*, 2nd juan). DZ59/TT31. Ca. 600.
*Yunji qiqian* 雲笈七籤. DZ1032/TT677–702. Compiled by Zhang Junfang 張君房. Ca. 1025.
*Zhen longhu jiuxian jing* 真龍虎九仙經. DZ227/TT112. Commentaries attributed to Ye Fashan 葉法善 (ca. 616–720) and Luo Gongyuan 羅公遠 (ca. 655–758).

*Zhen'gao* 真誥. DZ1016/TT637–640. By Tao Hongjing 陶弘景 (456–536). Completed in 499.

*Zhengyi fawen tianshi jiaojie kejing* 正一法文天師教戒科經. DZ789/TT563. Ca. 255.

*Zhenxian zhizhi yulu* 真仙直指語錄. DZ1256/TT998. By Xuanquanzi 玄全子. Ca. 1300.

*Zhonghe ji* 中和集. DZ749/TT118. By Li Daochun 李道純 (fl. 1288–1306).

*Zhong-Lü chuandao ji* 鍾呂傳道集. In *Xiuzhen shishu* (DZ263/TT131) 14–16. Ca. 11th c.

*Zhongnan shan shuojingtai lidai zhenxian beiji* 終南山說經臺歷代真仙碑記. DZ956/TT605. Compiled by Zhu Xiangxian 朱象先. Late 13th c.

*Zhouyi cantong qi* 周易參同契. DZ999/TT621. Ca. 450–650.

*Zhuzhen neidan jiyao* 諸真內丹集要. DZ1258/TT999. Compiled by Xuanquanzi 玄全子. Ca. 1300.

*Zhuzhen shengtai shenyong jue* 諸真聖胎神用訣 (*The Holy Embryo*). DZ826/570. 12th c. or later.

*Zongyuan xiansheng xuangang lun* 宗玄先生玄綱論. DZ1052/TT727. By Wu Yun 吳筠 (d. 778).

*Zuowang lun* 坐忘論 (*Sitting and Forgetting*, version A). DZ1036/TT740. Attributed to Sima Chengzhen 司馬承禎 (647–735).

*Zuowang lun* 坐忘論 (*Sitting and Forgetting*, version B). In *Yunji qiqian* (DZ1032/TT677–702) 94/1a–16b. Attributed to Sima Chengzhen 司馬承禎 (647–735).


PRIMARY SOURCES OUTSIDE THE *TAOIST CANON*

*Bianzheng lun* 辯正論. *Taishō Canon*, no. 2110, vol. 50. By Falin 法琳 (572–640).

*Bidian zhulin* 祕殿珠林. In *Yingyin wenyuan ge siku quanshu* 影印文淵閣四庫全書, vol. 823. Compiled by Zhang Zhao 張照 (b. 1650), Liang Shizheng 梁詩正 (1697–1763), et al.

*Bore boluomiduo xin jing* 般若波羅蜜多心經. *Taishō Canon*, no. 245, vol. 8. Translated by Kumarajiva 鳩摩羅什 (344–413).

*Bore boluomiduo xin jing* 般若波羅蜜多心經. *Taishō Canon*, no. 251, vol. 8. Translated by Xuanzang 玄奘 (602–664).

*Chuxue ji* 初學記. Beijing: Zhonghua Shuju, 1965. Compiled by Xu Jian 徐堅 (659–729) et al. (659–729).

*Dacheng jieyao* 大成捷要. Taiyuan: Shanxi Renmin Chubanshe, 1988. Prefaces dated 1929 and 1933.

*Dafang guangfo huayan jing* 大方廣佛華嚴經. *Taishō Canon*, no. 279, vol. 10. Translated by Śikṣānanda 實叉難陀 (652–710).

*Er Cheng quanshu* 二程全書. *Sibu beiyao* 四部備要 edition. Shanghai: Zhonghua Shuju: 1927–1936. By Cheng Hao 程顥 (1032–1085) and Cheng Yi 程頤 (1033–1107). Edited by Zhu Xi 朱熹 (1130–1200).

*Foshuo anban shouyi jing* 佛說安般守意經. *Taishō Canon*, no. 602, vol. 15. Translated by An Shigao 安世高 (fl. 148–170).

*Foshuo guanfo sanmeihai jing* 佛說觀佛三昧海經. *Taishō Canon*, no. 643, vol. 15. Translated by Buddhabhadra (Foduobatuo 佛馱跋陀; 359–429).

*Foshuo sanchu jing* 佛說三廚經. *Taishō Canon*, no. 2894, vol. 85. 8th c.

*Guanzi* 管子. In *Sibu congkan chubian* 四部叢刊初編38. Attributed to Guan Zhong 管仲 (725–645). Warring States period (403–221 BCE).

*Han shu* 漢書. Beijing: Zhonghua Shuju, 1962. By Ban Gu 班固 (32–92).

*Houhan shu* 後漢書. Beijing: Zhonghua Shuju, 1965. By Fan Ye 范曄 (398–445). With commentary by Li Xian 李賢 (654–684).

*Huiming jing* 慧命經. In *Zangwai daoshu* 藏外道書, vol. 5. By Liu Huayang 柳華陽. 1794.

*Jigu lumu* 集古錄目. Nanjing: Jiangsu Guji Chubanshe, 1998. By Ouyang Fei 歐陽棐. 1069.

*Jin'gang bore boluomi jing* 金剛般若波羅蜜經. *Taishō Canon*, no. 235, vol. 8. Translated by Kumarajiva 鳩摩羅什 (344–413).

*Jingdian shiwen* 經典釋文. In *Sibu congkan* 四部叢刊, vols. 52–63. By Lu Deming 陸德明 (556–627).

*Jinshu* 晉書. Beijing: Zhonghua Shuju, 1974. By Fang Xuanling 房玄齡 (578–648) et al.

*Jinsi lu* 近思錄. Taipei: Guangwen Shuju, 1967. Compiled by Zhu Xi (1130–1200) and Lü Zuqian 呂祖謙 (1137–1181). With commentary by Jiang Yong 江永 (1681–1762).

*Laozi Xiang'er zhu* 老子想爾注. Dunhuang Manuscript Stein 6825. 2nd or early 3rd c.

*Liuzu dashi fabao tan jing* 六祖大師法寶壇經. *Taishō Canon*, no. 2008, vol. 48. By Huineng 慧能 (638–713). Edited by Zongbao 宗寶 in 1291.

*Mengzi* 孟子. *Sibu congkan chubian* 四部叢刊初編 4. By Meng Ke 孟軻 372–289 BCE. With commentary by Zhao Qi 趙岐 (ca. 108–201).

*Miaofa lianhua jing* 妙法蓮華經. *Taishō Canon*, no. 262, vol. 9. Ca. 50–150. Translated by Kumarajiva 鳩摩羅什 in 406.

*Miaofa lianhua jing wenju* 妙法蓮華經文句. *Taishō Canon*, no. 1748, vol. 34. By Zhiyi 智顗 (538–598).

*Nan jing jizhu* 難經集注. In *Sibu congkan chubian* 四部叢刊初編 38. Compiled by Wang Jiusi 王九思 (1468–1551) et al. Main text attributed to Qin Yueren 秦越人 (Warring States [403–221]).

*Nanyue Si dachanshi lishiyuan wen* 南嶽思大禪師立誓願文. *Taishō Canon*, no. 1933, vol. 46. By Huisi 慧思 (515–577).

*Nanyue zongsheng ji* 南嶽總勝集. *Taishō Canon*, vol. 51, no. 2097. By Chen Tianfu 陳田夫. 1163.

*Sandong fengdao kejie yifan* 三洞奉道科誡儀範. Dunhuang Manuscript Pelliot 2337. Ca. early 7th c.

*Sanguo zhi* 三國志. Beijing: Zhonghua Shuju, 1959, 1962 (Shanghai). By Chen Shou 陳壽 (233–297). With commentary by Pei Songzhi 裴松之 (372–451).

*Shiji* 史記. Beijing: Zhonghua Shuju, 1959. By Sima Qian 司馬遷 (145–86 BCE).

*Suishu* 隋書. Beijing: Zhonghua Shuju, 1973. By Wei Zheng 魏徵 et al. 636.

*Taiping yulan* 太平御覽. Beijing: Zhonghua Shuju, 1960. By Li Fang 李昉 et al. 984.

*Taishō shinshū daizōkyō* 大正新修大藏經 (*Taishō Canon*). Tokyo: Taishō Issaikyō Kankōkai, 1924–1932.

*Tianji biwen* 天機秘文 (*Dacheng jieyao*). Taipei: Zhenshanmei Chubanshe, 1966. Ca. early 20th c.

*Tianxian zhengli zhilun zengzhu* 天仙正理直論增註. In *Zangwai daoshu*, vol. 5. By Wu Shouyang 伍守陽 (1573–1640).

*Xianfo hezong yulu* 仙佛合宗語錄. In *Zangwai daoshu*, vol. 5. By Wu Shouyang (1573–1640).

*Xiao jing* 孝經. In *Shisan jing zhushu* 十三經注疏, by Ruan Yuan 阮元 (1816). Beijing: Zhonghua shuju, 1960. Attributed to Zeng Shen 曾參 (ca. 509–436).

*Xin Tangshu* 新唐書. Beijing: Zhonghua Shuju, 1975. By Ouyang Xiu 歐陽修 et al. 1060.

*Xiuxi zhiguan zuochan fayao* 修習止觀坐禪法要. *Taishō Canon*, no. 1915, vol. 46. By Zhiyi 智顗 (538–598).

*Xunzi* 荀子. Taipei: Shangwu Yinshu Guan, 1964. By Xun Kuang 荀況 (ca. 313–238).

*Yixin fang* 醫心方 (*Ishinpō*). Beijing: Huaxia Chubanshe 華夏出版社, 1996. By Tanba no Yasuyori 丹波康賴. 984.

*Yiwen leiju* 藝文類聚. Beijing: Zhonghua Shuju, 1965. Compiled by Ouyang Xun 歐陽詢 (557–642). Completed in 624.

*Za ahan jing* 雜阿含經. *Taishō Canon*, no. 99, vol. 2. Translated by Guṇabhadra 求那跋陀羅 between 435 and 443.

*Zangwai daoshu* 藏外道書. Chengdu: Bashu Shushe, 1992–1994. Compiled by Hu Daojing 胡道靜 et al.

*Zhenzheng lun* 甄正論. *Taishō Canon*, no. 2112, vol. 52. By Xuanyi 玄嶷 (fl. 684–704).

*Zhong ahan jing* 中阿含經. *Taishō Canon*, no. 26, vol. 1. Translated by Saṃghadeva 僧伽提婆. Ca. 376–396.

# Index

alchemy, laboratory, 116, 123, 140–141, 145, 212, 327n46
ancient precedents. See *Laozi*, the; *Neiye*, the; *Zhuangzi*, the
Assandri, Frederike, 184–185

Bai Lüzhong, 117, 123, 328n50
Baoguan (Treasure Crown), 258
*Baopuzi neipian* (Ge Hong), 254–255
Benn, James, 227
Bodhidharma (Damo), 257–258
*Bodhidharma's Lesson* (*Damo dashi zhushi liuxing neizhen miaoyong jue*): and Embryonic Breathing theory, 27, 257, 348n28; and "Marvelous Functions Lesson," 269; and Mysterious Female, 259; and respect for parents, 265–266; and "true embryonic breathing," 270, 294
Bokenkamp, Stephen, 62, 63, 64, 65, 66, 67, 68, 69–71, 72, 74, 291
Buddhism, integrating: earlier phase, 143–180; overview, 22–23, 143, 308n17. See also *Original Arising*; *Western Ascension*
Buddhism, integrating: Emptiness and the Twofold Mystery, 181–210; overview, 23–24, 181. See also *Clarity and Calmness*; *Five Kitchens*; *Original Juncture*

Cavern Chamber, 109–110, 112–113, 117, 125–126
Chen Jingyuan, 144
Chen Shixiang, 62
Chen Shou, 29
Chongxuanzi, 144
Cinnabar Radiance-Firm Protection (Zidan Guangjian), 100–101
*Clarity and Calmness, The* (*Qingjing jing*), 201–209, 282–283; on attaining serenity, 206, 283; beginning of narrative, 202; and *Daoist Canon*, 201; dating of, 201; and doing away with desires, 206–207; and enigmatic passage, 202–203; and entering the true Dao,

*Clarity and Calmness, The* (continued) 207–208; and "heaven and earth will all return," 205, 299; influence of, 201, 338n40; and *Laozi* themes, 208–209; and Ma Yu interpretation of passage, 205; and "Mr. Anonymous" and Ms. Han incident, 203–205; and recitation of text, 282, 283; and religious paradox, 208; and Ren, 205–206; serenity as goal in, 209; summary of, 209

*Classic of Filial Piety* (*Xiao jing*), 201, 338n42

Confucius (Kong Qiu), 8–11, 120, 152, 215–216

*Contemplating the Baby* (*Rushi si chizi fa*), 104–118, 279–280; after Baby lodges in Cavern Chamber, 112–113; and ascending *yuan*, 108–109, 117–118, 297–298; and Baby takes shape, 110; background of, 104, 322n24; and Cavern Chamber location, 117; and Elixir Field location, 117; and focus on heart, 109–110; format of, 105; and Genuine Person arrives, 110–111, 112, 113; and Great Dao is encountered, 114, 115–116; and the Hall of Light, 117; and human head discussion, 116–117; and illusions to be disregarded, 114, 115; and kidney pacification, 108–109; Laozi's description of "his" Dao, 105–107, 322nn26–27; Laozi's meditation directions, 107–108, 279–280; and LLS#4, 132, 133, 134; and proper times for meditation, 107, 118, 126–127, 233nn28–29; and Queen Mother of the West, 113–114; and quitting regimen after 100 days, 116, 118; and red snake notifies Baby's ascension, 111–112, 118, 288, 349n1; and spontaneous visions, 107; and tangible benefits of regimen, 116; and text ambiguities, 114–115; and visions experienced, 236; summary of, 117–118. See also *Manifest Dao* (*Xiandao jing*)

Contemplation of the Great Cavern, 138

Counting and Measuring (3), 45–46

Crimson Palace (*jianggong*), 76, 126, 170, 175, 176

*Daodao jialing jie*, 62–63, 314nn42–43

*Daodian lun*, 57

Daoist Canon: and *Clarity and Calmness*, 201; and Dongzhen section, 2; and *Embryonic Breathing* (versions A and B), 256–257, 346n22; and *Five Kitchens*, 194; and *Great Peace*, 35; and *Inscription* (versions A and B), 241–242; and Ming dynasty, 33; and *Original Arising*, 161; and 2nd and 9th *juan*, 181–182; and Shangqing scriptures, 2; and *Sitting and Forgetting*, 212; and *Stability and Observation* (versions A and B), 230; texts missing from, 62; and *Tianyinzi*, 213, 340n6; and *Western Ascension*, 143–144; and Zhang Yuchu, 201

Daoist religious movements (earliest known), 29–74; overview, 20–21, 29–31. See also *GP Instruction*; *GP Synopsis*; *Great Peace*; *Laozi-Xiang'er zhu*; Taiping Group texts

*Daoji jing*, 77
deities, visualization of, 42–43, 55–57, 156–157, 178, 311n23
Dharma Body (*dharmakaya*; *fashen*), 166–167, 187–188, 191, 332n14, 345n8
*Dianlüe* (Yu Huan), 29
Divine Elixir, 212, 228–229
dramatic physical and sensory effects. *See* physical and sensory effects
drugs, 58–60, 140
Du Guangting, 195, 196–197
Dunhuang, caves of, 182

Elixir, Divine, 212, 228–229
Elixir Field (*dantian*): being full of *qi*, 245; contemplation of, 88–89; and Dao-*qi* emergence from, 21, 26, 89–92, 298, 320nn15–16; emphasis in Daoist texts, 117; and fasting, 249; focus on, 27, 284, 286–287; and natural satiation, 293; and shifting focus, 298; and visions of light from, 286
Elixir Field, Lower: and a conscious spirit in, 260; and eating, 83; focus on, 279–280, 285; location under navel, 126, 259, 268–269; and mentally directing *qi* toward, 266; and Mysterious Pearl in, 266–267; and overcoming hunger, 103, 256, 293; and shifting focus, 298. *See also* Gate of Life
Elixir Field, Middle, 126, 298
Elixir Field, Upper, 101, 126, 298
*Embryonic Breathing* (*Taixi jing zhu*), 254–275, 285–286, 301–302; overview, 25, 26–27, 52, 254; benefits of "Marvelous Functions Lesson," 273; and "circulating the *qi*," 254–255; colophon of version A, 257; and commentary, 259–262, 285, 301–302, 348nn29–30; dating of, 257; effects upon the body of, 262; and gaps supplemented in other treatises, 274; Huanzhen xiansheng (Mr. Huanzhen), 257, 346n24; and Huisi, 274, 349n37; and ingesting *qi*, 264; and *The Inscription*, 274, 285; interpretation difficulties with, 257; and "Marvelous Functions Lesson," 258, 269–270; and Mysterious Female (*xuanpin*), 259; and Neidan tradition, 274–275; and Oral Lesson on Embryonic Breathing, 255; origins of term, 254; and proactive breathing method, 256, 285, 346n20; and reverting to fetal conditions, 255–256, 345n19; satiation of hunger benefit of, 269–270; scripture in its entirety, 258; and spirit and *qi* in body, 258–261; and Taiping Group texts, 256; and unresolved questions, 263; and version A commentary, 262–263; and Wang Zhen's description, 254. *See also* *Bodhidharma's Lesson*; *Embryonic Origins*; *Embryonic Subtleties*; Ge Hong; *Holy Embryo*
*Embryonic Origins, The* (*Changsheng taiyuan shenyong jing*): breathing-related treatise, 26–27, 257, 347n25; and "Gate of Life," 268–269; on guarding of inner mother and child, 266; ingesting *qi* described in, 263–264; and "Marvelous Functions Lesson," 269,

*Embryonic Origins, The* (continued) 293, 295; and merging of spirit and *qi*, 267–268; and Mysterious Pearl in Elixir Field, 266–267; and visual technique, 270

*Embryonic Subtleties, The* (*Taixi jingwei lun*): and benefits of embryonic breathing, 272; breathing-related treatise, 26–27, 257; on guarding of inner mother and child, 266; and "Marvelous Functions Lesson," 269, 270–272; and Mysterious Female, 259; on obtaining long life, 265; and *qi* of sages, 271–272, 349n34; on respiration and inner spirit-*qi*, 268; value of sexual yogic techniques affirmed in, 273; on womb and *qi*, 264–265

Emptiness concept, 162–163. *See also* Naturalness of Empty Nothingness

"entering the room," 49–50, 123, 131

fasting, 79, 100, 249, 292. *See also* food intake, reduction of

Five Agents, 42, 47

*Five Kitchens, The* (*Wuchu jing*), 194–200, 282; authorship of, 194; and *Daoist Canon*, 194; and Du Guangting's interpretation of Yin, 196–197; and eating topic in final section, 198–199; and fasting not mentioned in, 197–198; and the five sprouts, 197, 337n30; and *Foshuo sanchu jing*, 194–195, 336n26; and harmony of the *qi*, 198, 282, 299, 337n31; plagiarism of, 195; and recitation of text, 282; and Twofold Mystery doctrine, 198, 282; and verses for overcoming hunger, 194–195, 336n27; versions A and B, 194, 335nn21–22; and *Wuling xindan zhang*, 194, 335n25; and Yin on human body of material elements, 199–200, 338n36; and Yin on mind of luminous wisdom, 338nn37–39; and Yin preface and commentary, 194; and Yin's commentary on final section, 199, 337nn32–34; and Yin's commentary on "*qi* of the one," 195–196, 200–201; and *Yunji qiqian*, 194, 335n24; summary of, 200–201. *See also* Buddhism, Emptiness and the Twofold Mystery; *Clarity and Calmness*; *Original Juncture*

Five Officials, 46–47

Five Peaks, 213, 340n8

Five Stages and Seven Phases, 230–231, 250–251, 300

Flying Transcendents, 167, 295, 333n15

food intake, reduction of: 42nd *juan* of *The Great Peace*, 54–55, 290; and *Laozi-Xiang'er*, 73–74, 291; and *Manifest Dao* (fasting manual), 79, 100, 292; 98th *juan* of *The Great Peace*, 53–54; and *Original Arising*, 170–171; and preparing to stop eating, 60–61; and satiating hunger, 249; 70th *juan* of *The Great Peace*, 58; and Taiping Group texts, 36, 50, 52–53; 36th *juan* of *The Great Peace*, 50–51, 290, 312n30; and *Western Ascension*, 158

Formless Divine Persons Entrusted to Qi, 54–55, 312n31

Four Meditations, 296–297, 350nn7–8

Fu Wuguang, 63
*fuming*, defined, 217–218

Gan Ji, 32, 163
Gate of Life (*mingmen*), 126, 268–269. See also Elixir Field, Lower
Ge Hong: and *Baopuzi neipian*, 254–255; and *Daoji jing* scripture, 77; and Embryonic Breathing, 256–257; and suspension of breathing, 275, 294. See also Embryonic Breathing
Gengsang Chu, 12
Genuine Man of the Great Ultimate (Taiji Zhenren), 191–192
Genuine Persons: becoming, 166; breathing of, 271–272; dwelling place of Zidan, 126; and Heavenly Master, 55–57; specters as intermediaries of, 96, 287, 321n19; visitations by, 114, 132
Genuine Spirit, 154–155, 167
Gong Chong of Langye, 32
*GP Instructions*: defined, 33; and Guarding the One, 38, 40–41, 53, 104; and Method of Guarding the One, 43, 311n24; and Shangqing School, 34; and Tang period, 34; and visualizing divine radiance, 286
*GP Synopsis*: and changing appearance, 138; defined, 33, 310n13; and the fetus, 51–52, 290–291, 297; and Guarding the One, 36–37, 278; joy attained by good *qi*, 39–40; and joyful radiance attracts spirits, 286; meditation in isolation and, 35–36; and Nine Rooms, 46–47; and preparing to stop eating, 60–61; and *qi* of naturalness, 52; and *qi* of *yin* and *yang*,

52; and Shangqing school, 34; and Tang period, 34
Great Cavern (*dadong*), 138–139
Great Harmony, 137
Great Naturalness of Empty Nothingness. See Naturalness of Empty Nothingness
*Great Peace, The*: cosmology of, 35; 86th *juan* of, 55; 42nd *juan* of, 54–55, 312n31; and Guarding the One, 48; length of, 30–31, 32; 98th *juan* of, 53, 291; 108th *juan* of, 49–50; and proactive meditation methods, 1–3, 44–46; *Taiping jing* and, 32; Zhang Jue and, 30, 31–32
Great Yang, 137
Great Yin, 137
Gu Baotian, 63
Guangchengzi, 14–15
*Guanzi*, the, 15, 307n11
Guarding the One, 150
"Guarding the One": and formlessness contemplated, 43–44; and Guarding the One Light, 39; and LLS#1, 127–128, 136; and the *Neiye*, 38; and Taiping Group texts, 36–37, 278; as vision-inducing method, 140

Hall of Light (*mingtang*), 76, 88–89, 109, 116–117, 125, 319n13, 320n14
Han dynasty, Daoism and, 3
heart. See Crimson Palace
*Heart Sutra of Clarity and Calmness Spoken by the Most High Lord Lao*, 201–202, 339n44
Heavenly Masters School, 32, 34, 104

Heavenly Worthies, 235–336, 290
Hendrischke, Barbara, 34–35, 310, 311
Heshanggong Commentary to the *Laozi*, 259, 348n29
*Holy Chronicle, The*: dating of, 135–136; and LLS#1, 136; and Lord Lao, 133, 135; and Nine Rooms, 135–136; and *True Record*, 119–121, 140–141, 280
*Holy Embryo* (*Zhuzhen shengtai shenyong jue*), 257, 269–270, 347n27
Huaisu, 201, 338n41
*huanglao*, defined, 31
*Huangting waijing jing* (Bai Lüzhong), 117, 123, 328n50
Huanzhen xiansheng, 257, 346n24
Huisi, 274, 349n37
Hundun, 163, 265

*Inscription, The* (*Cunshen lianqi ming*), 241–253, 284; overview, 25–26, 241–242; authorship of version B, 242, 344n4; A and B versions virtually same, 242; colophon of version A, 242; compassion ethic of, 253; dating of, 242; and Dharma Body, 247, 345n8; and Elixir Field, 245, 249, 284, 293; and Five Stages and Seven Phases, 230–231, 250–251, 300; and interpretation of "life," 248; and lament on insufficient study of "the Way," 252; and meditation, 245–246, 248–249; and mother-child metaphor, 244, 245, 302; and Neidan tradition, 253; and primal *qi* refining, 244–245, 249, 284; and satiating hunger, 249; and Seven Phases after calm condition, 251, 252–253; and sheer serenity, 242–243; and spirit and *qi* in body, 243–244, 252, 301–302; and Sun Simiao, 242; and text ambiguities, 246–250; summary of, 252–253
integrating Buddhism. *See* Buddhism, integrating: earlier phase; Buddhism, integrating: Emptiness and the Twofold Mystery
Intermediate Naturalness of Empty Nothingness. *See* Naturalness of Empty Nothingness

Jade Woman of Dark Radiance (Xuanguang Yunü), 76
*Jingdian shiwen*, 123–124, 328n51
*Jinye jing*, 123
*Jiudu jing*, 123
"Juegu shiqi fa" (fasting manual). See under *Manifest Dao* (*Xiandao jing*)

Kohn, Livia, 11, 144, 231, 243, 307n10
*kong* term, 158–159, 162, 163, 332n7
Kusuyama Haruki, 119, 124, 324n36

Laozi, 12, 31–32, 75, 120, 317n1
*Laozi*, the: absence of desires and, 4–5; and *Clarity and Calmness*, 208–209; embracing the One, 38; mental serenity (*qingjing*) and, 4–6; non-meditation-specific interpretations of, 7–8; page citations in, 307n6; as quoted in *Sitting and Forgetting*, 225, 343n18; renewed

interest in philosophy of, 3–4;
transmitted to Yin Xi, 123–126;
and *Western Ascension*, 145
*Laozi jiejie*, 123–124
*Laozi-Xiang'er* (*Laozi Xiang'er zhu*),
62–74, 279; and affinity to
*Manifest Dao*, 104; authorship of,
62–63; and binding together of
essence, 72, 316n54; and Dao as
both essence and *qi*, 64–65, 68–69;
and enabling the *qi* through clarity,
67, 315n50; English translations
of, 63; and food intake, 73–74,
291; and immortality of spirit, 71;
and indifference to worldly benefit,
66–67; and Mysterious Female,
71; and mystical experience of Dao
denied in, 65–66; as nonmystical document, 63, 279; and the
One, 64–65; and parallel between
world and humans, 67; and Plain
Way, 62, 279, 313n34; preservation of, 62; and *qi*-eating, 74; on
serenity, 63–64, 279, 315nn48–49;
and sexual activity, 69–73, 295,
315n51, 316n53, 317n55; sources
of, 62, 314nn35–36; and term
*xiang'er*, 63, 314n44
"Lesson on Entering and Refining the
Nine Cycle Reverted Cinnabar and
the Subduing of Fire," 123
Lévi, Jean, 242
Li Daochun, 202
Li Er. *See* Laozi
Li Rong, 144, 152–155, 158, 280
Li Simu, 201
Li Zhongqing, 182–183
Lingbao scriptures, 184
Liu Huayang, 73, 303

Liu Jinxi, 182–183
Liu Ningran, 213
Liu Renhui, 144
*Lizang jing*, 123, 327n49
LLS#1 ("Lord Lao said . . ."),
125–128, 136, 329n54
LLS#1–LLS#4 ("Lord Lao said . . ."),
questions on, 125, 130
LLS#2 ("Lord Lao said . . ."): and
Red Snake-Queen Mother vision
sequence, 131; and serenity,
128–130, 280, 288–289
LLS#3 ("Lord Lao said . . ."), 131
LLS#4 ("Lord Lao said . . ."): and
105-day juncture, 133–134;
and 150-day juncture, 134; and
180-day juncture, 134–135; and
280-day juncture, 135; and apparitions, 132–133; and appearance of
Great Dao, 132; and becoming a
Genuine Person, 135; and changing
appearance in solitude, 137–138;
and *Contemplating the Baby*,
132, 133, 134; and "entering the
room," 131–132; and First Room,
136–137; meditation of Ninth
Room, 138, 293; and Nine Rooms,
135, 136; and prodigies, 131; and
Red Snake-Queen Mother vision
sequence, 125, 130, 280, 287–288;
and remaining eight rooms, 137,
330n62
Lord Green Youth, 33, 34
Lord Lao (Laojun): as Genuine Spirit,
167; and *Original Arising*, 161; and
*Original Juncture*, 184; transformation of, 163. *See also entries beginning with* LLS; Laozi; *True Record*;
Yin Xi

*Lotus Sūtra* (*Miaofa lianhua jing*; *Fahua jing*), 148, 166, 186, 189, 290
Lü Dongbin, 131–132
Luo Yao, 29, 30

Ma Yu, 205, 209
Mādhyamika school of Mahāyāna Buddhism, 3–4
Mahāyāna Buddhist doctrine: abiding in realm of *saṃsāra*, 23, 166, 208–9; and Emptiness, 181; and *Huayan jing*, 297; influence of, 165, 302; and Li Rong, 158; and *Lotus Sūtra*, 186; and medieval Daoism, 302; and notion of supremely holy person, 162; and *Original Juncture*, 181, 184–185, 193–194, 335n19; school of, 3–4
*Manifest Dao, The* ("Sudao jie"), 79–100, 279; and aging process halt on Dao-*qi* accomplishment, 99; and another visualization meditation method, 100; and ascending lightly, 97–98; and both sexes may obtain the *qi*, 91–92; and breathing, 82; and celibacy, 79, 295; and Dao-*qi* emergence from Elixir Field, 89–91, 298, 320nn15–16; and Divine Palace (Hall of Light), 88–89, 319n13, 320n14; and eliminating grains, 83–86, 292, 318n10, 319n11; and Elixir Field contemplation, 88–89, 286–187; format of, 79–80; and invocation of five spirits, 88; and meditation, 79, 87–89; and not eating soon after meditation, 271; and Plain Way regimen, 80–82, 99–101, 279; and power of positive thinking, 97; and proof of Dao-*qi* accomplishment, 98–99; and proper conversation content, 97; and questions on 100 days, 87, 104; and questions on text of, 80; and radiance from Elixir Field, 92; and reclining position for meditation, 81–82, 87, 278; and regimen of secluded meditation, 81–83; on serenity, 79; and sexual activity, 86–87; and shaking and babbling, 95, 103, 287, 298; and specters as intermediaries of Genuine Persons, 96, 287; and Taiping Group texts, 103; and time period for Dao-*qi* accomplishment, 99; and visions experienced, 93–94, 103, 321n18. See also *Manifest Dao* (*Xiandao jing*)
*Manifest Dao, The* (*Xiandao jing*), 79; and affinity to *Laozi-Xiang'er*, 104; dating of, 77, 318n5; format of, 77; "Juegu shiqi fa" (fasting manual) at end, 79, 100, 292; "Juegu shiqi fa" and effects after 100 days, 102, 104; "Juegu shiqi fa" and elimination of foods, 100; "Juegu shiqi fa" and Middle and Upper Elixir Fields, 101; "Juegu shiqi fa" and *qi*-eating, 101; "Juegu shiqi fa" on later date than "Sudao jie," 101; "Juegu shiqi fa" varies from "Sudao jie," 102–103; Laozi discourses in section 1, 77–79. See also *Manifest Dao, The* ("Sudao jie")
Maoshan scriptures, 2
"Marvelous Functions Lesson": and authenticity of embryonic breathing, 272; and breathing through

nose suspended, 293–295; and
celibate Neidan traditions, 273;
and eliminating hunger, 293; and
failure to guard internal child and
mother, 270; four versions of, 269
Maspero, Henri, 255
Mencius, 17, 307n14
Meng Zhixiang, 34
mental serenity (*qingjing*), 1, 4–6,
145, 231, 237–238
"Merging of *Qi*" (sexual rite), 69–70,
315n51
Mogao Caves of Dunhuang, 62
Mollier, Christine, 195
"Mr. Anonymous" (Wuming shi),
202–205
Mt. Kunlun, 176
Muddy Pellet (*niwan*), 76, 125
Mysterious Female (*xuanpin*), *Embryonic Breathing* (*Taixi jing zhu*), 259
Mysterious Female term, 53–54, 71

Nanguo Ziqi, 12–13, 105
Nanjing, 2
Naturalness of Empty Nothingness,
and Intermediate, 166, 173
Naturalness of Empty Nothingness
(meditation methods): and affiliation with Lord Dao, 178; benefits
of, 164, 165–166; and breathing
faintly, 290; description of, 23,
44; in full title of *Original Arising*,
161, 162; and Great and Small,
176; and Intermediate, 174; and
superiority of Great, 280–281; and
superiority of three methods, 177;
techniques for achieving, 278. See
also *Original Arising*
Needham, Joseph, 255, 345n2

*neidan* ("inner elixir"), 135–136,
329n60
Neidan meditation: defined, 3,
306n4; literature of, 172–173,
333n16; theories of, 73, 130–131,
298, 303, 329nn55–56; tradition
of, 253, 274–275
*Neiye*, the, 15–19; ambiguity of
passage with *ding*, 17, 307n13;
buried in the *Guanzi*, 15; the Dao
and, 18; essence of *qi* and, 16;
and Guarding the One, 38; as rare
and crucial text, 4; section 13 and,
17–18; sections 15 and 16, 17;
serenity and longevity in, 15
Nine Contemplations (*jiusi*), 135–
136, 330n61
Nine Degrees (*jiudu*), 44–46, 162
Nine Rooms (*jiushi*): concept of, 136,
140; series of meditation techniques, 46–47; and Taiping Group
texts, 162; and *Way of Transcendence*, 130, 135–136
*nirvāṇa* term, 149

Ōfuchi Ninji, 62, 63
Oral Lesson on Embryonic Breathing, 255
*Original Arising, The* (*Xuwu ziran
benqi jing*), 161–179, 280–281;
Buddhist-influenced nature of,
161–162; and criticism of misguided meditation practices, 168;
dating of, 161, 162; Emptiness
concept missing from, 162; and
five paths, 165; and food intake
reduced, 170–171; and good deeds
required, 169–170; and graded
hierarchy of religious attainment,

166–167; and the Great Yang, 163; and highest attainment, 167–168, 299; and Intermediate Naturalness of Empty Nothingness, 166, 174–175; and *kong* term (empty space), 162, 163, 164; and Mahāyāna Buddhist doctrine, 165, 166; and meditation methods that "have action," 177–178; and meditation techniques, 170–172; and Neidan literature, 172–173, 333n16; and out-of-body experience, 172–173, 289, 295–296; principal assertion of, 23, 308n17; and proper spiritual grounding, 169; and series of cosmic emanations, 163–164; and Three Ones, 169–170; two versions of, 161; and visualization of deities, 178; and *xuwu ziran* term, 162; and *Yunji qiqian* referenced, 161. *See also* Naturalness of Empty Nothingness

*Original Juncture, The* (*Taixuan zhenyi benji miaojing*), 181–194, 281–282; overview, 23; authorship of, 182–183; and Buddhism, 184, 193–194, 299; condemnation of, 182–183; and contemplating the Dao, 189–190, 281; and correct insight attainment, 191–192; dating of, 181; and 8th *juan*, 191–192; fame and influence of, 183, 185; and 4th *juan*, 190–191, 335n18; and the *Laozi*, 193; and Lord Lao, 184; and *Lotus Sūtra*, 186; and Mahāyāna Buddhist doctrine, 162, 184–185; and reconstruction of, 182; and role of preacher, 183–184; and 2nd and 9th *juan*, 181–182; and 2nd *juan*, 185–186, 334n14; and Shangqing and Lingbao scriptures, 184; significance of, 194; and Twofold Mystery, 184–185, 299; and Xuanyi, 182–183. *See also* Primordial Heavenly Worthy

Pali Canon, 296, 350n7

Pei Songzhi, 29

physical and sensory effects, 75–142; overview, 21–22, 75–76. *See also Contemplating the Baby*; *Manifest Dao*; *True Record*

precedents, ancient. *See* ancient precedents

Primal Predecessor-Imperial Chamberlain (Yuanxian Diqing), 100–101

Primal Yang-Valley Mystery (Yuanyang Guxuan), 100–101

Primordial Heavenly Worthy (Yuanshi Tianzun): correct insight recommended by, 188–189; Daoist terminology used by, 187; preacher in 1st, 2nd, and 10th *juan*, 183; and promises of blessings, 189, 290; and *Stability and Observation*, 231; supreme deity of *Original Juncture*, 23; True Body equal to Dharma Body, 187–188, 191, 247; and True Body speech, 185–187, 290; and two ways of contemplating the Dao, 189–190. *See also Original Juncture*

prodigies, and Queen Mother of the West, 131–132

*qi*-eating: after invocations of three gods, 101; and celestial deities, 55–57; and *Embryonic Origins*, 263–264; Laozi's method of, 123; and *Laozi-Xiang'er*, 74; and substitutes for, 58; as vision-inducing method, 140; and wind-*qi*, 58–59
Qingli reign era of the Tang dynasty, 203, 339n48
Quanzhen Longmen Neidan theory, 73, 130–131, 329nn55–56
Quanzhen school, 24, 34, 201, 308n18
Queen Mother of the West, 113–114, 131–132

Rao Zongyi, 62
rebirth theme: and "Body of Response," 186; and Daoist worldview from Buddhism, 3, 22, 143, 146; and Four Meditations, 296–297; and Mahāyāna doctrine, 166; and *Original Arising*, 161–162; reappearance of, 148–149
red snake, defined, 111–112
Red Snake-Queen Mother vision sequence, 118, 125, 130–131, 139–140, 141
Ren, 205
Robinet, Isabelle, 2, 306n3
Roth, Harold, 4, 16, 17

Sagely Lord, 33, 34
Śākyamuni Buddha: and Four Meditations, 296–297; revelations not attributed to, 183; and Transformation Body, 166, 186; vision promised by, 290; and visualization preached by, 195

*Sandong zhunang*, 58–59
Schipper, Kristofer, 62, 63, 77, 318n5
Schmidt, Hans-Hermann, 201
Sea of *Qi*. See entries beginning with Elixir Field
serenity, primal *Qi* and embryonic breathing, 241–275; overview, 25, 241. See also *Embryonic Breathing*; *Inscription*
serenity and the reaffirmation of physical transformation, 211–239; overview, 24–25, 211. See also *Sitting and Forgetting*; *Stability and Observation*
Shangqing Daoism, 173
Shangqing school, 34, 213, 228, 315
Shangqing scriptures, 2, 76, 184, 275
Sima Chengzhen: and authorship of *Sitting and Forgetting* in doubt, 213–215, 243; background of, 213; and *Clarity and Calmness*, 201; and *Fuqi jingyi lun*, 213; and *Sitting and Forgetting* (version A), 211, 212; and *Sitting and Forgetting* (version B), 228–229; and *Tianyinzi* in *Daoist Canon*, 213, 340n6
*Sitting and Forgetting* (*Zuowang lun*), 211–230, 283; overview, 25; appendix to version A, 212; authorship of version A, 211, 212; authorship unknown of version B, 212; and benefits after obtaining the Dao (section 7), 222–225, 228, 283, 300; A and B versions in *Daoist Canon*, 212; colophon of version A, 212; content similar in both versions, 212; on the cultivation of serenity, 211–112;

*Sitting and Forgetting* (continued)
and Daoist anthology *Daoshu*, 212–213, 340n6; and Divine Elixir, 228–229; and English translation by Livia Kohn, 215; format of, 215, 341n13, 342n14; and the *Laozi*, 225–226, 343n18, 343n19; and meditation (section 6), 220–222; and meditation method (section 3), 216–220; and *Original Juncture*, 229; and passage in sixth chapter, 215–216; proactive meditation techniques absent from, 230; section 1: "Reverence and Faith," 215–216; section 2: "Severing Connections," 216; section 3: "Recollecting the Mind," 216–220; section 4: "Simplifying Affairs," 220; section 5: "True Observation," 220; section 6: "Peaceful Stability," 220–222; section 7: "Obtaining the Dao," 222; Sima Chengzhen's authorship in doubt, 213–215; and temptations encountered (section 4), 220; and Twofold Mystery doctrine, 218–219; variations between versions, 212, 226–228, 340n4; and version B conclusion, 228–230; and *Western Ascension*, chapter 4, 226; and Yan Hui, 152, 283; and Zhenjing, 212, 339n3; and *Zhuangzi*, 215–216, 271, 283; and "Zuowang pian," 212–215; summary of, 226–230

Small Naturalness of Empty Nothingness. *See* Naturalness of Empty Nothingness

specters, 94, 96, 287, 321n19

*Stability and Observation* (*Dingguan jing*), 230–239, 284; overview, 25, 26, 230; beginning of narrative, 231, 344n26; A and B versions virtually identical, 230; dating of, 231; and eliminating "moving mind," 231–232, 284; format of, 231; and Heavenly Worthies, 235–236, 290; and moderation, 233–234; and obtaining the Dao, 236–237; Phases 1 and 2 of transformation, 237; Phases 3 to 7 of transformation, 238; positive effects in body and mind required, 238–239; and "refined contemplation," 232, 234–235; and resistance to flaunting wisdom, 235; Seven Phases as possible add-on to, 239; and Seven Phases of transformation, 237–239; significance of, 231; and "true stability," 234; and trying too hard for calmness, 232–233, 284; and visions created by thoughts, 235–236; and *Zuowang shuyi*, 230

"Sudao jie" (Explanation on the Plain Way). See entries beginning with *Manifest Dao*

Sun Qi, 77

Sun Simiao, 25, 242–243

*Taiping dongji jing*, 34, 163

Taiping Group texts, 31–74, 277–279; bodily locations lacking in, 76; cosmological vision of, 48; and deities, 42–43; dietary restrictions and, 36, 50; "Guarding the One" and, 36–37, 278; and *Manifest Dao* ("Sudao jie"), 103, 104; meditation as major theme of, 35, 278–279;

and serenity, 41–42; substitutions for eating of *qi*, 58; and Three Corpses, 40–41; value of, 35; and visualization techniques, 43–44, 48, 278, 286. See also *GP Instructions*; *GP Synopsis*; *Great Peace*
*Taiping jing* scripture: 145th *juan*, 58–60; cherished in medieval Daoism, 32–33, 309n7; and Lord Lao, 163; propagation of, 48–49; textual history of, 34, 311n15
*Taiping qingling shu*, 32, 309n6
*Taiqing bafujing*, 123
*Taiqing guantian jing*, 123
*Taiqing zhenren luoming jue*, 77
*Taishang huangting waijing yujing*, 75
*Taishang Laojun zhongjing*, 75, 77, 117, 123, 317n1, 327n47
*Taixuan zhenyi benji miaojing*, 182
36th *juan* of *The Great Peace*, and dietary restrictions, 50–51, 290–291
Three Corpses, in Taiping Group texts, 40–41
Three Ones, Way of the, 136, 163–164, 169–170
Three Spirits, 137
*Tianyinzi*, the, in *Daoist Canon*, 213, 340n6
Trance of Complete Extinction (*miejin ding*), 296–297, 351nn10–12
*True Record, The* (*Taishang hunyuan zhenlu*), 47, 118–142, 280; authorship of, 118–119, 324n35; as composite of lore over centuries, 125; conclusion of, 139; and eating of *qi*, 123; and "entering the room," 131; format of, 121;

and *Holy Chronicle*, 119, 120, 280; and laboratory alchemy teachings, 123, 327n46; and LLS#3, 131; and LLS segments, 125–126; and Lord Lao, 121–122, 325n45; and Nine Rooms, 47; and Red Snake-Queen Mother vision sequence, 119, 287–288; and "times of Yin and Zhou," 121–124; and visions experienced, 236; and *Way of Transcendence*, 119–121, 280, 325n40; and *Western Ascension*, 22, 120–121, 124; and Yin Wencao, 119, 324n36; Yin Xi, 121–122; summary of, 124, 139–141. See also entries beginning with LLS

Upper Elixir Field, 126

vision-inducing methods, 140
visualization techniques, 43–44, 48, 76, 278, 279, 286

Wang Tu, 77
Wang Zhe, 201, 202
Wang Zhen, 254
Warring States period, Daoism and, 4
Way of the Five Pecks of Rice: and early role in Daoist religion, 31, 75; and isolated contemplation, 30, 49; and *Laozi Xiang'er*, 62; and Zhang Daoling, 20; and Zhang Xiu, 29
Way of the Great Peace. See *Great Peace*
Way of the Heavenly Masters. See Way of the Five Pecks of Rice
*Way of Transcendence, The*, 119–121, 130, 135–136, 280
Wei Jie, 144, 157, 159, 280, 301

*Western Ascension, The (Xisheng jing)*, 143–161, 280; and being without knowledge, 149–150; and Buddhism, 145–149; and A and B versions, 143–144; as companion volume to the *Laozi*, 145; and Dao-*qi* returning (version A), 159–160; dating of, 144; and destiny in own hands, 152–153; and detached calmness, 159; Emptiness concept missing from, 162; and guarding the body, 154, 300; and inner serenity techniques, 157–158; and *karma*, 149; and Mahāyāna Buddhist doctrine, 158; and meditation techniques, 155–156, 280; and mental serenity as theme of, 145; and mind-body relationship, 150–152, 155; and *nirvāṇa*, 149–150; and rebirth theme, 148–149, 299–300; and sagely governance theme, 150; and self-pity, 152–153; significance of, 160, 332n8; and spirit needs body, 155, 301; as teachings of Laozi/Lord Lao to Yin Xi, 22, 143; and thirty-sixth chapter on the Dao, 220, 300–301; variations between versions of, 144, 159, 331n4; and visualization of deities, 156–157; and wisdom, 148; and word *kong* (empty), 158–159, 332n7; and *wuwei* term, 149; and Yin Xi, 22; summary of, 160–61. See also *True Record*
Wu Chi-yu, 182
Wu Shouyang, 73, 298, 303, 317n57
Wu Yun, 257, 293
*wuwei* term, 149

*Xiandao jing*. See entries beginning with *Manifest Dao*
Xu Daomiao, 144, 160
Xuanquanzi, 130
Xuanyi, 182–183
*Xuanyuan huangdi shengji*, 119

Yan Hui: and Confucius, 215–216; *Sitting and Forgetting* inspired by, 152, 283; and the *Zhuangzi*, 8–11
Yancheng Ziyou, 12
Yellow Court (*huangting*), 76
Yellow Emperor (Huangdi), 14, 31
Yellow Spirit, 163
Yin Wencao, 119
Yin Xi: disciple of Lord Lao, 22, 47, 79; and Lord Lao's ascension revealed to, 125; and Red Snake–Queen Mother vision sequence told to, 130–131, 136; and resignation from government post, 130, 136; and study of Dao completed by, 139; and teachings of Lord Lao, 119, 121–124; and *Western Ascension*, 22. See also Lord Lao; *True Record*
Yin Yin. See under *Five Kitchens*
Yu Huan, 29
*Yuli zhongjing*, 123

Zeng Zao, 212, 213, 214, 215, 340n11
Zhang Daoling (first Heavenly Master), 62, 184
Zhang Jue: apparent Daoist leanings of, 31, 32; uprising led by, 29. See also Way of the Great Peace
Zhang Lu (third Heavenly Master), 62

Zhang Xiu, 29, 30, 308n1. *See also* Way of the Five Pecks of Rice
Zhang Yuchu, 201
Zhang Zhongli, 63
Zhao Jian, 214
Zhao Jingyuan, 213
Zhenjing: and *Sitting and Forgetting* (version A), 339n3; and *Sitting and Forgetting* (*Zuowang lun*), 212
Zhou Zhixiang, 34
Zhuang Zhou (Master Zhuang), 8–10, 272
*Zhuangzi*, the: chapter 2 anecdotes, 11–12; chapter 4 anecdotes, 8–10, 214–215; chapter 6 anecdotes, 10–11; chapter 11 anecdotes, 14; chapter 23 anecdotes, 12–13; and passage in sixth chapter, 152; serenity in "Outer Chapters," 14–15; and *Sitting and Forgetting*, 215–216, 271, 283
*Zhuzhen neidan jiyao*, 130
Zidan (Guangjian), 126, 163
*Ziran jing*, 123, 327n48
*Zuowang lun*, 214
"Zuowang pian," and *Sitting and Forgetting* (*Zuowang lun*), 212–213, 214, 215
*Zuowang shuyi*, appendix to *Sitting and Forgetting*, version A, 230
*Zuowang shuyi* (Wings of the Pivot of Sitting and Forgetting), 212